Joel Munsell

Collections on the History of Albany

From its Discovery to the Present Time

Joel Munsell

Collections on the History of Albany
From its Discovery to the Present Time

ISBN/EAN: 9783337098643

Printed in Europe, USA, Canada, Australia, Japan

Cover: Foto ©ninafisch / pixelio.de

More available books at **www.hansebooks.com**

Appeared before me Johannes La Montagne, in the service of, etc, in the presence of the honorable Sander Leendersen [Glen] and Jan Verbeeck commissaries of the same jurisdiction, the honorable Michiel Janssen [Van Edam] burgher and inhabitant here, who declares that he has granted and transferred as by these presents he does grant and transfer in real and actual possession to the behoof of Lowies Cobussen, his heirs or assigns a house lying in Fort Orange, which aforesaid house the grantor received by conveyance from Frans Barentse Pastoor of date the 20th of November, A.D., 1656, and the said Frans Barentse, from Jacob Janse Hap [or Stoll], who received a patent from the Heer director general and council of New Netherland of date the 3d of July, A.D., 1649: with all the right, title and interest which the grantor has had therein, and therefore promises said house to free from all claims and pretensions which may hereafter arise against the same, pledging his person and estate, real and personal, present and future, and submitting the same to all laws and judges.

Done in Fort Orange the 14th of August, A.D., 1659.

MACHGHYEL JANSE.

Appeared before me Johannes La Montagne, in the service of, etc., in the presence of the honorable Francoys Boon and Anderies Herbertsen, commissaries of the same jurisdiction, Roeloff Swartwout, who declares that he has granted and transferred, as by these presents he does grant and transfer in real and actual possession for the behoof of Philip Pieterse Schuyler his heirs or assigns a garden lying in the village of Beverwyck, to the east, the road, to the west, Dominic Schaets, to the south, Annatie Bogardus, which said garden was granted by the Heer director general and council of New Netherland to Antony De Hooges deceased, former husband of the wife of said Roeloff Swartwout, the length and breadth according to the patent which shall be delivered to the grantee together with all the right, title and interest which the grantor has had therein, who promises to free the same from all claims, demands or pretensions which may arise against the same, pledging his person and estate, real and personal, present and future, putting the same in subjection to all laws and judges.

Done in Fort Orange the 15th of August, A.D., 1659.

ROELOFF SWARTWOUT.

Francoys Boon,
Andries Herberts.

Acknowledged before me,

LA MONTAGNE, clerk in Fort Orange.

Appeared before me Johannes La Montagne, in the service of, etc., in the presence of the honorable Sander Leendersen [Glen] and Jan Verbeeck, commissaries of the same jurisdiction, Stoffel Janse [Abeel], who declares that he has granted and conveyed, as by these presents he does grant and convey, in real and actual possession, to the behoof of the honorable Francoys Boon, his heirs and assigns, a house and lot lying in the village of Beverwyck, east, west, and north, a street, south, Gillis Pieterse [Timmerman,] length and breadth according to the patent or as it stands in fence, which patent was given to the grantor by the Heer Director General and council of New Netherland of date the 25th of

October, A.D., 1653, together with all the right, title and interest which the aforesaid Stoffel Janse has had in the same, who also acknowledges that he has had satisfaction therefor, and therefore promises to free said house and lot from all claims, demands or pretensions which may hereafter arise against the same, pledging his person and estate, real and personal, present and future, putting the same in subjection to all laws and judges.

Done in Fort Orange the 15th of August, A.D., 1659.

STOFFEL JANSE ABEEL.

Sander Leenersen
Jan Verbeeck,

Acknowledged before me,

LA MONTANGE, clerk at Fort Orange.

Appeared before me Johannes La Montagne, in the service of, etc., in the presence of honorable Francoys Boon and Anderries Herbertsen, commissaries of said jurisdiction, Teunis Cornelisse Slingerland, who declares that he has granted and conveyed as by these presents he does grant and convey in real and actual possession to the behoof of the honorable Johan Dareth, burgher and inhabitant of the aforesaid village, his heirs or assigns a house and lot, lying in the Village of Beverwyck, to the north, the grantor, to the south, Henderick Gerritse [Van Wie], to the east, the street, to the west, Jacob De Brouwer, length thirty feet, and breadth twenty-eight wood feet; which aforesaid lot the grantor received by conveyance from the patent of Jacob De Brouwer, with whom the said patent remains, with all the right, title and interest, which the aforesaid Slingerland has had therein, who also acknowledges that he has had satisfaction therefor; and promises the said house and lot to free from all claims, demands or pretensions, which may hereafter arise against the same, pledging his person and estate, real and personal, present and future, and submitting the same to all laws and judges.

Done in Fort Orange, the 15th of August, A. D. 1659.

TUENYS CORNELIS SLYNGHERLANT.

Francoys Boon.
Andries Herberts.

Acknowledged before me,

LA MONTAGNE, Clerk in Fort Orange

Appeared before me Johannes La Montagne, in the service of, etc. in the presence of the honorable Sander Leendersen Glen and Jan Verbeeck, commissaries of the same jurisdiction, Leendert Philipse [Conyn], burgher and inhabitant of the aforesaid village. who declares that he has granted and conveyed as by these presents he does grant and convey in real and actual possession, to the behoof of Henderick Hendericksе his heirs or assigns, a house and lot, lying in the Village of Beverwyck to the south, Claas Janse, to the north, the grantor, to the east, the river bank, to the west, the highway, length nine rods, and breadth thirty six wood feet, which lot is a part of the patent of Anderies Herbertsen, granted him by the Heer director general and council of New Netherland, of date the 23d of April, A. D. 1652, for which house and lot the grantor acknowledges that he has had satisfaction and promises the same to free from all claims, demands and pretensions which may hereafter arise against the same, pledging his person and estate, real and personal, present and future, submitting the same to all laws and judges.

Done in Fort Orange, the 15th of August, A. D. 1659.

LEENDERT PHYLIPSE.

Sander Lenrsen.
Jan Verbeeck.

Acknowledged before me,

LA MONTAGNE, Clerk in Fort Orange.

Appeared before me Johannes La Montagne, in the service of, etc., in the presence of Sander Leendersen [Glen] and Jan Verbeeck, commissaries of the same jurisdiction, Henderick Henderickse, who declares that he has granted and conveyed as by these presents he does grant and convey in real and actual possession to the behoof of Stoffel Janse [Abeel], his heirs or assigns, a house and lot, lying in the Village of Beverwyck, to the south, Claas Janse, to the north, Leendert Philipse [Conyn], to the east, the river bank, to the west, the highway, length nine rods, and breadth thirty-six wood feet, which lot is a part of the patent of Anderies Herbertsen, granted him by the Heer director general and council of New Netherland, of date the 23d of April, A. D. 1652, for which aforesaid house and lot the grantor acknowledges that he has had satisfaction, and accordingly promises to free the same from all claims or pretensions which may hereafter arise against the same, pledging his person and estate, real and personal, present and future, submitting the same to all laws and judges.

Done in Fort Orange, the 15th of August, A. D. 1659.

HENDERICK HENDERICKSEN.

Sander Lenrsen.
Jan Verbeeck.

Acknowledged before me,

LA MONTAGNE, Clerk at Fort Orange.

Conditions on which Pietertie Janse proposes to sell at public sale to the highest bidder some household articles, to be paid for on the date hereof within twenty-four hours in good whole merchantable beavers.

Done in Beverwyck, the 15th of August, 1659.

Arnout Cornelise [Viele], two pewter pans,..........................	*f*	8.00
Anthony Janse, 3 ditto plates and one ditto pan,..................	*f*	6.00
Cornelis Teunisse, a silk cloak,..	*f*	14.00
Idem, a black coat,...	*f*	32.00
	f	60.00

Appeared before me Johannes La Montagne, in the service of, etc., in the presence of the honorable Sander Leendersen [Glen] and Jan Verbeeck, commissaries of said jurisdiction, Roeloff Swartwout, who declares that he is well, truly and honestly indebted to the honorable Jan Bastiaensen Van Gudsenhoven in the sum of one hundred and forty-seven guilders in good whole merchantable beavers, and promises to pay the same on the first of July of the coming year, 1660; for the payment of which aforesaid sum he, Roeloff Swartwout, aforesaid mortgages and specially pledges his house and lot, lying in the Village of Beverwyck, where he at presents dwells, as also the patent which is in the custody of the said Gudsenhoven, until the time of the full payment, all on pledge of his person and estate, real and personal, present and future, submitting the same to all laws and judges.

Done in Fort Orange, the 16th of August, A. D. 1659.

ROELOFF SWARTWOUT.

Appeared before me Johannes La Montagne, in the service of, etc., on the date underwritten in the presence of the afternamed witnesses, Claes Cornelisse, husband and guardian of Ariaentie Leenders, widow of the late Symon Tyssen, who declares that he has appointed as by these presents he does appoint and empower the honorable Stoffel Janse [Abeel] in the subscriber's name and for his sake to demand and receive from the honorable officers of the Orphan's Hall at Amsterdam, all such moneys as to the said Ariaentie Leenders are due from Dirck Janssen, her uncle deceased, and for receipts acquittance to pass and in the matter to act as if the subscriber were himself present provided that the attorney shall be holden to give a proper statement and return of his transactions and receipts, promising to hold as good and true all that the attorney shall do in the matter on pledge of his person and estate, real and personal, submitting the same to all laws and judges.

Done in Fort Orange, the 16th of August, A.D., 1659, in presence of Sacharias Sickels and Johannes Provoost.

CLAES CORNELIS.

This is the mark + of Ariaentie Leenders, with her own hand set.

Sacharyas Syckelse,

Johannes Provoost, witness.

Acknowledged before me,

LA MONTAGNE, clerk at Fort Orange.

Conditions on which Symon Symonse Groot proposes to sell at public sale to the highest bidder his house and lot lying in the village of Beverwyck. *Firstly*, the house with all that is fast by earth and nailed, shall be delivered to the buyer, except a horse stable; the house is twenty feet square with a lot four rods in breadth, and seven and a half rods long.

* * *

[This paper is incomplete and not signed.]

Appeared before me Johannes La Montagne, in the service of, etc., in the presence of the Honorable Frans Barentse Pastoor and Jan Verbeeck, commissaries of the same jurisdiction, Jan Martensen [De Wever] burger and inhabitant of the aforesaid village, who declares that he is well, truly and honestly indebted to Nicolas Meyer, merchant at Amsterdam, in New Netherland, in the sum of five hundred and seventy-six guilders in good whole merchantable beaver skins, for invoices of goods to his content received, and promises the aforesaid sum of five hundred and seventy-six guilders to pay next spring on the first of May, 1661, wherefore he mortgages and specially pledges his house and lot and garden lying in the village of Beverwyck, and at present occupied by him for the payment of the said sum in order that if need be the same may be recovered without loss or damage, also pledging his person and estate, real and personal, present and future, submitting the same to all laws and judges.

Done in Fort Orange, the 2d of August, A.D. 1660.

This is the mark + of Jan Martensen, with his own hand set.

Jan Verbeeck,
Frans Barens Pastoor.

Acknowledged before me,

LA MONTAGNE, clerk at Fort Orange.

Appeared before me Johannes La Montagne, in the service of, etc., in the presence of the honorable Sander Leenderse [Glen] and Rutger Jacobsen commissaries of the same jurisdiction, Pieter Lockermans senior, burger and inhabitant of said village, who declares that he has granted and conveyed as by these presents he does grant and convey in real and actual possession to the behoof of Jan Costerse Van Aken his heirs or assigns, his house and lot lying in the village of Beverwyck adjoining to the south Henderick *De Backer*, to the north the grantor the lot and house is in front on the street one rod eleven feet and nine inches wide, length north and south five rods less three inches, to the west the breadth is one rod and eleven feet, which lot is a part of the patent to him, the grantor, given by the Heer director general and council of New Netherland, of date the 7th of July, A. D., 1653; for which house and lot the grantor acknowledges that he has satisfaction and promises the same to free from all demands, claims and pretensions which may hereafter arise against the same, pledging his person and estate, personal and real, present and future, and submitting the same to all laws and judges.

Done in Fort Orange the 2d of August, 1660.

PIETER LOOCKERMANS.

Sander Lenrsen,
Rutger Jacobsen.

Acknowledged before me,

LA MONTAGNE, Clerk at Fort Orange.

Appeared before me Johannes Provoost, clerk of the court of Fort Orange and village of Beverwyck, Nicolaes Meyer merchant at Amsterdam in New Netherland, who declared in presence of the afternamed witnesses that he had appointed and empowered as by these presents he does appoint and empower Jan Costersen Van Aken. burger and inhabitant of the aforesaid village of Beverwyck, to appear before the court in his absence, and to defend his action for injuries done against the subscriber by Pieter Adriaensen Soogemackelyck, and further the same by process of law, the affidavits and other evidences to produce for the advantage of the subscriber; to proceed against the said Pieter Adriaense, and all things to do and perform which the subscriber being present might or could do; and if the matter requires greater and more special authority than stands expressed herein, promising at all times to hold good and true all that shall be done by virtue of this paper, on pledge of his person and estate, personal and real.

Thus done in Fort Orange the 3d of August, A. D. 1660, in presence of Reyndert Pieterse [Baroquier] and Pieter Bronck as witnesses hereto invited

NICOLAES MEYER.

This is the mark **R P** *of Reyndert Pieterse with his own hand set.*
Pieter Bronck.

Appeared before me Johannes La Montagne, by the Heer director general and council of New Netherland admitted vice director and clerk at Fort Orange and village of Beverwyck, residing at said Fort, in the presence of the honorable Rutger Jacobsen and Evert Janse Wendel, commissaries of the same jurisdiction, Pieter Bronck burger and inhabitant of the aforesaid village, who declares that he is well, truly and honestly indebted to Reyndert Pietersen [Baroquier,] in the sum of eight hundred and thirty-two guilders in good whole merchantable beaver's skins for goods to his content received with the interest on the same; which above written sum of eight hundred and thirty-two guilders together with the interest aforesaid. he promises to pay on the first of July, 1661, and specially he pledges his brewery and lot lying in the village of Beverwyck as a mortgage for the payment of the aforewritten sum, as also his person and estate real and personal, present and future, submitting the same to all laws and judges.

Done in Fort Orange the 4th of August, A.D., 1660.

PIETER BRONCK

Rutger Jacobsen,
Evert Janse Wendel.

Acknowledged before me,

LA MONTAGNE, Clerk at Fort Orange.

I. the undersigned Reyndert Pieterse, acknowledge that the above mortgage which stands as a charge against Pieter Bronck is wholly paid and satisfied.

Done in Fort Orange the 5th of August, A.D., 1662.

This is the mark of **R P** REYNDERT PIETERSE, with his own hand set.

In my presence,

J. PROVOOST, Clerk

Appeared before me, Johannes Provoost, in the service of, etc. Madame Johanna Ebbinghs, wife of Jeronimus Ebbinghs, who declares in the presence of the afternamed witnesses, on the one side. that she has sold, and Aert Pieterse [Tack,] and Jan Willemsen, of the other side, that they have bought a piece of land lying in the Esopus in New Netherland, adjoining to the north and to the west the seller, to the south the thicket [*kreupel bosch,*] to the east the hill, comprising forty-eight morgens and seventy-two rods. for the sum of six hundred and fifty guilders to be paid in three installments; the first, on the first of June, A.D. 1661, two hundred guilders, in good whole beavers; the second. on the first of June, A.D. 1662 half in grain at market price, and the other half in beavers as before; and the third installment on the first of June, A.D. 1663 two hundred and fifty guilders in grain, whole beavers as specified above

Thus done and with the friendship and amity of all, contracted and agreed in the presence of Arent Van den Bergh and Gillis den Necker as witnesses hereto invited on this 5th of August, A.D. 1660, at Fort Orange.

JOHANNA EBBINCK.

This is the mark of ⍊ AERT PIETERSE with his own hand set

This is the mark of ⊥ JAN WILLEMSEN with his own hand set.

This is the mark of **AB** *Arent Van den Bergh,*
with his own hand set.

This is the mark of + *Gillis den Necker,*
with his own hand set.

Appeared before me Johannes La Montagne, by the Heer director general etc., in the presence of honorable Jan Veerbeek and Frans Barentse Pastoor, commissaries of the same jurisdiction, Sander Leendersen Glen, who acknowledges that he is well, truly and honestly indebted to Dirck Janssen Croon, in the sum of five hundred and seventy-six guilders, with interest on the same at ten per cent, to begin from this date to be paid in good whole merchantable beaver skins, at eight guilders a piece, which aforesaid sum of five hundred and seventy-six guilders Sander Leenderse aforesaid promises to pay to the said Dirck Janssen Croon, or his attorney, in the month of June, 1661, specially pledging therefor his house and lot, lying in the Village of Beverwyck, adjoining to the east, Jan Tomassen, to the west, Annetie Bogardus, and which Jan Vinhagel at present occupies, as a fast pledge and mortgage for the payment of the aforesaid sum, and on a pledge of his person and estate, real and personal, present and future, the same submitting to all laws and judges.

Done in Fort Orange, the 13th of August, A. D. 1660.

SANDER LENRSEN.

Jan Verbeeck.
Frans Barentse Pastoor.

LA MONTAGNE, Clerk at Fort Orange.

Appeared before me Johannes La Montagne, in the service of, etc., Adriaen Janssen Croon, now about to depart for *patria*, who declares, in the presence of the afternamed witnesses, that he has appointed and empowered, as by these presents he does, the honorable Adriaen Gerritsen [Papendorp] in the subscriber's name and for his sake to demand, collect and receive here in Fort Orange, in New Netherland, or elsewhere in Manhatans such debts and moneys as to him are due, according to the evidences thereof, of his receipts acquittance to pass, and in case of refusal of payment, to procure by law and the rigor of justice, sentence and extreme execution, and even by arrest to proceed against persons and goods, and moreover all things to do and perform which he, the subscriber being present might or could do, promising at all times to hold as good and true all that shall be done by virtue of this paper, under pledge according to law.

Thus done in Fort Orange, the 20th of August, A. D. 1660, in presence of Johannes Provoost and Nataniel Pieterse [Van Leyden], as witnesses.

ADRYAEN JANSE CROON.

Johannes Provoost, witness.
Nathaniel Pieterse.

Appeared before me Johannes La Montagne, by the Heer director general etc, the honorable commissaries of this jurisdiction in the persons of Anderies Herbertsen and Rutger Jacobsen, who declare that they have granted and conveyed as by these presents they do grant and convey in real and actual possession to the behoof of Adriaen Janse Van Ilpendam and Catalyn Berx widow of the late Dirk Bensinck, their heirs or assigns, a certain lot lying in the village of Beverwyck, to the south Dirk Bensick deceased, to the north Adriaen Janse Van Ilpendam, east and west a street, breadth twenty-eight feet and four inches length from one street to the other to wit east and west, which lot the aforesaid grantors in the aforementioned character promise to free from all claims or pretensions which may hereafter come against it, arising from the interest which the community of this place or the village of Beverwyck may have in the same.

Done in Fort Orange the 23d of August A. D. 1660.

ANDRIES HERBERTS.

Acknowledged before me.

LA MONTAGNE, Clerk in Fort Orange.

Appeared before me Johannes LaMontagne, by the Heer director general etc., in the presence of the honorable Johan Verbeeck and Evert Jansen Wendel, commissaries of the same jurisdiction, Catalyn Berex widow of the late Dirck Bensick who declares that she has granted and conveyed as by these presents she does grant and convey in real and actual possession to the behoof Jacob Tyssen Van der Heyden, his heirs or assigns, a certain house and lot lying in the village of Beverwyck adjoining to the south Adriaen Jansen Van Ilpendam and to the north the grantee, the lot to the north is ten rods long, to the south the same, East and west the breadth is one rod, eleven feet and six inches, which lot is a part of the patent granted to Daniel Rinchout by the Heer director general and council of New Netherland, of date the 25th of October, A D. 1653, which the grantor aforesaid has received from him by conveyance; also her part of the lot received by conveyance from the honorable commissaries of this jurisdiction; for which the grantor acknowledges that she has received full satisfaction and therefore promises the same to free from all demands, claims or pretensions which may hereafter arise, on a pledge of her person and estate personal and real, present and future, submitting the same to all laws and judges.

Done in Fort Orange the 23d of August, A. D. 1660.

This is the mark × of Catalyn Berex with her own hand set.

Jan Verbeeck.
Evert Janse Wendel.

Acknowledged before me,

Clerk at Fort Orange.

(Copy).

Appeared before us undersigned magistrates [Schepenen] of the city of Amsterdam in New Netherland, Tryntie Janse the wife of Rut Jacobsen dwelling at Fort Orange in the village of Beverwyck, and acknowledges that she is well and truly indebted to the Heer Cornelis Steenwyck magistrate of the city aforesaid in the sum of five thousand four hundred and eighty-two guilders and two stuivers growing out of the matter of an obligation of date the 24th of November, 1657, passed by her husband to him, Heer Steenewyck, which aforesaid five thousand four hundred and eighty-two guilders and two stuivers, she, the subscriber, by virtue of a power of attorney of date the 27th of August, 1658, from her husband Rut Jacobsen aforesaid, wherein was approved whatever shall be done by her in this matter; promised to satisfy and pay next May, 1659, with interest on the same at one per cent a month beginning on the first of May, 1658 and ending in May, 1659 aforesaid, in good whole beavers at eight guilders apiece, pledging therefor as a special mortgage her house and lot standing and lying here in the Manhattans, to the north, the High street, to the west, the house and lot of William Herck, as also the subscriber's certain house and lot standing and lying in Fort Orange; also her person and estate, real and personal, nothing excepted, subject to all laws and judges. In witness of the truth, this is subscribed by her as well as by the Heer magistrates, Johannes De Peyster and Isaac De Foreest this 4th of September 1658, in Amsterdam, in New Netherland, and confirmed by the Heer president, the city seal being affixed.

Below stood, agrees with the original aforesaid, and was subscribed.

JOHANNES NEVIS, Secretary.

Appeared before me Johannss La Montagne by the Heer director general, etc., the honorable Rutger Jacobsen, commissary of the same jurisdiction, who has requested that the above mortgage should be recorded in the Register of this Court, which in presence of Anderies Herbertsen and Evert Janse Wendel, magistrates of said court is done, to be used in fitting time and place.

Done in Fort Orange, the 24th of August, A.D. 1660.

RUTGER JACOBSEN.
EVERT WENDEL.

Appeared before me, Johannes La Montagne, by the Heer director general etc., in the presence of honorable Andries Herbertsen and Frans Barentsen Pastoor, magistrates of said court, Jan Martensen [de Wever,] who acknowledges that he is well, truly and honestly indebted to Mr. Jan Bastiaensen Van Gudsenhoven in the sum of one thousand and forty-two guilders two stuivers and eight pennies in good whole merchantable beaver skins at eight guilders apiece, growing out of the receipt of invoices of goods and merchandise, which said sum of one thousand and forty-two guilders two stuivers and eight pennies, the aforesaid Jan Martensen promises to pay to the said Jan Bastiaensen Gudsenhoven, or his attorney on the first of July, 1661, for which the aforesaid Jan Martensen specially pledges and mortgages his house lot and garden lying in the village of Beverwyck and not at present occupied, to secure the payment if need be of the aforesaid sum without cost and loss; also his person and estate, real and personal, present and future, nothing excepted submitting the same to all laws and judges.

Done in Fort Orange the 24th of August. A.D. 1660.

This is the mark of + JAN MARTENSE with his own hand set.

Andries Herbertsen,
Jan Barentsen Pastoor.

Acknowledged before me,

LA MONTAGNE, Clerk at Fort Orange.

Appeared before me, Johannes La Montagne, in the service of, etc., Daniel Rinckhout inhabitant of Beverwyck, who declares in the presence of the afternamed witnesses that he has appointed and enpowered as by these presents he does appoint and empower Sacharius Janssen, dwelling at Munnekendam in Holland in the subscriber's name and for his sake to request of Nicholaes Broeck, dwelling at Amsterdam, one of the guardians of the subscriber, a statement and return of the administration of the guardianship which he has exercised over the effects belonging to the subscriber by way of the estate of Johannes Rinckhout deceased, the subscriber's uncle, acquittance to pass for said statement and return to be received, and in said matter to act as the subscriber himself, being present could or might do without any exception ; and in case of refusal the said Nicolaes Broeck to sue, and before a competent judge to carry the matter to a definitive sentence, from said sentence to appeal or acquiesce therein, according as he shall judge proper, with power in case of need, for furthering the business, in his place one or more persons to substitute; promising to hold good and true all that the attorney in the matter shall do, renouncing all customs and laws which might militate against his good intentions (provided that the attorney shall make a statement and return to the subscriber of his doings), on pledge of his person and estate, real and personal, present and future, submitting the same to all laws and judges.

Done in Fort Orange in New Netherland the 25th of August, A.D. 1660, in presence of Johannes Provoost and Zacharias Sickels as witnesses hereto invited.

DANIEL RINGHOUT

Zacharius Syckels,
Johanness Provoost, witness.

LA MONTAGNE, V.D., and Clerk at Fort Orange.

Appeared before me, Johannes Provoost, clerk, etc., Carel Janssen at present about to depart for *Patria*, who declares in presence of the aftername witnesses, that he has appointed and empowered, as by these presents he does appoint and empower Pieter Gillissen dwelling in the aforesaid village of Beverwyck in the subscriber's name, and for his sake, to demand, collect and receive here in Fort Orange in New Netherland, or elsewhere in Manhatans, such outstanding debts and moneys as to him, the subscriber, are coming according to the evidences and writings thereto serving; of the receipts quittance to pass, and in case of refusal, payment to compel by law and rigor of justice to sentence and extreme execution, and to proceed by arrest against persons and goods ; moreover all things to do and perform which he the subscriber himself being present could and might do, provided that the attorney shall be holden a proper statement and return to make to the subscriber, on pledge of his person and estate, real and personal.

Thus done in Fort Orange in presence of Dirk Hendrickse and Andries Hanssen as witnesses hereto invited, on this 27th of August, A.D., 1660.

CAREL JANSE.

This is the mark of H *Dirk Hendrickse.*
This is the mark of + *Andries Hanssen.*

Acknowledged before me,

JOHANNES PROVOOST, Clerk.

Appeared before me Johannes Provoost, in the service of, etc., Teunis Pieterse Temper, at present ready to depart for *patria*, who declares, in the presence of the afternamed witnesses, that he has appointed and empowered as by these presents he does appoint and empower Pieter Gillissen and Dirk Carstensen, at present dwelling in said village, in the subscriber's name and for his sake, to demand, collect and receive here in Fort Orange, in New Netherland, or elsewhere in Manhatans, such outstanding debts and moneys as to him, the subscriber, are owing according to the evidences and writings thereto serving, for the receipts quittance to pass, and in case of refusal payment to compel by law and rigor of justice to sentence and extreme execution, also to proceed by arrest against persons and goods, and further all things to do and perform which the subscriber himself being present, might or could do, provided that the attorney be holden a proper statement and return to make to the subscriber of his doings, on pledge of his person and estate, real and personal.

Thus done in Fort Orange, in presence of Dirk Hendrickse and Anderies Hanse [Scherp ?], as witnesses hereto invited, on the 27th of August, A. D. 1660.

THUENES PIETERSEN TEMPER.

This is the mark of H *Dirk Hendrickse.*
This is the mark of × *Anderies Hanssen.*

Acknowledged before me,

JOHANNES PROVOOST, Clerk.

Appeared before me Johannes La Montagne, in the service of, etc., in the presence of honorable Anderies Herbertsen and Evert Wendel, magistrates of said jurisdiction, Marretie Pieterse, widow of the late Anderies Van der Sluys, who acknowledges that she is well, truly and honestly indebted to the honorable Gerrit Bancker and Harmen Albertse Vedder, in the sum of five hundred Carolus guilders in good whole merchantable beaver skins, at eight guilders a piece, which sum of five hundred guilders she promises to pay to said Bancker and Harmen Vedder or to their attorneys, as soon as possible; and she specially mortgages her house, lot and garden, lying in the Esopus, next to Thomas Chambers, for the payment and satisfaction of the aforesaid sum, on a pledge of her person and estate, real and personal, present and future, nothing excepted, the same submitting to all laws and judges.

Done in Fort Orange, the 28th of August, 1660.

This is the mark of + MARRETIE PIETERSEN, with her own hand set.

Andries Herberts.
Evert Janse Wendel.

Acknowledged before me,

LA MONTAGNE, Clerk at Fort Orange.

Appeared before me Johannes La Montagne, in the service of, etc., in the presence of the honorable Frans Barentsen Pastoor and Evert Wendel, magistrates of the same jurisdiction, Pieter Meessen Vrooman, who declares, that he has granted and conveyed as by these presents he does grant and convey to the behoof of Cornelis Cornelisse Sterrevelt his heirs or assigns, a house and lot, lying in the Village of Beverwyck (together with a garden, lying on the third [Vossen] kil. to the east, Albert De Ramaker, length nine rods; to the north, Anderies De Vosch, breadth five rods seven feet six inches; to the east a low (*leegh*) lot, length seven rods; to the south, a cartway, breadth five rods seven feet six inches); to the south, Symon Groot, length seven rods four feet; to the east, a road, breadth four rods; to the north, Eldert de Goyer, length seven rods and four feet; to the west, a road, breadth four rods; which lot the grantor received by patent, of date the 17th of August, 1660; for which aforesaid house, lot and garden the grantor acknowledges that he has had satisfaction, and in consequence promises to free the same from all demands, claims and pretensions, which may hereafter arise, on pledge of his person and estate, real and personal, present and future, submitting the same to all laws and judges.

Done in Fort Orange, the first of September, A. D. 1660.

PIETER MEESE VROOMAN.

Frans Barentsen Pastoor.
Evert Janse Wendel.

Acknowledged before me,

LA MONTAGNE, Clerk in Fort Orange.

Appeared before me Johannes La Montagne, in the service of etc., in the presence of the honorable Anderies Herpertsen and Jan Verbeeck, magistrates of the same jurisdiction, Cornelis Cornelise Sterrenvelt, who declares that he has granted and conveyed as by there presents he does grant and convey in real and actual possession to the behoof of Cornelis Teunissen Bosch, his heirs or assigns a house and lot lying in the village of Beverwyck, to the south Symon Groot, length seven rods four feet, to the east a road breadth four rods, to the north Eldert Degojer, length seven rods four feet; to the west a road breadth four rods together with a lot for a garden lying on the kil, to the east Albert De Ramaker, length nine rods, to the north Anderies De Vosch, breadth five rods seven feet six inches, to the west a low lot length seven rods, to the south a cart road breadth five rods seven feet six inches, which lot and garden was granted by patent from the Heer director general and council to Pieter Meese

Vrooman of date the 17th of August 1660, from whom the grantor received the same by conveyance, and promises to free the same from all demands, claims or pretensions which may hereafter arise on pledge of his person and estate, real and personal, submitting the same to all laws and judges.

Done in Fort Orange the first of September A.D., 1660.

CORNELIS CORNELISSEN STERRENVELT.

Andries Herberts.
Jan Verbeeck.

Acknowledged before me,

LA MONTAGNE clerk at Fort Orange.

Appeared before me Johannes La Montagne, in the service of etc., in the presence of the honorable Anderies Herbertsen and Jan Verbeeck, magistrates of the same jurisdiction, Rem Janssen Smit burger of the aforesaid village of Beverwyck; who declares that he has granted and conveyed as by these presents he does grant and convey in real and actual possession to the behoof of Cornelis Teunisse Bosch his heirs or assigns a house and lot lying in the village of Beverwyck, adjoining to the east Adriaen Gerritsen [Papendorp] to the west Jan Tomassen, is two rods and two feet broad in front on the road, to the west and east length six rods three feet, to the north breadth two rods and eight feet, which lot was granted to Rut Adriaensen by the Heer director general and council of New Netherland by patent of date 23d of April 1652, and by him conveyed to Frederick Gerritsen from whom the grantor received it by conveyance, for which aforesaid house and lot the grantor acknowledges that he has had satisfaction and promises to free the same from all demands claims or pretensions which may hereafter come against the same, pledging his person and estate personal and real present, and future, submitting the same to all laws and judges.

Done in Fort Orange, on this 3d of September A.D., 1660.

REM YANSEN.

Andries Herberts.
Jan Verbeeck.

Acknowledged before me.

LA MONTAGNE Clerk at Fort Orange.

Appeared before me Johannes La Montagne, in the service of etc., in the presence of the honorable Jan Verbeeck and Evert Wendel, magistrates of the same jurisdiction, Rem Janssen Smit burger and inhabitant of the aforesaid village, who declares that he has granted and conveyed as by these presents he does grant and convey in real and actual possession to the behoof of Jan Tomassen also burgher and inhabitant here, his heirs or assigns, a house and lot lying in the aforesaid village of Beverwyck, adjoining to the west Jan Van Aecken, and to the east Cornelis Teunisse Bosch, in breadth in front on the street two rods one foot and six inches, to the east length six rods three feet, to the north breadth one rod, six feet, to the west length six rods and three feet, which lot was granted to Rut Adriaensen by patent of the Heer director general and council of New Netherland, of date the 23d, of April 1652, and by him conveyed to

Henderick Gerristen, by whom it has been received by conveyance by the grantor, who promises said house and lot to free from all demands, claims and pretensions, which may hereafter arise, on pledge of his person and estate, real and personal, present and future, submitting the same to all laws judges.

Done in Fort Orange the 3d of August A.D., 1660,

REM YANSEN.

Jan Verbreck.
Evert Janse Wendel.

Acknowledged before me,

LA MONTAGNE Clerk, at Fort Orange.

Appeared before me Johannes La Montagne, in the service of, etc., in the presence of the honorable Frans Barentse Pastoor and Evert Jansen Wendel, magistrates of the same jurisdiction, Philip Henderickse [Brouwer], who acknowledges that he is well, truly and honestly indebted to Henderick Anderiesse [Van Doesburgh], in the sum of three thousand one hundred and forty-four guilders, payable in good whole merchantable beavers skins, at eight guilders a piece, growing out of the purchase of a house and brewery, which aforesaid sum of three thousand one hundred and forty-four guilders the said Philip Henderickse promises to pay on the first of July, A. D. 1661, and specially therefor pledges his aforesaid house, brewery and lot, as a fast mortgage for the payment of the aforesaid sum, that in case of necessity said sum may be recovered without cost and loss, on a pledge also of his person and estate, real and personal, present and future, nothing excepted, submitting the same to all laws and judges.

Done in Fort Orange, the 2d of September, A. D. 1660.

PHILIP HENDERICKSEN

Frans Barentse Pastoor.
Evert Janse Wendel.

Acknowledged before me,

LA MONTAGNE, Clerk at Fort Orange

Appeared before me Johannes La Montagne, in the service of, etc., Wouter Aertsen Van Nieukerck, who declares, in the presence of the afternamed witnesses, that he has appointed and empowered as by these presents he does appoint and empower the honorable Harmen Albertsen Vedder, in the subscriber's name and for his sake, in fatherland to ask for, demand and receive from the right honorable the Heeren directors of the privileged West India Company at the Chamber of Amsterdam, a certain hundred and nine guilders fourteen stuivers and two pennies, due to him, the subscriber, for his monthly wages and subsistence earned in their service as a soldier, according to the settlement, signed Willem Kieft, the aforesaid sum of one hundred and nine guilders fourteen stuivers and two pennies to receive, and being received quittance to pass, which shall be valid as if the same was given by the subscriber; further, all things to do and perform which he, the subscriber, being present might or could do even although the matter requires greater and more special authority than stands expressed herein; promising to hold good and true all that shall be done by virtue of this paper, on a pledge of his person and estate, real and personal.

Thus done in Fort Orange, the 3d of September, A. D. 1660, in presence of J. Provoost and Jan Pieterse Muller.

This is the mark + of WOUTER AERTSEN,
with his own hand set.

Johannes Provoost, witness.
Jan Pieterse Mulder.

Acknowledged before me,

LA MONTAGNE, Clerk at Fort Orange.

Appeared before me Johannes La Montagne, in the service of etc., Henderick Andericssen [Van Doesburgh] dwelling in the aforesaid village, who declares in the presence of the after named witnesses that he has appointed and empowered, as by these presents he does appoint and empower, Mr. Abel Wolff dwelling at Amsterdam, in the subscriber's name and for his sake to demand, collect and receive of Mr. Gerrit Barentsen Koers also dwelling at Amsterdam, the five thousand six hundred and ninety-one guilders and fifteen stuivers due to the subscriber according to the writings and proofs hereto annexed, of the receipt quittance to pass, and in case of refusal the payment to compel by law and rigor of justice unto sentence and extreme execution; also to proceed by arrest against persons and goods. Further to do and perform all that he shall judge proper, with power in case of need to further the business, one or more persons in his place to substitute, promising to hold good and true all that the attorney in said business shall do, renouncing all customs and laws which might militate against his good intentions, provided that the attorney be holden to make a proper statement and return, on pledge of his person and estate personal and real, present and future, and submitting the same to all laws and judges.

Done in Fort Orange in New Netherland in presence of Gysbert Van Imborgh and Johannes Provoost as witnesses hereto invited on the 10th of September, A. D., 1660.

HENDRYCK ANDRIESEN.

Gysbert Van Imbroch.

Acknowledged before me,

LA MONTAGNE, Clerk at Fort Orange.

Appeared before me Johannes La Montagne, in the service of etc., Madame Johanna De Laedt assisted by the Honorable Jeronimus Ebbinck as husband and guardian of the same, on the one side, and Tjerck Claessen [DeWit] inhabitant of the Colony of Rensselarswyck of the other side, who have agreed and contracted with each other as follows: to wit, that the said woman Johanna De Laet grants *per forma* of exchange two pieces of land lying in the Esopus north-west of the inner [binne] kil of Esopus and lying beyond the same; the north field comprises five and thirty morgens and one-hundred and fifty-five rods, and the other adjoining the west side consists of thirty-five morgens and one-hundred and ten rods; in exchange for which Tjerk Claessen aforesaid has given his house twenty feet long and with the passage way [uytlaet] thirty feet broad, and lot (the lot is ten rods and nine and twenty feet long) lying in the village of Beverwyck, adjoining on the east side the street, on the west side the garden of Henderick Anderiessen and Lambert Van Neeck, and on the north side the house of Lambert Van Neck, and on the south side the house of Hendrick de Backer, provided that the respective parties shall deliver proper contracts and instruments securing perfect possession on the first of May, A. D., 1661, without craft or guile, on pledge of their persons and estates, personal and real, present and future, submitting the same to all laws and judges.

Done in Fort Orange the first of September, A. D., 1660, in presence of Jan Picterse Mulder and Arent Janse.

JOHANNA DE LAET.
JERONIMUS EBBINCK.
TJERK CLAESSEN DEWITT.[1]

Jan Picterse Mulder.
Arent Janse.

LA MONTAGNE, V. D., and Clerk at Fort Orange.

Appeared before me, Johannes La Montagne, in the service of, etc., Mr. Daniel Verveelen, merchant here, who declares that he has appointed and empowered by these presents, Wouter Albers, burgher and inhabitant of the village of Beverwyck, in his name and for his sake to ask and demand payment of such moneys and of such persons as the settlements and other papers which the subscriber has given into the hands of the attorney shall indicate, against said persons to proceed by process of law to definitive sentence, from said sentence to appeal or acquiese therein, as he shall think proper, for moneys received acquittance to pass, and in said matter to act as if the subscriber were himself present, provided the attorney shall be bound, of his doings and receipts a settlement and return to make to the subscriber, promising to hold good and true all that the attorney in this matter shall do, on pledge of his person and estate, real and personal, present and future, submitting the same to all laws and judges.

Done the 18th of September, 1660, in presence of Jan Picterse and Geurt Hendrickse [Van Schoonoven.]

DANIEL VERVEELEN.[2]

Jan Pieterse,
Geuert Heyndrycksen.

LA MONTAGNE, Clerk at Fort Orange.

Appeared before me, Johannes La Montagne, in the service of, etc., Madame (*Juffrou*), Johanna De Laet, wife of Jeronimus Ebbinck, who declares in presence of the afternamed witnesses, on the one side that she has sold, and Aert Jacobsen on the other side, that he has bought, a certain piece of land lying in the Esopus in New Netherland, adjoining on the northeast side the land of Jan Schoon and Aert Pieterse Tack, on the northwest side Tierck Claessen [De Witt], southwest the hill, containing forty-seven morgens and two hundred and fifteen rods, for the sum of six hundred guilders, half beavers and half wheat at market price,

---

[1] The above contract was probably carried out as Tjerk Claese soon after this became an inhabitant of Ulster county.

[2] In 1687 Daniel Verveelen probably lived at Spuyting Duyvil; he petitons for a renewal of a grant for a ferry there, formerly held by his father.—*Eng. Manuscripts*. XXV. 135.

in three installments, to wit, in June, 1661, the third part of said sum, in June, 1662, another third part, and the remaining third part in June, 1663, the said Madame promising to free said lot from all demands and pretensions which may come against said land, the respective parties for maintenance of said contract pledging their persons and estates, real and personal, present and future, and submitting the same to all laws and judges (as the acceptant also does his person).

Done in Fort Orange the 17th of September, 1660, in presence of Jan Pieterse Muller and Geurt Hendrikse as witnesses.

JOHANNA DE LAET,
AERT JACOBSEN.

Jan Pieterse Mulder,
Geurt Heyndrycksen.

Acknowledged before me,

Clerk at Fort Orange.

On the last day of September, A.D., 1660, the slaughter excise was offered at public sale by the honorable clerk and commissaries of Fort Orange according to the conditions of the year 1659, and Marcelis Janse [Van Bommel] remained the last bidder for the sum of seven hundred and twenty guilders, for which sum his sureties were Cornelis Teunissen Bosch and Gerrit Slechtenhorst, each for all, as principals, on pledge of their persons and estates, real and personal, present and future, submitting the same to all laws and judges. Done *ut supra.*

MARCELYS JANSEN,
CORNELIS THONISSE BOS,
GERRIT SLICHTENHORST.

Acknowledged before me,

LA MONTAGNE, Clerk at Fort Orange.

Appeared before me, Johannes La Montagne, in the service of, etc., Rem Janssen Smit, who declares in the presence of the afternamed witnesses that he has appointed and empowered, as by these presents he does appoint and empower, Daniel Rinckhout, burger and inhabitant of the aforesaid village, in his name and for his sake, to demand, collect and receive here in Fort Orange such debts and moneys as to him the subscriber are due according to the following specification: first from Jan Helmersen [1] the sum of sixty-five guilders in beavers or wheat, from Eldert Gerbertsen, forty-one guilders payable as before, and from Evert Pels forty-two guilders; from Jan Tyssen [Goes] [2] thirty-six guilders; from Gysbert Van den Bergh thirty-two guilders; and in case of refusal, payment to compel by law and rigor of justice to definitive sentence and extreme execution, also to proceed by arrest against persons and estates; further all things to do and perform, which he, the subscriber, being present would or might do, although the matter may require greater and more special authority than stands expressed in this paper, provided the attorney is holden to make to the subscriber a proper statement and return, on pledge of his person and estate, real and personal.

---

[1] *Alias* Jan de Bock.

[2] Jan Tyssen Goes came to Rensselaerwyck in 1630 as a trumpeter in the fort. By his wife Styntje Janse Van Hoesen he had eight children, seven of whom are spoken of in his will made Feb. 9, 1666-7. He died 31st May, 1705.—*Albany Church Records.*

Thus done in Fort Orange, New Netherland in presence of Jan Cloet and Johannes Provoost as witnesses hereto invited, on this 3d day of October, A.D., 1660.

REM YANSEN

Johannes Clute,
Johannes Provoost, witness.

Acknowledged before me,

LA MONTAGNE, Clerk at Fort Orange.

Appeared before me Johannes La Montagne, in the service of, etc., in the presence of the honorable Frans Barentse Pastoor and Evert Janssen Wendel, commissaries of the same jurisdiction, Cornelis Segersen [Van Voorhout,] who declares that he has granted and conveyed as by these presents he does grant and convey in real and actual possession to and for the behoof of Gerrit Slichtenhorst, his heirs and assigns, a house and lot lying in the village of Beverwyck on the hill, adjoining to the south Marcelis Janssen, to the northeast and west the street; the lot is twenty rods long, breadth to the east five rods one foot, or two exclusive, to the west the hill, breadth seven rods and a half, which lot before this, was granted by patent from the heer director general and council of New Netherland to Jan Roeloffse, from whom the grantor received it by conveyance, and promises the same to free from all demands, claims and pretentions, which may hereafter come against the same, pledging his person and estate, real and personal, present and future, submitting the same to all laws and judges.

Done in Fort Orange the 10th of December, A.D., 1660.

CORNELIS SEEOERZEEN.

Janse Barentse Pastoor,
Evert Janse Wendel.

Acknowledged before me,

LA MONTAGNE, Clerk at Fort Orange.

Appeared before me Johannes La Montagne, in the service, etc., in the presence of the honorable commissaries of the same jurisdiction, Cornelis Teunissen Bosch, who declares that he has granted and conveyed, as by these presents he does grant and convey, in real and actual possession, to and for the behoof of the aforesaid commissaries, a certain lot, being taken by their honors for public use for a street, adjoining to the south of the house of Jan Teunissen, *alias* de Paep (the priest), length thirteen rods and breadth two rods, which lot is a part of the patent to him, the grantor, given by the Heer director general and council of New Netherland, of date 23 April, 1652, for which lot the grantor aforesaid acknowledges that he has satisfaction, and promises the said lot to free from all demands, claims or pretensions, which may hereafter arise, on pledge of his person and estate, real and personal, present and future, submitting the same to all laws and judges.

Done in Fort Orange, the 10th of December, A. D. 1660.

CORNELIS THONISEN BOS.

Andries Herberts.
Jan Verbeeck.

Acknowledged before me,

LA MONTAGNE, Clerk at Fort Orange.

Appeared before me Johannes La Montagne, in the service of, etc., in the presence of the honorable Frans Barentsen Pastoor and Evert Jansen Wendel, Annetien Bogardus, who declares that she has granted and conveyed, as by these presents she does grant and convey, in real and actual possession, to and for the behoof of David Pieterse Schuyler his heirs or assigns, a part of a lot, lying in the Village of Beverwyck, adjoining to the west, the grantor, to the south and to the east, Sander Leendersen [Glen], to the north, the street; the aforesaid lot is six rods and three feet long to the west on the grantor, in front on the street one rod six feet and eight inches broad, to the east on Sander Leendersen six rods three feet, to the west one rod seven feet and eight inches broad, which aforesaid lot is a part of the patent to the grantor, given by the Heer director general and council of New Netherland, of date the 23d of April, A. D. 1652; for which the grantor aforesaid acknowledges, that she has had satisfaction, and promises to free the same from all demands, claims or pretensions, which may hereafter arise, on pledge of her person and estate, real and personal, present and future, submitting the same to all laws and judges.

Done in Fort Orange, the 22d of December, A. D. 1660.

This is the mark + of ANNETIEN BOGARDUS, with her own hand set.

Frans Barentsen Pastoor.
Evert Janse Wendel.

Acknowledged before me,

LA MONTAGNE, Clerk at Fort Orange.

Appeared before me Johannes La Montagne, by the Heer director general and council of New Netherland admitted, etc., Pieter Adriaensen Soogemackelyck, inhabitant of the Colony of Rensselaerwyck, who acknowledges in the presence of the aforenamed witnesses, that he is well, truly and honestly indebted to Mr. Gerrit Slichtenhorst as bookkeeper of the Diaconate, in the number of thirty-three and a half pieces of good whole merchantable beaver skins at eight guilders a piece, growing out of a purchase of seewant which he has received at fifteen guilders the beaver to his content, so the said Pieter Adriaensen promises the aforesaid number of thirty-three and a half beavers to pay, in the year 1661, the half in June, on pledge of his person and estate. * *

[This paper was not executed.]

Appeared before me Johannes La Montagne in the service of etc., Pieter Adriaensen Soogemackelyck inhabitant of the colony of Rensselaerwyck, who declares in presence of the afternamed witnesses that he has received from the hands of Mr. Gerrit Slichtenhorst book-keeper of the Diaconate the sum of five-hundred guilders in seewant for his use for one year from this date and no longer, for which use, the said Pieter Adriaensen promises to pay interest at 10 per cent, and at the end of said year to return the principal sum, for which he pledges his person and estate real and personal, present and future, nothing excepted, and submitting the same to all laws and judges.

Done in Fort Orange the 2d of February, A. D. 1661, in presence of.

[This bond and mortgage was not executed.]

* * * * [wanting) * * merchantable beaver skins at eight guilders apiece, growing out of the purchase of a house and lot that he the subscriber has bought at public sale of the aforesaid Francoys Boon, and as he failed in furnishing the two sufficient sureties which the conditions required, he Jochem Wesselse Backer mortgages and specially pledges the aforesaid house and lot, together with the house and lot that are at present occupied by him, for the payment of the aforesaid sum of one-thousand five-hundred and two guilders, to be collected therefrom without cost and loss after the expiration of the time stipulated in the conditions of the purchase aforesaid.

Done in Fort Orange the 1st of December, A. D., 1661.

JOCHEM BACKER.

Frans Barentse Pastoor.
Evert Janse Wendel.

Acknowledged before me,

LA MONTAGNE, Clerk at Fort Orange.

Appeared before me Johannes La Montagne, in the service of, etc., in the presence of the honorable Philip Pieterse Schuyler and Adriaen Gerritse [Papendorp,] commissaries of the same jurisdiction, the honorable Jan Dareth,[1] inhabitant of the aforesaid place, who declares that he has granted and conveyed as by these presents he does grant and convey in real and actual possession to and for the behoof of Jacob Joosten Van Covelens, his heirs or assigns, a lot for a house and a garden lying in the village of Beverwyck, to the east of the road, length, six rods, to the west, Tomas Pouwel, length, six rods, to the south, the plain, breadth three rods, according to the patent given to him, the grantor, by the Heer director general and council of New Netherland, of date the 5th February, A.D., 1660; and the grantor, promises to free said lot from all demands, claims, or pretensions which may hereafter arise, on pledge of his person and estate, real and personal, present and future, submitting the same to the authority of all laws and judges.

Done in Fort Orange the 2d of February, 1662.

JAN DARETH.

Philip Pietersen,
Andriaen Gerritsen.

Acknowledged before me,

LA MONTAGNE, Clerk at Fort Orange.

Appeared before me, Johannes La Montagne, in the service of, etc., in the presence of the honorable Aenderics Herbertsen and Evert Janssen Wendel, commissaries of the same jurisdiction, Jan Labite, inhabitant of the colony of Rensselaerwyck, who declares that he has granted and conveyed as by these presents he does grant and convey, in real and actual possession to and for the behoof of Evert Pels also an inhabitant of the colony of Rensselaerwyck, his heirs or assigns, a house standing in Fort

[1] Jan Dareth (Dret or Droit) from Utrecht, married Ryckje Van Dyck also from Utrecht, Nov. 1, 1654, in New Amsterdam — *Valentine's Manual.* In 1657, he bought a house and lot in Beverwyck, Deeds, I. 100.

Orange, making the curtain on the east side and adjoining to the south side of the gate, with a garden without the aforesaid fort, according to patent to him, the grantor given by the Heer director general and council of New Netherland of date the 12th of April, A.D., 1650; and promises to free it from all claims, demands or pretensions which may hereafter arise, on pledge of his person and estate, real and personal, present and future, the same submitting to all laws and judges.

Done in Fort Orange the 4th of February, A.D., 1661.

JAN LABATIE.

Andries Herberts,
Evert Janse Wendel.

Acknowledged before me,

LA MONTAGNE, Clerk in Fort Orange.

Appeared before me Johannes La Montagne, in the service of, etc., in the presence of the honorable Andries Herbertsen and Evert Janssen Wendel, commissaries of the same jurisdiction, Evert Pels inhabitant of the colony of Rensselaerwyck, who declares that he has granted and conveyed as by these presents he does grant and convey to and for the behoof of Jan Barentsen Wemp his heirs or assigns, a house standing in Fort Orange making a part of the east curtain, to the south the gate, with a garden without the said fort all according to the patent to Jan Labite granted by the heer director general and council of New Netherland, of date the 12th of April, A.D., 1650, and to him conveyed by the said Jan Labite, for which house and garden the grantor acknowledges that he has had satisfaction, and promises to free the same from all demands, claims and pretensions which may hereafter arise, on pledge of his person and estate, real and personal, present and future, submitting the same to all laws and judges.

Done in Fort Orange the 4th of February, A.D. 1661.

EVERT PELS.

Andries Herberts,
Evert Janse Wendel.

Acknowledged before me,

LA MONTAGNE, Clerk in Fort Orange.

Appeared before me Johannes La Montagne, in the service of, etc., two Indians named Maghsapeet *alias* Machackniemanauw, the other named Sansewaneuwe, also an Indian named Paneenseen, and a squaw (*wildin*), named Nipapoa, being joint owners of the island named Pachonakellick, in the presence of Aepjen and Nietamozit, being among the chiefs of the Mahikanders, who declare that they have sold, granted and conveyed as by these presents they do sell, grant and convey to and for the behoof of Anderies Herbertsen and Rutger Jacobsen inhabitants of the village of Beverwyck, a certain island named Pachonakellick lying in the river obliquely opposite Betlehem, and by the Dutch named the Long or Mahikander's island, with all the right and ownership, which they therein possess, for a certain sum in goods (*kargosaen*) to them paid and they the grantors acknowledge that they have received satisfaction therefor.

Thus Done in the village of Beverwyck in presence of Gerrit Bancker and Johannes Provoost as witnesses hereto invited on this 8th of February, A.D. 1661.

This is the mark of | | the squaw NIPAPOA, with her own hand set.

This is the mark of [mark] MACHACKNIEMANAUW, with his own hand set.

This is the mark of > SANSEWANOUWE, with his own hand set.

This is the mark of — JAN SYMON, with his own hand set.

This is the mark of + *Aepjen.*
This is the mark of 8 *Nitamorit.*
Gerrit Bancker,
Johannes Provoost.

Acknowledged before me,

LA MONTAGNE, V.D., Clerk at Fort Orange.

Appeared before me J. La Montagne, in the service of, etc., Albert Gisbert Raedemaeker (wheelwright), inhabitant of the Village of Beverwyck, and his honor Mr. Arent Van Curler, councillor of the colony of Rensselaerwyck, who declare that they have respectively contracted with each other in manner following, to wit: that the said Albert Gisbert grants and conveys as by these presents he does grant and convey in real and actual possession to said Heer Arent Van Curler his heirs or assigns, his house, lot and garden, lying in the Village of Beverwyck, adjoining on the east side Jan Barentse Wemp, on the south Wouter de Raedemaeker, on the west the highway, on the north the pallisadoes (*deffentie*) of the Village of Beverwyck; the garden lies on the third [Vossen] kil, between Andries De Vos' land, for which house, lot and garden the aforesaid Heer Arent Van Curler has given in payment two horses and a cow of three years, which horses and cow the said Albert Gisbert acknowledges that he has received to his content, and promises the transferred house, lot and garden to free from all claims and demands, and a parchment patent of the same, to deliver into the hands of said Heer Arent Van Curler; all on pledge of his person and estate, real and personal, present and future, submitting the same to all laws and judges.

Done in Fort Orange, the first of March, 1661, in presence of Jan Meynardssen and Dirk Andriesse, witnesses thereto invited.

This is the mark + of ALBERT GISBERT, with his own hand set.

A. VAN CURLER.

Jan Meinersen.
This is the mark **HS** *of Dirk Andriese.*

Acknowledged before me,

LA MONTAGNE, Clerk at Fort Orange.

Appeared before me Johannes La Montagne, in the service of etc., in the presence of the honorable Frans Barentse Pastoor and Evert Janssen Wendel, commissaries of the same jurisdiction, Evert Pels, who declares that he has granted and conveyed, as by these presents he does grant and convey, in real and actual possession to and for the behoof of the Heer Jeremias Van Rensselaer, director of the colony Rensselaerswyck, on account of the Messiers Patroons of said colony, their heirs or assigns, a house and lot, lying in the Village of Beverwyck adjoining to the east the river, to the south on the adjoining garden of Sander Leendersen [Glen], to the west the street, to the north Volkert Janssen [Douwe], length eleven rods and breadth four rods and two feet, according to the patent, granted by the Heer director general and council of New Netherland. to Willem Frederickse Bout, of date the——, from whom the grantor received it by conveyance, provided he, the grantor, convey to the said Messieurs a garden, lying in said village, adjoining to the south Willem Teljer [Teller], and to the north Willem Bout, extending from the street to the river, length ten rods and breadth seven rods, granted by patent to Sander Leendersen [Glen], of date the 23d of April, A. D. 1652, for which house, lot and garden the grantor acknowledges that he has had satisfaction, and promises the same to free from all demands, claims or pretensions, which may hereafter arise, on pledge of his person and estate, real and personal, present and future, submitting the same to all laws and judges.

Done in Fort Orange, the 14 March, A. D. 1661.

EVERT PELS.

Frans Barentse Pastoor.
Evert Janse Wendel.

Acknowledged before me,

LA MONTAGNE, Clerk at Fort Orange.

Appeared before me Johannes La Montagne, in the service of etc., in the presence of Evert Janse Wendel and Frans Barentse Pastoor, commissaries etc., Willem Janssen Stol, husband and guardian of the widow of Claes Henderickse[1] deceased, who declares that he has granted and conveyed as by these presents he does grant and convey in real and actual possession to and for the behoof of Johan Verbeeck commissary of the aforesaid place his heirs or assigns, a house and lot lying in said village of Beverwyck adjoining to the south and west the common street, to the north Claes Janssen and to the east also a common street, breadth on the west side fifty-seven wood feet, and to the east breadth forty-seven wood feet which lot is a part of the patent granted by the Heer director general and council of New Netherland of date the 23d of April, A. D., 1652, to Jan Tomassen from whom the grantor received the same by conveyance; for which aforesaid house and lot the grantor acknowledges that he has had satisfaction and promises to free the same from all demands, claims or pretensions which may hereafter arise, on pledge of his person and estate personal and real, present and future, submitting the same to all laws and judges.

Done in Fort Orange the 15th of March, A. D. 1661.

WILLEM JANSE.

Frans Barentse Pastoor.
Evert Janse Wendel.

Acknowledged before me,

LA MONTAGNE, Clerk at Fort Orange.

---

[1] Claes Henderickse Van Schoonhoven *alias* Timmerman.

Appeared before me Johannes La Montagne, in the service of etc., in the presence of the honorable Jan Verbeeck and Anderies Herbertsen commissaries etc., Willem Jansen Stoll husband and guardian of the widow of the late Claes Henderickse, who declares that he has granted and conveyed as by these presents he does grant and convey in real and actual possession to and for the behoof of Jan Barentsen [Wemp] burger and inhabitant of the village of Beverwyck his heirs or assigns, a lot lying in the village of Beverwyck, adjoining to the east the street, to the south Abraham Staets, to the west the plain, to the north Claes Van Rotterdam, length twelve rods and two feet, and breadth two rods eight and a half feet, which lot is the just half of the patent to him the grantor given by the Heer director general and council of New Netherland of date the 15th of September, A. D., 1657, and promises the aforesaid lot to free from all demands, claims or pretensions which may arise on pledge of his person or estate, personal and real, present and future, the same submitting to all laws and judges.

Done in Fort Orange the 15th of March, A. D. 1661.

WILLEM JANSE.

Jan Verbeeck.
Andries Herberts.

Acknowledged before me,

LA MONTAGNE, Clerk at Fort Orange.

Appeared before me Johannes La Montagne in the service of etc., in the presence of the honorable Jan Verbeeck and Evert Jansen Wendel commissaries etc., Willem Janssen Stoll husband and guardian of the widow of Claes Henderickse [Van Schoonhoven] deceased, who declares that he has granted and conveyed as by these presents he does grant and convey in real and actual possession to and for the behoof of Claes Jacobsen Van Rotterdam his heirs or assigns, a lot lying in the village of Beverwyck adjoining on the east side the street, on the south side Jan Barentsen [Wemp,] on the west the plain, and on the north side Teunis Dirkse [Van Vechten,] length twelve rods and two feet and breadth two rods, eight feet and a half, which lot is the just half of the patent to Claes Henderickse deceased granted by the Heer director general and council of New Netherland of date the 15th of September, A. D. 1657, and promises the aforesaid lot to free from all demands, claims or pretensions which may arise, on pledge of his person and estate real and personal, present and future, submitting the same to all laws and judges.

Done in Fort Orange the 15th of March, A. D. 1661.

WILLEM JANSE.

Jan Verbeeck.
Evert Janse Wendel.

Acknowledged before me,

LA MONTAGNE, Clerk in Fort Orange.

* * * * [wanting] of the above written farming of the excise of [wine and beer.] Gerritse Van Marcken remained the last bidder for the sum of three thousand, eight hundred and sixty-seven guilders according to the above conditions, on pledge of his person and

estate, real and personal, nothing excepted, submitting the same to the authority of all laws and judges.

Done in the village of Beverwyck, the 18th of November, A.D., 1661.

J. G. V. Marcken.

On this 19th day of November, A.D., 1661, appeared before the honorable Messieurs, Farmers of the Excise, Jurriaen Teunisse [Glasemacker,] Pieter Adriaensen [Soogemackelyck,] and Arent Vanden Bergh, who offered themselves as sureties, each as principal, for the payment of the sum of three thousand, eight hundred and sixty-seven guilders for which Jan Gerritse Van Marcken became the Farmer of the Excise, according to the above conditions, for the payment of which, pledging their persons and estates, real and personal, present and future, nothing excepted, submitting the same to the authority of all laws and judges.

Done in Beverwyck, *ut supra*.

Jurejan Tunsen.
Pieter Andriaen.

This is the mark **AB** of Arent Van Den Bergh,
with his own hand set.

The above Farming of the Excise was made in presence of the Messieurs Clerk and Commissaries to which their honors bear witness.

La Montagne, Clerk at Fort Orange.
Rutger Jacobsen,
Frans Barentse Pastoor.
Evert Janse Wendel.
Adriaen Gerritse.

Appeared before me Johannes Provoost, clerk of the Court of Fort Orange and village of Beverwyck, Adriaen Symonse Boer, who declares in presence of the afternamed witnesses that he has granted and conveyed as by these presents he does, to Jan Fransen Van Hoesen two certain obligations, the one of Uldrick Kleyn for the sum of one hundred and sixteen guilders in beavers, with interest on the same; the other of Dirckjen Martensen amounting to two hundred guilders in beavers, also with proper interest, the same to be received in real ownership for the securing of the payment for board and other things, for which the assignor is indebted to the aforesaid Jan Fransen Von Hoesem, for which he pledges his person and estate, real and pers[illegible] present and future, putting the same in subjection to all laws and judges.

Done in Beverwyck the last of October, A.D. 1661, in presence of Juriaen Teunise [Glasemacker] and Aernout Cornelissen [Viele.]

Aryaen Symense.

Jurejan Tunsen, witness.
Arnout Cornelise Wilen.

Acknowledged before me,

Johannes Provoost, Clerk.

Conditions on which the clerk and commissaries of Fort Orange and village of Beverwyck, propose to farm out to the highest bidder the burgher wine and beer excise for the space of one year. The farming as well as the excise shall begin on the first of November of this year,

1661, and end on the last day of October, A.D. 1662, according to the ordinances of our fatherland. The farmer shall receive for a tun of strong beer one dollar, for a tun of small beer ten stuivers, for a hogshead of French wine six guilders, for an ancker of brandy, Spanish wine or waters [spirits] two guilders, at twelve white and six black seewants to the stuiver, and the farmer shall not refuse certificates (*ceelen*), to any burghers to whom the burgher excise has been granted (?). The collector shall be holden to furnish two sufficient sureties, each for all and as principals, to the content of the Messieurs farmers of the excise, to pay the aforesaid burger's excise, every quarter year a just fourth part of the whole sum, in good strung seewant at twelve white and six black seewants (*sewantiens*), a stuiver, and in case the collector fail of the aforesaid sureties, then the said farming shall be offered again at sale at his cost and charge, and whatever less it becomes worth he shall be holden to make good, and whatever more it shall become worth, no profit shall acrue to him. Marcelis Janse [Van Bommel] remained the last bidder for the above farming of the excise, for the sum of two thousand two hundred and eight guilders, the same to be paid at twelve white and six black seewants the stuiver, according to the above conditions, for the payment of which, Mr. Gysbert Van Imborgh and Jan Labite offer themselves as sureties and principals to the content of the Messieurs Farmers of the excise, on pledge of their persons and estates, real and personal, present and future, nothing excepted, putting the same in subjection to all laws and judges.

Done in Beverwyck the first of November, A.D. 1661.

MARCELYS JANSSEN,
JAN LABITIE,
GUYSBERT VAN IMBROCK.[1]

Appeared before me J. La Montagne, in behalf of the honorable messieurs directors of the general privileged West India company and their honors the director general and council of New Netherland, vice director and clerk at Fort Orange and the village of Beverwyck, in the presence of Philip Pieterse Schuyler and Adrian Gerritse [Papendorp,] commissaries, etc., Marcelis Janse inhabitant of the village of Beverwyck, who declares that he has granted and conveyed to Jan Gerritsen [Van Marcken,] also an inhabitant in this place, the burger excise of wine and beer here consumable, according to the above conditions, for which, Jurriaen Teunisse, Pieter Adriaenssen [Soogemackelyck] and Arent Vanden Bergh, stand sureties as principals, for which they pledge their persons and estates, real and personal, present and future, submitting the same to all laws and judges.

Done in Beverwyck the 25th of November, A.D. 1661.

J. G. MARCKEN,
MARCELYS JANSSEN
JUREJAN TUNSEN.

This is the mark **AB** of ARENT VANDEN BERGH,

Philip Pieterse [*Schuyler,*]
Adriaen Gerritse [*Papendorp.*]

Acknowledged before me,

LA MONTAGNE, Clerk at Fort Orange.

---

[1] Guysbert Van Imbrock was a surgeon, and settled at Wiltwyck or Esopus,

Appeared before me Johannes La Montagne, in the service of, etc., in the presence of the honorable Evert Wendel and Adriaen Gerritsen [Papendorp] commissaries, etc., Marcelis Janssen [Van Bommel] who declares by these presents that he makes over and pledges to Doctor [*Meester*] Gysbert Van Imborgh and Jan Labité, the two last payments on his house, which Asser Levy has bought at public sale; further all his estate, real and personal, present and future, nothing excepted, all of which grows out of the bail for the burgher excise, *synde lants middelen*, which abovewritten is to last until the final payment of the aforesaid excise.

Thus done in Beverwyck, the first of November, A. D. 1661.

MAERCELYS JANSSEN.

Evert Janse Wendel.
Adriaen Gerretsen.

Acknowledged before me,

LA MONTAGNE, Clerk at Fort Orange.

Appeared before me Johannes La Montagne, in the service of, etc., in the presence of Philip Pieterse Schuyler and Adriaen Gerritse [Papendorp], commissaries, etc., Pieter Bronck, who acknowledges and declares by these presents, that he is well, truly and honestly indebted to Jacob Geveck, in the sum of two thousand two hundred and seventy-two Carolus guilders, payable in good whole merchantable beaverskins, at eight guilders a piece, for which I, Bronck, promise to pay yearly as interest one guilder for each beaver [12½ per cent], which shall continue until the full payment of the principal sum; for which I pledge my person and estate, real and personal, present and future, nothing excepted, and especially I offer as a fast mortgage and special pledge my brewhouse and millhouse with the lot, for the recovery of the aforesaid sum of two thousand two hundred and seventy-two guilders with the interest thereon, if need be, without loss or cost.

Done in Fort Orange, the 17th of November, A. D. 1661.

PIETER BRONCK.

Philip Pietersen.
Adriaen Gerretsen.

Acknowledged before me,

LA MONTAGNE, Clerk at Fort Orange.

I, the undersigned Jacob Gevick, acknowledge that the above mortgage (standing against Pieter Bronk), is fully paid and satisfied.

Done in Fort Orange, the 5th of August, A. D. 1662.

This is the mark of + JACOB GEVICK,
with his own hand set.

In my presence,

J. PROVOOST, Clerk.

Conditions on which Mr. Francoys Boon proposes to sell at public sale to the highest bidder, his house and lot, lying in the Village of Beverwyck.—*First.* The buyer shall receive the aforesaid house, kitchen and lot, as it stands in fence, with all that is fast by earth and nailed. The delivery shall be made on the first of May, A. D. 1662, on the express condition, that the seller, after the delivery, shall occupy the aforesaid house and lot, as lessee, until the first day of November, for which the buyer shall deduct from the first payment thirteen beavers. Payment shall be made in two installments, in good whole merchantable beaver-skins, at eight guilders a piece, of which the first half shall be in June, A. D. 1662, and the second also in the month of June, 1663. With the last payment the patent shall be delivered to the buyer. The buyer shall be holden to furnish two sufficient sureties, each for all as principals, immediately, to the content of the seller. If the buyer cannot furnish the said sureties in said time, then said house and lot shall be offered for sale again at his cost and charge, and whatever less it comes to be worth, he shall make good, and whatever more it becomes worth, he shall derive no profit therefrom. The auction fees become a charge to the buyer. On the above conditions Jochem Wesselse Backer remained the highest bidder for the sum of one thousand five hundred and two guilders, on pledge of his person and estate, real and personal, present and future, nothing excepted, putting the same in subjection to all laws and judges.

Done in Beverwyck, the 18th of November, A. D. 1661.

This is the mark,- JOH BAKER,- of JOCHEM WESSELSE BACKER,
with his own hand set.

Acknowledged before me,

LA MONTAGNE, Clerk at Fort Orange.

Appeared before me Johannes La Montagne, in the service of, etc., in the presence of Frans Barentse Pastoor and Evert Janssen Wendel, commissaries, etc., Jochem Wesselse Backer, who acknowledges that he is well, truly and honestly indebted to Francoys Boon, in the sum of one thousand five hundred and two Carolus guilders, payable in good whole,
* * *,

[The remainder of this bond is wanting].

Appeared before me Johannes La Montagne, in the service of, etc., two Indians, the one named Sioketas, and the other named Sachemoes, the son of Keesje Wey, owners, and having authority from the other owners, of the land upon the north river, on the westbank between Marten Gerritse's [Van Bergen] island and the *Neuten Hoeck*, among the Indians, named Koxhackung; the cleared land being a parcel away in the woods (together with the kil), extending from said kil, which lies over against Marten Gerritse's island, westward unto the Katskil path, from thence southward along the path to the Stenekil, thence eastward until over against the Noten Hoeck, and thence northward along the river to the aforesaid kil, which lies over against Marten Gerritse's island; which land and kil the grantors declare they have sold, granted and conveyed, as they do by these presents, to Pieter Bronck, inhabitant of the Village of Beverwyck, with all the right and title, which they, the grantors, therein have, for a certain sum in goods, to be paid to them, amounting to about one hundred and fifty guilders in beavers, of which sum the buyer promises to pay the half next May, when he shall come to live there, and the other half on the first of May, A. D. 1663.

Thus done in Fort Orange, the 13th of January, A. D. 1662, in presence of Jan Verbeeck, Frans Barentse [Pastoor] and Jan Dareth, as witnesses hereto invited.

This is the mark + of SIOKETAS, with his own hand set.
This is the mark of + SIACHEMOES, with his own hand set.
PIETER BRONCK.

This is the mark of + Pawanoos, as witness.
Jan Verbeeck.
Frans Barentse Pastoor.
Jan Dareth.

Acknowledged before me,
LA MONTAGNE, Clerk at Fort Orange

Conditions on which the widow of Henderick De Backer, deceased, proposes to sell at public sale to the highest bidder her house and lot, lying in the Village of Beverwyck, to wit the same, which she at present occupies. * * * * *

[This paper is unexecuted and erased].

Conditions on which Jan Lambertsen [Van Bremen] proposes to sell at public sale to the highest bidder his house and lot, lying in the Village of Beverwyck and occupied by Marten Hoffman,[1] saddler (*saelmaker*). The buyer shall receive the house and lot next Amsterdam Fairday, with all that is therein fast by earth and nailed; the lot is six rods long and three rods broad, the patent of which the buyer shall receive on the last payment, with a proper conveyance. The payment shall be made in two installments in good whole merchantable beavers, the first on the delivery of said house and lot, and the second on the first of June, A. D. 1663. The buyer shall be holden to furnish two sufficient sureties, each for all as principals, immediately, to the content of the seller. If the buyer cannot furnish the above mentioned sureties in said time, then shall said house and lot be offered for sale again at his cost and charge, and whatever less it comes to be worth he shall be holden to make good, and whatever more it becomes worth, he shall derive no profit therefrom. The auction fees shall become a charge to the buyer. On the above conditions Cobus Janssen remained the buyer of the house of Jan Lambertsen, for the sum of four hundred Carolus guilders, according to said conditions; for which Frans Barentse Pastoor and Seger Cornelise [Van Voorhoudt] offered themselves as sureties and each as principals, to pay the aforesaid sum, if necessary, on pledge of their persons and estates, real and personal, present and future, submitting the same to the force of all laws and judges.

Done in Beverwyck, the 19th of January, A. D. 1662.

This is the mark of + COBUS JANSSEN,
with his own hand set.

Frans Barentse Pastoor

This is the mark [mark] *of Seger Cornelise, with his own hand set.*

Acknowledged before me,
LA MONTAGNE, Clerk at Fort Orange.

[1] Marten Hoffman was still living in Albany, in 1678, when he sold his house and lot to Cornelis Cornelise Van der Hoeve. — *Deeds*, I, 350.

Conditions on which Philip Henderickse [Brouwer] proposes to sell at public sale to the highest bidder, his brewery and millhouse, with the lot thereto belonging, except the mill, standing therein, lying in the Village of Beverwyck and at present occupied by the seller.—*First.* The buyer shall receive the aforesaid brewhouse and millhouse, as they stand with all that is fast by earth and nailed, except the mill and furniture therein, with the lot as large as it lies in fence; with the brewery shall be delivered a kettle, two tubs, a cooler, twenty-five half barrels, six beer tubs [*Vlooten*], a funnel, a scoop and a *neest* cloth. * * * * *

[This paper was not executed].

Appeared before me Johannes La Montagne, in the service of, etc., in the presence of the honorable Frans Barentse [Pastoor] and Evert Janssen Wendel, commissaries, etc., the honorable Rutger Jacobsen, who declares and acknowledges by these presents, that he is well, truly and honestly indebted to Jacob Gevick in the sum of one thousand two hundred guilders, with interest on the same at twelve per cent, beginning on the 23d of June, 1661, to be paid in good whole merchantable beaverskins, which said sum with the interest aforesaid he promises to pay in two installments, the first in this current year and the second in the year 1663, in wheat *(kooren)*, or beavers, or other wares, at beavers price; wherefore the mortgager, for the payment of the same, mortgages and specially pledges his portion of the island, named Mahikanders island, lying over against Betlehem, which he owns with Anderies Herbertsen, to secure if necessary the payment of said sum of one thousand two hundred guilders, with interest on the same, without loss and cost.

Done in Fort Orange, the 3d of March, A. D. 1662.

RUTGER JACOBSEN.

Frans Barentse Pastoor.
Evert Janse Wendel.

Acknowledged before me,

LA MONTAGNE, Clerk at Fort Orange.

Appeared before me Johannes La Montagne, in the service of, etc., in the presence of the honorable Philip Pieterse Schuyler and Adriaen Gerritse [Papendorp], commissaries, etc., the honorable Sander Leendersen Glen, who declares that he has granted and conveyed as by these presents he does grant and convey in real and actual possession to and for the behoof of Jan Tomase, inhabitant of the aforesaid village, his heirs or assigns, a lot, lying in said village, adjoining the hill, to the east the grantee, to the west the grantor, length to the east on the grantee six rods, to the west on the grantor length six rods, in front [south] on the street breadth one rod four feet and six inches, to the north breadth also one rod four feet and six inches, which lot is a part of the patent to the grantor, given of date the 23d of April, A. D. 1652, and he acknowledges also that he has received of the grantee satisfaction and therefore promises the same to free from all actions, demands and pretensions, which may hereafter arise, on pledge of his person and estate, real and personal

present and future, putting the same in subjection to all laws and judges.
Done in Fort Orange, the 17th of April, A. D 1662.

SANDER LENRSEN GLEN.

Philip Pieterse.
Adriaen Gerretsen.

Acknowledged before me,

LA MONTAGNE, Clerk at Fort Orange.

Appeared before me Johannes La Montagne, in the service of, etc., in the presence of the honorable Philip Pieterse Schuyler and Adriaen Gerretsen [Papendorp], commissaries, etc., Cornelis Vosch, who declares that he has granted and conveyed as by these presents he does grant and convey in real and actual possession, to and for the behoof Capt. Abraham Staets, his heirs or assigns, a lot for a garden, lying in the Village of Beverwyck, adjoining to the north Van Slichtenhorst's gate, on the west side Dirk Janssen [Croon ?], length seven rods and breadth five rods, according to patent to the grantor, given by the Heer director general and council of New Netherland, of date the 23d of April A. D. 1652; for which garden the grantor acknowledges that he has had satisfaction, and promises to free the same from all actions, claims or pretensions, which may hereafter arise, on pledge of his person and estate, real and personal, present and future, putting the same in subjection to all laws and judges.

Done in Fort Orange, the 5th of May, A. D. 1662.

CORNELIS VOS.

Philip Pieterse.
Adriaen Gerretsen.

Acknowledged before me,

LA MONTAGNE Clerk at Fort Orange.

Appeared before me Johannes La Montagne, in the service of, etc., in the presence of the honorable Francoys Boon and Jan Tomassen, commissaries, etc., Philip Henderickse [Brouwer], who declares by these presents, that for the payment of the sum of three thousand one hundred and forty-four guilders in beavers, growing out of the purchase of a brewery (on which aforesaid sum in the year 1661 was paid in diverse assignments the sum of six hundred and seventy-two guilders in beavers), said brewery on the 27th of September, A. D. 1660, stood pledged to the behoof of Henderick Anderiesse [Van Doesburgh], for the aforesaid sum, by virtue of a mortgage; so is it that he, the subscriber, for the further payment of said sum, to the behoof of the aforesaid Hendrick Anderiesse, hypothecates all his estate, real and personal, present and future. nothing excepted, specially his bouwery on the Great Flat (*Groote Vlachte*),[1] which he proposes to take possession of this summer,[2] with horses and

---

[1] De *Groote Vlachte*, more commonly called the *Bouwland*, extends from the city of Schenectady westerly along the Mohawk river, nearly three miles. It has been cultivated more than 200 years, and is noted for its fertility. It was originally divided into thirteen allotments.

[2] Schenectady was first setled by the proprietors of whom Philip Hendr. Brouwer was one, in the spring of the year 1662.

cattle, to secure the payment if necessary of the aforesaid sum, without cost and loss.

Done in Fort Orange, the 10th of May, A. D. 1662.

FLIP HENRIKSEN.

Francoys Boon.
Jan Tomase.

Acknowledged before me,

LA MONTAGNE, Clerk in Fort Orange.

Appeared before me Johannes Provoost, clerk, etc., two Indians, one named Pamitepiet, or in Dutch Kesjen Wey, and the other Hans Vos, or in Indian Tatankenat, both owners, and commissioned by the other owners, of the land, lying in the Klaverrack, on the east bank [of the river], who declare, in the presence of the afternamed witnesses, that they have sold, granted and conveyed as by these presents they do, to and for the behoof of Jan Franse Van Hoesem, a parcel of land, lying in the aforesaid Klaverrack, extending from the little kil (*killetie*) of Jan Henderickse, *alias root-haer*, to the land of Slichtenhorst; in which parcel of land are comprehended three of the *klavers*, on the south side of said *root-haer*, and extending towards the wood about an *uyrgaens*,[1] until beyond the great kil, and further, of such magnitude as the grantors have bounded it by the woods and kils; for a certain sum in goods to these grantees paid, amounting to about five hundred guilders in beavers, for which they promise the aforesaid land to free from further actions or pretensions of the other Indians, who may sinisterly lay claim thereto.

Thus done in the presence of Gerrit Fisbeek and Carsten Claessen [Timmerman], as witnesses hereto invited, on this 5th of June, A. D. 1662, in Fort Orange.

This is the mark + ●— of PAMITEPIET,
with his own hand set.

This is the mark ⌣⌣⌣ of TATANKENAT,
with his own hand set.

Gerret Visbeeck.

This is the mark ▷–| of Carsten Claessen, with his own hand set

Acknowledged before me,

LA MONTAGNE, Clerk at Fort Orange.

On this 11th day of June, A. D. 1664, appeared before me as above an Indian, named Sickaneeck, or by the Dutch named Teunis, one of the proprietors of the above written land, who acknowledges and declares that, on the 5th of June, 1662, with Pamitepiet and Keesie Wey, he sold the above mentioned land to Jan Franceen Van Hoesen, and was fully paid and satisfied therefor, and frees him from all claims of the other Indians.

Done *ut supra*.

This is the mark of SICKANEECK, *alias* TEUNIS,
with his own had set.

---

[1] As far as one can go in an hours time

Appeared before me Johannes La Montagne, in the service of, etc., in the presence of the honorable Philip Pieterse [Schuyler] and Adriaen Gerritsen [Papendorp], commissaries, etc., Wynant Gerritse Van der Poel, who acknowledges and declares by these presents that he is well, truly and honestly indebted to Doctor (*Meester*) Jacob Hendrickse Vervanger,[1] chirurgeon, in the number of sixteen hundred good merchantable boards, growing out of an agreement for twelve hundred and sixty-one guilders nineteen stuivers and four pennies, Holland money, which he promises to deliver here in the space of the six following years, every year a just sixth part of the whole number, of which one installment for this current year has already been furnished; for the delivery of the aforesaid boards, the subscriber offers as a fast mortgage and special pledge his house and lot, lying in the Village of Beverwyck, and by him at present occupied, to secure if necessary the delivery of the aforesaid number of sixteen hundred good merchantable boards, without cost and loss.

Thus done in Fort Orange, the 22d of June, 1662.

WYNANDT GERREYDTS VAN DER POELL.

Philip Pieterse Schuyler.
Adriaen Gerritsen

Acknowledged before me,

LA MONTAGNE, Clerk at Fort Orange.

Appeared before me Johannes La Montagne, in the service of, etc., in the presence of the honorable Abraham Staets and Philip Pieterse Schuller, commissaries, etc., Theunis Slingerlandt,[2] inhabitant of the Village of Beverwyck, who acknowledges and declares that he is honestly indebted to the honorable Ariaen Gerritse [Papendorp], commissary of said jurisdiction, in the number of twenty-seven pieces of merchantable beavers, at eight florins [guilders] a piece, which he promises to pay within a year from date, with interest on the same at ten per cent, on pledge of his person and estate, real and personal, present and future, and especially mortgaging and pledging for the full payment of said beavers and interest on the same, his house and the lot, which lies behind it, lying in the Village of Beverwyck, and which he at present occupies, renouncing all exceptions which might militate against the same

Done in Fort Orange, in New Netherland, the 25th of July, A. D. 1662.

TUENYES CORNELISE SLYENGHERLANDT.

Abram Staes.
Philip Pieterse.

Acknowledged before me,

LA MONTAGNE, Clerk at Fort Orange.

Conditions on which Gisbert Janse proposes to sell at public sale to the highest bidder his house and lot, with all that is fast by earth and nailed, lying in the Village of Beverwyck, where he at present dwells;

---

[1] He was a surgeon in the West India Company's service at New Amsterdam.

[2] Teunis Cornelise Slingerland, the first settler, married Engeltie Albertse Bratt, and left three sons: Arent, Albert, and Cornelis, who arrived to maturity. Many of his descendants settled in Onisquatha.

length thirty feet, Rynland measure, and breadth twenty-two feet fourteen inches. * * * * * *

[This paper is incomplete and unexecuted].

Conditions on which Jan Barentse Kunst proposes to sell at public sale to the highest bidder the house and lot of Jan Barentse Kunst, with all that is fast by earth and nailed, standing and lying in the Village of Beverwyck, adjoining to the south the house of Mr. Abraham Staats, to the north the house of Claas Van Rotterdam, as it stands in fence. * * * * * * *

[This paper is incomplete and unexecuted].

Conditions on which Teunis Cornelise Slingerlant proposes to sell at public sale to the highest bidder his two houses, with the lot attached to each, and all that is fast by earth and nailed. The largest house is thirty wood feet long and twenty-two wood feet broad; the small house is fifteen feet square; the lot as it stands in fence. * * * * *

[This paper is incomplete and unexecuted].

Conditions on which Pieter Bronck proposes to sell at public sale to the highest bidder his brewery, millhouse, stable and hayhouse, *so als reet ende seelt*, with all that is fast by earth and nailed, lying in the Village of Beverwyck, as it stands in fence, which the friends [*lieffhebbers*] can see, and the buyer shall receive the half barrels, *neest*-cloth, kettle, and other tools which are there. * * * * *

[This paper is incomplete and unexecuted].

Conditions on which Pieter Bronck proposes to sell at public sale to the highest bidder his blockhouse, with the lot and a rick (*schuurbergh*), with all that is fast by earth and nailed, lying in the Village of Beverwyck, as it stands fenced, which the friends (*lieffhebbers*) can see. * * * * * *

[This paper is incomplete and unexecuted].

Conditions on which Pieter Bronck proposes to sell at public sale to the highest bidder his little house, by the side of the blockhouse, with the lot as it stands fenced, lying in the Village of Beverwyck, which the friends can see. * * * *

[This paper is incomplete and unexecuted].

Conditions on which Pieter Bronck proposes to sell at public sale to the highest bidder his house and lot, lying on the hill in the Village of Beverwyck; the lot is twenty rods long and five broad, according to the patent thereof. * * *

[This paper is incomplete and unexecuted].

Appeared before me Johannes La Montagne, in the service of, etc., in the presence of the honorable Francoys Boon and Jan Tomase, commissaries, etc., Pieter Bronck, inhabitant of said Village of Beverwyck, who declares that he has granted and conveyed as by these presents he does grant and convey in real and actual possession to and for the behoof of

Jacob Gevick [1] and Reyndert Pietersen their heirs or assigns, his brewery, and the dwellinghouse in front, with the millhouse and horsestable, together with the well and the lot attached, lying in the said Village of Beverwyck, in breadth in front on the street three rods one foot six inches, to the south the blockhouse length eleven rods eight feet, to the east in breadth three rods six feet, to the north of Leendert Philipsen [Conyn], length eleven rods eight feet, which is a part of the patent by the Heer director general and council of New Netherland, to him, the grantor, given of date the 25th October, A. D. 1653; likewise the said Bronck has conveyed to the aforesaid Gevick and Reyndert Pietersen,[2] a house and lot, lying in the aforesaid Village of Beverwyck, on the hill, breadth five rods and length twenty rods, lying in a square, according to the patent thereof to him, the grantor, given by the said Heer director general and council of New Netherland, the 25th of October, A. D. 1653; which the grantor promises to free from all actions, claims and pretensions, which may hereafter arise, on pledge of his person and estate, real and personal, present and future, putting the same in subjection to all laws and judges.

Done in Fort Orange, the 5th of August, A. D. 1662.

PIETER BRONCK.

Francoys Boon.
Jan Thomas.

Acknowledged before me,

LA MONTAGNE, Clerk in Fort Orange.

Appeared before me Johannes La Montagne, in the service of, etc., in the presence of the honorable Abraham Staets and Jan Tomassen, commissaries, etc., the honorable Rutger Jacobsen, who declares that he has granted and conveyed as by these presents he does grant and convey in real and actual possession to and for the behoof of Mr. Cornelis Steenwyck,[3] merchant in Amsterdam, in New Netherland, his heirs or assigns, a house and lot, lying in the Village of Beverwyck, on the hill, bounding to the south the street, to the north the kil, to the west Barent Reyndersen and to the east Gysbert Janssen, where a common alley runs between both doors; breadth in front on the road forty-seven wood feet; breadth in the rear on the kil thirty-six feet, length to the east one hundred and thirty-five feet, to the west length as before; which lot is a part of the patent to him, the grantor, given by the Heer director general and council of New Netherland and promises to free the same from all actions, claims or pretensions which may hereafter arise, on pledge of his person and estate, real and personal, present and future, nothing excepted, putting the same in subjection to all laws and judges.

Done in Fort Orange, the 7th of August, A. D. 1662.

Abram Staes. RUTGER JACOBSEN.
Jan Thomas.

Acknowledged before me,

LA MONTAGNE, Clerk at Fort Orange.

---

[1] Jacob Gevick, Hevick or Heven, administered on the estate of Reyndert Pieterse, in 1673, (*Deeds*, I, 221), and was living in Beverwyck, in 1675. His wife was Geertruy Barentse.—*Deeds*, I, 337.

[2] Reyndert Pieterse died about 1673, when his estate was sold by his administrators.—*Deeds*, I, 221.

[3] For an account of Cornelis Steenwyck, see Valentine's *History of New York city*, page 121.

Appeared before me Johannes Provoost, clerk, etc., Gysbert Janssen of the one part and Harmen Albertsen Vedder of the second part, who declare in the presence of the afternamed witnesses that in all friendship and amity they have contracted and agreed with each other, namely that the aforesaid Gysbert Janssen to said Harmen Vedder has sold his house and lot, lying in said Village of Beverwyck, adjoining close upon Philip Pieterse Schuyler; the house is thirty feet long and twenty-two feet broad; likewise the lot is eleven rods long and twenty-two feet Rynland measure broad; also the said Harmen Albertse Vedder accepts the aforesaid purchase for the sum of a thousand and six hundred Carolus guilders in good whole merchantable beavers skins at eight guilders a piece, in three installments; the first on the delivery, which shall be within three or four days from date; the second one year after; the third on the first of August, A. D. 1664; it is also by these presents expressly stipulated that, as the buyer has hired the house of Pieter Hartgers for the time of two years, the seller shall remove thither and pay five quarters rent as the buyers lease requires.

Thus done and passed without any craft or guile, they mutually placing themselves in subjection to all laws and judges, in presence of Mr. Antony Van Aelst and Bastiaen De Winter, as witnesses hereto invited on this 10th of August, A. D. 1662, in Beverwyck.

GEYSBERT YANSEN.
HARMEN VEDDER.

Anthony Van Aelst.
Bastiaen De Winter.

Acknowledged before me,

JOHANNES PROVOOST, Clerk.

Appeared before me Johannes La Montagne, in the service of, etc., in the presence of Philip Pieterse Schuyler and Francoys Boon, commissaries, etc., Harmen Bastiaensen [Visscher], inhabitant of the aforesaid village, who declares that he has granted and conveyed as by these presents he does grant and convey in real and actual possession to and for the behoof of Carsten Claessen his heirs or assigns, a house and lot, lying in the Village of Beverwyck, adjoining to the north the grantor, to the south Jan Henderickse Van Bael, in breadth in front on the street twenty-seven wood feet and nine inches, length on the north side seventy-three wood feet, breadth to the south sixty-two wood feet and two inches, in the rear on the river breadth eight feet eight inches, which lot is a part of the patent to him, the grantor, given by the Heer director general and council of New Netherland, of date the 28th of April, A. D. 1652, and promises the same to free from all actions, claims or pretensions, which may hereafter arise, on pledge of his person and estate, real and personal, present and future, placing himself in subjection to all laws and judges.

Done in Fort Orange, the 12 August, A. D. 1662.

HARMEN BASTIAENS.

Philip Pieterse Schuyler.
Francoys Boon.

Acknowledged before me,

LA MONTAGNE, Clerk at Fort Orange.

Appeared before me Johannes La Montagne, in the service of, etc., in the presence of the honorable Francoys Boon and Jan Tomassen, commissaries, etc., the honorable Jan Verbeeck, who acknowledges and declares that he is well, truly and honestly indebted to Dirk Dirkse Keyser, merchant, in the sum of two hundred and fifty-five guilders, payable in good whole merchantable beaver skins, at eight guilders a piece, which said sum he promises to pay in the current year, failing of which he stands holden from year to year to the end of the payment, to pay interest at ten per cent, and for the payment of the same he, Jan Verbeeck, mortgages and specially pledges his old house and lot, also a little house standing on said lot by the water side, which he at present occupies, for securing if necessary the payment of said sum of two hundred and fifty-five guilders or the quantity of thirty-eight and seven-eighths beavers, without cost and loss.

Done in Fort Orange, the 15th of August, A. D. 1662.

JAN VERBEECK.

Francoys Boon.
Jan Tomasse.

Aknowledged before me,

LA MONTAGNE, Clerk at Fort Orange.

Appeared before me Johannes La Montagne, in the service of, etc., on the date underwritten and in the presence of the afternamed witnesses, Jan Barentse Dulleman, baker in the aforesaid village, who declares that he has appointed and empowered as by these presents he does appoint and empower the honorable Gerrit Janssen Kuyper, in his name and for his sake, to demand, collect and receive of the honorable Lucas Aertsen and Mattys Harmensen, dwelling at Zwoll, uncles and guardians of the subscriber, the five hundred Carolus guilders and other sums coming to him by way of inheritance from his deceased father and mother; for the receipts quittance to pass; and in case of refusal payment to compel by law and rigor of justice, and for that purpose all terms of the laws to observe; further, to do and perform all things which he, the subscriber, being present could or might do, provided that the attorney be holden a proper statement and return of his transactions to make; on pledge of his person and estate, real and personal.

Thus done in Fort Orange, in New Netherland, in presence of Herman Albertse Vedder and David Provoost, as witnesses hereto invited on the 16th of August, A. D. 1662.

JAN BARENTSEN DULLEMEN.

Harmen Veddere.
David Provoost.[1]

Acknowledged before me,

LA MONTAGNE, Clerk at Fort Orange.

Appeared before me Johannes Provoost, clerk, etc., Marcelis Janse, who declares, in the presence of the afternamed witnesses, that he has granted and fully conveyed, as by these presents he does. to and for the behoof of Jan Van Aken, the number of six and sixty and a half good

[1] David Provoost was an inhabitant of New Amsterdam and held various offices of trust.

whole merchantable beavers, to be received for a second payment for his house, through the hands of Asser Levy,[1] who the aforesaid house bought at public sale; and that in real ownership, to be used as his other proper estates, so that no one shall make any pretensions upon the same, or institute any overreaching claims, but the (*acceptant*) grantee, shall dispose of, use, or alienate, the aforesaid number of sixty-six and a half beavers as his other estate, on pledge according to law.

Thus done in Fort Orange, the 18th of August, 1662, in presence of Arent Van den Bergh and Harmen Vedder, as witnesses hereto called.

MAERCELYS JANSEN.

Harmen Veddere.
This is the mark of **AVB** *Arent Van den Bergh.*

Acknowledged before me,

JOHANNES PROVOOST, Clerk.

Appeared before me Johannes La Montagne, in the service of, etc., in the presence of the honorable Philip Pieterse Schuyler and Francoys Boon, commissaries, etc., the honorable Johan Labate, who declares that he has granted and conveyed, as by these presents he does grant and convey in real and actual possession to and for the behoof of Jacob De Hinse, chirurgeon, a house and lot, lying in the Village of Beverwyck, adjoining to the north the first kil and Jochem Wesselse, baker, west on the street, to the south the grantor, and to the east the river bank; breadth in front on the road nine rods, length on the south side thirteen rods, in the rear on the east side breadth four rods and nine feet, length on the north side seventeen rods; from which lot is to be deducted fourteen feet of the breadth in front on the street and twenty feet of the breadth in the rear; together with a garden in the rear of Fort Orange, which the grantor reserves to himself, also the patent hereof shall be delivered into the hands of the grantee, which patent was given the grantor by the heer director general and council of New Netherland, of date the 25th of October, 1653, and promises the same to free from all actions, claims or pretensions, which may arise, on pledge of his person and estate, real and personal, present and future, nothing excepted, putting himself in subjection to all laws and judges.

Done in Fort Orange, the 20th of August, A. D. 1662.

JAN LABATIE.

Philip Pieterse Schuyler.
Francoys Boon.

Acknowledged before me,

LA MONTAGNE, Clerk at Fort Orange.

On this the 7th day of September, A. D. 1662, appeared before me Johannes Provoost, clerk, etc., Mr. Asser Levy, merchant at Amsterdam, in New Netherland, of the first part, and Robert Sanders, of the second part, who declare, in the presence of the afternamed witnesses,

---

[1] Asser Levy was a Jewish trader, residing chiefly in New Amsterdam. He was in the colony as late as 1684.

that they, in all friendship and amity, have contracted and agreed with each other in regard to the following purchase, namely, that the aforesaid Asser Levy to said Robert Sandersen has sold a house and lot, lying in the Village of Beverwyck on the hill, the same that he, the seller, bought of Marcelys Janse at public sale, as it stands and lies in fence, with all that is fast by earth and nailed, together with a little house also on the side of the great house, which the seller has built since his purchase; in magnitude according to the patent thereof; so likewise the said Robert Sandersen acknowledges that he has bought the same, and promises to pay therefor the sum of one thousand nine hundred and twenty guilders, payable in good whole merchantable beaver skins at eight guilders a piece, besides three beavers also for a hat for the seller; it was also stipulated that as the aforesaid house is leased for the term of two years, so the buyer is holden to buy out and pay the lessee according to contract; delivery shall be made on the 1st of May, A. D. 1663; the payment shall be made in five installments: the first on the first of July, 1663, which shall be the number of fifty beavers, and the following payments from year to year, every time a just fifth part; further the aforesaid house and lot is to remain as a special pledge for the purpose of a complete payment, the buyer also pledging his person and estate, real and personal, present and future, nothing excepted, and putting himself in subjection to all laws and judges.

Thus done in the village of Beverwyck, in the presence of the honorable Frans Barentse Pastoor and Jacob Tyssen Van der Heyden, as witnesses hereto invited on the date above.

Actum ut supra.

ASSER LEEVI.
ROBBERT SANDERSE.

Frans Barentse Pastoor.
Jacob Teyssen.

Acknowledged before me,

JOHANNES PROVOOST, Clerk.

Appeared before me Johannes Provoost, clerk, etc., Reyndert Pieterse and Jacob Hevick of the one side, and Henderick Roosenboom of the other side, who declare in the presence of the afternamed witnesses, that in friendship and amity they have agreed and contracted with each other, namely, the aforesaid Reyndert Pieterse and Jacob Hevick declare that they have sold to said Henderick Roosenboom their house and lot, lying in the village of Beverwyck on the hill, which they bought of Pieter Bronck, as it stands with all that is fast by earth and nailed and as great as the patent thereof mentions; so also the said Henderick Roosenboom accepts and acknowledges that he has bought the aforesaid house for the sum of five hundred and fifty guilders, payable in good whole merchantable beavers, at eight guilders a piece, in two installments: the first on the first July, A. D. 1663, the just half, and the second on the first of July, A. D. 1664; the delivery of the house, which stands at the buyer's risk, shall be made of this date; for which the respective parties pledge their persons and estates.

Thus done in Beverwyck, in the presence of Frans Barentse Pastoor and Marcelys Janssen as witnesses hereto called, on this 13th of September, A. D. 1662.

This is the mark **RP** of Reyndert Pieterse,
with his own hand set.

This is the mark of X Jacob Hevick,
with his own hand set.

Henderyck Yansen Rooseboom.

Frans Barentsen Pastoor.
Maercelys Jansen.

Acknowledged before me,

Johannes Provoost, Clerk.

On the date underwritten, appeared before me Johannes Provoost, clerk, etc., Wouter Albertse [Van den Uythoff], who declares that he is surety and principal for the person of Henderick Rosenboom for the payment of the sum of five hundred and fifty guilders in beavers, growing out of the purchase of a house and lot, which the said Roseboom has purchased of Reyndert Pieterse and Jacob Gevick, and for the same pledges himself to the aforesaid sellers for the payment of the said sum in case of need, under a pledge of his person and estate, real and personal, present and future, putting himself in subjection to all laws and judges.

Done in Beverwyck, the 13th of September, A. D. 1662, in presence of Frans Barentse Pastoor and Marcelus Janssen, as witnesses hereto invited.

Wouter Albers.

Frans Barentsen Pastoor.
Macrcelys Jansen.

Acknowledged before me,

J. Provoost, Clerk.

On this the 13th day of September, A. D. 1662, appeared before me Johannes Provoost, clerk, etc., Reyndert Pieterse and Jacob Gevick, who declare, in presence of the afternamed witnesses, that they have settled with each other for all that they have owned in company, as house, brewhouse, etc., and that Reyndert Pieterse owns in the aforesaid brewery and house on the hill, bought by them from Pieter Bronck, the sum of fourteen hundred and fifty-six guilders, and to Jacob Gevick is coming two thousand five hundred and fifty-six guilders, the portions of each as they have settled at this date.

Thus done in presence of Frans Barentse Pastoor and Adriaen Janse Van Leyden, as witnesses hereto called on the above date.

Actum ut supra.

This is the mark of **RP** Reyndert Pieterse,
with his own hand set.

This is the mark of X Jacob Gevick,
with his own hand set.

Frans Barentse Pastoor.
Aran Janse Van Leyden.

Acknowledged before me,

J. Provoost, Clerk.

In the name of the Lord Amen, be it known by the contents of this present instrument, that in the year of our Lord Jesus Christ, sixteen hundred and sixty-two, on the 23d day of September, appeared before me Johannes La Montagne in the service of, etc., Jacob Gevick, born at Mecklenburgh, of the one part, and Geertruy Barents Van Dwingelo, widow of the late Henderick Hendericksе Van Harstenhorst, of the other part, who declare in the presence of the afternamed witnesses, that for God's honor they have contracted a future marriage; and before the same is consummated, have consented to the following conditions:— *First.* The aforesaid betrothed persons [*echteluyden*] for the maintenance of this marriage shall bring together all their present estates and effects of whatever nature, in whatever places and with whatever persons the same may be, nothing excepted of what they each at present possess and are entitled to, to be possessed jointly according to the law of our Fatherland; except that out of the bride's estate, to wit, of that left [by her late husband], the half shall be reserved for the remaining children of the late Henderick Hendericksе Van Harstenhorst, the one named Lysbet Hendericksе, aged about six years, and the other Judick Hendericksе, aged three years, which by the consent of the bride is charged by the orphan masters and the said witnesses, with a hundred good whole merchantable beaver skins, at eight guilders a piece; further in case the bridegroom comes to die before the bride without children by them, the bride shall remain in full possession of all the estate, as the sole heir of the same, and on the other hand should the bride decease before the bridegroom also without children by them, the bridegroom shall be bound to reserve for her children the half of the estate remaining to be paid to the same over and above the hundred beavers before mentioned, on which account he shall remain in possession of the whole estate; provided also that after the decease of the above mentioned bride, there shall come to the aforesaid children as their inheritance all their mother's clothing, also gold rings and silver ware, which belong to her; *item* that the aforesaid betrothed persons shall bring up in the fear of the Lord and maintain in food and clothes the aforesaid children to their majority and married state, without diminishing their patrimonial and assigned estate; which marriage contract said bridegroom and bride promise to maintain without craft or guile, on pledge of their persons and estates, real and personal, present and future, nothing excepted, putting themselves in subjection to all laws and judges.

Thus done in the presence of the honorable Frans Barentse Pastoor and Anderies De Vos, as witnesses hereto called, on the date as above, in Beverwyck.

This is the mark of X JACOB GEVICK, with his own hand set.

This is the mark of △ GEERTRUY BARENTS VAN DWINGELOO, with her own hand set.

Frans Barentse Pastoor.
By me Andrys De Vos.
Evert Janse Wendel, as orphan master.

Acknowledged before me,

LA MONTAGNE, Clerk at Fort Orange.

Conditions on which the clerk and commissaries of Fort Orange and Village of Beverwyck propose to farm out to the highest bidder, at public sale, the slaughter excise for the time of one year. The farming of the aforesaid slaughter excise shall begin on the first of October of this year, and end on the last of September, A. D. 1663. The farmer shall receive for the slaughtered beasts whether ox, cow, calf, bull, hog, goat or sheep, for every guilder of the worth of the same one stuiver, to wit: for what is bought in beavers he shall give twenty stuivers in seewant per beaver, and in case of dispute an impartial apprisal is to be made. The farmer is to be holden to furnish two sufficient sureties for the excise money, to the content of those who farm out the excise. Every quarter year a just fourth part of the excise is to be paid in good current seewant, and if the farmer cannot furnish sufficient sureties, it shall be offered for sale again at his cost and charge, and whatever less it happens to be worth, he shall be holden to make good, and whatever more it becomes worth shall afford him no profit. After offering for sale the above excise, the Messieurs contractors stopped at seven hundred and fifty guilders; then appeared before them Jan Gerritsen Van Marcken, who accepted the aforesaid farming [*pacht*], and offered himself as farmer, for the sum of seven hundred and eighty guilders, according to the aforesaid conditions, and promises, because of his being released from furnishing sureties, to pay the half of the promise money within fourteen days or three weeks, for which he pledges his person and estates, real and personal, present and future, nothing excepted, putting himself in subjection to all laws and judges.

Done in Beverwyck, the 30th of September, A. D. 1662.

J. G. V. MARCKEN.

Appeared before me Johannes Provoost, in the service of, etc., in the presence of the honorable Adriaen Gerritse [Papendorp] and Goosen Gerritse [Van Schaick], commissaries, etc., Jan Gerritse Van Marcken on the one part, who declared that he had granted and conveyed as by these presents he does, to Henderick Janssen Rosenboom of the other part, the farming (*pacht*) of the slaughter excise, consumable in Fort Orange and Village of Beverwyck, according to the above conditions, just as the grantor has contracted for the same; so likewise the said Henderick Janssen Roseuboom declares himself the farmer of the aforesaid slaughter excise, for the payment of which Wouter Albertse [Van den Uythoff] and Gerrit Slichtenhorst offer themselves as sureties and principals, to the end that the sum of seven hundred and eighty guilders may be paid; on pledge of their persons and estates, real and personal, present and future, nothing excepted, placing themselves in subjection to all laws and judges.

Done in Beverwyck, the 5th of October, A. D. 1662.

J. G. V. MARCKEN.
HENDERYCK YANSSEN ROOSEBOOM.
WOUTER ALBERTSE.
GERRIT VAN SLICHTENHORST.

Adriaen Gerretsen.
Goosen Gerretsen.

Appeared before me Johannes La Montagne, in the service of, etc., in the presence of the honorable Philip Pieterse Schuyler and Adriaen Gerretsen [Papendorp], commissaries, etc., Paulus Martensen [Van Benthuysen], who declares that he has granted and conveyed, as by these presents he does grant and convey, in real and actual possession to and for the behoof of Claes Cornelise Van den Bergh, his heirs or assigns, a house and lot, lying in the Village of Beverwyck, near Fort Orange, bounded on the north by Capt. Abraham Staets, to the south by the aforesaid Fort, as large as it now lies in fence, according to the patent thereof granted by the Heer director general and council of New Netherland, to Jacob Luyersen, deceased, of date the 25th of October, A. D. 1653, and the grantor acknowledges that he is paid and satisfied therefor, and promises the same to free from all actions, claims or pretensions, which may hereafter arise; on pledge of his person and estate, real and personal, present and future, placing himself in subjection to all laws and judges.

Done in Fort Orange, the 12th of October, A. D. 1662.

PAULUS MARTEN.

Philip Pieterse Schuyler.
Adriaen Gerritsen.

Acknowledged before me,

LA MONTAGNE, Clerk at Fort Orange.

Appeared before me Johannes La Montagne, in the service of, etc., in the presence of the honorable Adriaen Gerritsen [Papendorp] and Goosen Gerritse [Van Schaick], commissaries, etc., the honorable Adriaen Janssen Van Leyden, surnamed Appel, who acknowledges and declares by these presents, that he is well, truly and honestly indebted to the Heer Johannes Baptist Van Rensselaer, in the sum of six hundred and forty-three guilders and six stuivers, payable in good whole merchantable beaver skins, at eight guilders a piece, growing out of goods and merchandise, which he has received to his content; which aforesaid sum he, the subscriber, promises to pay to the aforesaid Johannes Baptist Van Rensselaer, or his attorney Jeremias Van Rensselaer, on the 12th of July, A. D. 1663, with proper interest thereon, to begin from the 12th of July, A. D. 1662, for which he pledges and specially mortgages his house and lot, lying in the Village of Beverwyck, to secure if needfull the payment of the aforesaid sum of six hundred and forty-three guilders and six stuivers, with the interest on the same, without cost and loss.

Done in Fort Orange, the 15th of October, A. D. 1662.

ADRIAEN JANSE VAN LEYDEN.

Adriaen Gerretsen.
Goosen Gerretsen.

Acknowledged before me,

LA MONTAGNE, Clerk at Fort Orange.

Appeared before me Johannes La Montagne, in the service of, etc., in the presence of the honorable Philip Pieterse Schuyler and Adriaen Gerritse [Papendorp], commissaries, etc., the honorable Sander Leendersen Glen, who declares that he has sold, granted and conveyed, as by these presents he does sell, grant and convey, in real and actual possession to and for the behoof of Jan Bastiaensen Van Gudsenhoven, his heirs or assigns, his house with the stone front [*geerl*], where he at present dwells, with the lot and garden; also a little house, standing behind the great house, all as large as it at present lies in fence, with a barn also and lot and garden behind said barn, lying on the west side of the street, over against the aforesaid great house, all as it stands in fence, with all that is fast by earth and nailed, together with two gardens also behind Fort Orange, according to the patent thereof; for the sum of three thousand two hundred guilders, payable in beavers, by a deduction from an obligation by the said Sander Leendersen, passed on the 7th of May, A. D. 1661; also the seller of the aforesaid sold estate, acknowledges that he is paid and perfectly satisfied; further the seller delivers to him the little house, standing over against the great house, as it has before this lain in fence, also the said seller promises that the little house, which stands to the north of the great house, and is leased to him, shall be removed within the space of one year and not set up nearer to the great house than the space of nine feet, which shall be used as an alley for the accommodation of the seller; further the grantor promises to free all from any action, claim or pretension, which may arise hereafter, under a pledge of his person and estate, real and personal, present and future, nothing excepted, putting the same in subjection to all laws and judges.

Done in Fort Orange the 25th of October, A. D., 1662.

SANDER LENRSEN GLEN.

Philip Pieterse Schuyler.
Adriaen Gerretsen.

Acknowledged before me,

LA MONTAGNE, Clerk at Fort Orange.

Appeared before me Johannes La Montagne, in the service of, etc., in the presence of the honorable Goosen Gerritse [Van Schaick] and Jan Tomassen, commissaries, etc., the honorable Sander Leendersen Glen, who declares that he has granted and conveyed, as by these presents he does grant and convey, in real and actual possession to and for the behoof of Tomas Poulussen his heirs or assigns, a house and lot, lying in the village aforesaid, next to Dominie Schaets, bounded to the south and west by the street, to the north Jan Bastiaeuse [Van Gudsenhoven], length to the north ten rods, breadth in front on the street two rods and ten feet, length to the south ten rods eight and a half feet, to the west along the fence of Jan Bastiaensen breadth five rods and three feet, which lot is a part of the patent to the grantor given, by the Heer director general and council of New Netherland, of date the 23d of April, A. D. 1652, and acknowledges that he is paid and satisfied for the aforesaid house and lot, and therefore the grantor promises to free the same from all actions, claims or pretensions, which may hereafter arise, on pledge of his person and estate, present and future, nothing excepted, putting the same in subjection to all laws and judges.

Done in Fort Orange, the 26th of October, A. D. 1662.

SANDER LENRSEN GLEN

Goosen Gerretsen.
Jan Tomase.

Acknowledged before me,

LA MONTAGNE, Clerk at Fort Orange.

Conditions on which the Messieurs clerk and commissaries propose, in the name and for the sake of the Heer director general and council of New Netherland, to farm out to the highest bidder, the excise of all wines, beers and spirits (*gebrande wateren*), to be drawn and consumed by the innkeepers, tapsters and retailers (*uytventers*), in and about Fort Orange, village of Beverwyck and colony of Rensselaerswyck. The farming out as well as the collecting of the excise shall be done according to the laudable customs of our Fatherland, and the published ordinances and placards of their High Mightinesses the States General promulgated with regard to the finances. The farming shall begin on the first of November [1662], and end on the last of October, 1663, being the time of twelve months, during which time the farmer may collect and receive for all wines, beers and spirits to be drawn or consumed by the tapsters and innkeepers, in or about Fort Orange and village of Beverwyck, as follows:

for a ton of domestic brewed beer,..................................	*f*	4.00
for a ton of foreign beer,..	*f*	6.00
for a hogshead of French wine,....................	*f*	20.00
for an anker of ditto,........................	*f*	4.00
for an anker of Spanish wine, brandy or spirits,..................	*f*	7.00
for an anker of cider,..	*f*	2.00

greater or less casks after the same rate, and that in beavers or else in seewant at twelve white or six black ones to the stuiver at the choice of the payer. The farmer is holden to furnish sufficient sureties to the content of the Messieurs contractors for the excise money, to be paid every three months in beavers or in seewant at twelve white or six black to the stuiver, a just fourth part of the promised excise money. To provide against cavils, misunderstandings and frauds, it is stipulated that after the expiration of the farming, and when the new farming is again made, the new farmer shall be free on the day of the new farming, or on the following day, at least within the time of three days after the farming, in the presence of the late farmer, if he wishes to be present, to make a guaging of the remaining wines, beers and spirits, held by the tapsters and innkeepers, and return two-thirds of the receipts, or excise due the old or preceeding farmer to his successor or the old [new ?] farmer. The Messieurs contractors (*verpachters*) reserve to themselves the interpretation and enlargement of this paper, and promise the farmer all proper aid and assistance. For the above farming, Jan Gerritse Van Marcken remained the last bidder for the sum of four thousand guilders, according to the above conditions, for the payment of which Jurriaen Teunissen [Glasemaker] and Jochem Wesselse [Backer] stood as sureties and principals, and as such, they bind their respective persons and estates, real and personal, present and future, nothing excepted, subjecting themselves to the authority of all laws and judges.

Done in the village of Beverwyck, the last of October, A. D. 1662.

J. G. V. Marcken.
Jurejan Tunsen.
Jochem Backer.

On this, the last day of October, the above farming was made in our presence, according to the foregoing conditions, which we affirm.

LA MONTAGNE, Clerk (*commis.*).
PHILIP PIETERSE SCHUYLER.
ADRIAEN GERRETSEN [PAPENDORP].
GOOSEN GERRETSEN [VAN SCHAICK].

Acknowledged before me,

JOHANNES PROVOOST, Clerk.

Conditions on which the Messieurs clerk and commissaries of Fort Orange and village of Beverwyck propose to farm out to the highest bidder the burgher excise of wine and beer for the time of one year. The farming and excise shall begin on the first of November, 1662, and end on the last of October, 1663, according to the ordinances of our Fatherland. The farmer shall receive for a tun of strong (*goede*) beer one dollar, for a tun of small beer ten stuivers, for a hogshead of French wine six guilders for an anker of brandy, Spanish wine or spirits two guilders, at twelve white and six black seewants (*sewantiens*) a stuiver; and the farmer aforesaid shall not refuse any burghers, permits (*celen*), which have been entered in the burgher excise. The farmer shall be holden to furnish two sufficient sureties, one for all and each, as principals to the content of the Messieurs contractors, to pay said burgher excise, every quarter year, a just fourth part of the whole sum, in good strung seewant, at twelve white and six black seewants a stuiver, and in case the aforesaid farmer fails to furnish the said sureties, then said excise shall be offered for sale again, at his cost and charge, and what ever less it comes to be worth, he shall be holden to make good, and whatever more it becomes worth, he shall receive no profit therefrom. Jan Gerritse Van Marcken remained the last bidder, and farmer for the sum of two thousand two hundred and twenty guilders, according the foregoing conditions, and for the payment of said sum Jurriaen Teunisse [Glazemaker] and Jochim Wessselse [Backer] stood as sureties and principals, for which they pledge their persons and estates, real and personal, present and future, nothing excepted, subjecting themselves to the authority of all laws and judges.

Done in the village of Beverwyck, on the last of October, A. D. 1662.

J. G. V. MARCKEN.
JUREJAN TUNSEN.
JOCHEM BACKER.

On this 31st day of October, A. D. 1662, the above farming was made in our presence, according to the aforesaid conditions, which we the undersigned attest.

LA MONTAGNE, *Commis.*
PHILIP PIETERSE SCHUYLER.
ADRIAEN GERRETSE [PAPENDORP].
GOOSEN GERRETSEN [VAN SCHAICK].

Acknowledged before me,

JOHANNES PROVOOST, Clerk.

Conditions on which the administrators of the estate of Andries Herbertsen with said Herbertsen's wife, propose to sell at public sale to the highest bidder, the house and lot of said A. Herbertsen, with a barn on said lot, lying in the village of Beverwyck, together with all that appertains thereto, as it is occupied by said wife.—*First.* The buyer shall receive said house, lot, barn, and all that appertains to the same, as they lie enclosed in fence, with all that is fast by earth and nailed, on the first of May, A. D 1663. The payment shall be made in two installments, in good whole merchantable beaver skins; the first on the first of July, A. D. 1663, and the second on the first of July, A D. 1664. The buyer shall be holden to furnish two sufficient sureties, one for all and each, as principals, immediately, to the content of the seller. If the buyer cannot furnish said sureties in said time, then said house and lot, with all that appertains thereto, shall be again offered for sale at his cost and charge, and whatever less they shall become worth, he shall be holden to make good, and whatever more they become worth, he shall receive no profit therefrom. The auction fee becomes a charge to the buyer, payable as before. After offering the property for sale on the aforesaid conditions, Jurriaen Janse [Groenwout] remained the last bidder, for the sum of one thousand three hundred and fifty guilders, for the payment of which Jacob Schermerhooren and Henderick Janssen Rosenboom stood as sureties and principals, according to the said cond'tions (provided that the said house, lot and barn remain pledged and mortgaged as security for said sureties); under a pledge of their persons and estates, real and personal, submitting themselves to the authority of all laws and judges.

Done in Beverwyck, the 16th of November, A. D. 1662.

This is the mark of JURRIAEN JANSSEN,
with his own hand set.
JACOB JANSEN SCHERMERHOOREN.
HENDERYCK YANSSEN ROOSEBOOM.

Acknowledged before me,

LA MONTAGNE, *Commis.* at Fort Orange

Conditions on which the administrators of the estate of Anderies Herbersen, with the wife of the same, propose to sell at public sale to the highest bidder the pantile bakery and lot of Anderies Herbersen, lying in the colony of Rensselaerswyck—*First* The buyer shall receive the pantile bakery and lot and all the fixtures, with all that is fast by earth and nailed, according to the conveyance and bill of sale thereof, except a little point (*hoeckjen*), one board broad and in length to the point on the south side of the brick kiln (*steenbackerij*) of Pieter Bont, which is sold to said Pieter Bont; also Kees Pott, tile baker, is to remain in possession one year, to work according to contract made between him and Anderies Herbersen; provided that the buyer be holden to pay the patroon two guilders yearly, as an acknowledgment. Delivery shall be made the current year, 1662, so soon as the goods shall be got off. Payment shall be made in three installments in good whole merchantable beaver skins, or half of each installment in seewant at twenty guilders a beaver, the first of which installments shall be paid on the first of July, A. D. 1663, the second on the first of July, A. D. 1664, and the third on the first of July, A. D. 1665. The buyer shall be holden to furnish two sufficient sureties, one for all and each, as principals, immediately, to the content of the purchaser. If the buyer cannot furnish said sureties in said time, then the aforementioned pantile bakery shall be exposed for sale again at his cost and charge, and whatever less it comes to be worth, he shall be holden to make good and whatever more it comes to be worth, he shall receive no profit therefrom. The auction fees become a charge to the buyer Gerrit Slichtenhorst remained the last bidder, according to the above conditions, for the sum of one thousand nine hundred guilders, for the payment of which Wouter Albertse [Van den Uythoff] and David Schuyler stood as sureties and principals, according to the aforesaid conditions, provided the pantile bakery remain as a pledge and special mortgage, as a security for said sureties, under a pledge of their persons and estates, real and personal, subjecting themselves to the authority of all laws and judges.

Done in Beverwyck, the 16th of November, A. D. 1662.

GERRIT VAN SLICHTENHORST.
WOUTER ALBERS.
DAVYDT SCHUYLER.

Acknowledged before me,

LA MONTAGNE, *Commis.* at Fort Orange.

Conditions on which the administrators of the estate of Anderies Herbertsen, with the wife of the same, propose to sell at public sale, to the highest bidder, the half island, which belongs to him and Rut Jacobsen, lying obliquely opposite Betlehem. The buyer shall receive the half island, according to patent, with half of the house barn and two ricks (*bergen*); the island is sown with fifty-three schepels of winter grain (*kooren*), of which the buyer's portion is the half. Delivery shall be made at once, but the seller shall have permission to thresh out the grain that is now in straw there. The payment shall be made in two installments in grain at beaver price, the first on the last of November, 1663, and the second on the last of November, 1664. The buyer shall be holden to furnish two sufficient sureties, one for all and each, as principals, immediately, to the content of the seller. If the buyer cannot furnish said sureties, then shall said half island be offered for sale again at his cost and charge, and whatever less it comes to be worth, he shall be holden to make good, and whatever more it comes to be worth, he shall derive no profit therefrom. The auction fee is a charge to the buyer. Jeremias Van Rensselaer remained the last bidder, on the foregoing conditions, for the sum of a thousand three hundred and eighty-five guilders, for the payment of which Gerrit Swart and Dirrick Van Schelluyne stood as sureties and principals, according to the above conditions, under pledge of their persons and estates, real and personal, submitting themselves to the force of all laws and judges.

Done in Beverwyck, the 16th of November, 1662.

JEREMIAS VAN RENSSELAER.
G. SWART.
D. V. SCHELLUYNE. 1662.

Acknowledged before me,

LA MONTAGNE, *Commis.* at Fort Orange.

Conditions on which Jochem Wessels [Backer] proposes to sell at public sale, to the highest bidder, his house and lot, lying in the village of Beverwyck, formerly belonging to Mons. Boon — *First.* The buyer shall receive said house and lot, immediately, with all that is fast by earth and nailed. The payment shall be made in three installments, half in seewant and half beavers, the seewant reckoned at twenty guilders the beaver, the first installment on the first of June, A. D 1663, the second a year after, and the third in like manner. With the payment of the last installment, a proper conveyance and the patent shall be delivered to the buyer. The buyer is holden to furnish two sufficient sureties, one for all and each, as principals, immediately, to the content of the seller If the buyer cannot furnish sufficient sureties, then shall the aforesaid house and lot be offered for sale again, and whatever less it comes to be worth, he shall be holden to make good, and whatever more it becomes worth, he shall derive no profit therefrom. The auction fees become a charge to the buyer, payable as before. On these conditions David Schuyler became the last bidder, for the sum of one thousand and seven guilders, for the payment of which Philip Pieterse Schuyler and Gerrit Slichtenhorst stood as sureties and principals, according to the aforesaid conditions, under pledge of their persons and estates, real and personal, submitting themselves to the authority of all laws and judges.

Done in Beverwyck, the 15th of November, A. D. 1662.

DAVYDT SCHUYLER.
GERRIT SLICHTENHORST.

Acknowledged before me,

LA MONTAGNE, *Commis.* at Fort Orange.

Conditions on which Jan Bastiaensen [Van Gutsenhoven], commissioned of the *meesters* of Johannes Van Twillert, in the presence of Jeremyas Van Rensselaer, proposes to sell at public sale, to the highest bidder, a house lying in Fort Orange named the house of Johannes Van Twillert, according to the patent thereof, with a garden behind said Fort. * *

[This paper is incomplete and unsigned].

Conditions on which David Pieterse Schuyler proposes to sell, at public sale, to the highest bidder, his house and lot lying in the village of Beverwyck on the hill to the west of Annetien Bogardus. The buyer shall receive said house and lot, immediately, with all that is earth and nail fast; length six rods and three feet; breadth in front on the street, one rod six feet and eight inches; to the east Sander Leendertsen [Glen] length six rods three feet; to the north breadth one rod seven feet and eight inches, according to conveyance, with a *hansioos* little house in the rear where in are a chimney and bake oven. * * * *

[This paper is incomplete and unsigned]

Conditions on which Hans Carelsen [Noorman] proposes to sell, at public sale to the highest bidder, his house and lot lying in the village of Beverwyck, by the side of the hill on the plain where he at present dwells. * * * * * * * *

[This paper is imperfect and unsigned].

Appeared before me Johannes La Montagne in the service of, etc., Jan Martense [De Wever], inhabitant of said village, who declares that he has sold to the Honorable Goosen Gerritse [Van Schaick], commissary of said place, seven head of cattle great and little, for the sum of five hundred and eighty guilders payable in beavers, for which sum said Jan Martensen acknowledges that he is fully satisfied and paid; in witness of which he has subscribed this with his own hand.

Done in Fort Orange the 15th of March, A.D. 1663, in presence of J. Provoost and David Provoost.

This is the mark of ┬ JAN MARTENSEN
with his own hand set.

Johannes Provoost wit:
David Provoost.

Acknowledged before me,

LA MONTAGNE, *Commis.* at Fort Orange.

Appeared before me Johannes La Montagne in the service of, etc., in the presence of the Honorable Goosen Gerritse [Van Schaick] and Jan Tomassen commissaries etc., the honorable Jan Costersen Van Aecken, who declares that he has granted and conveyed, as by these presents, he does grant and convey, in real and actual possession to and for the behoof Arnout Cornelissen [Viele], his heirs or assigns, a house and lot lying in the village of Beverwyck; to the south Jochem Kettelheym, length eight rods six feet three inches, on the road, breath two rods and ten feet; to the north Wynandt Gerritsen [Van Der Poel] length six rods eleven feet; breadth in the rear three rods and ten feet, according to patent to the grantor given by the Heer director general and council of New Netherland, of date the 7th of March, 1661, for which aforesaid house and lot, the grantor acknowledges that he is paid and satisfied and therefore promises the same to free from all actions, demands or pretensions, which may hereafter arise, under pledge of his person and estate movable and immovable, present and future, nothing excepted, submitting himself to the authority of all laws and judges.

Done in Fort Orange the 17th of March, A.D. 1663.

JAN KOSTER VAN AACKEN.

Goosen Gerretsen,
Jan Tomas

Appeared before me Johannes Provoost, clerk, etc., Roeloff Willemse [Van Heerden] and Geurt Hendericksе [Van Schoonhoven], who declare in presence of the after named witnesses, that, in friendship and amity they have agreed with each other as follows, namely, Roeloff Willemse aforesaid acknowldges, by these presents, that he has sold to said Geurt Hendericksе his certain cellar and shed (*afdack*) over it with the lot attached, of magnitude both as to length and breadth, as mentioned in the patent thereof; in like manner also said Geurt Hendericksе accepts and acknowledges that he has bought of said Roeloff Willemse, said cellar and lot, for which he promises to pay the sum of two hundred and seventy-five guilders in good strung seewant, the delivery of said cellar to be made of this date at the buyers risk.

Thus done without craft or guile in presence of Jacob Janssen [Flodder] and David Provoost as witnesses hereto invited, on this 23d of March, A.D. 1663, in Fort Orange.

Roelef Willemsen,
Geurt Hendrycksen.

Jacob Jansen Flodder,
David Provoost.

Acknowledged before me,

J. Provoost, Clerk.

In the name of the Lord Amen, be it known by the contents of this present instrument, that in the year sixteen hundred and sixty-three the eighteenth day of May, appeared before me, Johannes La Montagne in the service of, etc., Meyndert Frederickse [Smith], widower of the late Cataryna Burger, who declares in the presence of the afternamed witnesses, that for God's honor he has contracted a future marriage with Pietertien Teunise, spinster (*jonge dochter*), and before the consummation of the same, he, the subscriber, assents to the following conditions, firstly, that the aforesaid betrothed persons, for the maintenance of said marriage, will collect and bring together, all such existing estates and effects of whatever nature; in whatever place, and with whatever persons, the same may be lying or deposited, nothing excepted, which each now has and possesses, to be by them possessed in common, according to the law of our Fatherland, except that out of the bridegroom's estate, to wit, from the estate left by Catarina Burger deceased, be reserved the sum of eight hundred guilders payable in beavers, for the children left by her; to wit Frederick Meyndersen aged six years and Burgert Meyndersen aged three years, being their maternal? (*matrimoniale*) inheritance; moreover said married persons shall be holden to bring up said children in the fear of the Lord, to teach them to read and write in the schools, to maintain them in food and clothing till their majority or married state, without diminishing their maternal estate, which the subscriber promises without craft or guile, and for the same binding his person and estate, real and personal, present and future, nothing excepted, subject to all laws and judges.

Thus done in presence of Heer Arent Curler and Jan Dareth and Pieter Bronck, guardians of the aforesaid children, with Jan Verbeeck and Evert Janse Wendel orphan masters.

Adij ut supra.

This is the mark of Meyndert Fredericksе, with his own hand set.

A. Van Curler,
Jan Dareth,
Jan Verbeeck,
Evert Jansen Wendel,
as *Wees Mysters,*
Pyeter Bronck.

Acknowledged before me,

La Montagne, *Commis* at Fort Orange.

Appeared before me, Johannes La Montagne, in the service of, etc , in the presence of the honorable Goosen Gerritse [Van Schaick] and Jan Tomassen, commissioners, etc., Harmen Tomassen [Hun, or Van Amersfort], husband and guardian of Catarina Berex, widow of Dirk Bensingh deceased, who declares that he has granted and conveyed, as by these presents he does grant and convey to Tjerck Claessen De Wit his heirs or assigns a lot lying in the village of Beverwyck; bounded to the south by Lambert Van Neck, to the north by Hans Coenraetse [Backer], and to the west by the street; length ten rods and breadth two rods three feet, which lot the grantor's predecessor [Bensingh] received by conveyance from Michiel Ryckertsen, of date the 29 April, Ao. 1656; and the grantor acknowledges that he is fully paid and satisfied for the purchase and transfer of the same, and therefore, promises to free the same from all claims, demands or pretensions, which may hereafter arise, pledging therefor his person and estates, real and personal, present and future, and submitting himself to all laws and judges.

Done in Fort Orange the 28th of May, 1663.

HARMEN TOMASSE.

Goosen Gerretsen,
Jan Tomasse

Acknowledged before me,

LA MONTAGNE, *Commis* at Fort Orange.

Appeared before me, Johannes La Montagne, in the service of, etc., in the presence of the honorable Goosen Gerritse [Van Schaick] and Jan Tomasse commissaries, etc., Harmen Tomasse [Hun of Amersfort], husband and guardian of Cataryna Berex, widow of the late Dirk Bensingh, who declares that he has granted and conveyed, as by these presents he does grant and convey in real and actual possession to and for the behoof of Lambert Albertse Van Neck his heirs or assigns, a house and lot lying in the village of Beverwyck, adjoining to the north Tjerck Claessen [De Wit], to the south Frans Barentsen [Pastoor], length ten rods and breadth five or six and twenty feet, which lot is a part of the patent granted by the heer director general and council of New Netherland, to Daniel Rinckhout, of date the 25th of October, 1653; acknowledging that he, the grantor, is fully paid and satisfied for said house and lot, and therefore he promises to free the same from all claims, actions, or pretensions, which may hereafter arise, under pledge of his person and estate, real and personal, present and future, submitting himself to the authority of all laws and judges.

Done in Fort Orange the 28th of May, 1663.

HARMEN TOMASSE.

Goosen Gerretsen,
Jan Tomasse.

Acknowledged before me.

LA MONTAGNE, *Commis* at Fort Orange.

Appeared before me Johannes La Montagne, in the service of, etc , in the presence of the honorable Jan Tomasse and Johan Verbeeck, commissaries, etc., Gillis Pietersen [Timmerman], who declares that he has granted and conveyed, as by these presents he does grant and convey, in real and actual possession to and for the behoof of Harmen Tomasse

[Hun of Amersfort], husband and guardian of Cataryna Berex, widow of the late Dirk Bensingh, his heirs or assigns, a lot, lying in the village of Beverwyck, adjoining to the south Evert Janse Wendel, north and west the street; length on the south side nine and a half rods, and on the north side five rods, breadth on the west side seven and a half rods, on the east side eight rods, which lot the grantor received by patent from the Heer director general and council of New Netherland, of date the 14th of April, A. D. 1654, and acknowledges that he, the grantor, has been fully paid and satisfied for the purchase of the same, and, therefore, promises to free said lot from all actions, claims or pretensions, which may arise, binding therefor his person and estate, real and personal, present and future, nothing excepted, and subjecting himself to the authority of all laws and judges.

Done in Fort Orange, the 28th of May, A. D. 1663.

JELIS PETERSE.

Jan Tomase.
Jan Verbeeck.

Acknowledged before me,

LA MONTAGNE, *Commis* at Fort Orange.

Appeared before me Johannes La Montagne, in the service of, etc., in the presence of the honorable Jan Verbeeck and Gerrit Slichtenhorst, commissaries, etc., Harmen Tomassen [Hun of Amersfoort], husband and guardian of Catarina Berex, widow of Dirk Bensingh, deceased, who declares that he has granted and conveyed, as by these presents he does grant and convey in real and actual possession to and for the behoof of Maritien Damens, widow of the late Henderick Andriessen [Van Doesburgh], her heirs or assigns, a lot, lying in the village of Beverwyck, to the south the lots length nine rods nine feet six inches to the north the grantor length seven rods eight feet, to the east Tjerck Claessen [De Wit], breadth three rods, to the west the road, breadth three rods, which lot is a part of the patent to Gillis Pieterse, granted by the heer director general and council of New Netherland, of date the 19th of April, A. D. 1654; and acknowledging that he, the grantor, is fully paid and satisfied for the purchase of said lot, he therefore promises to free the same from all actions, claims or pretensions, which may arise hereafter, pledging therefor his person and estate, real and personal, present and future, and submitting himself to the authority of all laws and judges.

Done in Fort Orange, the 29th of May, A. D. 1663.

HARMEN THOMASE.

Jan Verbeeck.
Gerrit Slichtenhorst.

Acknowledged before me,

LA MONTAGNE, *Commis* at Fort Orange.

Conditions on which the heirs of Annetien Bogardus, deceased, propose to sell at public sale, to the highest bidder, her house and lot, lying in the village of Beverwyck on the hill.—*First.* The buyer shall receive, on the first payment, the aforesaid house with an alley (*uytlaet*) on the east side, and a hen yard on the place with the lot, length to the west with the house five rods nine feet, and to the east five rods eight and a half feet, breadth to the north two rods eight and a half feet, and to the south two rods seven feet, with all that is fast by earth and nailed, except the little shed (*afdackjen*) that stands on the west (east?) side of the house, and to the east the little Indian house, and which remains with said little Indian house to the behoof of Jonas [1] and Pieter [1] Bogardus. * * * * *

[This paper is incomplete and unexecuted].

Appeared before me Johannes Provoost, clerk, etc., the heirs of the late Annetien Bogardus of the one side, and Dirk Wesselse [Ten Broeck] of the other side, who declare in presence of the afternamed witnesses, that in friendship and amity, they have agreed and contracted with each other that the aforesaid heirs (being the surviving children of said Annetien Bogardus, deceased,), have sold to said Dirk Wesselse, as by these presents they do, their late mother's house and lot, lying in the village of Beverwyck, adjoining to the east Jonas and Pieter Bogardus, and to the west Evert Janse Wendels, the same lot which she occupied to the day of her death; length to the west with the house five rods nine feet, and to the east five rods and eight and a half feet, breadth to the north two rods eight and a half feet, and to the south two rods seven feet, together with a shed (*afdack*) to the east side of said house, that has been rented out three months to the date of this purchase, and the rent of which the buyer shall receive; for which house and lot the said Dirk Wesselse, as buyer, promises to pay the sum of one thousand guilders, payable in good whole merchantable beaver skins, at eight guilders a piece, in three installments: the first immediately, the second on the first of July, 1664, and the third or last on the first of July, 1665, each time a just third part of the whole sum; the buyer shall, with the first payment, receive the aforesaid house and lot, and in the meantime said house shall be occupied at his risk, also with the last payment the buyer shall receive a proper conveyance, all of which the parties aforesaid mutually promise to hold good and true, under pledge according to law.

Done in Beverwyck, in presence of Wouter Albertsen [Van den Uythooff] and David Provoost, as witnesses hereto called, on this 21st of June, A. D. 1663.

W. Bogardus.
Jan Roeloffse.
Cornelis Bogardus.
by order of the other heirs,
Dirk Wesselse Ten Broeck.

Wouter Alberts.
David Provoost.

Acknowledged before me,

Johannes Provoost, Clerk.

Conditions on which the administrators of the estate of Anderies Herbertsen and Rut Jacobsen propose to sell at public sale, to the highest bidder, all the grain (*kooren*) that is sown and stands on their island

[1] Sons of Annatie Janse Bogardus.

(lying obliquely opposite Betlehem). The aforesaid grain shall be delivered to the buyer, on the understanding, that the whole island is sowed with fifty-three schepels of winter grain of which eight schepels is rye and all the remainder is wheat, which the buyer may harvest and gather into the barn and rick there standing: also the buyer shall be permitted to lodge two men in the house there (at the close of the harvest), with their luggage, to plough and sow the land again. The payment shall be made on the 15 January, A. D. 1664, in beavers or grain at beavers price, within which time the buyer shall be holden to remove and carry away said purchased grain whether it be threshed out or not. * * * * *

[This paper is imperfect and not signed].

Conditions on which the administrators of the estate of Anderies Herbertsen propose to sell to the highest bidder, at public sale, the half island that belongs to him and Rutger Jacobsen in company, except the grain, which at present stands upon it. Said half island shall be delivered to the buyer so soon as the grain at present standing upon it is hauled off, that it may be properly ploughed, in such right, title and ownership, as the said Anderies Herbertsen had therein, according to the tenor and contents of the patent by the Heer director general and council of New Netherland granted him. The buyer shall permit the purchasers of the grain at present standing there, at their convenience to stow away and keep their grain in the barn and rick, and to thresh it out according to their contract, by the 15th of January, A. D. 1664. The buyer shall be holden his promised purchase money to pay in good whole merchantable beavers or grain at beavers price, in two installments: the first on the first of July, A. D. 1664, and the second on the first of July, A. D. 1665. The buyer shall be holden to furnish two sufficient sureties, one for all and each as principals to the content of the seller, in the time of twenty-four hours. If the buyer cannot furnish said sureties in said time, then said half island shall be offered for sale again, at his cost and charge, and whatever less it comes to be worth, he shall be holden to make good, and whatever more it comes to be worth, he shall enjoy no profit therefrom. The auction fees become a charge to the buyer, payable as above. Volckert Janse [Douw] remained the last bidder, according to the aforementioned conditions, for the sum of six hundred and twenty guilders, for the payment of which Adriaen Gerritsen [Papendorp] and Jan Tomassen stood as sureties and principals, for which they pledged their persons and estates, real and personal, present and future, subjecting themselves to the authority of all laws and judges.

Done in the village of Beverwyck, the 26th of June, A. D. 1663.

VOLKART JANSE.
ADRIAEN GERRETSEN
JAN TOMASE.

Acknowledged before me,

LA MONTAGNE, *Commis* at Fort Orange.

Conditions on which the administrators of the estate of Andries Herbertsen with Rutger Jacobsen proposes to sell, at public sale to the highest bidder, all the grain that is sowed and stands upon their island lying obliquely opposite Betlehem. The aforesaid grain shall be delivered to the seller, on the understanding that it is all sowed with 53 schepels of winter grain, to wit, 45 schepels of wheat and 8 schepels of rye, which the buyer may harvest and gather into the barn and rick, which now stand there. The buyer shall be holden to pay the promised money on the 15th of January, A. D. 1664, payable in good whole merchantable beaver skins or wheat at beaver price. The buyer shall be holden to furnish two sufficient sureties, one for all and each, as principals, immediately to the content of the sellers. If the buyer cannot furnish said sureties in said time then the aforesaid grain shall be offered for sale again at his cost and charge, and whatever less it comes to be worth he shall be holden to make good, and whatever more it comes to be worth he shall derive no profit therefrom. The auction fees become a charge to the buyer, payable as before. Rutger Jacobsen remained the last bidder, according to the above conditions, for the sum of five hundred and twenty guilders, pledging therefor his person and estate, real and personal, subjecting himself to the authority of all laws and judges.

Done in Beverwyck, the 26th of June, A. D. 1663.

RUTGER JACOBSEN.

On this 28th day of July, A.D. 1663, appeared before me Johannes La Montagne, in the service of etc., Jan Anderissen and Anderies Hanse Van Sweeden, who offered themselves as sureties and principals for the person of Rutger Jacobsen for the payment of half of the above mentioned sum of five hundred and twenty guilders (for the purchase of the aforesaid grain of Anderies Herbertsen, the said half) being two hundred and ninety-five guilders, which they accept and promise to pay to the administrators of said estate of Andries Herbertsen, in grain from the crop at present standing thereon, and that no grain shall be removed therefrom before that the said administrators are fully paid and satisfied, under pledge of their persons and estates real and personal, submitting themselves to the authority of all laws and judges.

Done in Fort Orange *ut supra.*

This is the mark of ⌒ JAN ANDERIESSEN,
with his own hand set.
This is the mark + of ANDERIES HANSE.
with his own hand set.

J. Provoost, witness.

Appeared before me, Johannes La Montagne, in the service of, etc., in the presence of Jan Tomassen and Stoffel Janse [Abeel] commissaries etc., Jan Lambertsen Van Bremen, who declares that he has granted and conveyed, as by these presents he does, in real and actual possession to and for the behoof of Pieter Janssen De Boer, his heirs or assigns, a house and lot lying in the village of Beverwyck, bounded according to the patent to the east Doctor (*Meester*) Jacob [D'Hinse] length six rods, to the west Jan Van Breemen length 6 rods, to the north the road, breadth three rods, to the south the plain breadth three rods which patent was given to him, the grantor, by the Heer director general and council of New Netherland of date the last of April, A.D. 1663, for which house and lot, the grantor acknowledges that he has had satisfaction, and therefore promises to free the same from all actions, claims, or pretensions, which may hereafter arise, pledging therefor his person and estate, real and personal, subjecting himself to the authority of all laws and judges

Done in Fort Orange the 29th of June, A.D. 1663.

This is the mark + of JAN LAMBERTSEN VAN BREEMEN.
with his own hand set.

Jan Tomase.
Stoffel Jonse.

Acknowledge before me,

LA MONTAGNE, *Commis* at Fort Orange.

In the name of the Lord Amen: Be it known by the contents of this present instrument, that in the year sixteen hundred and sixty-three, the 30th of June, appeared before me, Johannes La Montagne, in the service of, etc., the Honorable Evert Janssen Wendel, late commissary of this place, widower of the late Susanna De Truwe,[1] who declares in presence of the afternamed witnesses and of the honorable Jan Verbeeck commissary and orphan master, that for God's honor, he has contracted a future marriage with Maria Abrahamse[2] widow of the late Tomas Janssen Mingael, and before the consummation of the same, he, the appearer (*comparant*), has assented to the following conditions: Firstly, that the aforesaid betrothed persons, for the maintenance of this marriage, shall mutually collect and bring together all present and such estates and effects of whatsoever nature, in whatsoever place, with whatsoever persons the same may lie or be deposited, nothing excepted, which they each have and are furnished with, to be possessed by them in common, according to the law of our Fatherland; except that out of the appearer's [Wendel's] estate, to wit, from the estate left by Susanna De Truwe deceased, shall be reserved the sum of one thousand guilders . . beavers price, for her six remaining children, to wit; Elsie Wendel aged 16 years, Johannes Wendel aged 14 years, Diewer Wendel aged 10 years, Jeronimus Wendel aged 8 years, Philip Wendel aged 5 years, and Evert Wendel aged 3 years, being her matrimonial portion, and to this end the appearer [Wendel] not only makes said sum a lien upon his house and lot for the satisfying of the same, but specially mortgages and pledges the same for securing the payment of the aforesaid sum; for which purpose said appearer appoints as guardians the honorable Isaac Foreest and Symon Symonsen Groot, uncles of said children on their mother's side; meanwhile the aforesaid married people remaining holden said children to bring up in the fear of the Lord, to teach them in the schools to read and write, further to maintain them in food and clothing until their majority and marriage, without diminishing the matrimonial estate left by her; which contract the appearer [Wendel] promises to maintain without craft or guile, pledging for that purpose his person and estate, real and personal present and future, nothing excepted, subjecting himself to the authority of all laws and judges.

---

1 This name is now Truax.

2 She was the daughter of Abraham Pieterse Vosburgh.

Thus done in the presence of Adriaen Gerretsen [Papendorp] old commissary, and Johannes Provoost, as witnesses hereto called, of date *ut supra*

EVERT JANSE WENDEL.

Jan Verbeeck,
Adriaen Gerretsen,
Johannes Provoost, witness.

Acknowledged before me,

LA MONTAGNE, *Commis* at Fort Orange.

Appeared before me, Johannes La Montagne, in the service of, etc., in the presence of the honorable Jan Verbeeck and Stoffel Janse [Abeel] commissaries, etc., Arent Isaackse Van Hoeck burgher and inhabitant of the aforesaid village, who acknowledges and declares, by these presents, that he is well and truly indebted to Philip Hendericksе [Brouwer], inhabitant of Schannhectade, in the sum of four hundred guilders, which sum he, the subscriber, promises to pay in good whole merchantable beaver skins in the month of July, A.D. 1664, with interest on the same at ten *per cent*, to begin at this date; for which he pledges his person and estate, real and personal, present and future, especially the subscriber's house and lot lying in the village of Beverwyck, next to Philip Pietersen [Schuyler's] house, being the same that the subscriber bought of said Philip Hendericksе and which he offers as a fast pledge and special mortgage, that in case of necessity, the payment of said four hundred guilders may be collected without loss and cost.

Done in Fort Orange the 6th of July, A D 1663

ARENT ISAACKSE VAN HOECK.

Appeared before me, Johannes Provoost, clerk, etc., Teunis Cornelisse Slingerlandt, inhabitant of said village, who acknowledges and declares in presence of the afternamed witnesses, that he is well and truly indebted to Mr. Jeronimus Ebbinck, merchant of Amsterdam in New Netherland, in the sum of a hundred and seventy guilders twelve stuivers payable in good whole merchantable beaver skins, for which sum he, the subscriber, not only assigns, but fully grants and conveys over the second payment on his house bought by Antony De Milt, also dwelling at Amsterdam in New Netherland, from whom the subscriber is to receive it in June A.D. 1664, when the time of payment expires, and which payment the said De Milt will punctually make; to which end the subscriber is preferred, that he may be paid before any one else; wherefore he pledges his person and estate, real and personal, present and future, nothing excepted, subjecting himself to the authority of all laws and judges.

Done in Fort Orange the 21st of July, A.D. 1663.

TUENYES CORNELIS SLYENCHERLANDT.

This is the mark **AB** *of Arent Vanden Bergh,*
with his own hand set, witness.
This is the mark + of Ryck Rutgers,
witness, with his own hand set.

Acknowledged before me,

J. PROVOOST, Clerk.

Appeared before me, Johannes La Montagne, in the service of, etc., in the presence of the honorable Jan Verbeeck and Gerrit Slichtenhorst commissaries, etc., Leendert Philipsen [Conyn], inhabitant of said village, who acknowledges and declares that he is well and truly indebted to Mr. Johannes Vander Meulen, merchant at Amsterdam in New Netherland, in the sum of twelve hundred and two guilders in good whole merchantable beaver skins at 8 guilders a piece, growing out of goods and merchandise delivered, which he has received to his content out of the hands of Isaack De Haen, which said sum he promises to pay in the business season [1] (*handeltyt*) of the year 1663; for the payment of which he, the subscriber, offers for a fast mortgage and special pledge his house and lot lying in the village of Beverwyck where he at present dwells, likewise his person and estate, real and personal, present and future, nothing excepted, that in case of need the payment of said sum of one thousand two hundred guilders may be effected without loss and cost.

Thus done in Fort Orange the 27th of July, A.D. 1663.

LEENDERT PYLYPSE.

Gerrit Slichtenhorst,
Jan Verbeeck.

Acknowledged before me,

LA MONTAGNE, *Commis* at Fort Orange.

Appeared before me, Johannes Provoost, clerk, Geertruy Barentse Van Dwingeloo, being now about to depart for *Patria*, who declares in the presence of the afternamed witnesses, that she has appointed and empowered as by these presents she does, Pieter Claerbout and Wouter Albertse [Vanden Uythoff], burghers here, in her name and for her sake to demand, collect and receive here in Fort Orange in New Netherland, such out standing debts as are due to her according to the existing writings and evidences thereof; for receipts acquittance to pass, and in case of refusal of payment to proceed with law and rigor of justice; to that end all terms of laws to observe to sentence and extreme execution, and in case of need to proceed against persons and estates by arrest; and further all things to do and perform, which her attorneys may judge reasonable, promising to hold as good and true whatever shall be done and performed by the attorneys in the matter aforesaid, provided that they be holden to make a proper settlement and return of their transactions and receipts.

Thus done in Fort Orange in presence of Willem De La Montagne and Carsten Carstense [Noorman] as witnesses hereto called, on the 4th of August, A.D. 1663.

This is the mark ◁ of GEERTRUY BARENTSE,
with her own hand set.

Willem de la Montagne,
This is the mark Λ *of Carsten Carstensen.*

Acknowledged before me,

JOHANNES PROVOOST, Clerk.

---

[1] The *handeltyt* was June, July and August, when the beaver skins and other peltries were brought to Beverwyck by the Indians for exchange

Appeared before me, Johannes La Montagne, in the service of, etc., in the presence of the honorable Goosen Gerritsen [Van Schaick] and Jan Tomassen commissaries, etc., Geertruy Barents Van Dwingeloo assisted by Jacob Hevick her husband and guardian, at present being about to depart for *Patria*, who declares, as by these presents she does, that she has pledged and mortgaged her house and lot lying in the village of Beverwyck, for a hundred good whole merchantable beaver skins at 8 guilders a piece, which she assigned to the two remaining children of Henderick Henderickse Van Harstenhorst, her late husband after the expiration of 6 weeks from the death of said husband deceased; this she does at the desire of Pieter Claerbout and Wouter Albertse [Vanden Uythoff] guardians of said children and by the persuasion of the orphan master; and therefore she promises said hundred beaver skins to invest in fatherland and as a discharge of this trust a proper voucher to bring or send where and in what security said hundred beavers or the value of the same is invested; in her character pledging her estate, real and personal, present and future, nothing excepted, subjecting herself to the authority of all laws and judges.

Thus done in Fort Orange in New Netherland, the 4th of August, A D. 1663.

This is the mark < of Jacob Hevick,
with his own hand set.
Gerttruet Barens.

Pieter Claerboudt, as guardian.
Wouter Albers.

Appeared before me, Johannes Provoost, clerk, etc., and in the presence of the afternamed witnesses, Cornelis Cornelissen *de boer* and Jan Henderickse Bruyn, who declare that they, in all friendship and amity, have agreed and contracted with each other, to wit, that the aforesaid Cornelis Cornelissen *de boer* to said Jan Henderickse Bruyn has sold, as by these presents he does, his house and lot lying in the village of Beverwyck adjoining to the west Barent Van Marle, and to the east Dirk Janssen Kroon, in such title, magnitude and boundaries as he received it from Pieter De Maker, and according to the tenor of the conveyance received from him; for which the said Jan Henderickse Bruyn promises to pay the sum of one thousand two hundred and twenty-four guilders payable in good whole merchantable beaver skins, in two installments, the first on the last of July A.D. 1664, and the second on the last of July, A.D. 1665, for the performance of which the parties hereto pledge their persons and estates, real and personal.

Thus done without craft or guile, in presence of Pieter Van Ale and Lowies Cobussen as witnesses hereto called, on this 9th of August, A.D. 1663, in Fort Orange.

Cornelis Cornelissen *de boer*,
Jan Henderick Bruyns.

Pieter Van Allen,
Ludovicus Cobes.

Acknowledged before me,

Johannes Provoost, Clerk.

Appeared before me, Johannes Provoost, clerk, etc., and in the presence of the afternamed witnesses, Cornelis Cornelissen de Boer, who declares that he has appointed and empowered as by these presents he does appoint and empower, Hans Hendericksе and Pieter Van Alen in his name and for his sake to demand, collect and receive, such outstanding debts and moneys as to him are coming here at Fort Orange in New Netherland, according to writings and proofs thereof; for receipts acquittance to pass, and in case of refusal payment to compel by law and rigor of justice; to that end all terms of the laws to observe to a definitive sentence and extreme execution; also to proceed by arrest against persons and estates; furthermore all things to do and perform that they, the attorneys, shall judge reasonable, provided that they shall be holden a proper statement and returns to make of their transactions and receipts; the subscriber promising to hold as good and true all that shall be done and performed by them in the matter aforesaid.

Thus done in Fort Orange, in presence of Capt. Abraham Staets and Arent Van Den Bergh as witnesses hereto called, on this 16th of August, A.D. 1663.

CORNELIS CORNELISSEN DE BOER.

Abram Staas,
This is the mark **AB** *of Arent Vanden Bergh,*
with his own hand set.

Acknowledged before me,

J. PROVOOST, Clerk.

Appeared before me Johannes La Montagne, in the service of, etc., in the presence of the Honorable Francoys Boon and Goosen Gerritse [Van Schaick] commissaries, etc., Teunis Cornelisse Slingerlandt, who acknowledges and declares by these presents that he is well and truly indebted to the Honorable Pieter Dirkse, merchant, dwelling at Amsterdam, in the sum of five hundred and sixty-one guilders fourteen stuivers, for goods and merchandise to his content received, which aforesaid sum he, the subscriber, promises to pay to the aforesaid Pieter Dirkse, or to Mr. Nicolaes Meyer, also merchant, who is his attorney, in good whole merchantable beaver skins, in two installments, the first in the month of July, A.D. 1664, the just half, and the second in the month of July, A.D. 1665; for the payment of which aforesaid sum he, the subscriber, offers as a fast mortgage and special pledge his house and lot together with a garden and little house by the side of said house, lying in the village of Beverwyck, in which he at present dwells, that in case of need the payment of the aforesaid sum of five hundred and sixty-one guilders fourteen stuivers may be collected without loss or cost.

Done in Fort Orange the 27th of August, A.D. 1663.

TUENYES CORNELISE SLYENGHERLANT.

Francoys Boon,
Goosen Gerretsen.

Acknowledged before me,

LA MONTAGNE, *Commis* at Fort Orange.

Appeared before me, Johannes La Montagne, in the service of, etc., in the presence of the Honorable Jan Verbeeck and Gerrit Slichtenhorst commissaries, etc. Leendert Philipsen [Conyn], inhabitant of said village, who declares that he has granted and conveyed, as by these presents he does grant and convey in real and actual possession to and for the behoof of Mr. Nicolaes Meyer, merchant in Amsterdam, in New Netherland his heirs or assigns, a garden lying in the aforesaid village, to the west [east?] the river bank, to the east [west?] the street, to the south Pieter Bronck, to the north also the street, of such magnitude as it at present lies in fence, and shall shortly be measured by the surveyor, which garden the grantor received by conveyance from Anderies Herbertsen, who obtained the same from the Heer director general and council of New Netherland, by virtue of a patent of date the 23d of April, A.D. 1653; and the grantor acknowledges that he has been fully paid and satisfied for said garden with the number of fifteen beaver skins, and therefore promises to free it from all demands or pretensions, which may hereafter arise, pledging therefor his person and estate, real and personal, present and future, subjecting himself to the authority of all laws and judges.

Done in Fort Orange, the 27th of August, A.D. 1663.

LEENDERT PHYLES [PHILIPSE].

Jan Verbeeck,
Gerrit Slichtenhorst.

Acknowledged before me,

LA MONTAGNE, *Commis* at Fort Orange.

Appeared before me, Johannes Provoost, clerk, etc., and in the presence of the afternamed witnesses, Teunis Cornelise Slingerland, inhabitant of said village, who acknowledges and declares by these presents that he is well and truly indebted to Pieter Rens retailer, dwelling at Amsterdam, in the sum of two hundred and eighty Carolus guilders according to agreement by the subscriber with Mr. Nicholaes Meyer, merchant at Amsterdam in New Netherland, attorney for said Rens, growing out of goods and merchandise, which the subscriber received out of Holland from said Rens on bottomry, the principal sum of which was 330 guilders, the bottomry 78 guilders, and the interest thereon 48 guilders; which aforesaid sum of two hundred and eighty guilders, for which he has contracted, the subscriber promises to pay to said Rens or his attorney in good whole merchantable beaver skins, in two installments, the first in the month of July, A.D. 1665, and the second in the month of July A.D. 1666. *

[This paper is unexecuted].

Appeared before me La Montagne, in the service of, etc., and in the presence of the Honorable Messieurs Francoys Boon and Jan Verbeeck commissaries, etc., the Honorable Jan Cornelise Vander Heyden, citizen here, who declares that he appoints and empowers by these presents his father Cornelis Jacobsen Vander Heyden, dwelling at Sevenbergen in Brabant, specially to demand, collect, and receive from the hand of the heirs of his uncle and guardian, the late Jacob Van Duren, such inherited estate as is coming to him by the death of his grandmother the late Neeltien Black, from his mother Sarah Janssen Van Duren deceased, and his brother the late Jacob Cornelise Vander Heyden, whether by virtue of will or *ab intestato;* the condition and inventory of the estates to demand; the same to approve or disprove; his rights and hereditary portion receiving acquittance therefor to pass; and in case of opposition (without hope) the same to prosecute by means of justice; to which end. all terms of laws to observe to sentence and extreme execution, with powers also to agree, compromise and compound; likewise one or more persons if need be in his place to substitute; and further all things to do and perform, which may be needful and he shall think needful, promising at all times to hold good all that shall be done and performed in, the matter aforesaid by his father as his attorney, or by his substitute without any opposition, under pledge according to laws therefor provided.

Done in Fort Orange in New Netherland, the 3d of September, A D. 1663.

JAN CORNELISSE VANDER HEYDEN.[1]

Francoys Boon.

Acknowledged before me,

LA MONTAGNE, *Commis* at Fort Orange.

Appeared before me Johannes La Montagne, in the service of, etc., and in the presence of the Honorable Jan Tomassen and Jan Verbeeck commissaries etc., Willem Janssen Schut, who declares that he has granted and conveyed, as by these presents he does grant and convey in real and actual possession to and for the behoof of Cornelis Bogardus[2] his heirs and assigns, his house and lot lying in the village of Beverwyck, bounded on the westerly side by the house and lot of Anderies Herbertsen, present owner Jurriaen Janssen [Groenwout], on the northerly side by the highway, on the easterly side by Jacob Loockerman, and on the southerly side by the garden of said Jurriaen Janssen, (the lot is of such magnitude as it lies at present in fence according to the aforesaid boundaries); which said house stands on the lot bought, by the grantor, of said Anderies Herbertsen, being a part of the patent to said Herbertsen granted, by the Heer director general and Council of New Netherland of date the .... for which house and lot the grantor acknowledges that he is fully paid and satisfied with the sum of eighty good whole merchantable beaver skins, reckoned at eight guilders a piece, assigned as an offset for what he the grantor is indebted to Johannes Withart; therefore he promises to free the same from all actions, demands or pretensions, which may hereafter arise, pledging therefor his person and estate, personal and real, present and future, submitting himself to the authority of all laws and judges.

Done in Beverwyck the 11th of September, A.D. 1663.

WILLEM JANSEN SSCHUT.

As the above standing sum of eighty guilders, beaver skins, is nothing different (?) after a further settlement of outstanding [debts] between each other (that is between J. Withart and Willem Janssen Schut), so each one remains *daer van in syn geheel.*

Done the 11th of September A.D. 1663, in Beverwyck.

WILLEM JANSSEN SCHUET.
JAN JANSSEN
Attorney for JOAN WITHART.

Appeared before me Johannes Provoost, clerk, etc., and in the presence of the afternamed witnesses, Rutger Jacobsen, at present about to depart

---

[1] J. C. Vander Heyden made his will September 1, 1663, and speaks of his wife Aeltie Janse Wemp, born in the *Colonie*, Daughter of Jan Barentse Wemp deceased. *Notarial papers*, I. *Dutch Manuscripts*, x. 207.

[2] Cornelis Bogardus was son of Annatie Janse B.

for Manhattans, who declares that he has appointed and empowered as by these presents he does, Teunis Cornelisse Spitsbergen and Jacob Heveck, in the subscriber's name and for his sake, to sell at public sale to the highest bidder, the subscriber's half island named Constaple's Island, and in said matter to do and act, as the subscriber, being present, could or might do; promising to hold, as true and good, all that shall be done and performed by the attorneys in the matter of the aforesaid sale, provided that they make a proper statement and exhibit of their transactions. Thus done in Fort Orange in presence of Ryck Rutgersen as witness hereto called, on this 12th of September, A. D. 1663.

RUTGER JACOBSEN.

This is the mark of + *Ryck Rutgersen, with his own hand set.*

Acknowledged before me,

J PROVOOST, Clerk.

Conditions on which the Messieurs *commies* and commissaries of Fort Orange and village of Beverwyck propose to farm out, at public sale to the highest bidder, the slaughter excise for the time of one year. The farming of the said slaughter excise shall begin on the first of October of this year and end on the last of September, A. D. 1664. The farmer shall receive for the slaughtered beasts, whether ox, cow, calf, bull, hog, goat or sheep, one stuiver for every guilder of value of the same, to wit, for those bought for beavers shall be given twenty stuivers in seewant a beaver, in case of dispute to be valued by indifferent persons; the farmer is holden to furnish two sufficient sureties to the content of the Messieurs contractors, for the excise money; the just half of the promised excise money to be paid within the time of six weeks; the other half within the two last quarters, each quarter a fourth part of the whole sum, in good current seewant; if the farmer can not furnish sufficient sureties, it shall be offered for sale again at his cost and charge, and whatever less it comes to be worth, he shall be holden to make good, and whatever more it comes to be worth he shall receive no profit therefrom.

On the above conditions Henderick Rooseboom remained the last bidder and farmer, for the sum of seven hundred and ninety guilders; for the payment of which aforesaid sum, Philip Pieterse Schuyler and Wouter Albertse [Vanden Uythoff] offered themselves as sureties and principals under pledge of their persons and estates, personal and real, present and future, nothing excepted, placing themselves in subjection to all laws and judges.

Done in Beverwyck the 29th of September, A. D. 1663.

HENDERICK JANSSEN ROOSEBOOM,
PHILIP PIETERSE SCHUYLER,
WOUTER ALBERSEN.

Acknowledged before me,

LA MONTAGNE, *Commis*, at Fort Orange.

Appeared before me, Johannes La Montagne, in the service of, etc., and in the presence of the afternamed witnesses, an Indian named Wattawit with his mother named Pepewitsie, who declares that they have sold, granted and conveyed, as they do sell, grant and convey by these presents in real and actual possession to and for the behoof of Volckert Janssen [Douw] and Jan Tomassen, their certain land lying on the *goojer's kil* on

Apjen's island, or by the Indians called Schotack, their portion of said Apjen's island (which the buyers for the afternamed sum receive), is the north end, extending from the north end until right over against the south end of the Green flat (*groene plaet*), cutting obliquely over Apjen's island to the kil which makes the island; together with a piece of land on the east shore of the kil, being the fast bank, where the house of Machacknotas stood, and extending into the woods; for the sum of 442 guilders in beavers payable in merchandise, which the grantors acknowledge that they have received and to be paid, therefore, promising the aforesaid parcel of land as well on the fast bank as on the island, to free from all actions, claims, or pretentions of the other Indians, who might sinisterly make some pretention to the same.

Thus done in the village of Beverwyck, in presence of Tomas Schambert [Chambers] and Johannes Provoost, as witnesses hereto called, on this 4th of October, A.D. 1663.

This is the mark ⊥⊥ of Wattawit,
with his own hand set.
This is the mark ╲ of the mother of Wattawit,
with her own hand set.

Thomas Chambers
Johannes Provoost, Clerk.

Acknowledged before me,

La Montagne, *Commis* at Fort Orange.

At the same time, on the date above, appeared before me, Johannes La Montagne, *commies*, in the aforesaid character, an Indian with a squaw, the Indian named Naspahan or Pofpouick, and the squaw named Pasies, owners of the south end of Apjen's island named Schotack, who declare that they have sold, granted and conveyed, as by these presents they do grant and convey, in real and actual possession to and for the behoof of Volckert Janssen [Douw] and Jan Tomassen, their heirs or assigns, said south end of the aforesaid island, being the greatest half, beginning from a point over against the Green Flat (*groene plaet*), and running to the south end of said Apjen's island, so that the whole island of said Apjen belongs to these grantees; for the sum of 500 guilders in beavers in merchandise paid to them, which the grantors acknowledge they have received, and therefore promise to free the same from every action or demand of other Indians, who may present any claim to it.

Thus done in Beverwyck, in presence of Tomas Chambert [Chambers] and Johannes Provoost, as witnesses hereto called, on the 4th of October, A.D. 1663.

This the mark of Naspahan,
with his own hand set.
This is the mark of the squaw Pasies.
with her own hand set.

Thomas Chambers,
Johannes Provoost, Witness.

Acknowledged before me,

La Montagne, *Commis* at Fort Orange.

Appeared before me Johannes Provoost, clerk, etc., and in the presence of the afternamed witnesses. Stoffel Janssen Abeel, commissary, etc., who declares that he has appointed and empowered, as by these presents he does, the Honorable Pieter Jacobsen, merchant at Amsterdam in New Netherland, in the subscriber's name and for his sake, in all humility, to ask of the Heer director general and council of New Netherland, restitution for the subscriber's certain goods and merchandise, which were by the Heer fiscal retained, because said goods at Amsterdam in Holland, by mistake of the clerk Liefferingh, were not put into the invoice, about which error said Liefferingh has given a written explanation; not receiving the aforesaid goods in kind the director general to ask only that the same may serve as a payment for the liability (?) (*recognitie*); to which end all proper means to use, which, the subscriber himself being present, might or could use, although the matter should require more special authority than is herein expressed; the subscriber promising to hold good and true all that the attorney in the matter aforesaid shall do and perform, provided that he make a proper statement and return of his transactions and receipts; under pledge of his person and estate.

Thus done in Fort Orange in presence of Jan Harmensen and Harmen Tomassen [Hun of Amersfort] as witnesses hereto called on this 6th of October, A. D. 1663.

STOFFEL JANSE ABEEL.

Jan Harmensen Weendorp,
Harmen Tomase [Hun.]

J. PROVOOST, Clerk.

Conditions on which the Honorable Sander Leendersen Glen proposes to sell, at public sale to the highest bidder, his house and lot lying in the village of Beverwyck, on the hill, adjoining on the east side Wouter Albertsen [Van den Uythoff], and on the west side Jan Tomassen. Said house and lot shall be delivered to the buyer as it stands and lies in fence, with all that is earth and nail fast, and with the last payment a proper conveyance thereof shall be delivered to him. Payment shall be made in two installments, the first on the first of June, A. D. 1664, and the second on the first of June, A. D. 1665, in good whole merchantable beaver skins. The buyer shall be holden to furnish two sufficient sureties immediately, one for each and all, as principals, to the content of the seller. If the buyer can not furnish said sureties in the time aforesaid, said house and lot shall be offered for sale again at his cost and charge, and whatever less it comes to be worth, he shall be holden to make good, and whatever more it becomes worth, he shall receive no benefit therefrom. The auction fees become a charge to the buyer. On the above conditions, Jan Clute remained the last bidder, for the sum of six hundred and thirty guilders, for the payment of which, Jacob Tyssen Vander Heyden and Barent Reyndersen offered themselves as sureties and principals, on a pledge of their persons and estates, personal and real, placing themselves in subjection to all laws and judges.

Done the 17th of October, A D. 1663, in Beverwyck.

JOHANNES CLUTE

Jacob Theysen,
Barent Reyndersssen.

Conditions on which the Messieurs *Commies* and commissaries of Fort Orange and Beverwyck, propose, in the name and for the sake of the Heer director general and council of New Netherland, to farm out to the highest bidder the excise of all wines, beers, and spirts (*gebrande wateren*,) to be consumed and drawn by the innkeepers. tapsters, and retailers, in and about Fort Orange, village of Beverwyck and Colony Rensselaerswyck. The farming out (*verpachtinge*) as well as the farming (*pachtinge*) is done in accordance with the praiseworthy custom of our fatherland and the printed ordinances and placards of their high mightinesses the Heeren States General issued on the subject of the finances. The farming shall commence on the first of November [1663], and end on the last of October, A.D. 1664, being the time of 12 months, during which time the farmer may demand and receive for all wines, beers, or spirits to be consumed or drawn by the tapsters and innkeepers, in or about Fort Orange, and village of Beverwyck, as follows:

for a tun of domestic beer,..........	4	guilders.
for a tun of foreign beer,..	6	"
for a hogshead of French wine,................................	20	"
for an anker, do	4	"
for an anker of Spanish wine,..................................		
brandy, mead, or spirits,...	7	"
for an anker of cider,...	2	"

Greater or less casks (*fustagien*), proportionally, at beaver prices, or else 12 white or six black [sewants] for a stuiver, at the option of the payer. The farmer, or highest bidder, shall be holden to the content of the Messieurs contractors (*verpachters*) to furnish two sufficient sureties, for the *pacht* money a just fourth part to be paid every three months, in beavers or else in seewant, 12 white or six black a stuiver. To prevent all cavilling, misunderstanding, and frauds, it is stipulated that after the expiration of this farming, when a new farming out is made, the new farmer shall be at liberty, on the day of the new farming out, the following day, or at least within three days after the farming out (*verpachtinge*), in the presence of the late farmer, if he wishes to be present, to guage the remaining wines, beers, or spirits held by the tapsters and innkeepers, and two thirds parts of the receipts, or excise due, is to be returned by the old or out going farmer to his successor. The messieurs contractors reserve to themselves the interpretation and enlargement of this contract, and promise the farmer all proper support and assistance. Willem Frederickse Bout remained the last bidder for the above farming, for the sum of three thousand eight hundred [3,800] guilders, according to the aforesaid conditions, for the payment of which Harmen Bastiaense [Visscher] and Jan Vinhagen stood as sureties and principals, according to the aforesaid conditions, pledging therefor their persons and estates, personal and real, present and future, nothing excepted.

Thus done in Beverwyck the last October, A. D. 1663.

This is the mark of with his own WILLEM FREDRICKSE BOUT. hand set.

HARMEN BASTIAENS.

JAN DIRKSEN VINHAEGHEN.

Acknowledged before me, LA MONTAGNE, *Commis* at Fort Orange.

By order of the messieurs commissaries. J. PROVOOST, Clerk.

Conditions on which the Messieurs *Commis* and Commissaries of Fort Orange and village of Beverwyck, propose to farm out to the highest bidder the burgher's wine and beer excise for the time of one year. The farming out (*Verpachtinge*), as well as the farming (*pachtinge*), shall begin on the first of November in the year 1663; and end on the last of October, A.D. 1664, according to the ordinances of our Fatherland. The farmer shall receive for a tun of strong (*goet*) beer one dollar, for a tun of small beer ten stuivers, for a hogshead of French wine six guilders, for an anker of brandy, Spanish wine, or spirits two guilders, at 12 white and 6 black seewants (*sewantiens*) the stuiver, and the farmer aforesaid shall not refuse any burghers a permit? (*celen*) who is entered upon the burgher's excise. The farmer shall be holden to furnish two sufficient sureties, one for all and each, as principals, to the content of the Messieurs contractors (*verpachters*), for the payment of the aforesaid burgher's excise, every quarter year a just fourth part of the whole sum, in good strung seewant, at 12 white and 6 black seewants (*sewantiens*) the stuiver, and in case the farmer fails of furnishing the aforesaid sureties, then the aforesaid farming shall be offered for sale again, and whatever less it comes to be worth, he shall be holden to make good, and whatever more it shall become worth, he shall receive no profit therefrom. The messieurs contractors reserve to themselves the interpretation and enlargement of this contract and promise the farmer all proper aid and assistance. For the above farming Willem Frederickse Bout remained the last bidder and farmer, for the sum of two thousand five hundred guilders, for the payment of which Harmen Bastiaense [Visscher] and Jan Dirkse Vinhagen, stood as sureties and principals, according to the conditions aforesaid, pledging therefor their persons and estates, personal and real, present and future, nothing excepted.

Thus done in Beverwyck, the last of October, A.D. 1663.

WILLEM FREDERICKSE BOUT.
HARMEN BASTIAENS.
JAN DIRCKSEN VINHAEGHEN.

Acknowledged before me,

LA MONTAGNE, *Commis* at Fort Orange.

By order of the messieurs commissaries,

J. PROVOOST, Clerk.

Appeared before me, Johannes La Montagne, in the service of, etc., in the presence of the Honorable Jan Verbeeck and Goosen Gerritse [Van Schaick] commissaries, etc., Claes Janssen Van Baren, who acknowledges and declares that he is well and truly indebted to Anderies Jochimse in the sum of two hundred and forty-four guilders in beavers, growing out of the purchase of a lot, which aforesaid sum of two hundred and four and forty guilders in beavers, with interest on the same at ten per cent, to commence four years ago, and running until the final payment, he, the subscriber, promises to pay to the aforesaid Anderies Jochimsen or his attorney, on the first day of June, A.D. 1664, pledging therefor his person and estate, real and personal, present and future, nothing excepted, especially his house and lot lying in the village of Beverwyck, bounded to the south by Stoffel Janse [Abeel], and to the north by the aforesaid commissary Jan Verbeeck, as a fast mortgage and special pledge, to secure the payment, if need be, of the aforesaid sum and interest on the same without cost or loss. submitting to this end to all laws and judges.

Done in Fort Orange the 14th of November, A.D. 1663.

CLAES JANSE.

Goosen Gerretsen.
Jan Verbeeck.

Acknowledged before me,

LA MONTAGNE, *Commis* at Fort Orange.

Seletie Fredricx attorney for her husband Anderies Jochimsen, declares, with the transfer of the house, which she took in possession, and acknowledges, that she is fully paid and satisfied for the sum of two hundred and forty-four guilders in beavers and interest on the same, without claiming any thing more of Claes Janssen.

Done in Albany the 3d of August, 1665, old style.

SELYTIEN FREDERICKSE.

Acknowledged before me,

JOHANNES PROVOOST. Secretary.

Appeared before me Johannes Provoost clerk of, etc., and in the presence of the afternamed witnesses, the honorable Wouter Albertsen [Van den Uythoff], citizen of said village, who declares that he has appointed and empowered, as by these presents he does appoint and empower, Jan Pietersen Muller soldier in the service of the honorable company, lying in garrison at the Esopus in the village of Wildwyck, in the subscriber's name and for his sake, to demand, collect, and receive, such debts and outstanding moneys as to him are coming, in the Esopus aforesaid, according to the writings and evidences thereto serving; for receipts acquittance to pass, and in the case of unwillingness, payment to compel, by law and rigor of justice; for which end all terms of the laws to observe to definitive sentence and extreme execution; * * also to proceed by arrest against persons and estates; furthermore all things to do and perform, which the subscriber being present could or might do, although the matter should require greater and more special authority than stands expressed in this paper, provided that the attorney be holden, on request made, to render a proper statement and return of his transactions and receipts, under pledge of his person and estate personal and real.

Thus done in Fort Orange, in presence of Arent Van den Bergh and Jochim Lambertsen [Van Valkenburgh], as witnesses hereto called, on this 23d of November, A. D. 1663.

WOUTER ALBERTSEN.

This is the mark **AB** *of Arent Vandenburgh,*
with his own hand set.

Jochem Lambertse

Acknowledged before me.

JOHANNES PROVOOST, Clerk.

Found in the kitchen, 5 little earthen pots, also 17 ditto little and great, 10 pewter platters, 1 pewter mug, 4 pewter dishes, 11 pewter spoons, 1 copper frying pan. an iron pot hanger, 2 iron pots and 1 copper ditto, 1 copper kettle, 2 little wooden pails, 1 lantern, 1 little pail, 1 skimmer, 2 wooden bowls.

[The above is probably a part of the following inventory.]

Inventory of the goods of Jan Gerritsen Van Marcken [1] farmer of the excise, taken the 11th of December, 1663. A clothes press wherein were found a little box (*bosjen*) of black seewant. 4 blue aprons, 1 ivory tobacco box, 8 men's and women's shirts (*hemden*), also 2 shirts, 5 sheets. also 2 ditto, 2 white roundabouts (*wambas*), 1 coarse white bed blanket, 18 pillow biers great and little, also 1 ditto, 15 napkins, 3 table cloths, 5 towels, a child's woolen bed blanket, a woman's white under waistcoat, 1 white drawers, (*onder broeck*), 2 white aprons, 4 red towels, 1 patched tick, a little child bed basket, 2 small red flowered curtains. 2 pairs of gloves, 3 black hoods, a woman's red boddice. a little piece of stuff, 4 woman's black cloaks, (2 lost), 1 man's red waistcoat, (lost), 1 piece of red stuff, 1 pair of women's shoes, 3 woman's stomachers, (lost), 2 black aprons, (one lost), a little green garment, 1 blue coat (lost), 1 red coat and 2 black coats. (lost), a woman's gown, (the coat lost), 1 pair of man's and 1 pair of woman's stockings, (the woman's gone), 1 man's brown cloth suit, a man's serge suit (lost), 1 pair of drawers. 1 man's black coat, (gone), 3 children's garments, 2 swathing cloths, 2 green valances, (gone), 2 green curtains, (gone), 1 bed coverlet.

Goods which hang loose about the house. 2 guns, 2 pocket pistols, 1 looking glass, 1 hollow cane [*stickaet*], 2 books little and great, 3 pictures, 1 gridiron 1 smoothing iron, 1 iron pot hanger, 1 tongs, 3 earthen dishes, 1 *bort* almanac.[2]

Found in the garret. 15 little white earthen mugs, 12 white do plates, a parcel of wine glasses, (?) 3 earthen saltcellers, 4 white ditto bowls, 3 earthen platters, 3 woman's wooden * a parcel of * and trammels, bed and bolster.

Appeared before me Johannes Provoost, clerk, etc., and in the presence of the after named witnesses, Jan Classen [*Backer* Van Osanen] husband and guardian of Lysbet Donneur [D'Honneur] widow of Pieter Jacobsen Van Rinsborgh deceased, who acknowledges and declares by these presents, that he has agreed with the administrators of the estate of the aforesaid Pieter Jacobsen Van Rinsborgh, to wit, that he, the subscriber, renounces the said estate, for the sum of three hundred guilders in heavy (*swaert*) money, which he shall receive in merchandise from Mr. Johannes Withart, but from said sum shall be deducted the sum of one hundred guilders in light (*licht*) money, for the *Commies* Johannes La Montagne, to the behoof of the Honorable Company, which was furnished

[1] J. G. Van Marcken and wife Geertie Huybertse came over in the ship St Jacob, *Dutch Ms.*, xiv, 116,—received a patent for a lot near Fort Casimir in 1657,—was in New Amstel, 1659 from whence he was banished farmer of the excise in Beverwyck, 1662: and appointed sheriff of Schenectady 1673, where he resided several years.

[2] A broad side almanac or calendar ?

to said Pieter Jacobse Van Rinsborgh on his sick bed; therefore he, the subscriber, acquits said estate of any further claim or pretension, pledging thereto his person and estate personal and real.

Thus done in Fort Orange the 23d of November, Ano: 1663, in presence of Wouter Albertsen [Van den Uythoff] and Arent Van Den Bergh witnesses hereto called.

JAN KLASSEN.

Jan Verbeeck, Administrator,
Evert Wendel, do,
Wouter Albersen,
This is the mark of **AB** *Arent Van den Bergh,*
with his own hand set.

Acknowledged before me.

Appeared before me Johannes La Montagne, in the service of etc., and in the presence of the honorable Goosen Gerritse [Van Schaick] and Jan Tomassen, commissaries, etc., the honorable Sander Leendersen Glen, who declares that he has granted and conveyed, as by these presents he does grant and convey, in real and actual possession to and for the behoof of Jurriaen Teunisse [Glasemaecker] his heirs or assigns, two gardens lying together near *(omtrent)* the village of Beverwyck, aforesaid, behind the Heer Rensselaer's house, in the second street next to the hill, bounded to the south by Jan Bastiaense Van Gudsenhoven, and to the north by Goosen Gerritsen [Van Schaick,] each of such magnitude as before this they were by allotment distributed; for which aforesaid two gardens, the said Jurriaen Teunisse promises to pay the sum of one hundred and seventy-five guilders in seewant: wherefore, the grantor promises to free said two gardens from all actions, claims, or pretensions of all other persons, who may lay claim thereto, pledging therefor his person and estate, personal and real, present and future, nothing excepted, and submitting himself to all laws and judges.

Done in Fort Orange the 28th of December, 1663.

SANDER LENRSEN GLEN.
JUREJAEN TUNSEN.

Goosen Gerretsen
Jan Thomas.

Acknowledged before me,

LA MONTAGNE, *Commis* at Fort Orange.

Appeared before me Johannes La Montagne, in the service of, etc., and in the presence of the honorable Gerrit Slichtenhorst and Stoffel Janse [Abeel,] commissaries, etc., the honorable Sander Leendersen Glen, who declares that he has granted and conveyed, as by these presents he does grant and convey, in real and actual possession to and for the behoof of Caspar Jacobse [Halenbeck] his heirs, or assigns, a lot for a garden lying in Fort Orange aforesaid, bounded to the west by the lot of Jeremias Van Rensselaer, north by the lot of the grantee (*acceptant,*) length sixteen and a half rods, and breadth three rods eight and a half feet; which lot was conveyed to the grantor by patent of the Heer director general and council of New Netherland, of date the 13th July, A. D.

1658, and therefore, the grantor promises to free the same from all actions, claims, or pretentions, which may hereafter arise, pledging therefor his person and estate, personal and real, present and future, and submitting himself to all law and judges.

Done in Fort Orange, the 29th of December, A D. 1663.

SANDER LENRSEN GLEN

Gerrit Slichtenhorst.
Stoffel Janse.

Acknowledged before me,

LA MONTAGNE, *Commis* at Fort Orange.

Appeared before me Johannes Provoost, clerk, etc., and in the presence of the afternamed witnesses, two Mahikander Indians, the one named Panasit, the other Wapto, brothers and owners of the fast land on the east side of Apjen's island extending from the one end of said island to the other, who declare that they have sold, granted, and conveyed, as by these presents they do, in real and actual possession, to and for the behoof of Jan Tomassen and Volkert Janse [Douw,] their heirs or assigns, the aforesaid land on the east bank [of the Hudson river,] extending as above, and further more, running into the woods; for a certain sum in goods, to them paid, which the grantors acknowlege that they have received, and for the aforesaid land are fully paid and satisfied; and therefore renounce said land on said east bank, and promise to free the same from every claim or pretension of the other Indians, who may sinisterly lay claim to the same.

Thus done in the village of Beverwyck, in the presence of Rutger Jacobsen and Doctor (*meester*) Jacob de Hince, as witness hereto called, on the 17th of January, A. D. 1664.

This is the mark 4 of PAENSIT.
with his own hand set.

This is the mark of WAPTO.
with his own hand set.

Rutger Jacobsen.
J. Dehinsse.

Acknowledged before me,

J. PROVOOST, Clerk.

On this the 21st day of February, A. D. 1664, appeared before me Johannes Provoost, clerk, etc., and in the presence of the afternamed witnesses, the honorable Goosen Gerritse [Van Schaick,] commissary of said place, of the one side, and Gerrit Ryersen, his half brother, for his portion, of the other side, who declare, by these presents, that they have made with each other a dissolution and buying out of a certain contract, commenced the 11th of August, A. D. 1662, between their people and Hendrick Coster, in partnership with Gerrit Reyerse, in respect to a certain six thousand guilders, which they, the people of Goosen Gerritse, at their expense have employed to be used the space of two years, conditioned on the payment of interest thereon at ten *per cent*, the dissolution thereof to be made in manner following: Gerrit Ryerse shall deliver over, by inventory, all such goods and merchandise as he has on hand, and likewise assign, by these presents, for the sake of the above mentioned sum, all the outstanding debts due him with the account book; he shall also collect the outstanding debts, or else on his departure to *Patria*, obtain from the debtors proper obligations and acknowledgements for the debts; and as some beavers are held as a return to Holland and something is to be paid there, Goosen Gerritse shall receive and take to himself the surplus, which comes from Holland in merchandise; wherefore the said Goosen Gerritse, to buy out said Gerrit Reyersen, promises to pay the number of thirty good whole beaver skins, likewise ninty-nine guilders, which Gerrit Reyersen owes the capital personally, without farther claim therefor; together with a hundred and twelve guilders in seewant, and two beavers, by way of moneys disbursed, which Goosen Gerritsen shall also pay to him; for the due performance of which the respective parties pledge below their persons and estates, personal and real.

Thus done without craft or guile, in the presence of Dirk Van Schelluyne and Pieter Van Alen, as witnesses hereto called, on the date as above.

GOOSEN GERRETSEN
GERRIT REYERSE

D. V. Schelluyne, 1664.
Pieter Van Alen

Acknowledged before me,

JOHANNES PROVOOST, Clerk.

25th of March, 1664.

Inventory taken for the second time, of the goods of Jan Gerritse Van Marcken, as he has broken the seal and opened the press and abstracted goods therefrom, which press with some goods therein, is brought to the house of Jochem Wesselse [Backer] for safe keeping, to be hereafter inventoried.

Loose Goods.— 3 earthen platters, with 2 little ditto and a little porcelain cup, 7 pewter platters, 1 pewter mug, and ditto little cup, 8 pewter spoons and 2 copper ditto, 5 earthern plates, 1 white earthern cullender, 2 little red earthern and ditto white cups, 1 copper smoothing iron, 1 copper skimmer, 1 iron trivet, 1 iron chopping knife, 1 pot hanger and 1 ditto hook, 1 wooden spoon-rack (*lepel bortie*), 1 copper lamp, 1 shot-pouch (*schiet-tas*), 1 little copper kettle, 1 iron pot, 2 pewter wine measures, 1 pewter mustard pot, 1 candle box, 1 white earthern oil pot, 1 little white earthern mug, 1 gridiron and pan, 1 red cullender, 1 red earthern platter, 3 little earthern pots, 1 red wooden bowl, 1 tick-tack board, 1 picture, 1 can rack, 1 round table, 1 gun, 1 case with six bottles, 1 old wooden pail, 3 dusters, a rolling pin and board, 1 bat, 1 wood axe, 1 water pail, 1 bed with bolster and 2 pillows, 3 coverlets which are left in the house of Jan Gerrits, for his convenience, 2 green curtains, 2 iron tongs, 15 pewter plates, 1 box with trellice, (*tralien off [illegible]nskasie*).

Brought from the garret.—4 white earthern plates, 1 red earthern stew pan, 5 (say 5) little earthern platters, 10 white earthern mugs and a blue ditto, 5 white earthern mustard pots, 1 ditto oil pot, 3 white earthern salt cellars, 4 little white earthern pots, 4 little earthern pots, 3 little white platters, 1 earthern pot with 8 little rumbling pots[1] therein, 7 earthern pots, little and great, a lantern, 2 market pails. 1 duster, 1 iron pot cover, 1 iron pot hanger, 8 iron door locks, 13 iron scissors, 4 pairs of iron pot hooks, 1 church [foot] stove. 2 latches, 2 iron hammers, with some little rings, 8 great wine glasses, 21 *stroo rissen* with wine glasses, 1 hat case, 1 little basket, 1 iron weight of ten pounds, a parcel of pipes lying loose up garret.

On the first of March, 1664, the press of Jan Gerritse Van Marken was opened and therein were found: 3 pieces of false parchment, 3 *bossen piet*, 2 little square pictures, 8 pocket handkerchiefs. 4 tin spyglasses, 3 rubbing brushes, 2 pocket pistols, 3 little copper rods (*roetiens*), 1 farthingale, 1 pair of little child's stockings, one little child's knitted waist coat, 1 one old green valance, one riding coat, 3 children's *doeckentiens*, 1 green, 2 white, 1 pair of man's grey stockings patched, 1 green valance, 1 red swathing cloth, 1 man's drawers, half red and half white, 1 man's brown suit, 2 silk damask valances, 1 green swathing cloth, a piece of apple blossom cloth, a little black mantel without sleeves 1 black grogram apron, 1 silk grogram hood, a bundle or roll of very coarse linnen, a woman's stays in a white linnen cloth, 1 *kral* basket. 2 pairs of knit gloves, 1 black and 1 pair gray, 1 ivory tobacco box, 1 pair of woman's shoes, 1 silver frontlet[2] (*silvervooriser*). 2 white linnen aprons. 2 white men's coats, 5 pillows, also 3 pillows, 1 linnen bag, 1 piece of white bombazine, and 1 piece of white woolen, a man s and a woman's shirt, 1 blue checked (*dobbelsteentiens*) valance, 1 woman's black petticoat, 1 white bombazine drawers, (*onderbroeck*), 5 pillows, also 2 ditto small, 1 woman's white underwaist coat, 1 little red garment (*kleetje*), 1 woman's shift, 1 little old black mantel, a woolen cloth in which are found some children's clothes, a cloth with a parcel of seewant, 2 old silk caps, 2 chair cushions, 5 blue aprons, a woman's old bandage [*kebasje*,] 16 books great and little, a little white basket with some trumpery therein, 2 books with maps, a portmanteau, 3 little pictures, 1 great looking-glass, a perpetual almanac, a green coverlet, a little piece of bed tick, 3 table clothes, 18 napkins, little and great, 6 towels and a sash (*gezondheyt*), in a red swathing cloth, a large and small brush, a wooden bowl in which are 11 hoods and caps, 4 night neckkerchiefs, 3 fine neckkerchiefs, 3 rags (*doekjins*) 3 tuckers (*neerstucken*), and 3 *santees*, 1 cane wherein is a rapier blade, 5 pocket handkerchiefs attached to each other, 15 tuckers (*neerstucken*), 2 *santeen*, 2 woman's neckkerchiefs, 2 white aprons, 8 hoods, 1 woman's stiched cap, 1 pocket handkerchief, a signet, a white apron, in which is wrapped a whole parcel of trumpery.

A chest wherein was found, 20 girls and boy's caps and some gloves, 10 wooden flutes (*fluyten*), 1 pair of yellow stockings for a child, 1 pair of man's leather stockings, 3 chair cushions, 1 blue linnen drawers, one woman's old linnen under-waistcoat, 1 stuff breeches, 1 scarlet underwaistcoat with silver buttons, 1 man's serge suit, 1 black hat, a cloth with starch, a pilot's *boogh*, and 2 compasses.

On this 12th day of March, A.D. 1664, by these presents, the honorable Abraham Staets on the one side, and Jan Anderiessen the Irishman, of the other side, have contracted and agreed together in the manner

---

[1] *Rommelcrytiens*, a shrovetide play toy [2] An ornament for the head.

following, to wit: the aforesaid Abraham Staets leaves to the said Jan Anderiessen, his *bouwery* lying in the Klaverrack, with the land, house, barn, and rick, as it at present stands, for the time of the four and a half next following years, commencing on the first of April of this year, and ending on the first of September, A. D. 1669, with which he delivers six milk cows, two horses, a mare and stallion, and six sows; for which Jan Anderiessen promises to pay rent as follows: for the first half year, he shall at the end of the lease leave in the ground, for the behoof of the lessor, three *mudde*, [about 12 bushels] of wheat, and a tight fence, the year following one hundred guilders, each of the three next years one hundred and fifty guilders in beavers, or grain at beavers price; and promises furthermore, to keep the buildings in good repair; likewise the increase of the aforesaid cattle shall be shared alike by the lessor and lessee, and a slaughtered hog from each of the six sows, yearly; at the end of the lease, the lessee shall be holden to deliver again the full number of beasts; as it respects the orchard, the parties shall receive each the half of the fruit, provided also that they together take care and defray the expense of the fence, but the lessee shall take all possible care that the fruit be not destroyed.

Thus done in Beverwyck in amity and friendship, and in presence of me, J. Provoost, clerk, *datum ut supra.*

ABRAM STAETS.

This is the mark S of JAN ANDERIESSEN the Irishman, with his own hand set.

Acknowledged before me.

Copy. J. PROVOOST, Clerk.

I, the undersigned, acknowledge that I am indebted to Philip Pieterse Schuyler, in the sum of 50 guilders, Holland money, for my fare, bespoken for my benefit of Skipper Pieter, because I did not pay the same in Holland; and likewise 2 beavers, one lent to me formerly, the other now, with 10 guilders, silver money, which sum I promise to pay him to his content, when I return next year from Holland. In acknowledgment of the truth of which I have subscribed with my own hand. Was signed,

ANTHONY TOINEL.

60 guilders Holland money, and two beavers.

Done the 12th of August, 1662, in Fort Orange in N. Netherlant.

In the name of the Lord Amen, be it known that in the year of our Lord Jesus Christ sixteen hundred and sixty-four, the 19th day of April, appeared before me Johannes La Montagne, in the service of, etc., the honorable Willem Teller, widower of the late Margariet Donckesen, who declares in the presence of the afternamed witnesses, that for God's honor he has contracted a future marriage with Maria Verlet, widow of the late Paulus Schrick, and before the consummation of the same, he, the subscriber, has made up and exhibited for the seven remaining children of Margariet Donckesen (the subscriber's late wife), the sum of three thousand five hundred carolus guilders in beaver's price, exclusive of all debts hitherto made, which he undertakes to pay, to be distributed as follows, to wit: to Anderies Teller aged 22 years, Helena Teller 19 years, Martjen? 16 years, Elysabeth Teller 12 years, Jacob Teller 9 years,

Willem Teller 7 years, and Johannes Teller 5 years, being her matrimonial inheritance, and for the payment of the aforesaid sum, the subscriber offers all his estate personal and real, as a pledge and mortgage; to which end said subscriber appoints, as guardians, the honorable Sander Leendertse Glen [1] and Pieter Loockermans, uncles of said children; in the meantime the subscriber shall remain holden to bring up the aforesaid children to wit, the minors, in the fear of the Lord, to teach them to read and write; furthermore, to maintain them in food and clothing, until their majority and marriage, without any diminution of their matrimonial [maternal?] estate; all which the subscriber promises to do, without craft or guile, pledging therefor his person and estate, real and personal, present and future.

Thus done in the village of Beverwyck, in the presence of the honorable Evert Wendel and Johannes Provoost, as witnesses hereto called, of date *ut supra.*

WILLEM TELLER.

Evert Janse Wendel, as witness.
Johannes Provoost, witness

Acknowledged before me,

LA MONTAGNE, *Commis* at Fort Orange.

Conditions upon which the administrators of the estate of Philip Hendrickse [Brouwer] propose to sell, at public sale to the highest bidder, the house, brewery and mill house of said Philip Hendrickse. Firstly, the buyer shall immediately receive the aforesaid house and brewery, together with a kettle, two tubs and a cooler, with the mill house reserving the mill, also the lot and garden of such size as it lies in fence. Payment shall be made in good whole merchantable beaver skins, in three installments, the first on the 15th of July, of this year 1664, the second one year thereafter, and the third on the 15th of July, 1666. The buyer shall be holden to furnish two sufficient sureties, one for all and each, as principals, immediately, to the content of the seller. If the buyer can not furnish said sureties in said time, then said house, brewery, mill house, lot and garden, shall be again offered for sale at his cost and charge, and whatever less it comes to be worth, he shall be holden to make good, and whatever more it becomes worth he shall receive no profit therefrom. The auction fees become a charge to the buyer payable as above. After publishing the above conditions, Jan Dirckse Van Eps.[2] remained the last bidder of the brewery, for the sum of one thousand one hundred and fifty guilders, for the payment of which, Cornelis Van Nes and Pieter Van Alen, stood as sureties and principals.

Thus done in the village of Beverwyck, on the 29th of April, A.D. 1664.

JAN DIERCKSE VAN EPS.
PIETER VAN ALEN.
CORNELIS VAN NES.
LA MONTAGNE, *Commis* at Fort Orange.

---

[1] S. L. Glen married Catalyn Doncasseen or Dongan, sister of William Teller's first wife.

[2] Jan Dirkse Van E., was the son of Dirk Van E. and Maritie Damens. He married Elizabeth Janse, and was one of the original proprietors of Schenectady. In the massacre at Schenectady Feb. 9, 1690, he was killed with his two children. From his surviving sons Jan Baptist and Evert, have sprung the families of this name in Schenectady and vicinity

On this 29th day of April, A. D. 1664, appeared before me Johannes Provoost, clerk, etc., Hester Douwese [Fonda], assisted by her son, Douwe Gillis [Fonda], and her daughter, Geertien Gillis, on the one side, and Jan Costersen Van Aken of the other side, who declare that they have made a purchase, as follows, to wit: Hester Douwese sells, by these presents, to the aforesaid Jan Van Aken, two distiller's kettles, to be delivered in May, else interest for the money shall be given, which Jan Aken accepts, and promises, in the month of May next, to pay therefor, the sum of four hundred guilders in good strung seewant, which purchase the parties promise to hold fast. Thus done, without craft or guile.

Done in Beverwyck, in presence of Jan Schekel, *datum ut supra.*

HESTER DOUWES
DOUWE GELLISE.
Jan Scheckel. JAN KOSTER.
JOHANNES PROVOOST, Clerk.

Conditions on which the administrators of the estate of Philip Henderickse [Brouwer] propose to sell at public sale to the highest bidder, the *bouwery*, house, lot, and garden of Philip Henderickse Brouwer aforesaid of Schenhechtade, consisting of a lot of about twenty-five morgens, or so much as shall be allotted to each of the other inhabitants. Firstly, the buyer shall receive the aforesaid *bouwery* or lot, immediately, and of such size as is above recited, all being broken up land, a part sowed with nine and a half schepels of winter wheat and two and a half schepels of summer wheat; furthermore, the house lot is two hundred feet square, and the garden as it lies in fence, on which is a barn thirty by twenty-four feet, besides the gangway, two ricks, the one of four and the other of five rods [square], a passable cart, a stretcher (*span-touwen*), and an after plough (*achter plocgh*). The payment shall be made in good whole merchantable beaver skins, in three installments, the first on the 15th of July of this year, 1664, the second on the 15th of July, A. D. 1665, and the third or last installment on the 15th of July, 1666. The buyer shall be holden to furnish two sufficient sureties, one for all and each as principals, immediately, to the content of the seller, but if the buyer cannot furnish said sureties in said time, then it shall be offered for sale again at his cost and charge, and whatever less it comes to be worth, he shall be holden to make good, and whatever more it become worth, he shall receive no benefit therefrom. The auction fees shall be a charge on the buyer, payable as above. Having offered it for sale, Cornelis Van Nes remained the last bidder for the *bouwery*, for the sum of one thousand two hundred and eighty seven guilders, according to the above standing conditions, for which sum Volkert Janse [Douw] and Jan Dirckse Van Eps stood as sureties and principals, according to the aforesaid conditions.

Done in the village of Beverwyck on the 29th of April, A. D. 1664.

CORNELIS VAN NES.[1]
VOLCKERT JANSE.
JAN DIERCKSE VAN EPS.

Acknowledged before me

---

[1] Cornelis Van Nes's first wife was a daughter of Jan Oothout, by whom he had three sons, Hendrick, Jan and Gerrit. His second wife was Maritie Damens, the mother of Jan Dirkse Van Eps, who afterwards possessed the property described above

Conditions on which the administrators of the estate of Anderies Herbertsen, together with Cornelis Van Nes, husband and guardian of Maritie Damens, each owning a half, propose to sell at public sale to the highest bidder, a house and lot lying in the village of Beverwyck, bounded northerly by David Schuyler, and south by Wouter the wheelright, according to the patent thereof. Firstly, the buyer shall receive said house and lot immediately, in breadth four rods, and length eight rods, according to the patent. The payment shall be made in good whole merchantable beaver skins, or else seewant at twenty guilders the beaver, in two installments, the first on the first of July of this year, 1664, and the second on the first of July, A. D. 1665. The buyer shall be holden to furnish two sufficient sureties, one for all and each as principals, immediately, to the content of the seller. If the buyer cannot furnish said sureties in said time, then the aforesaid house and lot shall be offered for sale again at his charge and cost, and whatever less it comes to be worth, he shall make good, and whatever more it becomes worth shall be no benefit to him The auction fees become a charge to the buyer, payable as before. Having offered it for sale on the above conditions, Cornelis Van Nes remained the last bidder, for the sum of two hundred and seventy-two guilders, for which Jan Dirkse Van Eps stood surety as principal.

Done in the village of Beverwyck, on the 29th of April, A. D. 1664.

CORNELIS VAN NES.

Pieter Van Alen. JAN DIERCKSE VAN EPS.

Acknowledged before me.

Conditions on which the administrators of the estate of Philip Henderickse [Brouwer] propose to sell some horses and cattle, together with a horse mill, as it stands, to be paid for on the 15th of July of this year, 1664, in good whole merchantable beaver skins. The auction fees to become a charge to the buyer, payable as above.

Done the 29th of April, A. D. 1664, Beverwyck.

Jan Van Eps, a mare named *Snel* (quick),.............	*f*	175.00
Idem, also a horse being a gelding, for	*f*	160.00
Idem, also a yearling colt, for.	*f*	110.00
Idem, also a cow with a heifer calf, ...	*f*	119.00
Matteuwes Abrahamse [Vandeusen], a cow,..................	*f*	118.00
Jan Eps, a heifer of two years,..................................	*f*	84.00
Jacob Tyssen [Vander Heyden], a heifer of a year,............	*f*	40.00
Jan Eps, 5 sows, ...	*f*	77.00
Cornelis Teunise Bos, the running works of a horse mill......	*f*	112.00
	f	1004.00

I, Harmen Harmense Van Gansevoort,[1] offer myself as surety for the person of Jacob Tyssen, for the payment of forty guilders for the purchase of a calf.

HARMEN VAN GANSEVORT.

(Jacob Tyssen has paid forty guilders for the calf)

---

[1] H. H. Van G. married Marritie Leendertse Conyn: the baptisms of five of their children are recorded in first church records, between 1683 and 1690, of whom the eldest was Leendert. In 1677, he bought the lot on the south corner of "Cow street," now Broadway and Maiden lane, of Paulus Martense Van Benthuysen: here he erected a brewery.—*Deeds*, I 335.

Cornelis Teunisse Bos, by these presents, declares himself surety and principal for the person of Teuwes Abrahamsen, for the payment of the sum of one hundred and eighteen guilders in beavers, for the purchase of a cow.

Done in Beverwyck, the 29th of April, 1664.

CORNELIS TONISSEN BOS.

Likewise Mateuwes Abrahamsen offers himself as surety for Cornelis Bos, for the payment of one hundred and twelve guilders, for the purchase of a horse mill.

This is the mark M of MATEUWES ABRAHAMSEN, with his own hand set

I, the undersigned Jan Dirckse Van Eps, am the bidder and buyer of three horses, a cow, a calf, a heifer of two years, and five hogs, amounting to the sum of seven hundred and thirty-four [guilders], for which we, Cornelis Van Nes and Pieter Van Alen, stand as sureties and principals for the payment of said sum, in case of the failure of the buyer.

Done in Beverwyck the 29th of April, A. D. 1664.

JAN DIERCKSE VAN EPS.
CORNELIS VAN NES.
PIETER VAN ALEN.

Appeared before me Johannes Provoost, clerk, etc., Cornelis Teunisse Bos, who declares in presence of the afternamed witnesses, that he has conveyed, as by these presents he does, to Jan Dirckse Van Eps, the horse mill, which he bought at public sale, of the administrators of the estate of Philip Henderickse (and which the grantee accepts), for the same price which he paid for it, amounting to the sum of one hundred and twelve guilders in beavers, to be paid as the conditions specify, renouncing, furthermore, all claims and pretensions which he has therein.

Thus done in Fort Orange, the first of May, A. D. 1664.

CORNELIS THONISSEN BOS.
JAN DIERCKSE VAN EPS.

Acknowledged before me,

J. PROVOOST, Clerk.

Appeared before me, Johannes Provoost, clerk, etc., and in the presence of the afternamed witnesses, Jan Martensen [Wever], who acknowledges that he is well and truly indebted to Harmen Vedder in the sum of two hundred and eighty-six guilders and eleven stuivers in beavers, and thirty-one guilders and five stuivers in seewant, for goods and merchandise to his content received, which beforementioned sum he, the subscriber, promises to pay on the first day of May, A. D. 1665, for which he pledges his person and estate, real and personal, present and future, especially seventeen hogs, which he has on his *bouwery*, and which, in case of failure of payment, shall be turned over, according to their value, to said Harman Vedder, in preference of any one else, as an offset to said sums.

Thus done in the village of Beverwyck, on the first of May, A D 1664, in presence of Barent Reyndersen and Jan Byvanck as witnesses.

This is the mark + JAN MARTENSEN
with his own hand set.

Barent Reynders.
Jan Byvanck.

Acknowledged before me,

JOHANNES PROVOOST, Clerk.

Appeared before me Johannes Provoost, clerk, etc., and in presence of the afternamed witnesses, Jan Martensen [Wever,] who declares that he has appointed and empowered, as by these presents does, Harmen Vedder, in his name and for his sake, to demand, collect, and receive, of diverse persons, as well in the village of Wiltwyck, as here in Beverwyck, the following moneys to him, the subscriber owing, to wit: of Jan Van Aemsfort six schepels of wheat, eighteen guilders; from Cornelis Slecht fifty-four guilders in wheat; from Geertruy Haps *f.* 40, four in wheat; Henderick Jansen, *alias* Ribbide sixty-one guilder in beavers; Aert Otterspoor forty-five guilders in beavers; Poulus de Noorman twenty-eight guilders; from Jurriaen Westvael, according to obligation, one hundred and forty-one guilders in wheat; for the receipts acquittance to pass, and in case of unwillingness, payment to exact by law and rigor of justice, to which end all terms of the laws to observe, to definitive sentence and extreme execution, and to proceed by arrest against persons and estates, furthermore, to do and act as the subscriber being present might, or could do, provided that the attorney be holden to give a proper statement to him of his transactions and receipts, but shall keep for himself the previously received sum of two hundred and eighty-six guilders and eleven stuivers in beavers, and thirty-one guilders and five stuivers in seewant, for the payment of an obligation made on this date.

Thus done in Beverwyck, on the first of May, A. D. 1664, in the presence of Jan Henderickse, and Jan Janse Bleecker as witnesses.

This is the mark + of JAN MARTENSEN,
with his own hand set.

This is the mark **IH** *of Jan Henderickse, with his own hand set.*
Jan Jansen Bleecker.

Acknowledged before me,

J. PROVOOST, Clerk.

Conditions on which Adrian Gerritse [Papendorp,] attorney for Dirck Janse Kroon, proposes to sell at public sale to the highest bidder, some furniture and household goods, to said Kroon belonging; for which payment must be made in good, whole merchantable beaver skins, in the time of one month from this date; and whatever is other than beaver, the buyer shall pay at twenty-two guilders the beaver. Who ever buys more than one lot (*perceel*), the sum for each shall be reckoned up, and be reduced to whole beavers. The buyer shall also be holden to furnish sufficient sureties, immediately, for the purchase money

The auction fees become a charge to the buyer payable as above. (one bed for 140 guilders retained).

Gerrit Slichtenhorst, a lantern,.. *f* 3.05
Jochem Wesselse [Backer], a tin (*blickse*) cullender,................ *f* 4.00
Philip Pieterse [Schuyler], a great tin pail,........................ *f* 5.00
Mr. Jan Leck, a pewter mug and salt cellar,........................ *f* 7.05
Mr. Jacob [D'Hinsse], a pewter tankard,............................ *f* 4.05
Adriaen Gerritsen [Papendorp], a pewter chamber pot,.......... *f* 5.00
Jurrian Teunissen [Glasemaker] a tin sugar box,................ *f* 3.00
Idem, a pewter cullender,.. *f* 5.05
Philip Pieterse a copper mortar,.................................... *f* 8.15
Adriaen Gerritse, 2 pewter platters,................................ *f* 7.15
Idem, a copper chafing dish,.. *f* 7.10
J. Provoost, 2 pewter platters,.. *f* 7.00
Adriaen Gerritse, a little oil pot, ... *f* 3.05
Philip Pieterse, a funnel, a great copper spoon,................ *f* 5.00
J. Provoost, 2 copper candlesticks,.................................. *f* 8.00
Stoffel Janse [Abeel], 2 copper snuffers,........................ *f* 2.08
Adrien Gerrit, a pewter platter,...................................... *f* 4.10
Henderick Rosenboom, a copper stewpan,.......................... *f* 15.15
Jan Van Aken, an iron candlestick,.................................. *f* 2.05
Gysbert the tailor, a hand candlestick,............................ *f* 1.10
Stoffel Janse, an iron candlestick,.................................. *f* 1.00
Isaac DeHaen a pewter beaker gilt,................................ *f* 2.15
Philip Pieterse, a do .... *f* 2.15
Isaack De Haen, a hand candlestick,................................ *f* 1.00
Jan Clute, an iron pepper mill,...................................... *f* 3.00
Henderick Rosenboom, an iron chaffing dish,.................... *f* 3.00
Jan Vinhagel. 2 little pewter platters,............................ *f* 2.00
Philip Piterse, a pewter mug,.. *f* 3.10
Willem Brouwer, a pewter beaker,.................................. *f* 2.15
Volckert Janse [Douw], a pewter pint measure,.................. *f* 2.10
Idem, 2 little pewter platters,...................................... *f* 2.10
Philip Pieterse, 2 little pewter cups,.............................. *f* 2.00
Adriaen Gerritsen, a pewter pint measure,........................ *f* 2.10
Gerrit Slichtenhorst, a skimmer, ... *f* 3.15
Adriaen Gerritse, a mustard pot,.................................... *f* 1.10
Idem, a little copper pan .... *f* 5.00
Jan Clute, a pewter mug,.. *f* 5.00
Slichtenhorst, a little pewter beaker,.............................. *f* 1.00
Volckert Janse, a do.. *f* 1.00
J. Provoost, a pewter salt cellar,.................................... *f* 1.15
Adriaen Gerritse, 6 pewter plates,.................................. *f* 7.00
Johannes Provoost, a pewter platter,.............................. *f* 5.10
Idem, 2 andirons,.. *f* 7.10
Jan Henderickse Bruyn, 6 pewter spoons,........................ *f* 2.05
Isaack De Haen, a tin powder box,.................................. *f* 2.10
Gysbert the tailor, a chopping knife,.............................. *f* 2.10
C. Bogardus, a lamp and candlestick,.............................. *f* 3.00
Henderick Rosenboom, a chain pot hanger,........................ *f* 4.05
Volckert Janse, an iron tongs,.. *f* 2.05

Carried forward,.................................... *f* 89.05

Brought forward,	*f*	89.05
Adriaen Gerritsen, a frying pan,	*f*	2.15
Jan Van Aken, an iron do.,	*f*	1.10
Adriaen Gerritse, a pot hanger,	*f*	6.00
Jan Van Aken, a looking glass,	*f*	10.00
Barent the smith, 2 copper cocks,	*f*	2.15
Dr. Jacob [D'Hinsse], 4 pictures,	*f*	31.00
Robbert, 2 little pictures,	*f*	8.05
Jurriaen Teunisse, 2 do.,	*f*	6.05
Cornelis Bogardus, a *bort* almanac,	*f*	3.10
Rosenboom, a do.,	*f*	2.00
Jan Bastiaense [Van Gutsenhoven], 3 little pictures,	*f*	3.00
Dr. Adriaen, 3 do.,	*f*	4.05
Dr. Adriaen, also 3 pictures,	*f*	4.50
Wouter the Wheelwright, 3 ditto,	*f*	3.10
Dr. Adriaen, 3 ditto,	*f*	2.05
Rosenboom, 3 ditto,	*f*	2.05
Idem, 3 ditto,	*f*	1.15
Robbert Sandersen,[1] 3 ditto,	*f*	1.15
J. Provoost, 2 curtains and a valance,	*f*	20.10
Gerrit Lansingh, 2 curtains,	*f*	11.05
Adriaen Gerritse, a coverlet,	*f*	13.05
Jan Bastiaense, 3 little earthern platters,	*f*	3.00
Jurriaen Teunisse, 3 ditto,	*f*	1.10
Rosenboom, 3 ditto,	*f*	1.10
C. Bogardus, 3 ditto,	*f*	1.15
Jurriaen Teunisse, 2 ditto,	*f*	2.05
Rosenboom, 2 ditto,	*f*	2.00
Dirck Wesselse [Ten Broeck], 2 little pictures,	*f*	5.00
Rosenboom, 2 ditto,	*f*	3.10
Poulus Martense [Van Benthuysen], 2 ditto,	*f*	3.15
Adriaen Gerritsen, a brush,	*f*	2.05
Jacob Schermerhoorn, 2 chair cushions,	*f*	6.00
Adriaen Gerritsen, 2 sheets,	*f*	14.00
Antony Janse, 2 ditto,	*f*	8.00
Jan Hendr. Bruyn, 2 ditto,	*f*	8.00
Rosenboom, *hele* and an old pillow bier,	*f*	5.00
Volckert Janse, 1 wooden bowl and 7 or 8 wooden plates,	*f*	1.00
Goosen Gerritse, a duster,	*f*	1.10
Poulus Martense, 3 little pictures,	*f*	2.10
Barent the smith 3 ditto,	*f*	2.15
Goosen Gerritse, 1 great chest,	*f*	11.00
Jan Janse Ouderkerck, 3 chairs,	*f*	4.00
	f	427.05

[1] Robert Sanders son of Thomas S. of Amsterdam, and Sarah Van Gorcum, was baptized in New Amsterdam, 10 Nov. 1641. He came to Albany with his father before 1654; by his wife Elsie Barentse he had one son Barent and three daughters. In 1697 he was a merchant in New York, and admitted freeman in 1698.

On this 14 day of May A.D. 1664, appeared before me Johannes La Montagne in the service, of etc., in the presence of the honorable Jan Henderickse Van Bael and Jan Costersen Van Aken, commissaries etc., the following Indians, named Queskimiet, son of Pacies, Aepie, Wickepe, Kleyn Davidtie [Little David], who testify and declare, at the request of Jan Tomasse and Volckert Janse [Douw] as follows; translated by Jan Dareth. First, they say that eighteen years ago, Jacob Janse Flodder bought the Gojers kil, but no land with it, only a little piece north of said kil, which was granted him to make a garden, for the hire of which, these deponents, the owners of the same, have received only a piece of cloth. The deponents being asked if Jacob Janse Flodder had bought some land at Schotack, thereupon answered unanimously, No, but that he only had a small piece of land that they rented to him to sow oats upon, furthermore, that he had a rick there to house his grain in for the winter, but that he never had any ownership therein. Again the deponent being asked who are the lawful owners of Schotack and of the fast bank extending the whole length of the island, declared that Jan Tomasse and Volckert Janse [Douw] are the lawful owners, who bought and paid for the same, and nobody else. They declare likewise, according to the conveyance of Wattawit, of date the 4th of October, A.D. 1663, that the land on the fast bank (*vaste wal*) where the house of Machack Notas stood, was justly owned by Wattawit, all of which aforesaid facts they declare were stated yesterday the 13th of this month, at the house of the Heer Rensselaer, in presence of the interpreter, Jan Dareth and Marten Gerritse [Van Bergen].

Thus Done in Fort Orange, the 14th of May, A.D. 1664.

This is the mark with his own [mark] of QUESKIMIET hand set.

This is the mark with his own [mark] of AEPJE; hand set.

This is the mark with his own [mark] of WICKEPE, hand set.

This is the mark with his own [mark] of DAVIDIE. hand set.

In acknowledgment of the truth this is subscribed by us the above mentioned commissaries.

J. H. Van Bael.
Jan Koster.
Jan Dareth.

LA MONTAGNE, *Commis* at Fort Orange.

Appeared before me Johannes La Montagne, in the service of, etc., Volckert Janse [Douw] and Jan Tomassen, who declare by way of complaint, that on the 12th of this month, the Heer Renselaer with the *Schout* Swart and the Secretary Schelluyne were upon the island Schotack, and there forbade Jan Martensen [Wever], the subscriber's tenant, to proceed farther with the plowing and sowing, on account of which prohibition the tenant was afraid to proceed with the tillage. So it is that the subscribers free said tenant, Jan Martensen, from all harm which might come upon him by reason of said prohibition with respect to the tillage of the land, which is done without producing offence except to complain to the officer and the subscribers in regard to the violence that may be done him.

Done in Fort Orange 15th May, A D. 1664.

VOLCKERT JANSE,
JAN THOMAS.
LA MONTAGNE, *Commis* at Fort Orange.

Appeared before me Johannes La Montagne, in the service of, etc., in the presence of the honorable Jan Verbeeck and Gerrit Slichtenhorst, commissaries of the same jurisdiction, Pieter Janssen the boor (*de Boer*) who acknowledged and declared by these presents that he is well, truly, and honestly indebted to Mr. Pieter Ryverdingh, in the sum of eighty guilders Holland money, for goods and merchandise to his content received, which aforesaid sum of eighty guilders Holland money, the subscriber promises to pay on the first of July, A.D. 1665, to said Ryverdingh or his attorney Adriaen Janssen V. Leyden; and in case said subscriber, Pieter Janssen fails, he promises to pay interest on the same at 12 *per cent* to begin from this date; for which he pledges his person and estate, personal and real, present and future, specially mortgaging his house and lot lying in the village of Beverwyck next to Claes Vylspic and Lambert Van Valckenborgh, to secure the payment of said sum, if need be, without cost and loss.

Done in Fort Orange, the 10th of June, A.D. 1664.

This is the mark + of PIETER JANSSEN DE BOER.
with his own hand set.

Gerrit Slichtenhorst,
Jan Verbeeck.

Acknowledged before me,

LA MONTAGNE, Clerk, at Fort Orange.

Appeared before me Johannes La Montagne, in the service of, etc., in the presence of the honorable Jan Hendricksen Van Baelen and Jan Van Aken commissaries, etc., Jacus Cornelis [Van Slyck] [1] dwelling at Schonhechtede, who declared and acknowledged that he is well, truly and honestly indebted to Sweerus Teunise [Van Velsen], in the sum of six hundred and ninety-three guilders in beavers, for goods and sundries to his content received; which aforesaid sum he, Jacus Cornelisse, promises to pay in the year of our Lord 1668, in the month of May; for the payment of said sum, pledging his person and estate, real and personal, more especially mortgaging the Island lying at Schonechtede named *Marten's island*, renouncing all exceptions which might militate against this obligation.

Done in Fort Orange, the 3d July, A.D. 1664.

The mark of, ACKES, JACUS CORNELISSEN.

---

[1] Jaques Cornelise Van Slyck, *alias* Gantsh, *alias* Itsychosaquachka, was one of the three children of Cornelis Antonissen V. S. *alias* Broer Cornelis and a Mohawk woman; Jaques had a brother Marten, who gave name to the great Island lying west of Schenectady, and a sister Hilletie, who was a well known interpretress and married Pieter Danie se Van Olinda; she is the person in whom Messrs. Dankers and Sluyter took such interest during their visit to Schenectady in 1680. See their Journal, page 304, etc.

Appeared before me Johannes La Montagne, in the service of, etc., in the presence of the honorable Jan Verbeeck and Jacob Schermerhoorn commissaries, etc., Jan Van Eeckelen,[1] who acknowledged and declared that he is, well, truly and honestly indebted to Cornelis Teunisse Bos, trustee for the estate of Cornelis Maçrsen, in the number of thirty-two and a half beavers growing out of an assignment of a debt due by Albert Gerritse to said estate; which aforesaid number of thirty-two and a half beavers he (*comparant*) by agreement made with said trustee promises to pay within the time of three years from this date with interest at the rate of ten *per cent*, to commence from the 6th of August next coming; for which the subscriber pledges his person and estate, personal and real, present and future, specially mortgaging and pledging his house and lot lying in the village of Beverwyck, bounded north by Jan Dareth and south by Pieter Loockermans, to secure the payment of the aforesaid number of thirty-two and a half beavers, if need be, without loss and cost.

Done in Fort Orange, the 7th of July, A.D. 1664.

JAN JANSEN VAN EECKEL.

Jan Verbeeck.
Jacob Schermerhooren.

Acknowledged before me,

LA MONTAGNE, Clerk at Fort Orange.

Appeared before me Johannes La Montagne, in the service of, etc., in the presence of Gerrit Slichtenhorst and Stoffel Janssen [Abeel] commissioners, etc., Francoys Boon, old commissary of the aforesaid place, who declared that he had granted and transferred, as by these presents he does grant and transfer, in real and actual possession to and for the behoof of Jochim Wesselse Backer, his heirs or assigns, a house and lot lying in the village of Beverwyck bounded east, west and south by the highway, and north by the house of Gillis Pieterse [Timmerman] as large as it lies enclosed in fence, with all the right and title which the grantor has had therein, by virtue of a conveyance to him given by Stoffel Janssen Abeel of date the 15th of August A.D. 1659, and the grantor at the same time acknowledges that he is paid and satisfied for the sale of the same, and therefore promises the aforesaid house and lot to free from all claims, actions, and pretensions, which may arise save the lord's right, pledging therefor his person and estate, personal and real, present and future, submitting himself to all laws and judges.

Done in Fort Orange the 17th of July, A.D. 1664.

FRANCOYS BOON.

Gerrit Slichtenhorst.
Stoffel Janse Abeel.

Acknowledged before me.

LA MONTAGNE, Clerk at Fort Orange.

Appeared before me Johannes Provoost, clerk, etc., and in the presence of the afternamed witnesses, Rutger Jacobsen, who declares by these presents that he has sold, granted and transferred to Jacob Hevick, his portion of the grain, which stands upon the seller's island, being the

[1] A Johannes Van Eeckelen, perhaps the above, was a schoolmaster in Flatbush in 1691; the minister and elder of the church desired his removal from office because he had been an active partizan of Leisler.—*English Manuscripts.*

fourth part thereof, for the number of five and thirty good whole merchantable beaver skins, which the aforesaid Jacob Hevick promises to pay to said Rut Jacobsen by an abatement on the mortgage, which the said Hevick holds upon the seller's island; furthermore, the seller makes over said grain and, by these presents, gives the buyer authority to harvest the same without any let or hindrance from any one from whom he also promises to protect him.

Thus done without craft or guile, in Fort Orange, in the presence of Claes Jacobsen, and Sacharias Sickels, as witnesses hereto invited, on this 16th July, A.D. 1664.

RUTGER JACOB.

This is the mark χ of JACOB HEVICK.

with his own hand set.

Claes Jacobse.
Sacharias Seckels.

Appeared before me Johannes La Montagne, in the service of, etc., in the presence of honorable Jan Verbeeck and Gerrit Slichtenhorst magistrates etc., the honorable Francoys Boon old commissary of said place, who declares that he has granted and transferred, as by these presents he does grant and transfer, in real and actual possession to and for the behoof of Jurriaen Teunisse [Glasemaker] his heirs or assigns, a garden lying in the village of Beverwyck behind Fort Orange, adjoining to the west and north the highway, of such magnitude as it lies enclosed in fence with all the right and title which the grantor has had therein, and acknowledges that he is fully paid and satisfied for the purchase, and therefore pledges his person and estate, real and personal, present and future, submitting himself to all laws and judges.

Done in Fort Orange the 16th of July, A.D. 1664.

FRANCOYS BOON.[1]

Gerrit Slichtenhorst.
Jan Verbeeck.

Acknowledged before me,

LA MONTAGNE, Clerk in Fort Orange.

Appeared before me Johannes La Montagne, in the service of, etc., in the presence of honorable Jan Hendrickse Van Bael and Jan Coster Van Aken, magistrates of the same jurisdiction, Jan Roeloffsen [De Goyer] inhabitant of said village, who declares that he has granted and transferred, as by these presents he does grant and transfer in real and actual possession to and for the behoof of William Brouwer his heirs and assigns, a garden lying in the village of Beverwyck, hard by Fort Orange, adjoining on the rear of Heer Renselaer's lot, to the south of the heirs of Annetien Bogardus, to the east of the road, and to the north of Abraham Staets, length seven rods, and breadth five rods, which lot was granted, by the Heer director general and council of New Netherland, by patent of date the 25th of October 1653, to Albert Gerritsen, from whom the grantor received the same by conveyance of date the 4th of July A.D. 1658, and the grantor acknowledges that he is fully paid and satisfied

[1] See Valentine's *History of New York*, p. 99.

for the purchase, promising said garden to free from all actions, claims or pretensions, which hereafter may arise, therefor pledging his person and estate, personal and real, present and future, placing himself in subjection to all laws and judges.

Done in Fort Orange the 24th of July A.D 1664.

JAN ROELOFFSE.

Jan Koster.

Acknowledged before me.

LA MONTAGNE, Clerk at Fort Orange.

Appeared before me Johannes La Montagne, in the service of, etc., in the presence of the honorable Jan Verbeeck and Stoffel Janssen Abeel magistrates, etc., Willem Brouwer, inhabitant of said village, who declares, by virtue of a conveyance to him, the grantor, given of this date, by Jan Roeloffsen, that he has again granted, transferred, and made over, as by these presents he does grant and transfer in real and actual possession to and for the behoof of Capt. Abraham Staets old commissary of said place, his heirs or assigns, a garden lying in the village of Beverwyck hard by Fort Orange, adjoining on the rear of Heer Rensclaer's lot, to the south of the heirs of Annetie Bogardus, to the east of the road, and to the north of the grantee, length seven rods and breadth five rods, which garden was granted to Albert Gerritsen by patent, by Heer director general and council of New Netherland, of date the 25th of October, A.D. 1653; and the grantor acknowledges that he is paid and satisfied for the purchase and delivery of the same, and promises to free the aforesaid garden from every action, claim or pretension, which may hereafter arise, therefor pledging his person and estate, personal and real, present and future, submitting himself to all laws and judges.

Done in Fort Orange, the 24th of July, 1664.

WILLEM BROUWER.

Jan Verbeeck.
Stoffel Janse.

Acknowledged before me,

LA MONTAGNE, Clerk at Fort Orange.

Appeared before me Johannes Provoost, clerk, etc., the Honorable Nicolaes Gouverneur, substitute for the honorable Cornelis Steenwyck,[1] attorney for Barent Van Marle, of the first part, and Jan Hendrickse Bruyn of the second part, who declare in presence of the afternamed witnesses, that they have agreed and contracted about the purchase of the house and lot of Barent Van Marle deceased, lying in the village of Beverwyck in the manner following: — Firstly, said Claes Gouverneur sells to said Jan Hendrickse Bruyn the house and lot of said Van Marle deceased, by virtue of a power of attorney (*procuratie*), of such magnitude and bounds as said Barent Van Marle purchased it from Cornelis Vos, according to conveyance of date the 30th of July, A.D. 1661, and shall deliver said house and lot within fourteen days from date free and unincumbered save the lord's right; for which Jan Hendrickse Bruyn promises, on delivery,

[1] See Valentine's *History of New York*, 121.

to pay in one sum the number of sixty good whole merchantable beaver skins and fourteen half beavers, and no more; and on said payment a proper conveyance shall be given to the buyer.

Thus done in presence of Gerrit Swart and Jacob De Hince, without craft or guile, in Fort Orange, the 14th of August, A.D. 1664.

CLAES GOUVERNEUR.
JAN HENDRICKSE BRUYN.

G. Swart.
J. De Hinsse.

Acknowledged before me,

J. PROVOOST, Clerk.

Appeared before me Johannes La Montagne, in the service of, etc., in the presence of the honorable Jan Verbeeck and Stoffel Janssen [Abeel] commissaries etc., the honorable Sander Leendersen Glen old commissary who declares that he has sold, granted and transferred, as by these presents he does in real and actual possession to and for the behoof of the honorable Jan Hendrickse Van Bael commissary etc., his heirs or assigns, a house and lot lying in the village of Beverwyck on the Hill, adjoining to the north Jan Tomassen, to the south Hendrick Kuyler, east and west the highway, of such magnitude as it is enclosed in fence, which lot the grantor bought at public sale of the Heeren commissaries under an execution made on the person of Marten Gerritse [Van Bergen]; and the grantor acknowledges that he is fully paid and satisfied for the purchase and delivery of the same, with the sum of eight hundred and seventy-six guilders in beavers; therefore he promises to free the aforesaid house and lot from all actions, claims, or pretensions, which may hereafter arise, excepting only the lord's right, pledging his person and estate, personal and real, present and future, and submitting himself to all laws and judges.

Done in Fort Orange the 18th of August, 1664.

SANDER LENRSEN GLEN

Stoffel Janse Abeel.
Jan Verbeeck.

Acknowledged before me,

LA MONTAGNE, Clerk at Fort Orange.

Appeared before me Johannes La Montagne, in the service of, etc., in the presence of honorable Gerrit Slichtenhorst and Jan Hendrickse Van Bael commissaries etc., Jan Francen Van Hoesem, inhabitant of said village, who acknowledges and declares, by these presents, that he is well, truly and honestly indebted to Mr. Nicolaes Meyer, alderman and merchant at Amsterdam in New Netherland, in the sum of one thousand three hundred and forty-six carolus guilders and eleven stuivers in good whole merchantable beaver skins, growing out of goods and merchandise delivered, together with moneys loaned according to an honest statement thereof received, which aforesaid sum of one thousand three hundred and forty-six guilders and eleven stuivers, the subscriber promises to pay in two installments, the first of which shall be on the first day of August, A.D. 1665, the just half; and the other half on the first of July, 1666, with interest on the same at ten *per cent*, beginning from this date and continuing until the full payment of the same, but the interest is to continue no longer than the mortgagee (*acceptant*) shall please, for which said Jan Francen Van Hoesen pledges his person and estate, personal and real, present and future, specially mortgaging and hypothecating both his houses, with the lot and garden behind the same as they stand, situated in the village of Beverwyck, adjoining to the north of Jochem Wesselse [Backer], and said Meyer shall likewise draw and use the house rent of the mortgageor's house where Cornelis Van Dyck dwell ; likewise his, the mortgageor's Bouwery and lands lying in the Claverack, to secure the payment if necessary, of said sum without cost and loss

Thus done in Fort Orange the 26th of August, A.D. 1664.

This is the mark of JAN FRANCEN VAN HOESEM, with his own hand set

Gerrit Slichtenhorst.
J. H. Van Bael.

Acknowledged before me,

LA MONTAGNE, Clerk at Fort Orange.

Appeared before me Johannes La Montagne, in the service of, etc., in the presence of honorable Stoffel Janse Abeel and Jan Hendrickse Van Bael commissaries, etc., Mr. Claes Gouverneur, trustee for the estate of Barent Van Marle, who declares that he has granted and transferred, as by these presents he does grant and transfer, in real and actual possession to and for the behoof of Jan Hendrickse Bruyn, his heirs or assigns, a house and lot lying in the village of Beverwyck, adjoining to the south the street, to the north the kil, to the east the grantee (*acceptant*), and to the west Juriaen Teunisse [Glasemacker,] full length nine rods, breadth in the rear on the kil, seventeen feet and a half, in front as broad as the house, with an alley on the east side of the house, three and a half feet wide; which lot is a part of the patent granted by the Heer director general and council of New Netherland, to Cornelis Vos; and the grantor acknowledges that he is fully paid and satisfied for the purchase and delivery of the same, whereof the Heer Jeremias Van Renselaer has received the sum of three hundred and ninety-six guilders in beavers, which was due to him by virtue of a mortgage upon said house and lot, and the grantor promises to free said house and lot from all actions, claims or pretensions, which may hereafter arise, pledging his person and estate, personal and real, present and future, nothing excepted, submitting himself to all laws and judges.

Thus done in Fort Orange, the 28th of August, A.D. 1664.

CLAES GOUVERNEUR.

Stoffel Janse Abeel.
J. H. Van Bael.

Acknowledged before me,

LA MONTAGNE, Clerk at Fort Orange.

Appeared before me Johannes Provoost, clerk, etc., in the presence of honorable Stoffel Janse and Jan Hendrickse Van Bael, commissaries, etc., the Heer Jeremias Van Renselaer, who acknowledges by these presents, that he has received from Mr. Claes Gouverneur, trustee of Barent Van Marle deceased, the sum of three hundred and ninety-six guilders in beavers, payment, in part, for a mortgage which he holds upon the second installment due on the house of Cornelis Vos, which the aforesaid Barent Van Marie bought, and said Renselaer promises said Gouverneur in his office of trustee as his successor, to free the same from all actions, claims, or pretensions, which may hereafter arise

Done in Fort Orange the 28th of August, A D. 1664.

JEREMIAS VAN RENSSELAER.

Stoffel Janse Abeel.
J. H. Van Bael.

Appeared before me Johannes La Montagne, in the service of, etc., in the presence of the honorable Jan Hendrickse Van Bael and Jan Coster Van Aken, commissaries, etc., Pieter Adriaense [Soogemackelyck,] [1] inhabitant of Schanhectade, who declares that he has granted and transferred, as by these presents he does grant and transfer, in real and actual possession to and for the behoof of the honorable Philip Pieterse Schuyler, his heirs or assigns, a house and lot lying in the village of Beverwyck, adjoining to the north Adriaen Appel and to the south Jan Barentse Poest, deceased, to the west the street, length ten rods and breadth four rods; which lot was granted to said grantor, by the Heer director general and council of New Netherland of date A.D. 16—; he, the grantor, acknowledging that he is fully paid and satisfied for the purchase and delivery of the same and therefore promises to free the same from all actions, claims, or pretensions, which may hereafter arise, pledging his person and estate, personal and real, present and future, and submitting himself to all laws and judges.

Done in Fort Orange, the 11th of September, A.D. 1664.

PIETER ADRIAENSE.

J. H. Van Bael.
Jan Koster.

Acknowledged before me,

LA MONTAGNE, Clerk at Fort Orange.

Appeared before me Johannes La Montagne, in the service of, etc., in the presence of the honorable Jan Verbeeck and Stoffel Jansen commissaries, etc., Tomas Poulus [Powell], inhabitant of said village, who acknowledges and declares, by these presents, that he is well, truly, and honestly, indebted to the honorable Jan Koster Van Aken, in the number of twelve pieces of good whole merchantable beaver skins, for goods and merchandise to his content received, and promises the aforesaid twelve beavers to pay on the first of May. A.D. 1665, and failing of said payment, he shall be holden to pay proper interest; for which the mortgageor pledges his person and estate, real and personal, present and future, and specially mortgages his house and lot lying in the village of Beverwyck, on the west side of the street, right against Jan Labatie's, to secure the payment of said twelve beavers, if need be, without loss or cost.

Done in Fort Orange, the 15th of September, A.D. 1664.

THOMAS POWELL.

Jan Verbeeck.
Stoffel Janse Abeel.

Acknowledged before me,

LA MONTAGNE, Clerk at Fort Orange.

---

[1] Sometimes called Van Woggelum.

Appeared before me Johannes La Montagne, in the service of, etc., in the presence of the honorable Jan Hendrickse Van Bael and Jan Koster Van Aken, commissaries of the same jurisdiction, Reyer Albert, inhabitant of said village, who declares that he has granted and transferred, as by these presents he does grant and transfer, in real and actual possession to and for the behoof of Heer Johannes Baptist Van Rensselaer and Goosen Gerritse [Van Schaick], old commissaries of this place, their heirs or assigns, a house and lot lying in the village of Beverwyck aforesaid, on the third (*Vossen*) kil, adjoining to the north and west the grantor, and to the south and east the highway, length six rods and breadth four rods; which lot is a part of the patent to him, the grantor, given by the Heer director general and council of New Netherland, of date the 25th of October, A.D. 1653, and the grantor acknowledges that he is fully paid and satisfied for the purchase and delivery of the same, and therefore promises the aforesaid house and lot to free from all actions, claims, or pretensions, which may arise, pledging therefor his person and estate, personal and real, present and future, and subjecting himself to the force of all laws and judges.

Done in Fort Orange, the 15th of September, A.D. 1664.

This is the mark ✝ of Reyer Albertsen.

Jan Koster.
J. H. Van Bael.

Acknowledged before me,

La Montagne, Clerk at Fort Orange.

Appeared before me Johannes La Montagne, in the service of, etc., in the presence of the honorable Jan Verbeeck and Jan Koster Van Aken commissaries, etc., the Heer Jeremias Van Rensselaer empowered by his brother Johan Baptist Van Rensselaer, who declares, by virtue of a conveyance of this date given to him, the grantor, and Goosen Gerritse [Van Schaick] by Reyer Albertse, that he has again granted and transferred, as by these presents, he does grant and transfer, in real and actual possession to and for the behoof of said Goosen Gerritse his heirs or assigns, his portion of the house and lot (being one half of the same), which he with the grantee in company have bought, lying in the village of Beverwyck on the third [*Vossen*] kil, adjoining to the north and west the said Reyer Albertse, to the south and east the highway, whole length six rods and breadth four rods; and the grantor acknowledges that he is fully paid and satisfied for the purchase and delivery of the same, and therefore promises to free the same from all actions, claims, or pretensions, which may hereafter arise (save the lord's right), pledging his person and estate, personal and real, present and future, and putting himself under the authority of all laws and judges.

Done in Fort Orange, the 15th of September, A.D. 1664.

Jeremias Van Rensselaer.

Jan Koster.
Jan Verbeeck.

Acknowledged before me,

La Montagne, Clerk at Fort Orange.

Appeared before me Johannes La Montagne, in the service of, etc., in the presence of the honorable Jan Verbeeck and Jan Koster Van Aeken commissaries etc., the honorable Goosen Gerritse [Van Schaick] old commissary, who declares that he has granted and transferred, as by these presents he does grant and transfer, in actual and real possession to and for the behoof of Hendrick Koster his heirs or assigns, a house and lot lying in the village of Beverwyck on the hill, adjoining to the north Henderick Rosenboom, to the south the widow[1] of Henderick Anderisse [Van Doesburgh], east and west the highway, is in breadth five rods and length twenty rods, according to the patent thereof granted, by the Heer director general and council of New Netherland, to Lourens Lourense of date the 25th of October, 1653; and the grantor acknowledges that he is fully paid and satisfied for the purchase and delivery of the same, and therefore promises said house and lot to free from all claims, actions, or pretensions which may hereafter arise, (saving only the lord's right) under a pledge of his person and estate, real and personal, present and future, submitting himself to all laws and judges.

Done in Fort Orange the 15th of September, A.D. 1664.

GOOSEN GERRITSE.

Jan Verbeeck.
Jan Koster.

Acknowledged before me,

LA MONTAGNE, Clerk at Fort Orange.

Appeared before me Johannes La Montagne, in the service of, etc., in the presence of the honorable Jan Verbeeck and Jan Koster Van Aken commissaries, etc., Marcelus Janssen [Van Bommel], inhabitant of the colony Rensselaerswyck, who declares that he has granted and transferred as by these presents, he does grant and transfer, in real and actual possession to and for the behoof of Asser Levy, merchant of Amsterdam in New Netherland, his heirs or assigns, a house and lot lying in the village of Beverwyck aforesaid on the hill, adjoining to the north Gerrit Slichtenhorst, to the south the lot of Claes Ripse, [Van Dam], east and west the highway, length according to the patent twenty-one and a half rods, and breadth six rods, except thirty feet in breadth taken off for the behoof of said Claes Ripse [Van Dam], which patent was granted to Goosen Gerritse [Van Schaick], by the Heer director general and council of New Netherland of date the 25th of October, A.D. 1653, from whom the grantor (*transportant*) received a conveyance; and the grantor (*cedant*) acknowledges that he is fully paid and satisfied for the purchase and delivery of the same, and therefore promises said house and lot to free from all actions, claims, or pretensions, which may hereafter arise (excepting the lord's right), pledging his person and estate, personal and real, and submitting himself to the force of all laws and judges.

Done in Fort Orange the 15th of September, A.D. 1664.

MAERCELYS JANSSEN.

Jan Verbeeck.
Jan Koster.

Acknowledged before me,

LA MONTAGNE, Clerk at Fort Orange.

---

[1] Maritie Damens who afterwards married Cornelis Van Nes.

Appeared before me Johannes La Montagne, in the service of, etc, in the presence of honorable Jan Verbeeck and Jan Koster Van Aken commissaries, etc., the honorable Philip Pieterse Schuyler old commissary of this place, who declares that he has granted and transferred, as by these presents, he does grant and transfer, in real and actual possession, to and for the behoof of Goosen Gerritse [Van Schaick,] his heirs, or assigns, his portion of the house and lot (being one half) that he holds in company with the grantee (*acceptant*), lying in the village of Beverwyck, aforesaid on the hill, adjoining to the north Henderick Rosenboom, and to the south the widow of Henderick Anderiessen [Van Doesburgh.] east and west the highway, whole length twenty rods, and breadth five rods, according to the patent thereof granted, by the Heer director general, and council of New Netherland, to Lourens Lourense, of date the 25th of October, A. D. 1653, and the grantor acknowledges that he is fully paid and satisfied for the purchase and delivery of the same, and therefore promises to free the same from all actions, claims, or pretensions, which may hereafter arise, pledging therefor his person and estate, personal and real, present and future, and submitting himself to all laws and judges.

Done in Fort Orange the 15th of September, A. D. 1664.

PHILIP PIETERSE SCHUYLER.

Jan Verbeeck.
Jan Koster.

Acknowledged before me,

LA MONTAGNE, Clerk at Fort Orange

Appeared before me Johannes La Montagne, in the service, etc., in the presence of Jan Verbeeck and Jan Koster Van Aken commissaries, etc., the honorable Abraham Staets, old commissary of this place, who declares that he has granted and transferred, as by these presents, he does grant and transfer, in real and actual possession, to and for the behoof of honorable Philip Pieterse Schuyler also old commissary, his heirs, or assigns, a lot lying in the village of Beverwyck, adjoining to the east (?) the hill, to the west a common alley, to the south the street to the north the kil, in breadth from the common alley westward six rods two feet, length from the street to the kil; which lot is part of the patent given to him, the grantor, by the Heer director general and council of New Netherland, of date the 25th of October. A. D. 1653; and the grantor acknowledges that he is fully paid and satisfied for the purchase and delivery of the same, and therefore promises to free said lot from all actions, claims, or pretensions, which may hereafter arise, pledging therefor, his person and estate, real and personal, present and future, submitting himself to all laws and judges.

Done in Fort Orange the 15th of September, A. D. 1664.

ABRAM STAES.

Jan Verbeeck.
Jan Koster.

Acknowledged before me,

LA MONTAGNE, Clerk at Fort Orange.

Appeared before me Johannes La Montagne, in the service of, etc., in the presence of Hon. Stoffel Janssen [Abeel] and Jan Koster Van Aken commissaries, etc., the honorable Philip Pieterse Schuyler, who declares that he has granted and transferred, as by these presents, he does grant and transfer, in real and actual possession to and for the behoof of Gysbert Janssen, his heirs or assigns, a lot lying in the village of Beverwyck on the hill, adjoining to the east the grantor, to the west a common alley or the house of Cornelis Steenwyck, to the south the street, to the north the kil, breadth one rod ten feet less two and a half inches, length from the street to the kil in the rear, which lot is a part of the patent granted to the honorable Abraham Staets of date the 25th of October, 1653, from whom the grantor received the same by conveyance; and the grantor acknowledges that he is fully paid and satisfied for the purchase and delivery of the same, and therefore promises to free it from all claims, actions, or pretensions, which may hereafter arise, pledging therefor his person and estate, personal and real, present and future, and submitting himself to the force of all laws and judges.

Done in Fort Orange the 15th of September, A.D. 1664.

PHILIP PIETERSE SCHUYLER.

Stoffel Janse Abeel.
Jan Koster

Acknowledged before me,

LA MONTAGNE, Clerk at Fort Orange.

Appeared before me Johannes La Montagne, in the service of, etc., in the presence of Gerrit Slichtenhorst and Stoffel Janssen [Abeel] commissaries, etc., Gysbert Janssen, who declares that he has granted and transferred, as by these presents he does grant and transfer, in real and actual possession to and for the behoof of Harmen Albertsen Vedder his heirs or assigns, a house and lot lying near Fort Orange in the village of Beverwyck on the hill, adjoining to the east Philip Pieterse Schuyler, to the west a common alley or the house of Mr. Cornelis Steenwyck, to the south the street, to the north the kil, breadth one rod ten feet less two and a half inches, length from the street to the kil in the rear; which lot the grantor received by conveyance from said Philip Pieterse Schuyler, by virtue of a patent granted to honorable Abraham Staets, of date the 25th of October, A D. 1653, whereof this lot is a part; and the grantor acknowledges that he is fully paid and satisfied therefor, and promises to free the aforesaid house and lot from all claims, actions, or pretensions; which may hereafter arise, therefor pledging his person and estate, personal and real, present and future, and submitting himself to all laws and judges.

Done in Fort Orange the 15th of September, A.D. 1664.

GYSEBERT YANSEN.

Stoffel Janse Abeel.

Acknowledged before me,

LA MONTAGNE, Clerk at Fort Orange

Conditions according to which the Heeren commissaries of Albany propose to farm out at public sale to the highest bidder, the slaughter excise for the time of one year. The farming of the slaughter excise shall begin on the first of October of this year, and end on the last day of September A.D 1665, old style. The farmer shall receive for the slaughtered beasts, whether ox, cow calf, bull, hog, goat, or sheep, for every guilder according to the value of the same, to wit, what is purchased for beavers shall give twenty stuivers in seewant for a beaver, and in case of dispute to be determined by an indifferent person. The farmer shall be holden to furnish two sufficient sureties as principals for the payment of the excise money, to the content of the Heer contractors, and in the time of six weeks from this date he shall pay the just half of the promised sum, and the other half on New Years day, being the first day of January, 1665, old style, in good current seewant, and if the farmer can not furnish sufficient sureties, then it shall be offered for sale again at his cost and charge, and whatever less it comes to be worth he shall make good, and whatever more it becomes worth he shall enjoy no profit therefrom. The farmer shall receive what has been paid in since the first of October new style, for the slaughtered beasts. After offering it for sale according to the above standing conditions, Henderick Rosenboom remained the highest bidder and farmer, for the sum of seven hundred and eighty guilders, for which he offered, as sureties and principals, Jan Tomassen and Evert Janssen Wendel, who pledge their persons and estates, personal and real.

Done in Albany the 27th of September, A.D. 1664.

HENDERYCK ROOSEBOOM.
JAN THOMASSE.
EVERT JANSE WENDEL.

Appeared before me Johannes Provoost by the Heeren commissaries of Albany admitted clerk of their Honors' court, and in the presence of the honorable Gerrit Slichtenhorst and Jan Koster Van Aken chosen witnesses out of their honorable college [court], Volckert Janssen [Douw] and Adriaen Van Ilpendam trustees of the estate of Andries Herbertse, who declares that they have granted and transferred, as by these presents they do grant and transfer, in real and actual possession to and for the behoof of Jurinen Janssen, his heirs or assigns, a house and lot lying in the village of Albany on the hill, adjoining on the south Jacob Schermerhorn, on the north and east the road, on the west the hill; breadth five rods, and length twenty rods, according to patent thereof granted to Gysbert Cornelis Van Wesap of date the 25th of October 1653, which lot said Anderies Herbertsen received by conveyance from Francoys Boom, for which house and lot the grantors acknowledge that they are fully paid and satisfied, and therefore promise to free the same from all actions, claims, or pretensions, which may hereafter arise, pledging therefor their persons and estates, personal and real, present and future, and submitting themselves to the force of all laws and judges.

Done in Albany the first of October 1664, old style.

VOLCKERT JANSE.
ADRIAEN VAN ILPENDAM.

Gerrit Slichtenhorst.
Jan Koster.

Conditions according to which the highest officer and the Heeren commissaries of Albany propose, in the name and by the authority of the Heer governor of New York, to farm out to the highest bidder, the excise of all the wines, beers and distilled liquors to be consumed and drawn by the innkeepers, tapsters, and retailers, in and about Albany and the colony Rensselaerswyck. The farming shall begin on the 22d day of October, old style, and 1st of November new style, and end on the 22d of October old style, *Anno* 1565: being the time of 12 months, during which time the farmer may take and receive for all wines, beers, or distilled liquors, to be drawn and consumed by the tapsters and innkeepers, as follows:

For a tun of domestic brewed beer,..................................	*f*	4 00
For a tun of foreign beer,..	*f*	6.00
For a hogshead of French [wine],........	*f*	20.00
For an anker do, ...	*f*	4.00
For an anker of Spanish wine, brandy, or distilled liquors,......	*f*	7.00
For an anker of cider,..	*f*	2.00

Greater and lesser measures in proportion; in beaver currency or else 16 white or 8 black seewants for a stuiver at the choice of the payer. The farmer shall be holden, to the content of the Heeren contractors, to furnish two sufficient sureties, one for each and all as principals, to pay every three months in beavers, or else in seewant, 16 white or eight black the stuiver, a just fourth part of the promised excise money. To prevent all cavil, misunderstanding and fraud, it is stipulated and agreed that, after the expiration of this farming, when a new farming is made, the new farmer shall be permitted on the day of the new farming, the day following, or at least within three days after the farming is let to make a guaging in presence of the late farmer if he wishes to be present, of the remainders of the wines, beers, and distilled liquors held over by the tapsters and innkeepers, and two-third parts of the receipts or dues for excise is to be made over and returned by the old or preceding farmer to his successor or following farmer. The Heeren contractors reserve to themselves the interpretation and amplification of this paper, and promise the farmer all proper aid and assistance. On the date above written the aforesaid farming being offered for sale, not more than 1000 guilders was offered for it, so Willem Bout on the 22d of October, was accepted? by the highest officer and the Heeren commissaries of Albany at the house of Antony Janse innkeeper, and upon the aforesaid conditions, for the tapster's excise promises to pay twenty-nine hundred guilders, and next Monday to furnish sufficient sureties according to the import of this paper. In accordance with the above written conditions, Harmen Bastiaense and Jan Vinhagen, offered themselves as sureties and principals, on pledge of their respective persons and estates, personal and real, present and future, nothing excepted.

Done in Albany, the 24th of October, 1664.

This is the mark with his own hand set. of WILLEM FREDERICKSE,

HARMEN BASTIAENSE.
JAN VINHAEGEN.

Passed in presence of the highest officer [La Montagne] and Heeren commissaries of Albany. * * *

LUDOVICUS COBES. * * *

Conditions according to which the Heeren commissaries of Albany, farm to the highest bidder, the burgher wine and beer excise, for the time of one year. The farming shall begin on the 22d of October, old style, and on the 1st of November, new style of the year 1664, and end on the 22d of October, old style *anno* 1665. The farmer shall receive for a tun of strong (*goet*) beer one dollar; for a tun of small beer ten stuivers; for a hogshead of French [wine] six guilders; for an anker of brandy, Spanish wine, or liquor, two guilders at twelve white, and six black seewants the stuiver, and the farmer aforesaid shall not refuse a licence (*ceelen*) to any burgher, who has been entered upon the burgher excise. The captain shall be free from this burgher excise, and the soldiers shall be free from the excise for small beer, also the preacher's excise shall be free from this farming. The farmer shall be holden to furnish two sufficient sureties, one for all and each as principals, to the content of the Heeren contractors, to pay the aforesaid excise every quarter year, a just fourth part of the whole sum in good strong seewant at twelve white, and six black [seewants] the stuiver, and in case the farmer fail in the aforesaid sureties, said farming shall be offered for sale again at his cost and charge, and whatever less it comes to be worth, he shall make good, and whatever more it becomes worth he shall enjoy no benefit therefrom. The Heer contractors reserve to themselves the interpretation and amplification of these conditions, and promise the farmer proper aid and assistance.

[This paper is incomplete.]

Appeared before me Johannes La Montagne, in the service of, etc., Willem Janssen Schut, who declares himself surety for the person of Lucas Eldersen, for the use of a canoe being *inquessit* (?) wi h Cornelis Cornelisse and Jan Henderickse Bruyn. In witness of wh ch this is subscribed with his own hand.

Done in Fort Orange the last day of March, A. D. 1661, in presence of Johannes Provoost.

WILLEM JANSSEN.

Appeared before me Johannes La Montagne, in the service of, etc., Willem Janssen Stoll, at present about to depart for the Esopus, who declares in presence of the afternamed witnesses that he has appointed and empowered, as by these presents he does, Mr. Evert Janssen Wendel, burgher and inhabitant of the village of Beverwyck, in the subscriber's name and for his sake, to demand, collect, and receive from Claes Janssen *timmerman* [carpenter] certain thirty and a half beavers due to the subscriber, growing out of the purchase of a lot; among which thirty and a half beavers there are twenty-four on which the attorney, is to collect interest for the time of three years at ten *per cento;* and in case of delay, the payment to urge with law and the rigor of justice to definite sentence and extreme execution; and to proceed also to the arrest of persons and goods, and to do and perform all things which, the subscriber being present could or might do, provided that the attorney be holden to make a proper exhibit and return of his transactions and receipts on pledge of his person and estate, real and personal.

Thus done in Fort Orange the 20th of April, A.D. 1661, in presence of Eldert Gerbertsen, and J. Provoost.

WILLEM JANSSEN STOL.

Elbert Gerbertsen Cruis.
Johannes Provoost witnesses.

Acknowledged before me,

LA MONTAGNE, clerk at Fort Orange.

Appeared before me Johannes La Montagne, in the service of, etc., Elderd Gerbertsen Kruiff, and Willem Janssen Stoll, who declare that they have contracted with each other, that Eldert Gerbertsen shall undertake to perform the contract between him and Claes Hendrickse for the repairing and finishing of the house which the aforesaid Kruiff bought of said Claes Henderickse; to keep an account of expenses which shall be paid according to the liquidation of the parties, and in case he uses more than the money he has in hand amounts to, Willem Janssen Stoll is to pay the excess, whatever less he uses he shall return again to the aforesaid Willem Janssen Stoll.

Thus done in Fort Orange the 20th of April, A.D. 1661, in presence of Evert Wendel, and J. Provoost.

ELBERT GERBERTSE CRUIF.
WILLEM JANSE STOL.

Evert Janse Wendel.
J. Provoost, clerk.

Acknowledged before me,

LA MONTAGNE, clerk at Fort Orange.

Appeared before me Johannes La Montagne, in the service of, etc., the honorable commissaries of said place, who declare that they have granted and transferred, as they do by these presents, in real and actual possession to and for the behoof of Juriaen Teunissen [Glasemacker], his heirs or assigns, a parcel of land lying in the middle of his lot, surveyed and to be used as a highway, in length from the road to the kil, and breadth three rods and four feet, therefore their honors promise him the grantee, to free it from all actions, claims, or pretensions, which may hereafter arise.

Thus done in Fort Orange the 1st of May A.D. 1661.

ANDRIES HERBERTS.
JAN VERBEECK.
FRANS BARENTSE PASTOOR.
EVERT JANSE WENDEL.

Acknowledged before me,

LA MONTAGNE, Clerk at Fort Orange.

Appeared before me Johannes La Montagne, in the service of, etc., in the presence of the honorable Philip Pieterse Schuyler and Adriaen Gerritsen [Papendorp] commissaries etc., Henderick Gerritse [Van Wie], inhabitant of the aforesaid village, who declares that he has granted and transferred as by these presents he does grant and transfer in real and actual possession to and for the behoof of Arent Vandenbergh *adelborst* (gentleman soldier) here under the honorable [West India] company, his heirs or assigns, a lot for a garden lying near or behind the aforesaid Fort [Orange], breadth in front on the road four rods two feet and a half, to the south the grantor length eight rods, to the west Jeremias Van Rensselaer breadth four rods, to the north Gerrit Baucker length eight rods, all of such title and ownership as the grantor has possessed, promising the grantee to free it from all actions, claims, or pretensions, which may hereafter arise, on pledge of his person and estate real and personal, present and future subjecting the same to the authority of all laws and judges.

Done in Fort Orange the 10th of May, A.D. 1661.

HENDERICK GERRITSE.

Philip Pieterse.
Adriaen Gerritse.

LA MONTAGNE, Clerk at Fort Orange.

Appeared before me Mattheus De Vosch notary public commissioned by the honorable Heeren director general and council of New Netherland residing [at New Amsterdam] and in the presence of the afternamed witnesses, the honorable Alexander Leendersen [Glen] dwelling in the village of Beverwyck near Fort Orange and acknowledged for himself and his heirs that he, the subscriber, is well and truly indebted to the honorable Mr. Jan Sebastiaensen Van Gutsenhoven, in the sum of nine thousand seven hundred and fifty-three guilders twelve stuivers and eight pennies, growing out of wares and merchandise delivered according to the tenor of the settlement placed in the hands of the subscriber, who declares that he has received all that is mentioned in said account to his content; which aforesaid sum of 9753 guilders 12 stuivers and 8 pennies he, the subscriber, promises and undertakes to pay or cause to be paid to Mr. Jan Sebastiaensen Van Gutsenhoven or his order therefor properly qualified, at the farthest in the month of September next coming, 1661, with good merchantable beaver skins at eight guilders apiece, and for the punctual performance of all the aforesaid, the subscriber pledges his person and all his estate, personal and real, present and future nothing in anywise excepted, wherever it may lie, submitting the same to all laws and judges, promising by these presents to give, or in his name to cause to be given, knowledge of his estate to all counsellers or magistrates, nothing excepted, until the claims aforesaid of said Mr. Jan Sebastiaensen shall be fully paid, under submission as before.

Done in good faith at Amsterdam in New Netherland in presence of Jacques Cortelyou and Harmanus Letschoo inhabitants of this city witnesses, who with the mortgagor have subscribed this paper, this seventh day of May, 1661.

Was subscribed, "this agrees with the original minute *quod attestor Mattheus de Vos, Notary Public.*"

The above written copy was, by me J. La Montagne clerk of Fort Orange and village of Beverwyck, at the request of Mr. Jan Sebastiaensen Van Gutsenhooven, registered in this record, for his service in proper time and place.

Done in Fort Orange the 2d of June, A.D. 1661.

Quod Attestor LA MONTAGNE, Clerk at Fort Orange.

Conditions and proposals according to which Juriaen Tennisse [Glasemacker] is minded to sell at public sale to the highest bidder his house, lot and garden lying in the village of Beverwyck, to the east on Jochem De Backer and by the seller at present occupied.

Firstly the aforesaid house, lot and garden shall be delivered to the buyer with all that is fast by earth and nailed. Delivery shall be made eight days after old Amsterdam fair day next coming.

[This paper is unexecuted and incomplete.]

Appeared before me Johannes La Montagne, etc., Jacob Vander Coelen, who in the presence of the afternamed witnesses, declared that he had transferred, granted and made over, as by these presents he does, to and for the behoof of Maercelus Janssen [Van Bommel], inhabitant of said village, his whole credit due by the honorable West India company for wages and subsistence earned in the service of *lantspasaet*, furthermore by these presents appointing and empowering said Jacob Vandercoelen [Marcelis Janse ?] or the lawful holder of this instrument, to ask for, demand and receive the aforesaid moneys at Amsterdam in New Netherland from the Heer treasurer of the honorable West India company at the treasury of the same, and having received the same acquittance to give, which shall be valid as though given by the subscriber himself; and furthermore all things to do and perform to obtain the aforesaid wages and subsistence money, which he, the subscriber, being present could or might do although the matter may require greater and more special authority than stands herein expressed; promising at all times to hold good all that shall be done by virtue of this power under pledge of his person and estate personal and real.

Thus done in Fort Orange in presence of Nataniel Pietersen and Wallerom du Mon as witnesses hereto invited on this 29th of June, A.D. 1661.

JACOB VANDER COULEN.

Nattaneiel Petterse.
Woullerand du Mont.

Acknowledged before me,

LA MONTAGNE, Clerk at Fort Orange.

Conditions according to which Pieter Adriaensen [Soogemackelyck] is minded to sell at public sale to the highest bidder, his house and lot standing and lying in the village of Beverwyck, to the north Adriaen Janse Van Leyden and to the south Jan Barentsen [Wemp]. *Firstly*, the house and lot shall at once be delivered to the buyer as it stands with all that is fast by earth and nailed, which house is thirty-seven and a half feet long and twenty-six feet broad and fitly built up with stone on all sides; with the lot attached thereto ten rods long and four rods broad, for which the buyer with the last payment shall receive the patent and a proper conveyance. The payment shall be made in three installments; the first installment within six weeks from this date in good whole merchantable beavers at eight guilders a piece; the second in the month of May, A.D. 1662, in good current seewant to be paid at the rate of ixteen guilders the beaver; and the third or last installment on the first of August, A.D. 1662, in good whole merchantable beavers as before. The buyer shall be holden to furnish two sufficient sureties, one for all and each as principals, immediately, to the content of the seller. If the buyer can not furnish said sureties in the time aforesaid the said house and lot shall be offered for sale again at his cost and charge, and whatever less it shall come to be worth he shall be holden to make good, and whatever more it shall become worth he shall enjoy no profit therefrom. The auction fees become a charge to the buyer. After many offers, Philip Pieterse Schuyler remained the last bidder for the sum of one thousand three hundred and six guilders according to the aforesaid conditions, for which the honorable Adriaen Gerritse [Papendorp] and Harmen Vedder offered themselves as sureties and principals for the payment of the aforesaid sum, on pledge of their persons and estates, personal and real, present and future, subjecting themselves to the authority of all laws and judges.

Done in Beverwyck on the 15th of September, A.D. 1661.

PHILIP PIETERSE SCHUYLER.
ADRIAEN GERRETSEN.
HARMEN VEDDEREN

Acknowledged before me,

LA MONTAGNE, Clerk at Fort Orange.

Proposals and conditions on which Pieter Adriaensen [Soogemackelyck] is minded to sell at public sale to the highest bidder his house and lot and garden, lying in the *colonie* Rensselaerswyck and at present inhabited by him. *Firstly*, the aforesaid house lot and garden as it stands and lies in fence shall be delivered to the buyer with all that is fast by earth and nailed, except the fruit trees which are therein, free and unincumbered without any claim standing against the same save the lord's right. Delivery shall be made on the first day of May, A.D. 1662. * *

[This paper is incomplete and unexecuted].

Conditions on which Marcellus Janssen [Van Bommel] is minded to sell at public sale to the highest bidder, his house and lot as it is at present occupied by the seller with all that is fast by earth and nailed. *Firstly*, the aforesaid house shall be delivered to the buyer with the lot as it is at present occupied by him and stands in fence according to the patent thereof. The delivery of the aforesaid house and lot shall be made on the first of May, A.D. 1662, with a conveyance of the same. Payment shall he make in good whole merchantable beaver skins in three installments, the first on the first of June, A.D. 1662, the second one year after date on the first of June, A.D 1663 and the third one year after the second installment being on the first of June, A.D. 1664. With the last payment the patent shall be delivered The buyer shall be holden to furnish two sufficient sureties one for all and each as principals, immediately, to the content of the seller. If the buyer can not furnish said sureties then the aforesaid house and lot shall be offered again for sale, and whatever less it comes to be worth he shall be holden to make good, and what more it becomes worth he shall derive no profit therefrom. The auction fees become a charge to the buyer. On the above standing conditions Asser Levy remained the last bidder for the sum of one thousand seven hundred and nine guilders, for which the honorable Johan Verbeeck and Jochim Wesselse [Backer] offered themselves as sureties and principals for the payment of the aforesaid sum, on pledge of their persons and estates, personal and real, present and future.

Done in Fort Orange this 15th of July, 1661.

ASSER LEEVI.
JAN VERBEECK.
JOCHEM BACKER

Acknowledged before me,

LA MONTAGNE, Clerk at Fort Orange.

Appeared before me Johannes La Montagne, etc., Henderick Jochemsen,[1] burgher and inhabitant of the village of Beverwyck, who declares in the presence of the honorable Frans Barentsen Pastoor and Adriaen Gerritsen [Papendorp] commissaries etc., that he had granted and transferred as by these presents he does grant and transfer in real and actual possession to the behoof of Captain Abraham Staets also burgher and inhabitant of the same place his heirs or assigns, his house and lot without Fort Orange according to the patent, and act of concession for a certain parcel [of ground] to said lot annexed, for a certain sum for which he the grantor, acknowledges that he has had payment and satisfaction, promising to free said house and lot from all actions and claims on pledge of his person and estate personal and real, present and future, and submitting himself to all laws and judges.

Thus done in Fort Orange the 20th of July, A.D. 1661.

HENDRICK JOCHEMSE.

Frans Barentse Pastoor.
Adriaen Gerretsen.

Acknowledged before me,

LA MONTAGNE, Clerk at Fort Orange.

Proposals and conditions on which Cornelis Vosch proposes to sell at public sale to the highest bidder, his house and lot standing and lying in the village of Beverwyck, to the east Daniel Verveelen. *Firstly*, the aforesaid house shall be delivered to the buyer with all that is fast by earth and nailed, except the little leanto on the east side of said house, with the chimney and oven which thereto belongs; the house is five and twenty feet long and eighteen feet broad, and if it happens that the buyer comes to repair or remove the house or replace it by another, he shall be holden to leave a proper drip for both this and Daniel Verveelen's house; the lot that shall be delivered to the buyer is altogether nine rods long, breadth in the rear on the kil seventeen feet and a half, in front as broad as the aforesaid house, together with an alley of three and a half feet.

[This paper is incomplete and unexecuted].

Proposals and conditions on which Cornelis Vosch proposes to sell at public sale to the highest bidder his lot lying in the village of Beverwyck

[1] Henderick Jochemsen was a citizen of Beverwyck in 1654, the following year he kept a public house and was lieutenant of the burgher company.—*Deeds* II, 68, 104. *Dutch Manuscripts*, XVI, 103.

next to his house. *Firstly*, the aforesaid lot shall be delivered to the buyer in length nine rods, breadth in front on the road three and twenty feet and in the rear on the kil six and thirty feet. The lot aforesaid shall be delivered to the buyer on the first of May, A.D. 1662.

[This paper is incomplete and unexecuted].

Proposals and conditions on which Henderick Jochemsen proposes to sell to the highest bidder at public sale his house and lot lying in the *colonie* Rensselaerswyck. *Firstly*, the aforesaid house and lot shall be delivered to the buyer with all that is fast by earth and nailed, and the lot as it lies in fence.

[Incomplete].

Appeared [1] before me Johannes La Montagne in the service of the Privileged West India Company, by the director general and council of New Netherland admitted vice director and clerk (*commies*) at Fort Orange and village of Beverwyck, certain sachems (*oversten*) of the Mohawks' land named Cantuquo, Sonareetse, Aiadne, Sodachdrasse, owners of a certain piece of land named in Dutch the Great Flat and lying behind Fort Orange, between the same and the Mohawks' lands, who declare that they have granted and transferred as by these presents they do grant and transfer, in real and actual possession and ownership to the behoof of Mr. Arent Van Corlaer, the said piece of land or Great Flat by the Indians named Schonowe, in its compass and circumference with its woods and kils, for a certain number of cargoes, for which the grantors acknowledge they have had satisfaction, renouncing henceforth and forever all ownership and pretensions, which they to said pieces of land heretofore have had, and promising to free it from all pretensions which the other Indians may have.

Done in Fort Orange, the 27th of July, A. D. 1661, in presence of Marten Mouris [2] and Willem Montagne, hereto invitted.

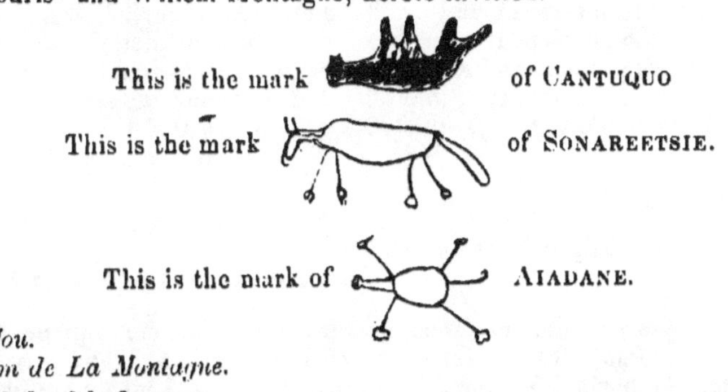

This is the mark of CANTUQUO

This is the mark of SONAREETSIE.

This is the mark of AIADANE.

M. Mou.

Willem de La Montagne.

Acknowledged before me,

LA MONTAGNE, V. D. and Clerk at Fort Orange.

---

[1] The following paper is the first conveyance of the land on which Schenectady stands and of the *Bouwland* lying west of the city. Arent Van Curler was the leader of the little company who settled there the following year.

[2] Marten Mouris was a half breed and brother of Jacques Cornelise Van Slyck. He gave name to the great island, lying west of Schenectady in the Mohawk river, called "Marten's island." Jacques was owner of one half of it.

On this day, date underwritten, in the presence of the afternamed witnesses, Abraham Staets purchased at public sale from Pieter Jacobsen Bosboom,[1] a brick kiln (*steen backery*) excepting the bricks (*steenen*) which are now therein, with the lot belonging thereto of such magnitude as the patent mentions, for the sum of three hundred and fifty guilders in good current seewant to be paid in two installments; the first within one month from date, and the other on the first of May, A.D. 1662; meanwhile the buyer remains holden to provide for the auction fees and pay to the vendue master a stuiver for every guilder, on pledge of his person and estate, personal and real, present and future, subjecting himself to the force of all laws and judges. Done in Beverwyck, this 28th day of July, A D. 1662.

ABRAM STAES.

Ludovicus Cobes, witness.
Johannes Provoost, witness.

Acknowledged before me,

LA MONTAGNE, Clerk at Fort Orange.

Appeared before me Johannes La Montagne, in the service of, etc., in the presence of the honorable Abraham Staets and Adriaen Gerritsen [Papendorp,] commissaries, etc., Mr. Jan Verbeeck, old commissary, who acknowledges that he is well, truly and honestly indebted to Mr. Jan Bastiaensen Gudsenhoven in the sum of four hundred and sixty-two guilders and seven stuivers, growing out of bills of goods and merchandise, which he during the time of three or four years has received to his content, which aforesaid sum of four hundred and sixty-two guilders and seven stuivers, he, the subscriber, promises to pay to the aforesaid Jan Bastiaensen or his attorney, in good whole merchantable beaver skins at eight guilders a piece, at the furthest in the time of one year from this date punctually without longer delay, therefor pledging his person and estate, personal and real, present and future, nothing excepted, specially mortgaging his new house and lot annexed, standing and lying in the village of Beverwyck and by the mortgagor occupied, as a fast pledge to secure the payment if need be of the aforesaid sum of four hundred and sixty-two guilders and seven stuivers, without loss and cost, all on pledge as before and submitting himself to all laws and judges.

Done in Fort Orange, this 30th of July, A.D. 1661.

JAN VERBEECK.

Abram Staes.
Adriaen Gerretsen.

Acknowledged before me,

LA MONTAGNE, Clerk at Fort Orange.

Appeared before me Johannes La Montagne, etc., in the presence of the honorable Rutger Jacobsen and Evert Janssen Wendel, commissaries, etc., the honorable Leendert Philipsen [Conyn] inhabitant of the aforesaid village, who acknowledges that he is well, truly and honestly indebted to Mr. Jan Bastiaensen Van Gudsenhooven in the sum of one thousand one hundred and thirty-seven guilders and eight stuivers, growing out of invoices of goods and merchandise, which he to his content and satisfaction has received, which aforesaid sum of one thousand one

---

[1] This *Steenbacker* was one of the early settlers of Schenectady.

hundred and thirty-seven guilders and eight stuivers with interest on the same at ten *per cento* yearly to begin from this date and running till the full payment, he, the subscriber, promises to pay to Jan Bastiaensen, or his attorney, in good whole merchantable beaver skins at eight guilders a piece, at the farthest within one year from date punctually without longer delay, on pledge of his person and estate, personal and real, present and future, nothing excepted, and specially mortgaging as a fast pledge and special hypothecation, his house and lot lying in the village of Beverwyck, and at present occupied by him, to secure the payment of the aforesaid sum of one thousand one hundred and thirty-seven guilders and eight stuivers with interest on the same, if need be, without loss or cost, all on pledge as before, and submitting himself to all laws and judges.

Done in Fort Orange, the 30th of July, A.D. 1661.

LEENDERT PHYLES [PHILIPSE].

Rutger Jacobsen
Evert Wendel.

Acknowledged before me,

LA MONTAGNE, Clerk at Fort Orange.

Proposals and conditions on which Cornelis Vos proposes to sell at public sale to the highest bidder his house and lot lying in the village of Beverwyck, to the east Daniel Verveelen. *Firstly*, the aforesaid house and lot shall be delivered to the buyer, as it stands; the aforesaid house is 25 feet long and 18 feet broad except the leanto on the east side of the same; the aforesaid lot with the house is nine rods long, breadth in the rear on the kil seventeen and a half feet, in front on the road as broad as the aforesaid house, with a gangway on the east side of three and a half feet, provided the buyer when he comes to remove the house and build another in its place, shall leave a proper drip to both his and Daniel Verveelen's houses. The delivery shall be made on the first of May, A.D. 1662. The payment shall be made in good whole merchantable beaver skins at eight guilders apiece, in two installments, the first on the delivery; the second on the first of July, A.D. 1663. The buyer shall be holden to furnish two sufficient sureties one for all and each as principals, to the content of the seller immediately. If the buyer can not furnish said sureties in said time, then the house and lot, shall be offered for sale again at his charge and cost, and whatever less it comes to be worth, he shall be holden to make good, and whatever more it becomes worth he shall enjoy no benefit therefrom. The auction fees become a charge to the buyer payable as before. On the above standing conditions Barent Van Marle remained the highest bidder for the sum of one thousand and twenty guilders, for which the honorable Jan Verbeeck and Andries Herbertsen offer themselves as sureties and principals for the payment of the aforesaid sum, on a pledge of their persons and estates personal and real, present and future, submitting themselves to all laws and judges.

Done in the village of Beverwyck, this 30th of July, A.D. 1661.

BARENT VAN MARLE.
JAN VERBEECK.

Acknowledged before me, ANDRIS HERBERTS.

LA MONTAGNE, Clerk at Fort Orange.

Appeared before me Johannes La Montagne, in the service of, etc., Mrs. Sophia Van Wyckersloot, assisted by her husband Mr. Toinel, who declares in presence of the afternamed witnesses, that she has sold and transferred to Mr. Asser Levy, all the goods and merchandise, which she is expecting out of *Patria* by the ship Beaver, consigned to her by her father, for which the aforesaid Asser Levy is holden to pay seventy-five *per cento* advance on their cost in Holland, besides also the freight, of the aforesaid goods to the skipper; appointing and empowering by these presents the said Asser Levy out of the honorable company's warehouse to receive, open and inspect said goods, and for injury (if there be any) restitution to demand, furthermore to do in the matter as she, the subscriber, being present could or might do, promising to hold as good and true all that the attorney by virtue of these presents shall do, provided he be holden of his transactions and receipts to render to the subsciber a proper statement and return, and payment according to the above written conditions, under pledge of her estate personal and real, present and future, the same submitting to all laws and judges.

Done in Fort Orange, in presence of Johannes Provoost and Jan. Pieterse as witnesses here to invited on this 1st day of August, A.D. 1661.

Sophia Van Wyckersloot.
Anthony Toinel.

Jan Pieterse Mulder.
Johannes Provoost, wit.

Acknowledged before me,
La Montagne V. D. and *Commies* at Fort Orange.

Appeared before me Johannes La Montagne, in the service of, etc., in the presence of the honorable Rutger Jacobsen and Frans Barentse Pastoor commissaries, etc., Mr. Jan Verbeeck old commissary, who acknowledges that he is well, truly and honestly indebted to Mr. Barent Van Marle in the sum of two hundred and sixty-six guilders and ten stuivers growing out of invoices and merchandise which he to his content, has received, which aforesaid sum of two hundred and sixty-six guilders and ten stuivers he the subscriber promises to pay to said Barent Van Marle or his attorney in good whole merchantable beaver skins at eight guilders a piece, within one year from this date, on pledge of his person and estate personal and real, present and future, nothing excepted, especially his new house and lot standing and lying in the village of Beverwyck, and by him at present occupied, as a fast security and special pledge for the payment of said sum if need be, without loss or cost.

Thus done in Fort Orange, this 2d of August, A.D. 1661.

Jan Verbeeck.

[The above mortgage is crossed out].

Appeared before me Johannes La Montagne, in the service of, etc., in the presence of the honorable Frans Barentse Pastoor and Evert Wendell commissaries etc., Jan Lambertsen Van Breemen, who acknowledges and declares that he is well, truly, and honestly indebted to Mr. Jan Bastiaense Van Gudsenhooven, in the sum of sixty guilders and fifteen stuivers, growing out of invoices and merchandise which he received in the year 1656 to his content, which aforesaid sum of sixty-five guilders and fifteen stuivers, he, the subscriber, promises to pay to said Jan Bastiaense Van Gudsenhooven or his attorney, with interest on the same at ten per cent, commencing on this date and extending to the complete payment, in good whole merchantable beaver skins at eight guilders a piece, within the time of one year from date and no longer; for which the subscriber aforesaid pledges as security and special mortgage, his house and lot standing and lying in the village of Beverwyck, and at present occupied by him, for the payment of the aforesaid sum of sixty-five guilders and fifteen stuivers without cost or loss, with interest on the same, on pledge of his person and estate, personal and real, present and future, submitting himself to all laws and judges.

Done in Fort Orange, this 11th of August, A.D. 1661

This is the mark + of JAN LAMBERTSEN VAN BREEMAN.
with his own hand set.

Frans Barentse Pastoor.
Evert Wendell.

Acknowledged before me,

LA MONTAGNE, Clerk at Fort Orange.

Appeared before me Johannes La Montagne, in the service of, etc., in the presence of honorable Frans Barentse Pastoor and Evert Janssen Wendel commissaries, etc., Cristoffel Davidts, who declares that he has granted and transferred as by these presents he does grant and transfer in real and actual possession to and for the behoof of Geertruy Anderiesen widow of Jacob Janssen Stoll deceased, her heirs or assigns a piece of cleared land lying in the Esopus, adjoining to the north Madame Ebbingh and to the south Jurriaen Westvael, in two parcels, together about thirty-six morgens, also a piece of pasture land of about twenty morgens, extending to the woods; for the sum of fourteen hundred guilders, for which aforesaid sum, he, the grantor, acknowledges that he has had satisfaction, except six hundred guilders in seewant, which he assigns and transfers to Jeremias Van Rensselaer by the agreement of the grantee according to the conveyance of the aforesaid Jacob Janssen Stoll deceased dated the 13th July, A.D. 1657, which aforesaid sum of six hundred guilders, she, the grantee, undertakes to pay to said Rencelaer within one year from next November, in good winter wheat reckoned at four guilders the skipple, and other grains; he, the grantor, promising to free the aforesaid land from all claims, actions or pretensions, which may hereafter arise on pledge of his person and estate, personal and real, present and future, submitting himself to all laws and judges.

Done in Fort Orange, the 15th of August, A.D. 1661.

This is the mark CD of CHRISTOFFEL DAVIDS,
with his own hand set.

This is the mark of GEERTRUY ANDRIESEN,
with her own hand set.

Frans Barentse Pastoor.
Evert Wendel.

Acknowledged before me,

LA MONTAGNE, Clerk at Fort Orange.

Appeared before me Johannes La Montagne, in the service of, etc., in the presence of honorable Rutger Jacobsen and Adriaen Gerritsen [Papendorp] commissaries, etc , who acknowledges and declares that he is well, truly and honestly indebted to Mr. Barent Van Marle, in the sum of two hundred and sixty-six guilders and ten stuivers, growing out of invoices and merchandise to his content received, which said sum of two hundred and sixty-six guilders and ten stuivers, he, the subscriber, promises to pay to the aforesaid Marle or his attorney on the first of June, A.D. 1662, in good whole merchantable beaver skins at eight guilders a piece, wherefore he pledges and mortgages his old house and lot behind the same where he at present dwells, to secure the aforesaid sum without cost or loss, on pledge also of his person and estate, personal and real, present and future, and submitting himself to all laws and judges.

Done in Fort Orange, this 16th of August, A.D. 1661.

JAN VERBEECK.

Rutger Jacobsen.
Adriaen Gerretsen.

Acknowledged before me,

LA MONTAGNE, Clerk at Fort Orange.

Appeared before me Johannes La Montagne, in the service of, etc., in the presence of the honorable Rut Jacobsen and Adriaen Gerritsen [Papendorp] commissaries, etc., Jan Michielsen [Van Edam] inhabitant, who acknowledges and declares that he is well, truly and honestly indebted to Mr. Nicolaes Meyer in the sum of sixty-four guilders for goods received to his content, which aforesaid sum of sixty-four guilders he promises to pay to the aforesaid Meyer or to his attorney on the first of June, A.D. 1662, in good whole merchantable beaver skins at eight guilders a piece for which he pledges and specially mortgages his house and lot where he at present dwells, for the payment of the aforesaid sum, without cost or loss, on pledge also of his person and estate, personal and real, present and future, nothing excepted, and submitting himself to all laws and judges.

Done in Fort Orange, this 18th of August, A.D. 1661.

JAN MYCHGHYELSOON.

Rutger Jacobse.
Adriaen Gerretsen.

Acknowledged before me,

LA MONTAGNE, Clerk at Fort Orange.

Appeared before me Johannes La Montagne, in the service of, etc., in the presence of the honorable Evert Wendel and Adriaen Gerritsen [Papendorp] commissaries, etc., Henderick Gerritsen [Van Wie], inhabitant of the aforesaid place, who acknowledges and declares by these presents that he is well, truly and honestly indebted to Mr. Nicolaes Meyer, in the sum of fifty-six guilders, for goods and merchandise received to his content, which sum of fifty-six guilders, he promises to pay on the first day of May, A.D. 1662, in good whole merchantable beaver skins at eight guilders a piece, for which he pledges and specially mortgages his two houses and lots, the one occupied by himself and the other by Jan de

Kuyper, together with his garden lying behind Fort Orange together with the rent of the house occupied by Jan de Kuyper for the space of one year, amounting to the sum of one hundred and fifteen guilders in seewant to secure the payment of the sum of fifty-six guilders without loss or cost, on pledge also of his person and estate, personal and real, present and future, nothing excepted, and submitting himself to all laws and judges.

Done in Fort Orange, the 18th of August, A.D 1661.

HYNDRICH GERISEN.

Evert Wendel.
Adriaen Gerretsen.

Acknowledged before me,

LA MONTAGNE, Clerk at Fort Orange.

Appeared before me Johannes La Montagne, in the service of, etc., in the presence of the honorable Evert Wendel and Adriaen Gerritse commissaries, etc , Mr. Daniel Verveelen trader, who declares that he has granted and transferred as by these presents he does grant and transfer in real and actual possession to and for the behoof of Cornelis Cornelissen de Boer, his heirs or assigns, his just half of the house and lot that he and the grantee bought in company of the attorney of Pieter De Maker, of such form, size and limits as received by them by conveyance from the aforesaid attorneys, to wit, Stoffel Janse [Abeel] and Jan Costerse Van Aken, for which half part of said house and lot the grantor acknowledges that he has had satisfaction, and promises to free the same from all actions, claims and pretensions which may hereafter arise, on pledge of his person and estate, personal and real, present and future, nothing excepted, submitting himself to all laws and judges.

Done in Fort Orange, this 25th of August, A.D. 1661.

DANIEL VERVEELEN.

Evert Wendel.
Adriaen Gerretse.

Acknowledged before me,

LA MONTAGNE, Clerk at Fort Orange.

Appeared before me Johannes La Montagne, in the service of, etc., in the presence of the honorable Rutger Jacobson and Frans Barentse Pastoor, commissaries, etc., the honorable Jan Mangelsen[1] of said place, who declares and acknowledges by these presents, that he is well, truly and honestly indebted to his father-in-law Pieter Adriaensen [Soogemackelyck] dwelling in the *colonie* Rensselaerswyck, in the sum of six hundred guilders in seewant and the number of ten good whole beaver skins, for seewant and other goods which he to his content has received; which sum he promises to pay in the time of ten days, wherefore he pledges his person and estate, personal and real, present and future, nothing excepted, for the payment of said sum, submitting himself to the force of all laws and judges.

Done in Fort Orange, the 25th of August, A.D. 1661.

JAN MANGELSEN.

---

[1] Jan Mangelse was in Beverwyck as early as 1656, probably a trader. *Deeds* I, 124. *Dutch manuscripts.*

The honorable court do not find it proper that the above standing commissaries shall witness this obligation, before the sentence in favor of both Jan Claessen Backer and others is paid and satisfied.

Done at their session in Fort Orange the 30th of August, A.D. 1661.

By the order of the honorable court,

JOHANNES PROVOOST, Clerk.

Appeared before me Johannes La Montagne, in the service of, etc., in the presence of the honorable Rutger Jacobsen and Frans Barentse Pastoor, commissaries, etc., Pieter Jacobse Borsboom, who declares that he has granted and transferred as by these presents he does grant and transfer in real and actual possession to and for the behoof of Captain Abraham Staets and the honorable Goosen [Gerritse Van Schaick] their heirs or assigns, a lot lying by the First [Bever] kil, to the north the hill breadth five rods, to the east length twenty-three rods, to the south the road breadth sixteen rods, to the west length seventeen rods, according to patent to him granted by the Heer director general and council of New Netherland, of date the 23d of February, A.D. 1660; for which lot the grantor acknowledges that he has had satisfaction, and promises the same to free from all actions, claims and pretensions which may arise, on pledge of his person and estate personal and real, present and future and submitting himself to all laws and judges.

Done in Fort Orange, the 29th of August, A.D. 1661.

PIETER JACOBSEN BORSBOOM.

Rutger Jacobsen.
Frans Barentse Pastoor.

Acknowledged before me,

LA MONTAGNE, Clerk at Fort Orange.

Appeared before me Johannes La Montagne, by the Heer director general, etc., in the presence of the honorable Rutger Jacobsen and Frans Barentse Pastor, commissaries, etc., Marcelus Janssen [Van Bommel] burgher of said place who acknowledges and declares by these presents that he is well, truly, and honestly indebted to Cornelis Jacobsen [By] in the sum of two hundred and two guilders and sixteen stuivers in good whole merchantable beaver skins at eight guilders a piece, which said sum he promises to pay with interest on the same at ten per cent, on the first of June, A.D. 1662, for the first payment on his house which Asser Levy has bought at public sale and which remains as a fast pledge and special mortgage for the payment of the aforesaid sum, on pledge of his person and estate, personal and real, present and future, nothing excepted and submitting himself to all laws and judges.

Done in Fort Orange the 30th of August, A.D. 1661.

MAERCELYS JANSSEN.

Rutger Jacobsen.
Frans Barentse Pastoor.

Acknowledged before me,

LA MONTAGNE, Clerk at Fort Orange.

On this fourth of June 1663, appeared before me Johannes La Montagne, in the service of, etc., Pieter Claessen Kay attorney for Cornelis Jacobsen, [By] who acknowledges and declares that the above standing mortgage for the behoof of the aforesaid Cornelis Jacobsen, and standing as an incumbrance against Marcelis Janse is fully paid and satisfied, and that he has no further claim upon said Marcelis Janse.

Done *ut supra.*

PIETER CLAESSE KAY.

Acknowledged before me,

LA MONTAGNE.

Appeared before me Johannes La Montagne, in the service of, etc , in the presence of the honorable Frans Barentse Pastoor and Evert Janssen Wendel, commissaries, etc., the honorable Rutger Jacobsen, who acknowledges and declares by these presents that he is well, truly, and honestly indebted to Tunis Cornelise Vander Poel[1] in the sum of three hundred and fifty-two guilders in good whole merchantable beaver skins, at eight guilders a piece, besides two *toebevers* and two otters, which aforesaid sum of three hundred and fifty-two guilders, two *toebevers* and two otters he promises to pay on the first of January, A.D. 1662, and failing therein, the mortgagor shall be holden to pay interest on the aforesaid sum, and for the securing of said payment both principala nd interest, offers as a fast pledge and special mortgage, his whole portion of the island lying obliquely over against Betlehem, which he and Andries Herbertsen hold in company, on pledge of his person and estate, personal and real, present and future, nothing excepted, and submitting himself to all laws and judges.

Done in Fort Orange, the last day of August A.D. 1661.

RUTGER JACOBSEN.

Frans Barentse Pastoor.
Evert Janse Wendel.

Acknowledged before me,

LA MONTAGNE, Clerk at Fort Orange.

Appeared before me Johannes Provoost, in the service of, etc., Marcelus Janssen, burgher of the aforesaid village, who declared in the presence of the afternamed witnesses that he had granted and transferred to Cornelis Cornelisse de Boer the number of ten and a half good whole merchantable beaver skins at eight guilders a piece for the first payment on the grantor's house, which Asser Levy at public sale bought, and from whom the *acceptant* [De Boer] is to receive them, and the half of a preferred debt due from Seger Cornelisse, assigned by Adriaen Symonse [Boer] and accepted by the grantor; for the full payment of which he pledges his person and estate, personal and real, present and future, nothing excepted, under subjection to all laws and judges.

Done in Fort Orange, the 31st of August, A.D. 1661, in presence of J. Verbeeck and Segger Cornelissen.

MAERCELYS JANSEN.

Jan Verbeeck.
Segger Cornelissen.

Acknowledged before me,

J. PROVOOST, Clerk.

---

[1] Teunis Cornelise Vander Poel made his will 17th June 1687, in which he speaks of his wife Catherine Jans Croon and thre daughters, Elizabeth widow of Sybrant Van Schaick, then wife of Bennony Van Corlaer, Maria wife of Anthony Van Schaick, and Johanna wife of Barent Lewis. He died soon after the date of his will leaving to his widow a house and lot in Amsterdam, which she devised to her three daughters.— *Annals of Albany*, III, 196 197.

Appeared before me Johannes Provoost, clerk of the court of Fort Orange and village of Beverwyck, Marcelus Janssen [Van Bommel] burgher of said place, who declared that he had granted and transferred to Seger Cornelissen [Van Voorhoudt] the number of four and thirty good whole merchantable beaver skins, for the first payment on his house bought by Asser Levy at public sale from the grantee (*acceptant*), growing out of an assignment from Adriaen Symonsen accepted by the grantor and transferred for the aforesaid payment on his house; wherefore in full payment of the same he pledges his person and estate, personal and real, present and future, nothing excepted, submitting himself to all laws and judges.

Done in Beverwyck, the 31st August, A.D. 1661, in presence of the honorable Jan Verbeeck and Cornelis Cornelissen de Boer.

MAERCELYS JANSSEN.

Jan Verbeeck.
Cornelis Cornelissen de Boer.

Acknowledged before me,

JOHANNES PROVOOST, Clerk.

Appeared before me Johannes La Montagne, in the service of, etc., in presence of the honorable Evert Wendel and Philip Pieterse Schuyler, commissaries, etc., the honorable Rutger Jacobsen dwelling in the aforesaid village, who declares that he has granted and transferred in real and actual possession to and for the behoof of Mr. Gerrit Bancker, trader here, his heirs or assigns, a lot lying in said village of Beverwyck, adjoining to the east Goosen Gerritsen [Van Schaick], to the west Barent Reyndersen, to the south the kil, to the north the grantee (*acceptant*); the length extends to the kil, the breadth to the south three rods and ten inches, breadth to the north the same; which lot is a part of the patent to the grantor given by the Heer director general and council of New Netherland of date the 23d of April, A.D. 1652, and he promises to free said lot from all actions, claims or pretensions which may hereafter arise, on pledge of his person and estate, personal and real, present and future, submitting himself to all laws and judges.

Done in Fort Orange, the 2d of September, A D. 1661.

RUTGER JACOBSEN.

Evert Janse Wendel.
Philip Pieterse.

Acknowledged before me,

LA MONTAGNE, Clerk at Fort Orange.

Appeared before me Johannes Provoost, in the service of, etc , Reynier Wisselpenningh about to depart for Manhatans, who declares in presence of the afternamed witnesses that he has appointed and empowered, as by these presents he does appoint and empower Lowies Cobussen, court messenger here, in the subscriber's name, and for his sake, to appear before the said court against the person of Tomas Lodewyckse [1] to plead in the suit which they have, about the fitting out of the sloop (*jaght*) which they have begun in company; and against said Tomas Lodewyckse to proceed in a legal manner, to definite sentence and extreme execution;

[1] Thomas Lodewyckse and Reynier Wisselpenningh in an action against the church, May 1, 1658, for constructing a baptistry (*doophuysje*) in the church recovered 270 guilders.—*Dutch Manuscripts*, A. 31–5.

and moreover, all things to do and perform, which he, the attorney, shall judge proper, promising to hold good and just all that said attorney shall do in said matter, provided he make a proper return of his transactions

Thus done on this 5th of September, A. D. 1661, in presence of Harmen Henderickse Van Barnewel.

REINIER WYSSELPENGH.

Heremen Hendrick.

Acknowledged before me,

J. PROVOOST, Clerk.

Appeared before me Johannes La Montagne, in the service of, etc., in the presence of the honorable Philip Pieterse Schuyler and Adriaen Gerritse [Papendorp], commissaries, etc., Cornelis Vosch, who declares and acknowledges, that he is well, truly and honestly indebted to Mr. Gerrit Bancker, in the sum of three hundred guilders in good whole merchantable beaver skins, at eight guilders a piece, for goods to his content received, and promises said sum of three hundred guilders to pay next year, A. D. 1662, in the business season (*handeltyt*), and failing of that in the year 1663; and for the payment of which he specially mortgages and pledges his lot lying in the village of Beverwyck, adjoining to the east Barent Van Marle, to the west the street, to the south the first [Bever] kil, and to the north the street, for the payment of the aforesaid sum of three hundred guilders, if need be without cost or loss, on a pledge also of his person and estate, personal and real, present and future, and submitting himself to the authority of all laws and judges.

Done in Fort Orange, the 9th of Sept., A. D. 1661

CORNELIS VOS.

Philip Pieterse.
Adriaen Gerretsen.

Acknowledged before me,

LA MONTAGNE Clerk at Fort Orange.

Appeared before me Johannes La Montagne, in the service of, etc., in the presence of the honorable Frans Barentsen Pastoor and Evert Janssen Wendel, commissaries, etc., the honorable Rutger Jacobsen, who declares that he has granted and transferred, as by these presents he does grant and transfer in real and actual possession, to and for the behoof of Barent Reyndersen, his heirs, or assigns, a lot lying in the village of Beverwyck, adjoining to the west Gerrit Bancker, to the east the grantor, to the south the street, to the north the kil, length from the front on the street to the kil, and breadth in the rear on said kil twenty-seven feet; which lot is a part of the patent to the grantor, given by the Heer director general and council of New Netherland, of date the 23d of April, A. D. 1652, and he promises the aforesaid lot to free from all claims, actions, or pretensions, which may hereafter arise, on pledge of his person and estate, personal and real, present and future, and submitting himself to all laws and judges.

Done in Fort Orange, the 9th of September, A. D. 1661.

RUTGER JACOBSEN.

Frans Barentse Pastoor.
Evert Janse Wendel.

Acknowledged before me,

LA MONTAGNE, Clerk at Fort Orange.

Appeared before me Johannes La Montagne, in the service of, etc., in the presence of the honorable Frans Barentse Pastoor and Evert Wendel, commissaries, etc., the honorable Rutger Jacobsen who acknowledges that he is well, truly, and honestly indebted to Pieter Simonsen [Van Oostsanen] in the sum of one thousand and thirty-two guilders for goods to his content received, which aforesaid sum of one thousand and thirty-two guilders, the subscriber promises to pay to said Pieter Simonsen or his attorney on the first of July, A.D. 1662, in good whole merchantable beaver skins at eight guilders a piece; and for the full payment of the aforesaid sum the subscriber specially pledges and mortgages his sloop (*jacht*) of which Abraham de Truwe is skipper, for the payment of said sum of one thousand and thirty-two guilders in beavers if need be without loss or cost, on pledge also of his person and estate, personal and real, present and future, submitting himself to all laws and judges.

Done in Fort Orange, the 10th of September, 1661.

RUTGER JACOBSEN.

Frans Barentse Pastoor.
Evert Janse Wendel.

Acknowledged before me,

LA MONTAGNE, Clerk at Fort Orange.

Appeared before me Johannes La Montagne, in the service of, etc., on the date underwritten, in presence of the afternamed witnesses, the honorable Henderick Anderiesse [Van Doesburgh] at present about to depart for *Patria*, who declares that he has appointed and empowered, as by these presents he does, the honorable Frans Barentse Pastoor, commissary, etc., in his name and for his sake so far as he can, to demand, collect and receive from Philip Hendericksе Brouwer of this place, certain three thousand one hundred and ninty-four guilders in beavers, which are coming to him, the subscriber, growing out of the sale of a brewery as it stands with its appurtenances, and if so be the aforesaid Philip Henderickse comes to sell said brewery, to lay hands upon the money and if said brewery does not fetch so much as said sum of three thousand one hundred and ninty-four guilders in beavers, he shall the further payment seek to obtain by law and rigor of justice; to which end all terms of the laws to observe to definitive sentence and extreme execution; also if need be to proceed by arrest of persons and goods; for receipts acquittance to pass, furthermore all things to do and perform, which he, the attorney, shall judge proper; promising at all times, to hold as true all that said attorney shall perform in the aforesaid matter, provided that the attorney shall be holden when asked, to make a proper exhibit of his transactions.

Thus done and passed in presence of Johannes Provoost and Walleran du Mont as witnesses hereto called, on this 13th of September, A.D. 1661, in Fort Orange.

HENDRICK AENDRIESEN.

Johannes Provoost, witness.
Wallerand du Mont.

Acknowledged before me,

LA MONTAGNE, Clerk at Fort Orange.

Appeared before me Johannes La Montagne, in the service of, etc., in the presence of the honorable Evert Wendel and Philip Pieterse Schuyler, commissaries, etc., the honorable Anderies Herbertsen, who acknowledges and declares by these presents that he is well, truly, and honestly indebted to the honorable Goosen Gerritse [Van Schaick] in the sum of one thousand and fifteen guilders and fourteen stuivers and eight pennies for goods which since the year 1657 to this date to his content and satisfaction he has received, which aforewritten sum of one thousand and fifteen guilders fourteen stuivers and eight pennies, he the subscriber, promises to pay to the aforesaid Goosen Gerritse or his attorney on the first of June, A.D. 1662, in good whole merchantable beaver skins, at eight guilders a piece, and for all the time beyond the aforesaid date the subscriber shall be holden to pay proper interest; for the full performance of which he pledges and specially mortgages his house and lot lying in the village of Beverwyck where he at present dwells, to secure the payment if need be of the aforesaid sum without loss or cost, on pledge of his person and estate, personal and real, present and future, nothing excepted, submitting himself to all laws and judges.

Done in Fort Orange, the 13th of September, A.D. 1661.

ANDRIS HERBERTS.

Evert Janse Wendel.
Philip Pieterse.

Acknowledged before me, LA MONTAGNE, Clerk at Fort Orange.

Appeared before me Johannes La Montagne, in the service of, etc., in the presence of the afternamed witnesses, Daniel Rinckhout dwelling in the said village, who declares that he has appointed and empowered as by these presents he does, the honorable Pieter de Maker house carpenter, dwelling at Amsterdam, in the subscriber's name and for his sake, to demand, and collect, of Sacharias Kreleman dwelling at Rotterdam guardian of the subscriber, such accounts and balances as are due to the subscriber by way of inheritance from Johannes Rinckhout deceased, the subscriber's uncle; for receipts acquittance to pass, seeking to procure said inheritance if necessary by law and rigor of justice; to which end all the terms of the law to observe to definitive sentence and extreme execution of the same; also if need be to proceed by arrest against persons and goods; furthermore all things to do and perform which he, the subscriber being present could or might do; provided that the attorney be holden of his transactions and receipts when requested a proper statement to make, promising at all times to hold good all that the attorney in said matter shall have done.

Thus done and passed on this 14th of September, A.D. 1661, in Fort Orange, in New Netherland in presence of Arent Vanden Bergh and Johannes Provoost as witnesses hereto called.

DANIEL RINGHOUTT.[1]

This is the mark **AB** *of Arent Vanden Bergh, with his own hand set.*
J. Provoost, witness.

Acknowledged before me, LA MONTAGNE, Clerk at Fort Orange.

---

[1] Daniel Rinckhout was in Beverwyck as early as 1657.— *Dutch Manuscripts*, xvi, 89. In 1662, Daniel Rinckhout born in Pomeren, aged about 36 years gave acquittance for the bequest of his uncle Jan R., of Munickendam (*Notarial Papers* I, 62), and makes his will giving to his brother Jan his house and all his property, save to his brother Aertman in Pomeren 25 guilders if living.— *Ibid.* p. 63. His brother Jan, baker of Albany in 1670, by his wife Elizabeth Drinckvelt, leased his house to Anthony Lespinard with privilege of baking for Christians and savages.— *Notarial Papers*, II.

Appeared before me Johannes La Montagne, in the service of, etc., Jan Van Aken, who declares in presence of the afternamed witnesses that he has appointed and empowered as he does by these presents the honorable Goosen Gerritsen [Van Schaick] in his name and for his sake, at Amsterdam in New Netherland, to ask, demand, and receive of the treasurer of the general Priviledged West India Company at the treasury of the same. certain three hundred guilders in beavers coming to him through Jan Cloet as appears by a statement subscribed by C. V. Ruyven;[1] of the receipt acquittance to pass which shall be valid as if done by the subscriber himself, furthermore all things to do and perform to obtain the aforesaid three hundred guilders which the subscriber himself being present might or could do, should the matter demand greater and more special authority than stands expressed herein, promising him at all times to hold good and true whatever he shall do by virtue hereof.

Thus done in Fort Orange, in presence of Sacharias Sickles and Johannes Provoost as witnesses hereto called this 14th of September, A.D. 1661.

This is the mark of  JAN VAN AKEN.
with his own hand set.

Zacharias Seckelse.
Johannes Provoost, witness.

Acknowledged before me,

LA MONTAGNE, Clerk at Fort Orange.

Appeared before me Johannes La Montagne, in the service of, etc., Goosen Gerritse [Van Schaick] dwelling in the aforesaid village, who declares in presence of the afternamed witnesses that he has appointed and empowered as he does by these presents, Mr. Jan Sibinck dwelling at Amsterdam to arrange and settle with Mr. Gillis Verbrugger also dwelling at Amsterdam in respect to goods and merchandise, likewise with respect to out standing debts which the subscriber holds in company with said Mr. Verbrugger, also to make a just partition giving him power to give or take *op taxatie* and if need be to substitute one or more persons in his place, promising to hold good and true all that the attorney or his substitute in the matter aforesaid shall have done, provided that he shall make a proper statement and exhibit thereof, on pledge of his person and estate.

Thus done in Fort Orange in New Netherland in presence of Jan Van Aken and Johannes Provoost, as witnesses hereto called on this 14th of September, A.D. 1661.

This is the mark H of GOOSEN GERRITSE.
with his own hand signed.

Appeared before me Johannes La Montagne, in the service of, etc., the honorable Jan Claessen Backer and Lambert Janse Vander Lange both at present about to depart for *Patria*, who together declare in presence of the afternamed witnesses that they have appointed and empowered as by these presents they do, Mr. Francoys Boon in their names to demand, collect and receive all the moneys and debts which are outstanding and

[1] Cornelis Van Ruyven was the provincial secretary residing at New Amsterdam.

coming to either of the subscribers here at Fort Orange in New Netherland according to the evidences and writings thereof; of receipts acquittance to pass, and in case of necessity to compel payment by law and rigor of justice; to that end all the terms of the laws to observe to definitive sentence and extreme execution (also if need be) to proceed by arrest against persons and goods; furthermore all things to do and perform which he, the attorney shall judge proper, provided that he be holden of his transactions and receipts when required a proper statement and return to make, on pledge of his person and estate, personal and real, present and future nothing excepted.

Thus done in Fort Orange, in presence of Sacharias Sickels and Arent Vanden Bergh as witnesses hereto called on this 15th of September, A. D. 1661.

JAN CLAESSE BACKER.
LAMMERT JANSE VANDE LAEN.

Zacharias Sickelse.
This is the mark of **AB** *Arent Van den Bergh, as witness.*

Acknowledged before me,

LA MONTAGNE, Clerk at Fort Orange.

Appeared before me Johannes La Montagne, in the service of, etc., Cornelis Jacobsen [By] trader, at present about to depart for *Patria* who declares in the presence of the afternamed witnesses that he has appointed and empowered the honorable Evert Wendel commissary of the aforesaid place, in the subscriber's name and for his sake to demand, collect and receive here in Fort Orange in New Netherland such outstanding debts and moneys as to him, the subscriber, are due according to the existing writings and evidences thereof; of receipts acquittance to pass, and if necessary, to further the payment of the aforesaid debts by law and the rigor of justice; to that end all terms of the laws to observe to definitive sentence and extreme execution, also (if need be) to proceed by arrest against persons and goods; furthermore, all things to do and perform which he, the subscriber, being present, might or could do, promising to hold good and true all that the attorney in the matter aforesaid shall have done or performed, provided said attorney be holden when required a proper statement and return of his transactions and receipts to make, on pledge of his person and estate, personal and real, present and future.

Thus done and delivered in Fort Orange, in presence of Sacharias Sickels and Johannes Provoost as witnesses hereto called this 15th of September, A.D. 1661.

CORNELIS JACOBZ.

Zacharias Seckelse.
Johannes Provoost, witness.

Acknowledged before me,

LA MONTAGNE, Clerk at Fort Orange.

Appeared before me Johannes de la Montagne, in the service of, etc., in the presence of Philip Pieterse Schuller and Ariaen Gerritse [Papendorp] commissaries, etc., Adriaen Simonse Bet trader at present dwelling in the village of Beverwyck, who declares that he has granted and transferred by these presents to the behoof of Barent Pieterse [Coeymans] his heirs or assigns, his house, lot, garden and all their appurtenances according to the patent thereof, said house to possess in real and actual possession, renouncing all claims and pretensions which he the grantor may have upon said house and freeing the same from all actions and claims, on pledge of his person and estate personal and real, present and future, submitting himself to all judges and laws.

Thus done in Fort Orange, the 22d of September, *Anno*, 1661.

ARIAN SYMENSE.

Philip Pietersen.
Adriaen Gerretsen.

Acknowledged before me,

LA MONTAGNE, Clerk at Fort Orange.

Appeared before me, Johannes La Montagne, in the service of, etc., Seger Cornelissen [Van Voorhoudt] who declares that he has granted and transferred as he does by these presents, to Cornelis Cornelissen de Boer certain thirty-four good whole merchantable beaver skins coming to him the subscriber for the first payment on the house of Marcelis Janssen by Asser Levy, purchased at public sale, which thirty-four good beavers the grantor received by conveyance from Marcelis Janssen to be paid by the hand of said Asser Levy as a payment aforesaid, from whom said Cornelis Cornelissen de Boer in place of the subscriber shall obtain receive and use them in full ownership as his other proper estate, without any future claim or action from the grantor; on pledge of his person and estate, personal and real, placing himself under the authority of all laws and judges.

Done in Fort Orange the 27th of September, A.D. 1661, in presence of Johannes Provoost.

SEGER CORNELISSEN.

Johannes Provoost, witness.

Acknowledged before me,

LA MONTAGNE, Clerk at Fort Orange.

Conditions on which the honorable Heeren *Commies* and commissaries of Fort Orange and village of Beverwyck, propose to sell at public sale to the highest bidder the slaughter excise for the time of one year. The farming of the aforesaid slaughter excise shall begin the first of October in the year 1661, and end on the last day of September, A.D. 1662. The farmer shall receive for the slaughtered beasts, whether ox, cow, bull, calf, hog, goat, and sheep, for every guilder of the worth of the same, one stuiver and in case of dispute to be decided by indifferent persons. The farmer shall be holden to furnish two sufficient sureties to the content of the Messieurs contractors for the excise money, a just fourth part to be paid every quarter year in good current seewant, and if the farmer cannot furnish sufficient sureties, it shall be offered for sale again at his cost and charge and whatever less it comes to be worth he shall be holden to make good, and whatever more it becomes worth he shall enjoy no benefit therefrom. Marcelis Janssen [Van Bommel] remained the last bidder for the above farming for the sum of six hundred and eight guilders, for which said sum Cornelis Teunissen Bosch and Gerrit Slichtenhorst offered themselves as sureties and principals for the payment of the same, on pledge of their persons and estate, personal and real, present and future, and placing themselves under the authority of all laws and judges.

Done in the village of Beverwyck, on the last day of September, A.D. 1661.

MAERCKLYS JANSEN.
CORNELIS THONISSEN BOS.
Acknowledged before me, GERRIT SLICHTENHORST.
LA MONTAGNE, Clerk at Fort Orange.

Proposals and conditions on which Reynier Wisselpenningh, proposes to sell at public sale to the highest bidder, his house lot and garden lying in the village of Beverwyck at present occupied by him. *Firstly*, the aforesaid house shall be delivered to the buyer with all that is fast by earth and nailed, together with the lot as it stands; length two and thirty wood feet, with the garden as it stands in fence, adjoining to the south the garden of Gerrit Bancker, to the north the garden of Henderick Gerritsen [Van Wie] except the crop therein. Delivery shall be made on the 20th of next month, October, of the year 1661. * * * *

[This paper is incomplete and unexecuted].

Conditions and proposals on which the *Commies* and commissares, propose in the name and for the sake of the honorable Heeren director general and council of New Netherland, to farm out publickly to the highest bidder, the excise of all wines, beers and distilled liquors to be drawn and consumed by the innkeepers, tapsters and retailers in and about Fort Orange, village of Beverwyck and colony of Rensselaerwyck. The farming out as well as the farming shall be done in accordance with the laudable customs of our fatherland, and in pursuance of the printed ordinance and placards of their high mightinesses the states general promulgated in respect to the finances. The farming shall begin on the first of November [1661], and end on the last of October, A.D. 1662, continuing the space of 12 months, during which time the farmer may collect, and receive for all wines, beers, or distilled liquors to be drawn and consumed by the tapsters and innkeepers in or about Fort Orange, village of Beverwyck or colony of Rensselaerwyck as follows:

For a tun of domestic brewed beer,....................................	*f*	4.00
For a tun of foreign beer,..	*f*	6.00
For a hogshead of French wine,..	*f*	20.00
For an anker of ditto,...	*f*	4.00
For an anker of Spanish wine, brandy, mead or distilled liquor,	*f*	7.00
For an anker of ditto,...	*f*	2.00

And for greater and less measures in proportion; in beaver or else in seewant at twelve white or six black [seewants] for the stuiver at the choice of the payer. The farmer shall be holden to furnish sufficient sureties to the content of the Messrs. contractors for the excise money to pay every three months in beavers or else in seewant at 12 white or six black [seewants] the stuiver a just fourth part of the promised excise money. To provide against misunderstandings and frauds it is stipulated, and agreed that at the expiration of this farming, when the new farming shall be again made, the new farmer shall have liberty on the day of the new farming, or the following day, or at furthest within three days after the farming is made, to make a guaging, in presence of the late farmer if he wishes to be present, of the liquors held over by the tapsters and innkeepers, of which wines, beers or distilled liquors found on hand two-thirds parts of the receipts, or excise due from the old or foregoing farmer is to be returned and made due to his successor, or the following farmer. The messieurs contractors reserve to themselves the interpretation and amplification of these conditions, and promise the farmer all proper aid and assistance.

[This paper is unexecuted].

On this $\frac{10}{18}$ of November, A.D. 1664, Jan Evertse,[1] Barent Meyndersen and Rut Arentsen, shoemakers by trade, affirm and declare that they were sent for at the request of Willem Brouwer, on account of dissatisfaction with some leather which he, Brouwer, says he had received from Abel Hardenk (?); therefore, we the deponents, having examined the leather, found that there was fourteen pounds of sole leather and inner sole leather, two skins of Spanish leather weighing one pound one and a half quarters, also a dressed calf's skin prized at two guilders; which as Willem Brouwer says, should be in payment of six ox hides, he is not content therewith, inasmuch as he has too little for his six hides; which aforesaid facts we attest if need be by our solemn oath.

Done in Albany *ut supra.*

This is the mark of χ JAN EVERTSE.
with his own hand set.
BARENT MEYNDERSE,
RUT ARENTSEN.

We the commissaries of the court of Fort Orange and village of Beverwyck, declare that we have granted and transferred as by these presents we do, to Sander Leendersen Glen, a house and lot lying in the village of Beverwyck on the hill, length and breadth as it lies enclosed in fence, which we do by virtue of an execution made on Marten Herbertsen of date ——, which lot he received by patent from the Heer director general and council of New Netherland, of date 23d of April, A.D. 1652, and as said Sander Leendersen has paid the promised money to the creditors of said Marten Herbertsen, he is freed from all actions, claims or pretensions, which may hereafter arise.

[This paper is not executed].

In the name of the Lord, Amen; Be it known by the contents of this present instrument that in the year of our Lord Jesus Christ sixteen hundred and sixty-four on the $\frac{12}{22}$ of November, appeared before me Johannes Provoost, clerk of the court of Albany, in presence of the officer Johannes La Montagne, and the honorable Jan Verbeeck and Evert Jansen Wendel, orphan masters, Cataryn Anderiese De Vos[2] widow of

---

[1] In 1717 one Jan Evertse had a lot on the east corner of Broadway and Maiden Lane.—*Albany Annals* VII, 72. In 1661 he was complained of for smuggling shoes.—*Dutch Manuscript*, IX, 716–7.

[2] Catalyntje Andriese De Vos was a daughter of Andries De Vos deputy director of Rensselaerwyck; her second husband was Barent Janse Van Ditmars whom she married in 1664, and who with his son was killed in the massacre at Schenectady, February 9, 1690. Soon after she married her third husband Claes Janse Van Boekhoven whom she also survived, and died in 1712.

the late Arent Anderiese [Bratt], who declares that for God's honor she purposes a future marriage, and before the consummation of the same, she has consented to the following conditions, to wit: that she assigns to her children left by the said Arent Andriese deceased, named Jesie aged 15 years, Ariaentie aged thirteen years, Anderics aged 11 years, Cornelia aged nine years, Samuel five years and Dirck Anderiese aged three years, and promises to pay to them conjointly, the sum of a thousand guilders in beaver currency, and no more, which they shall together receive as their patrimonial inheritance, each his portion at his majority; for the security of which, she, the subscriber, pledges and specially mortgages, her house and *bouwery* lying at Schanhechtade; whereto by request Anderies de Vos and Juriaen Teunise consent to act as guardians and overseers of said children; furthermore said subscriber promises to bring up said children in the fear of God, to teach them to read and write, to maintain them in food and clothing till their majority and marriage state without diminishing their patrimonial estate; which aforesaid conditions she, the subscriber, promises to abide by without craft or guile, on pledge of her person and estate, personal and real.

Thus done in N. Albany, *datum ut supra.*

This is the mark of K CATARYN ANDERIES DE VOS,
with her own hand set.

Jan Verbeeck, as meester.
Evert Janse Wendel, also as Weesmyster.
Andryes de Vos.[1]
Jurejan Tunsen.
La Montagne.

Acknowledged before me,

JOHANNES PROVOOST, Clerk.

Appeared before me Johannes Provoost, clerk of the court of Albany, and in the presence of Jan Verbeeck and Jacob Schermerhoorn commissaries of said court, the honorable Sander Lendersen Glen, who declares that he has granted and transferred, as by these presents he does grant and transfer in real and actual possession to and for the behoof of Adriaen Gerritse, attorney for Dirck Janssen Croon, his heirs or assigns, a house and lot lying in the village of Beverwyck on the hill, adjoining to the north the street, to the south Jan Henderickse Van Bael, to the east Jan Tomassen, to the west Wouter Albertse [Vanden Uythoff], of such magnitude as it lies in fence, which he does by virtue of a conveyance to him granted by the Heeren commissaries of Fort Orange, and village of Beverwyck; and the grantor acknowledges that he is fully satisfied and paid for the purchase and delivery of the same, by a deduction from an existing mortgage, of five hundred and seventy-six guilders and interst from the third of January, at ten per cent, together with a hundred guilders in seewant received in cash; wherefore the grantor promises to free the

[1] Andries De Vos deputy director of Rensselaerswyck was in Beverwyck as early as 1640, and a magistrate in 1648.— O'Callaghan's *History of New York*. i, 439. Besides Catalyntje he probabl had two other daughters, Cornelia wife of Christoffel Davidts (*Deeds* 164), and wife of Cornelis De Vos *alias* Van Schoenderwoert. He had a lot on the west corner of James and Columbia streets (*Annals of Albany*, viii, 243), afterwards owned by Harmanus Wendel 1726 (viii, 312). Also land north of Steuben and west of Pearl streets, (vi, 23, viii, 272); extending from Steuben north on the west side of Pearl street across the *Vossen* kil now Canal street.— *Deeds* 1, 356.

aforesaid house and lot from all actions, claims or pretensions which may, hereafter arise, therefor pledging his person and estate, personal and real, future and present, and submitting himself to all laws and judges.

Done in Albany the 12/22 of November, A.D. 1664.

SANDER LENRSEN GLEN

Jan Verbeeck.
Jacob Schemerhoorn.

We the commissiaries of the court of Fort Orange and village of Beverwyck, declare by these presents that we grant and transfer, as by these presents we do, to Sander Leendersen Glen his heirs or assigns, a house and lot lying in the village of Beverwyck on the hill, adjoining to the north the street, to the south Jan Henderickse Van Bael, to the east Jan Tomasse, and to the west Wouter Albertse Vanden Uythoff] of such magnitude as it lies enclosed in fence; which we do by virtue of an execution issued against the person of Marten Herbertsen, and by public sale, which lot was granted to him by patent of the Heer director general and council of New Netherland on the 23d of April, A.D. 1652, and as said Sander Leendersen has paid the purchase money to the creditors of said Marten Herbertsen, he is free from all claims or pretensions which may hereafter arise, on pledge according to law.

Done in Albany 12/22 of November, A.D. 1664.

JAN VERBEECK, as Receivor.
JACOB SCHERMERHOOREN.

We the undersigned Cornelis Van Nes and Jan Van Bael commissaries of Albany, colony Rensselaerswyck and Schanechtede, testify and declare by these presents, that the honorable David Pieterse Schuyler and Wouter Albertse Vanden Uythoff burghers and inhabitants in Albany have appeared before us; and David Pieterse Schuyler by these presents acknowledges and declares by these presents that in true rights, free ownership he grants, transfers, and makes over to and for the behoof of said Wouter Albertse Vanden Uythoff (who by these presents accepts the same), in a certain lot lying in Albany formerly named Beverwyck, together with the house and barn (?) (*vorder getimmer*) by the grantor built, standing thereupon, adjoining to the south and east Sander Leendersen to the north the street, and to the west the grantor; the lot being in length to the east six rods three feet, breadth in front on the street one rod six feet eight inches, to the east of Sander Leendersen length six rods and three feet, and to the west breadth one rod seven feet eight inches; by virtue of a patent for a greater lot to the late Annetie Bogardus granted by the Heer director general and council of New Netherland the 23d of April, 1652, and likewise by virtue of a deed of conveyance by Annetie Bogardus to him delivered on the 22d of December, 1660, perfectly free and unincumbered, with no claims standing upon or growing out of the same save the lord's right, without the grantors having, holding or reserving any further right of ownership, action, or pretension therein; also acknowledging that by the hand of the grantee he is fully paid and satisfied therefor the last penny with the first, and therefore giving *plenam actionem cessam* and full authority to the grantee his heirs, and successors, or those who may receive title from him, to do with, dispose of, and sell, the aforesaid house, lot, and buildings thereon standing, as he might do with his own patrimonial possessions; with a promise neither to do nor permit anything to be done with or without law in any manner whatsoever against the same, but to free the same from all claims and actions of each and every person, on pledge of his person and estate, personal and real, present and future, nothing excepted, under the authority of all laws and judges.

Done in Albany, on the first day of September, 1665, old style.

DAVYD SCHUILER.
WOUTER ALBERTSEN.

Cornelis Van Nes.
Jan Van Bael.

Acknowledged before me,

D. V. SCHELLUYNE, Secretary 1665.[1]

We, the undersigned, Cornelis Van Nes and Jacob Schermerhoorn, commissaries of Albany, colony Rensselaerwyck and Schanectede, attest and declare by these presents, that Juriaen Theunisse [Glasemaker] and Anthony Janse burghers and inhabitants here, have appeared before us, Juriaen Theunisse acknowledging that in true rights and free ownership he grants, transfers and makes over, and Anthony Janse that he has accepted the grantor's certain house, lot and garden, as the same is built, enclosed and fenced, standing and lying in Albany (formerly named Beverwyck), at present occupied by the grantee, as the same was received by conveyance from Wouter Albertse Vanden Uythoff of date the 2d of February, 1660, also a little piece of a lot included therein purchased from the Heeren commissaries, A.D. 1659, or 1660, according to the declaration of Heeren Jan Verbeeck and Evert Janssen Wendel of date $\frac{26}{6}$ $\frac{\text{Sept.}}{\text{Oct.}}$, 1665, the aforesaid house, lot and garden being in length, breadth and boundaries according to the tenor and contents of the aforesaid deeds of conveyance and declaration referred to in these presents and delivered over to the grantee; all free and unencumbered without any claim standing or issuing against the same, save the lord's right, without the grantor's having, holding or reserving any further right or claim of ownership therein, acknowledging according to bill of sale of date the 14th of January, 1662, that he is fully satisfied, content and paid for the same, the last penny with the first, and therefore giving to the grantor his heirs and successors or assigns *plenam actionem cessam* and full authority, to do with, dispose of, and sell the aforesaid house, lot and garden, as he could do with his own patrimonial estate, promising never more, either with or without law in any manner whatsoever to do or suffer any thing to be done against the same but to protect the aforesaid house, lot, and garden against each and every person and to free the same as is lawful, from all actions, trouble and claims, under pledge of his person and estate, personal and real, present and future, nothing excepted, under authority of all laws and judges.

Done in Albany the $\frac{26}{6}$ $\frac{\text{Sept.}}{\text{Oct.}}$, 1665.

JUREJAN TUNSEN.
ANTHONY JANSE.

Cornelis Van Nes.
Jacob Schermerhooren.

Acknowledged before me,

D. V. SCHELLUYNE, Secretary, 1665.

---

[1] This is the first paper acknowledged before Dirk Van Schelluyne as secretary of Albany.

We, the undersigned, Gerard Swart officer, and Jan Van Bael, commissaries of Albany, colony Rensselaerwyck and Schanechtede, attest and declare that upon the date underwritten, Harmen Tomassen [Hun,] of Amersfort, married to the widow of Dirck Bensingh, and Cobus Janssen, appeared before us, Harmen Tomassen acknowledging by these presents, that in true rights, ownership, he has granted, transferred, and made over to Cobus Janssen, who accepts the conveyance, in a certain house and lot, with a garden and what is fast by earth and nailed, as the same stand, enclosed and fenced, in Albany, built by the aforesaid Dirck Bensingh deceased, by virtue of a patent formerly granted to him by the Heer director general and council of New Netherland, of date the 25th of October, 1653, together with a little piece of a lot inclosed in the aforesaid fence, which the grantor received from Jillis Pieterse; adjoining to the east the highway, to the south Lambert Van Neck, to the west also the highway, and to the north Jacob Tyssen Van der Heyden; all free and unincumbered, with no claims standing against, or growing out of the same, save the lord's right, without the grantor's making the least pretension, on said lot any more; and moreover acknowledging that he is fully paid and satisfied therefor, by the hand of Cobus Janssen, the last penny with the first, and therefore giving *plenam actionem cessam*, and full power to said Cobus Janssen, his heirs and successors, or assigns, to do with and dispose of the same, as he could do with his own patrimonial estate, furthermore, promising the said house and lot to free and protect from all trouble and claims of each and every person, as is right, and never more to do or suffer any thing to be done against the same, either with or without law in any manner whatsoever, on pledge of his person and estate, personal and real, nothing excepted, in subjection to all laws and judges.

Done in Albany, the $\frac{19}{9}$ October, 1665.

This mark + is set by COBUS JANSSEN.
HARMEN THOMASSE.

As witnsss, G. Swart.
J. V. Bael.

Acknowledged before me,

D. V. SCHELLUYNE, Clerk, 1665.

We, the undersigned, Gerard Swart (*Schout*) and Jan Van Bael, commissary of Albany, colony Rensselaerwyck and Schanechtede, testify and declare, that on the date underwritten, Cobus Janssen and Mr. Jan Verbeeck, appeared before us, Cobus Janssen acknowledging that he has granted and transferred, and in true rights, ownership made over, and Jan Verbeeck holding the power of Frans Barentse Pastoor, that he has accepted, the grantor's certain lot and house, with what is therein fast by earth and nailed, in Albany aforesaid, as the same stands enclosed and fenced, and was received by purchase, by Dirck Bensingh, and by deed of conveyance, delivered this day from Harmen Thomase [Hun] of Amersfort, present husband and guardian of the widow of said Dirck Bensingh, adjoining on the east the highway, on the south Lambert Van Neck, on the west also the highway, and on the north Jacob Thyssen Van der Heyden; all free and unencumbered, with no claim standing, or issuing against the same, save the lord's right, without the grantor's having the least pretension thereto any more, likewise acknowledging that he is fully paid therefor to his satisfaction, the last penny with the first, and therefore giving *plenam actionem cessam*, and full power to the aforesaid Jan Verbeeck, in his aforesaid character [of attorney], his heirs, successors, or assigns, to do with and dispose of the same, as he might do with his patrimonial estate, promising to protect and free the aforesaid house and lot, from all trouble and claims of each and every person, as is right and never more to do or suffer any thing to be done against the same, either with or without law in any manner whatsoever, on pledge of his person and estate, personal and real, present and future, nothing excepted, subject to all laws and judges.

Done in Albany the $\frac{9}{19}$ of October, 1665.

This mark is set by COBUS + JANSSEN, aforesaid.

JAN VERBEECK.

As witness, G. Swart.

J. V. Bael.

Acknowledged before me,

D. V. SCHELLUYNE, Secretary, 1665.

We the undersigned Cornelis Van Nes and Jan Van Bael, commissaries of Albany, colony Rensselaerswyck and Schanechtede, testify and declare by these presents, that on the day and date underwritten, before us appeared Mr. Jan Verbeeck in character of attorney for Frans Barentse Pastoor and Jacob Tyssen Vander Heyden; the aforesaid Verbeeck acknowledging in his said character that in true rights free ownership he has granted, transferred and made over, and he, Jacob Tyssen Vander Heyden that he had accepted, of a certain house and lot with what is therein fast by earth and nailed, and as the same stands enclosed and fenced, in Albany aforesaid, formerly built by Dirck Bensingh deceased, and received by conveyance from Cobus Janssen, adjoining on the east the highway, on the south Lambert Van Neck, on the west also the highway, and on the north the aforesaid Vander Heyden; all free and unincumbered, with no claim standing or issuing against the same, except the lord's right, without the grantor's having the least pretension thereto any more; likewise acknowledging that he is fully paid and satisfied therefor, the last penny with the first, and therefore giving *plenam actionem cessam* and full power to the aforesaid Jacob Tyssen Vander Heyden, his heirs and successors, or assigns to do with and dispose of the same as he might do with his own patrimonial estate; promising, moreover, to free and protect the aforesaid house and lot from all trouble and claims of each and every person, as is right, and never more to do or suffer anything to be done against the same either with or without law in any manner whatsoever, on pledge of his person and estate, personal and real, present and future, nothing excepted, subject to all laws and judges.

Done in Albany the $\frac{10}{20}$ of October, 1665.

JAN VERBEECK.

JACOB TEYSSEN VANDER HEYDEN.

Cornelis Van Nes.

J. V. Bael.

Acknowledged before me,

D. V. SCHELLUYNE, Secretary, 1665.

We, the undersigned, Arent Van Curlor and Jacob Schermerhooren, commissaries of Albany, Rensselaerswyck and Schanechtade, testify and declare that Volckert Janse [Douw] and Mr. Arien Van Ilpendam in character of trustees of the estate of Andries Herbertsen, and Cornelis Van Nes, husband and guardian of Maritie Damens, last widow of the late Henderick Andriessen [Van Doesburgh], appeared before us; the aforesaid trustees acknowledging that in true rights free ownership they had granted, transferred and made over, and that he, Van Nes, had accepted, of the just half of a house and lot standing and lying in the village of Beverwyck, now called Albany, the other half of which the aforesaid Maritie Damens is the owner, by virtue of a conveyance by Theunis Theunisse *metselaer*, to the behoof of the aforesaid Andries Herbertse delivered on the 19th of February, 1660, with all that is fast therein by earth and nailed, as the same stands enclosed and fenced, adjoining to the north Pieter Adriaense [Soogemackelyk] now Philip Pieterse Schuyler, to the south Adriaen Janse Van Leyden, as it was bid in and bought at public sale by Van Nes on the 29th of April, 1664; all free and unencumbered, with no claim standing or issuing against the same, except the lord's right, without the grantor's having, holding, or reserving any action or claim thereon, likewise acknowledging that they are fully satisfied and paid by the hands of said Van Nes, the last penny with the first, moreover giving *plenam actionem cessam* and full power to the aforesaid Van Nes, his heirs and successors or assigns, to do with, dispose of, and sell the aforesaid just half house and lot, as he could do with his own patrimonial estate; furthermore promising to free and protect the said half house and lot from all trouble and claims of each and every person, as is right, and never more to do or suffer any thing to be done against the same either with or without law in any manner whatsoever, on pledge of their persons and estates, personal and real, present and future, nothing excepted, subject to all laws and judges.

Done in Albany the 1/21 November, 1665.

VOLKART JANSE.
ADRIAEN VAN ILPENDAM.
CORNELIS VAN NES.

A. Van Curler.
Jacob Schermerhooren.

Acknowledged before me,

D. V. SCHELLUYNE, Secretary, 1665.

We, the undersigned, Arent Van Curlor and Cornelis Van Nes, commissaries of Albany, etc., testify and declare that Mr. Andriaen Van Ilpendam in character of trustee of the estate of Andries Herbertsen, and Volckert Janse [Douw] have appeared before us; acknowledging the aforesaid Mr. Adriaen Van Ilpendam in his aforesaid character, that in true rights, free ownership he had granted transferred and made over, and he, Volckert Janse, that he had accepted of the half island that belongs to him, Adries Herbertsen, and Rutger Jacobsen deceased together in company, according to patent by the Heer director general and council of New Netherland granted, of date the 19th of March 1661, and as he, Volckert Janse, bid off and bought the same at public sale on the 26th of June, 1663; free and uinnucumbered with no claim standing or issuing against the same, except the lord's right; said island lies in the

North river in the aforesaid colony below Fort Albany; without the grantor's having, holding or reserving any right, claim or action any more therein, likewise acknowledging that he is fully satisfied and paid therefor through the hand of said Volckert Janse the last penny with the first, giving therefore *plenam actionem cessam* and full power to the aforesaid Volckert Janse, his heirs and successors to do with, dispose of and sell the aforesaid half island as he could do with his own patrimonial estate, promising to protect and free the aforesaid half island from all trouble and claims of each and every person as is right, and never more to do or suffer anything to be done against the same either with or without law in any manner, on pledge of his person and estate, personal and real, present and future, nothing excepted, subject to all laws and judges.

Done in Abany the $\frac{11}{21}$ of November, 1665.

ADRIAEN VAN ILPENDAM.
VOLKART JANSE.

A. Van Curler.
Cornelis Van Nes.

Acknowledged before me,

D. V. SCHELLUYNE, Secretary, 1665.

We, the undersigned, Arent Van Curlor and Cornelis Van Nes, commissaries of Albany, etc., testify and declare, that on the date of these presents, Volckert Janse [Douw] and Mr Adriaen Van Ilpendam as trustees of the estate of Andries Herbertse, Constapel, appeared before us and acknowledged that in true rights, free ownership they had granted, transferred and made over to and for the behoof of Anthony Janse who accepts this conveyance, of a certain lot for a garden, allotment No. 18, adjoining to the south Pieter Hartgers, north and east the highway, and west Jacob *de Brouwer*, breadth four and a half rods and length seven rods, as the same lies in fence in the village of Beverwyck now called Albany; by virtue of a patent for a larger lot by the Heer director general and council of New Netherland granted to the aforesaid Andries Herbertsen of date the 25th of October, 1653; free and unincumbered with no claim standing or issuing against the same except the lord's right; and without the grantors' having, holding or reserving any further action or claim on the same; likewise acknowledging that they are fully satisfied and paid therefor the last penny with the first; and therefore giving *plenam actionem cessam* and full power to the aforesaid Anthony Janse his heirs and successors or assigns, to do with, and dispose thereof, as he might do with his own patrimonial estate, therefore promising to protect and free the same from all trouble and claims of each and every person, as is right, with a further promise never more to do or suffer anything to be done against the same either with or without law in any manner, on pledge of their persons and estates nothing excepted, subject to all laws and judges.

Done in Albany, the $\frac{11}{21}$ of November, 1665.

VOLKART JANSE.
ADRIAEN VAN ILPENDAM.
ANTHONY JANSE.

A. Van Curler.
Cornelis Van Nes.

Acknowledged before me,

D. V. SCHELLUYNE, Secretary 1665.

We the undersigned Cornelis Van Nes and Jan Van Bael, commissaries of Albany, etc., testify and declare that on the date underwritten, before us appeared William Janse Schut, dwelling in the aforesaid colony, who declares that in true rights free ownership he had granted, transferred and made over by these presents, to and for the behoof of Cornelis Bogardus the grantor's certain house and lot as it came to him from Andries Herbertse, constapel (being the house which the grantor himself caused to be erected on the lot) standing and lying here in Albany, extending from the aforesaid Constapel's gate to the fence of Tryn Claesse, and further, as the same is enclosed and fenced, according to bill of sale of date the fourth of August, 1662, and other evidences thereof; without the grantor's having, holding or reserving the least action or claim any more against the same; likewise acknowledging that he is fully satisfied and paid therefor, by the hands of Johannes Withart, the last penny with the first; namely, with the sum of eighty-five whole merchantable beaver skins; therefore giving *plenam actionem cessam* and full power to the aforesaid Bogardus, his heirs and successors, or the aforesaid Withart, who by virtue of the aforesaid payment has right and claim thereto, to do with and dispose of the aforesaid house and lot as he might do with his own patrimonial estate and effects, promising never more to do or to suffer any thing to be done against the same either with or without law in any manner, on pledge of his person and estate, personal and real, present and future, nothing excepted, subject to all laws and judges.

Done in Albany, $\frac{6}{16}$ of May, 1666.

WILLEM JANSEN SCHUET.[1]

Cornelis Van Nes.
Jan Van Bael.

Acknowledged before me,

D. V. SCHELLUYNE, Secretary, 1666.

We the undersigned, Arent Van Curler and Cornelis Van Nes, commissaries of Albany, etc., testify and declare by these presents that on the date underwritten before us appeared Jochem Wesselse Backer, attorney for Pieter Janse *de Boer* dwelling in the aforesaid colony, who declares that in true rights free ownership, he has granted, transferred and made over, by these presents to and for the behoof of Henderick Bries, shoemaker here in Albany, in a certain house and lot, which he, Bries, purchased of Pieter Janse and at present occupies, by virtue of a patent and of the conveyance thereof of date the 29th of June, 1663, received by him from Jan Lambertse Van Bremen, all according to the purport and contents of the aforesaid deed of conveyance, to which reference has been made in these presents, and which with these presents, shall be handed over to him, Bries, giving him his heirs and successors full power to do with the same as he might do with his own patrimonial estates and effects, without the grantor's (in his aforesaid character) having the least claim thereto any more; likewise acknowledging that he is fully satisfied and paid the last penny with the first, and therefore promising to protect and free the aforesaid house and lot from all trouble and claims of each and every person as is right and especially from the mortgage

[1] W J Schuet, was a tailor in Beverwyck in 1654.—*Deeds*, I, 181; II, 11.

which Pieter Ryverdyngh, has upon the aforesaid house and lot of date the 10th of June, 1664, and for which Jochem Wesselse Backer aforenamed by these presents substitutes him in his place as surety and principal, the grantor and surety promising, furthermore, never more to do or suffer anything to be done against the samo, with or without law in any manner, on pledge according to law; all sincere and in good faith.

Done in Albany, on the $\frac{8}{18}$ of June, 1666.

JOCHEM BACKER.

A Van Curler.
Cornelis Van Nes.

Acknowledged before me,

D. V. SCHELLUYNE, Secretary, 1666.

We, the undersigned, Arent Van Curlor and Richard Van Renselaer, commissaries of Albany, etc., testify and declare by these presents, that on the underwriten date, before us appeared Volckert Janse for Hendrick Jochemse, who declares by virtue of a patent and conveyance of date the 23d of April 1652, and 16th of April of the year 1661, respectively thereof, likewise according to the bill of sale of date of $\frac{19}{29}$ February, also of this year 1666, that in true rights free ownership he has granted and transferred to and for the behoof of Philip Pieterse Schuyler, in a part of the lot of the aforenamed Hendrick Jochemse and the garden over the back street; the lot extending along the street thirty wood feet, in length to the rear to the fence of the brewery of Harmen Rutgers, breadth there the same, the little alley that runs to the garden being comprehended therein, said aforesaid part lot, and garden lies here in Albany, bounded according to the purport and contents of the aforesaid bill of sale, to which in these presents reference is made, as also by the aforesaid conveyance in the Esopus by Femmetie Albertse widow of Hendrick Janse Westercamp deceased, delivered to the aforesaid Hendrick Jochemse; without the grantor's (in his aforesaid charter) making the last claim any more to the same, likewise acknowledging that he is fully satisfied and paid therefor, the last penny with the first by the hand of the aforesaid Schuyler, therefore giving full power to the aforesaid Schuyler, his heirs and successors or assigns, to do with and dispose thereof as he might do with his own patrimonial estate and goods, promising to protect and free the aforesaid part of lot and garden from all trouble, claims and liens of each and every person as is right, and furthermore never more to do or suffer anything to be done against the same either with or without law in any manner on pledge according to law.

Done in Albany the $\frac{9}{19}$ of June, 1666.

VOLKART JANSE.

A Van Curler.
R. V. Rensselaer.

Acknowledged before me,

D. V. SHELLYUNE Secretary, 1666.

We the undersigned Jacob Schermerhoorn and Jan Van Bael, commissaries of Albany, etc., testify and declare by these presents that on the date underwritten, before us appeared Jurriaen Janse Groenwout, husband and guardian of Maritie Tomasse Mingael, deceased, last widow of the late Cornelis Theunisse Van Westbroeck,[1] and Poulus Martense Van Benthuysen, acknowledging, and he Jurriaen Janse declared that in true rights free ownership he had transferred to and for the behoof of Poulus Martense, in a certain lot upon which he, Poulus, has built a house, which aforesaid lot as enclosed, fenced and bounded lies here in Albany, as now occupied by Poulus Martense, by virtue of a bill of sale of date the 24th of April, 1660, and of a patent for a larger lot of date the 23d of April, 1652, also according to further proofs derived from a highway cut off from this lot, and released from the aforesaid Paulus Martense, furthermore on condition that the fence on the south side, (which now Mary Dyckman[2] has in use, or dwells next to it) on neither side shall be built up without the assent and permission of both parties; without the grantor's making the least claim thereto any more, likewise acknowledging that he is fully satisfied and paid therefor the last penny with the first, therefore giving him the aforesaid Paulus Martense, his heirs and successors or assigns full power and authority to dispose of the aforesaid lot as he might do with his own patrimonial estate, promising at all times to protect and free the aforesaid lot from all trouble and actions of each and every person as is right, and furthermore never more to do or suffer anything to be done against the same, either with or without law in any manner, on pledge of his person and estate, personal and real nothing excepted, subject to all laws and judges.

Done in Albany, the 26/8 July, 1666.

This mark is set by JURRIAEN [mark] JANSE,[3] aforesaid.

POULUS MARTEN.

Jacob Schermerhooren.
Jan Van Bael.
Jan Verbeeck, as guardian.
Stoffel Janse Abeel, as guardian.

In my presence,

D. V. SCHELLUYNE, Secretary, 1666.

We, the undersigned, Arent Van Curler and Abraham Staets commissaries of Albany etc., testify and declare, that on the date underwritten, before us appeared Tjarck Claesse De With[4] farmer in the Esopus, who declares that he has granted, transferred and in true rights free ownership made over by these presents to and for the behoof of Mr. Jeronimus Ebbingh, merchant of New York, in his certain house and lot standing and lying here in Albany, adjoining to the east the highway, on the south side of Hendrick De Backer, on the west side the garden of Hendrick Andriesse [Van Doesburgh] and Lambert Van Neck, and on the north side the garden of Lambert Van Neck, said lot being in breadth in front

---

[1] C. T. Van Westbroeck or Bos, came to Beverwyck in 1631.

[2] Maria Bosyns wife of Johannes Dyckman late *commies* or officer at Fort Orange.

[3] Jurriaen Janse Groenwout was a licensed butcher in Albany in 1670.— *Albany Annals*, iv, 10. Still living in 1677.— *Deeds* 1, 359.

[4] T. C. De Witt, was a citizen of Beverwck 1657 to 1668 when he was at Esopus.— *Deeds*, II, 236; *Dutch manuscripts*, XV: 48.

on the street thirty-two wood feet and four inches, and in length ten rods, as the aforesaid lot was received by him by purchase and delivery from the late Dirck Bensingh, according the deed of conveyance thereof, and the house thereon built by the grantor; with whatever is fast by earth and nailed, free and unincumbered. with no claim standing or issuing against the same, save the lord's right, acknowledging that he, the grantor, is fully paid and satisfied therefor, by certain lands in the Esopus by way of exchange with said Ebbingh and his wife, Madam Johanna De Laet, received by conveyance of date the 11th of September, 1660, without the grantor's having, holding or reserving the least claim or action any more against the said house and lot, but releasing the same to said Ebbingh his heirs and successors or assigns; promising to protect and free said house and lot from all trouble, actions and incumbrance of each and every person, and furthermore never more to do or suffer anything to be done against the same, either with or without law, in any manner whatsoever, on pledge of his person and estate, personal and real, present and future, nothing excepted, subject to all laws and judges.

Done in Albany the $\frac{14}{24}$ of July, 1666.

TIERCK CLAESSEN DE WITT.

A. Van Curler.
Abraham Staes.

Acknowledged before me,

D. V. SCHELLUYNE, Secretary, 1666.

We, the undersigned, Jan Van Bael and Abraham Staes, commissaries of Albany, etc., declare by these presents that on the day under written before us appeared, Bastiaen De Winter dwelling at Schanechtade aforesaid, who declares that he has appointed and empowered by these presents Daniel Janse Van Antwerpen,[1] the bearer of this, proposing to depart for Holland, to demand, collect and receive of Mr. Anthony Moore, merchant, at present dwelling at Amsterdam, or wherever his residence may be, a certain sum of one hundred and seventy-seven guilders at 20 stuivers each, the same being due to Mr. Mathys Oosterman dwelling at Meuwes (?) in the Caribean islands, according to obligation of date the 15th of May, 1655, whose right and action the subscriber has by assignment of date the 26th of June, 1658, in the English tongue, whereof a translation and copy of the obligation is placed in the lands of the attorney with this power; for receipts on the same acquittance to pass; if necessity require it to parry all demands, and in case of refusal to constrain him to payment of the aforesaid sum with cost, damage and interest on the same, with law and rigor of justice, to which end all terms of the laws according to the custom of the place to observe to sentence and extreme execution *van dien in cluys;* with power one or more persons *ad lites tantum* in his place to substitute, likewise to compromise, arrange and postpone, and furthermore to do, transact and perform what he shall think needful and proper; promising at all times to hold good all that shall be done and performed in the matter aforesaid by the attorney and his sub-

[1] D. J. Van Antwerpen was one of the early settlers of Schenectady. He was born in 1635, and by Mary Groot his wife had a numerous family. Besides a house lot in Schenectady he owned the Third Flat on the south side of the Mohawk river, about eight miles above the village.

stitute, without any gainsaying, provided that the attorney be holden when requested to make a proper statement of his aforesaid transactions and receipts. In confirmation of the same the *comparant* has in our presence subscribed this with his own hand in Albany the $\frac{16}{26}$ of July, 1666.

BASTEIAEN DE WINTER.[1]

Jan Van Bael.
Abram Staes.

Acknowledged before me,

D. V. SCHELLUYNE. Secretary, 1666.

We, the undersigned, Jacob Schermerhooren and Cornelis Van Nes, commissaries of Albany, etc., testify and declare, on the date underwritten, that before us appeared Theunis Willemse, husbandman, young man born in the district of Utrecht at Heyvelt, who declares that he has appointed and empowered by these presents his sister Evertie Willemse dwelling at Utrecht aforesaid with the honorable Heer Van Wulven, specially to demand, collect and receive from the heirs of the late Willem Theunise his deceased uncle, or whom it concerns, payment and satisfaction of an order entrusted with his aforesaid sister upon the aforesaid heirs and others, for what was inherited by him from his father Willem Theunise deceased, and his uncle Barent Theunise deceased, according to the tenor and contents of the aforesaid order; for receipts of the same acquittance to pass, and in case of delay to bring said order to execution, and all terms of the laws to observe according to the customs of the place, to which end if it be needful one or more persons or attorneys (*procureurs*) to substitute in her place *ad lites;* likewise to compromise, arrange and assign; and furthermore all things to do, transact and perform, which are needful and she may think proper; promising at all times to hold good all that his sister aforesaid and her substitute in the matter aforesaid shall do and perform without any opposition, provided that she be holden when requested, to make a proper statement of her transactions and receipts.

Done in Albany, the $\frac{17}{27}$ of July, 1666.

This mark is set by
THEUNIS [mark] WILLEMSE, aforesaid.

Jacob Schermerhooren.
Cornelis Van Nes.

Acknowledged before me,

D. V. SCHELLUYNE, Secretary, 1666.

We, the undersigned, Cornelis Van Nes and Rychard Van Rensselaer, commissaries of Albany, etc., testify and declare that on the date underwritten, appeared before us, Nicolaes Meyer, merchant at New York at present here in Albany, who declares that in true rights, free ownership, he has granted, transferred and made over by these presents to and for the behoof of Daniel Rinchout dwelling in Albany in a certain garden

---

[1] B. De Winter, a native of Middleburgh, early settled in Schenectady, where he sold, in 1670, his house, lot, and *bouwery* upon the Groote Vlachte to Jean Labatie, Elias Van Guyseling and Joris Aertse Van der Baast. He was probably deceased before 1678 when the Dutch church of Albany claimed and probably obtained his property for the use of the poor.— *English Manuscripts*, xxvii, 169, 180. *Notarial Papers. Deeds*, II, 788-9.

lying in Albany aforesaid, in magnitude according to the survey bill thereof (*meet brief*) of the surveyor, and bounded according to the tenor and contents of the deed of conveyance delivered by Leendert Philipse [Conyn] to the behoof of the grantor on the 23d of August, 1663, in Fort Orange, by virtue of said deed of conveyance and of a bill of sale of date the first of July, 1665, and a later deed of confirmation put on the back of the bill of sale and subscribed by Rinchout of date the 30th of April, 1666, together with a following sentence, of the honorable court here, of date the $\frac{5}{15}$ of this month, to all of which reference is made; without the grantor's having, holding or reserving the least action or claim any more on the aforesaid garden; likewise acknowledging that he is fully satisfied and paid therefor through the hands of the aforenamed Rinchout the last penny with the first, and therefore giving *plenam actionem cessam*, and full power and authority to the aforenamed Rinchout, his heirs and successors or assigns, to do with, dispose of and transact with the aforesaid garden, as he might do with his own patrimonial lands and effects; promising also to protect and free the same from all trouble, actions and claims of each and every person; and furthermore never more to do or suffer any thing to be done against the same, either with or without law, in any manner whatsoever, under pledge of his person and estate, personal and real, nothing excepted, subject to all laws and judges.

Done in Albany, the $\frac{19}{29}$ of July, 1666.

NICOLAES D. MEYER.

Cornelis Van Nes.
Richard Van Rensselaer.

Acknowledged before me,

D. V. SCHELLUYNE, Secretary, 1666.

We, the undersigned, Jan Van Bael and Jacob Schermerhooren, commissaries of Albany, etc., testify and declare by these presents, that before us appeared Anthony Janse, innkeeper here in Albany, who acknowledges, that he is well and honestly indebted to Jan Van Aecken, in the quantity of five and seventy good merchantable beavers, and to Goosen Gerritse [Van Schaick] for five and twenty beavers, growing out of a matter of money lent on the 2d of September, 1662, to his satisfaction received and employed for the first payment for the house and lot which he at present occupies, transferred to him by Jurriaen Theunisse; which aforesaid respective sums of seventy-five and twenty-five beavers, with proper interest on the same, commencing on the 2d of September, 1662, aforesaid, and running to the full and complete payment, he, the subscriber, promises to pay punctually within the time of one year from date without longer delay, therefor pledging his person and estate, personal and real, present and future, nothing excepted, especially the aforesaid house and lot, to secure the payment thereof if needful, without cost or loss, subject to all laws and judges.

Done in Albany the $\frac{9}{19}$ of August, 1666.

ANTHONY JANSE.

Jan Van Bael.
Jacob Schermerhooren.

Acknowledged before me,

D. V. SCHELLUYNE, Secretary, 1666.

We, the undersigned, Abraham Staets and Cornelis Van Nes, commissaries of Albany, etc., testify and declare, that before us appeared Cornelis Wyncoop, who declares that in true rights, free ownership, he has granted, transferred and made over by these presents, to Claes Ripse [Van Dam] in his certain house and lot which he received by conveyance from Marcelis Janse [Van Bommel], according to conditions of purchase at public vendue on the 10th and 17th of January, 1658, with all that is fast by earth and nailed, and in length and breadth according to the tenor and contents of the aforesaid deed of conveyance and conditions referred to in these presents as the aforesaid house and lot stands and lies here in Albany, without the grantor's making the least pretension or demand against the same any more; likewise acknowledging that he is fully paid and satisfied therefor by the hands of Claes Ripsen [Van Dam] the last penny with the first, and therefore giving *plenam actionem cessam*, and full authority to the aforenamed Claes Ripsen, his heirs and successors or assigns, to do with and dispose of the aforesaid house and lot as he could do with his own patrimonial estate; promising moreover to protect and free the aforesaid house and lot from all trouble, claims and actions of each and every person as is right; and furthermore never to do or suffer anything to be done against the same, either with or without law, in any manner whatsoever, on pledge of his person and estate, personal and real, nothing excepted, subject to all laws and judges.

Done in Albany the $\frac{15}{25}$ of August, 1666.

Abram Staes. CORNELIS WYNCKOOP.
Cornelis Van Nes.

In my presence, D. V. SCHELLUYNE, Secretary, 1666.

We, the undersigned, Cornelis Van Nes and Jacob Schermerhoorn, commissaries of Albany, etc., testify and declare, that on the date underwritten, before us appeared Mr. Jan Verbeeck, attorney for his brother-in-law Theunis Cornelisse [Slingerland], who declares that, by virtue of a patent for a greater lot of date 23d of April, 1652, in true rights, free ownership, he had granted, transferred and made over by these presents, to and for behoof of Willem Bout, in a certain lot received by him, Theunis Cornelise, lying here in Albany, adjoining to the north Jacques Thyssen [Vander Heyden], east and south the aforesaid Theunis Cornelise, and to the west the public street, the lot being in breadth in front and rear three rods Rynland measure, and in length as long as the lot of Jacques Thyssen aforesaid; without Theunis Cornelisse having the least claim on the aforesaid lot, also acknowledging that he is fully paid and satisfied therefor by the hands of said Willem Bout, the last penny with the first, and therefor giving *plenam actionem cessam*, and perfect power and authority to the aforesaid Willem Bout, his heirs and successors, to do therewith as he might do with his own patrimonial effects; promising to protect and free the said lot from all trouble, actions and claims of each and every person as is right, and furthermore, never more to do or suffer anything to be done against the same, either with or without law, in any manner whatsoever, on pledge of his person and estate, nothing excepted, subject to all laws and judges.

Done in Albany the $\frac{27}{5}$ of August, of September, 1666.

Cornelis Van Nes. JAN VERBEECK.
Jacob Schermerhooren.

In my presence, D. V. SCHELLUYNE, Secretary, 1666.

We, the undersigned, Jan Van Bael and Abraham Staes, commissaries of Albany, etc., testify and declare that on the date underwritten, before us appeared Claes Ripsen [Van Dam] master carpenter here in Albany, who declares, that in true rights, free ownership, he had granted, transferred and made over by these presents to and for the behoof of Omy La Grand, master tailor, in a certain house and lot (together with the just lowermost half of the lot lying thereby, to be measured from the top to the bottom, as the lot stands in its enclosure and fence), standing and lying here in Albany, and by him, La Grand, at present occupied, according to the bill of sale of date $\frac{16}{26}$ of January last, and by virtue of a conveyance of a greater lot from Cornelis Wyncoop to him delivered on the $\frac{15}{25}$ of the month of August last, whereto reference is herein made, without the grantor's making the least claim any more to said house, lot and just half lot; also acknowledging that he is fully paid and satisfied by the hands of said La Grand therefor, the last penny with the first, and therefore giving *plenam actionem cessam*, and full power and authority to the aforesaid La Grand,[1] his heirs and successors, to do with and sell the same as he might do with his own patrimonial effects; furthermore promising to protect and free the aforesaid house lot and just half lot from all trouble, actions and claims of each and every person as is right, and never more to do or suffer anything to be done against the same, with or without law, in any manner whatsoever, on pledge of his person and estate, nothing excepted, subject to all laws and judges.

Done in Albany the $\frac{21}{31}$ of August, 1666.

CLAES RIPSEN VAN DAM.

Jan Van Bael
Abram Staes.

Acknowledged before me,

D. V. SCHELLUYNE, Secretary, 1666.

We, the undersigned, Abraham Staets and Jan Van Bael, commissaries of Albany, etc., testify and declare by these presents, that on the date underwritten, before us appeared Willem Bout, who declared by these presents, that in true rights, free ownership, he had granted, transferred and made over to and for the behoof of Jan Clute, in a certain house and lot standing and lying in Albany, adjoining to the north Jacques Thyssen [Van der Heyden], to the east the lot on which the mill of Heer Rensselaer has stood, to the south Theunis Cornelisse and to the west the highway; by virtue of a conveyance passed on this $\frac{\text{27th of August,}}{\text{8th of September,}}$ 1666, breadth in front on the street thirty wood feet, and length to the aforesaid lot of Heer Renseelaer; without the grantor's making the least claim thereto any more, likewise acknowledging that he is fully paid and satisfied therefor by the hands of Jan Clute, the last penny with the first, and therefore giving *plenam actionem cessum*, and full power and authority to the aforesaid Jan Clute, his heirs and successors, to do with the same as he could do with his own patrimonial effects; promising moreover to protect and free the same from all trouble, claims and actions of all and every person as is right, and furthermore, never more to do or suffer anything to be done against the

[1] Omy De La Grange had by his wife, Annetje De Vries, five sons, Omy, Johannes, Christiaan, and Isaac, all of whom had families. The father early purchased land on the Normans kil, where most of his sons settled.

same, either with or without law, in any manner whatsoever, on pledge of his person and estate, nothing excepted, subject to all laws and judges.

Done in Albany the $\frac{27th\ of\ August,}{5th\ of\ September,}$ 1666.

This mark [mark] is set by WILLEM BOUT, aforenamed.

Abram Staes.
Jan Van Bael.

Acknowledged before me,

D. V. SCHELLUYNE, Secretary, 1666.

In Beverwyck, *Anno* 1656, on the 13th of May, we, the undersigned commissaries, acknowledge that we have contracted and agreed with Jan Van Aecken, that we shall have the liberty to set the church as far on his smithy (*in syn smit*), as the width of the door, on condition that we set up his house according to the regulation (*op de Rooye*) of Rem Janssen [*Smit*], and leave a proper lot for the bakery and remove the great house at our own expense. Was subscribed,

RUTGER JACOBSEN.
ANDRIES HERBERTSEN.
This is the mark H of GOOSEN GERRITSE [VAN SCHAICK.]
DIRCK JANSSEN CROON.

This is the mark of [mark] JAN VAN AECKEN.

Jacob Janse Schermerhoorn.
Philip Pieterse [*Schuyler*].

After a collation with the original of date, and subscription as above, this copy was found to agree therewith.

In Albany the $\frac{16}{26}$ of March, 1667.

By me

D. V. SCHELLUYNE, Secretary, 1667.

We, the undersigned, Arent Van Curler and Richard Van Rensselaer, commissaries of Albany, etc., testify and declare that on the date underwritten before us appeared Jan Coster Van Aecken, dwelling here in Albany, who acknowledges by these presents, according to agreement with the Heeren commissaries, made the 13th of May, 1656, and by virtue of a patent of a larger lot, of date the 25th of October, 1653, committed to the care of Carsten Fredericksе Smith, likewise according to a bill of sale of date the $\frac{29}{19}$ December, 1665, that in true rights, free ownership he has granted, transferred and made over to and for the behoof of Jan Clute, in the grantor's certain house and lot, in length and breadth as the same stands enclosed and fenced here in Albany, bounded according to the purport of said bill of sale, without the grantor's making the least claim thereto any more, likewise acknowledging that he is fully paid and satisfied therefor by Jan Clute, namely, with the sum of sixty beavers by him received, and a mortgage for the sum of four hundred and fifty guilders in beavers, passed by Jan Clute to his behoof; therefore giving *plenam actionem cessam*, and full power to the aforenamed Jan Clute, his heirs and successors or assigns, to do therewith as he might do with his own patrimonial effects; promising to protect and free the aforesaid house and lot from all trouble, actions and liens according to the aforesaid bill of sale, of all and every person as is right, and furthermore never more to do or suffer any thing to be done against the same, either with or without law, in any manner whatsoever, on pledge of his person and estate, personal and real, nothing excepted, subject to all laws and judges.

Done in Albany the $\frac{16^{th}}{26^{th}}$ of March, 1667.

JAN KOSTER.

A. Van Curler.
R. V. Rensselaer.

In my presence, D. V. SCHELLUYNE Secretary, 1667

We, the undersigned, Richard Van Rensselaer and Philip Pieterse Schuyler, commissaries of Albany, etc., testify and declare that on the date underwritten, before us appeared Jan Coster Van Acken, who declared, by virtue of a patent for a greater lot granted by the Heer director general and council of New Netherland, to Albert Gerritse, of date the 23d of April, A.D. 1652, in the keeping of Mr. Adriaen Van Ilpendam, that in true rights, free ownership, by these presents he had granted, transferred and made over, to and for the behoof of Gerrit Banckert, in the grantor's certain house and lot, standing and lying here in Albany at present occupied by Jan Dareth, adjoining to the north Jan Van Eeckelen, and to the south Myndert Fredericksе, as the same stands enclosed and fenced, breadth in front on the street three rods and four feet, in the rear ten and a half feet Rynland measure, according to the survey bill of the surveyor, Harmen Bastiaense [Visscher] of date the $\frac{12^{th}}{22}$ of March, 1667, without the grantor's making the least claim thereon any more, also acknowledging that he is fully paid and satisfied therefor, the last penny with the first, and therefore giving *plenum actionem cessam*, and full power to the aforenamed Gerrit Banckert or his assigns, to dispose thereof as he might do with his own patrimonial effects; promising to protect and free the aforesaid house and lot for his sake from all actions, trouble and claims of all and every person as is right, and furthermore, never to do nor suffer anything to be done against the same, with or without law, in any manner whatsoever, on pledge of his person and estate, nothing excepted, subject to all laws and judges.

Done in Albany the $\frac{8}{18}$ of April, 1667.

Richard Van Rensselaer. JAN KOSTER.
Philip Pieterse Schuyler.

In my presence, D. V. SCHELLUYNE, Secretary, 1667.

[Copy.]

Harmen Albertse Vedder declares by these presents that in true and free ownership he transfers and makes over to Gerrit Banckert, by these presents, the house and lot mentioned in the last conveyance, without his laying claim any more thereto, likewise acknowledging that he is fully paid and satisfied therefor, the last penny with the first, promising to protect and free the same from all trouble and claims of all persons as is right, and never more to do or suffer anything to be done against the same, either with or without law in any manner, on pledge of his person and estate, nothing excepted, subject to all laws and judges.

Done in Albany the $\frac{8}{18}$ of April, 1667, in presence of Heeren commissaries Philip Pieterse Schuyler and Richard Van Rensselaer.

Was subscribed, HARMEN VEEDER.

Philip Pieterse Schuyler.
R. V Rensselaer.

In my presence,

D. V. SCHELLUYNE, Secretary.

NOTE. The original of this paper stands on the conveyance passed before the vice director and *commys* La Montagne, of date the 14th of September, 1658.

We, the undersigned, Philip Pieterse Schuyler and Goosen Gerritse [Van Schaick], commissaries of Albany, etc., testify and declare that on the date underwritten, before us appeared Jurriaen Janse Groenewout, husband and guardian of Maritie Thomassen, last widow of the late Cornelis Theunisse Bos, assisted by Mr. Jan Verbeeck and Stoffel Janse Abeel, also appointed guardians of Weyntie Cornelisse, infant daughter of the aforenamed Cornelis Theunisse and Maritie Thomasse, who declared that in true rights, free ownership, they do grant, transfer and make over by these presents to and for the behoof of Symon Volckertse [Veeder de] *Backer*, dwelling at present at Schanechtade, in a lot lying here in Albany, whereon said Symon Volckertse has caused a house to be built, the lot being to the south along a common road twenty rods nine feet, to the west the street breadth four rods, to the north Theunis Cornelisse length twenty rods nine feet, to the east the river breadth nine feet, according to the survey bill of the surveyor, Jan Roeloffse, of date the 1st of April, 1661, by virtue of the patent granted by the Heer director general and council of New Netherland, to him, the late Bos, of date the 23d of April, A.D. 1652; without the grantor's in the aforesaid character, or in any manner, making the least demand or claim thereto any more, his aforenamed wife before the date of her marriage with the grantor, her present husband, acknowledging that she is fully paid and satisfied therefor, the last penny with the first, and therefore giving *plenam actionem cessam*, full authority and power to the aforenamed Symon Volckertse, his heirs and successors or assigns, to do with and dispose of the aforesaid lot and house thereon built, as he might do with his own patrimonial goods and effects; promising to protect and free the said lot from all trouble, actions and liens of all persons as is right, and furthermore never to do nor suffer anything to be done against the same, either with or without law, in any manner, on pledge of his person and estate, real and personal, nothing excepted, subject to all laws and judges.

Done in Albany the $\frac{9}{19}$ of April, 1667.

This mark ⋎ is set by,
JURRIAEN JANSE GROENEWOUT, aforesaid.

JAN VERBEECK.
STOFFEL JANSE ABEEL.

Philip Schuyler.
Goosen Gerritse.

In my presence, D. V. SCHELLUYNE, Secretary, 1667.

We, the undersigned, commissaries of Albany, etc , testify and declare, that on the date underwritten, before us appeared Jurriaen Janse Groenewout, husband and guardian of Maritie Thomasse, last widow of the late Cornelis Theunisse Bos, assisted by Messrs. Jan Verbeeck and Stoffel Janse Abeel, likewise the appointed guardians of Weyntie Cornelisse, infant daughter of the aforenamed Cornelis Theunisse and Maritie Thomasse, who declare that in true rights, free ownership they grant, transfer and make over by these presents to and for the behoof of Huybert Janse, in a certain lot, in length on the north side seven rods and nine feet, on the south side eight rods and ten feet, on the east side two rods six feet and on the west side two rods, likewise a garden over the highway lying on the river side in length on the north and south sides four rods, in breadth on the west side two rods and seven feet, and on the east side three rods, both lot and garden lying in Albany and adjoining on the south side the grantor, on the west and north sides the street and on the east side the river; by virtue of a patent for a greater lot of date the 23d of April, 1652, granted to the aforesaid Cornelis Theunisse by the director general and council of New Netherland; without the grantors' making the least claim thereto any more, Huybert Janse having fully paid for the same, the last penny with the first, and therefore giving *plenam actionem cessam*, and full power to the aforenamed Huybert Janse, his heirs and successors or assigns, to do with and dispose thereof as he might do with his own patrimonial lands; promising to protect and free the aforesaid lot and garden from all trouble, actions and liens of all persons as is right, and furthermore never to do nor suffer anything to be done against the same, either with or without law, in any manner, on pledge of their persons and estates, personal and real, nothing excepted, subject to all laws and judges.

Done in Albany $\frac{9}{19}$ of April, 1667.

This mark is set by JURRIAEN [mark] JANSE GROENEWOUT.

JAN VERBEECK.
STOFFEL JANSE ABEEL

Philip Pieterse Schuyler.
Goosen Gerritsen.

In my presence,

D. V. SCHELLUYNE, Secretary, 1667.

We, the undersigned, commissaries of Albany, etc., testify and declare, that on the date underwritten, before us appeared Jurriaen Janse Groenewout, burgher and inhabitant here in Albany, husband and guardian of Maritie Thomase Mingael, last widow of the late Cornelis Theunisse Van Westbrook,[1] who declares that in true rights, free ownership, he grants, transfers, and makes over by these presents to and for the behoof of Geertruy Barents, last widow of the late Henderick Henderickse and at present the wife of Jacob Heving, in the half of a lot with the house standing thereon, in length, breadth and compass according to conveyance, of date the 4th of June, 1658, whereto reference is here made, without the grantor's making the least claim thereto any more, acknowledging that he is fully paid and

[1] Van Westbrook, *alias* Bos --*Deeds* II, 641.

satisfied therefor, the last penny with the first, and promising therefore nevermore to do or suffer anything to be done in any manner against the same, on pledge of his person and estate, nothing excepted, subject to all laws and judges.

Done in Albany the $\frac{8}{18}$ of April, 1667.

This mark is set by JURRIAEN JANSE GROENEWOUT.

Philip Pieterse
Goosen Gerritse.

In my presence,

D. V. SCHELLUYNE, Secretary.

We, the undersigned, commissaries of Albany, etc., testify and declare, that on the date underwritten, before us appeared Hans Henderickse and Pieter Van Alen, attorneys of Cornelis Cornelisse de Boer, who declare that in true rights, free ownership, they do grant, transfer and make over by these presents, to and for the behoof of Jan Hendrickse Bruyns, in a certain house and lot standing and lying here in Albany, in length and breadth and with such rights and privileges as the same was received by said de Boer, by conveyance from Jan Coster Van Aeken, and Stoffel Janse [Abeel], attorneys for Pieter Maecker, to the behoof of said de Boer and Daniel Verveelen, passed the 8th of August 1659, and according to deed of conveyance by said Verveelen, to the behoof of the aforenamed de Boer on the 25th of August, 1661, likewise according to bill of sale between said de Boer and the afornamed Bruyns, made on the 9th of August, 1663, to all which reference is herein made; without the grantor's making the least claim thereto any more, likewise acknowledging that he is fully paid and satisfied by the aforesaid Jan Hendrick Bruyns, the last penny with the first, and therefore giving *plenam actionem cessam*, and full power to the aforesaid Bruyns, his heirs and successors or assigns, to dispose thereof as he might do with his own patrimonial effects; promising to protect and free the aforesaid house and lot as it regards the said de Boer, from all actions, trouble and liens of all persons, as is right, and further, never to do nor suffer anything to be done against the same, either with or without law, in any manner, on pledge of his person and estate, nothing excepted, subject to all laws and judges.

Done in Albany, $\frac{12}{22}$ of April, 1667.

HANS HEINDRICKSE.
PIETER VAN ALEN.

Philip Pieterse.
Richard Van Rensselaer.

In my presence,

D. V. SCHELLUYNE, Secretary, 1667.

We, the undersigned, commissaries of Albany, etc., testify and declare, by these presents, that on the date underwritten, before us appeared Hendrick Marcelis, who declares by these presents that in true rights, free ownership, he grants, transfers and makes over to and for the behoof of Robert Sandertse, smith, in his house and lot standing and lying here in Albany, adjoining to the south and east the street, to the north Harmen

Janse Ryckman, and to the west Volkie Jurriaense, widow of the late Jan Van Hoesen,[1] length to the east 5 rods and eight feet, length to the south 9 rods and 11 feet, to the west 4 rods 11 feet, and to the north 9 rods 8 feet 8 inches; by virtue of a patent for a greater lot to him, the grantor, given by the Heer director general and council of New Netherland, of date the 24th of March, sixteen hundred and fifty-four, for which aforesaid house and lot, he, the grantor, acknowledges that he is fully paid and satisfied, the last penny with the first, giving therefore *plenam actionem cessam*, and full power to the aforenamed Robert Sandertse, his heirs and successors or assigns, to dispose thereof as he might do with his own patrimonial effects; promising to protect and free the aforesaid house and lot from all actions and claims of all persons as is right, and never more to do nor suffer anything to be done, against the same, either with or without law, in any manner, on pledge of his person and estate nothing excepted, subject to all laws and judges.

Done in Albany $\frac{13}{23}$ of April, 1667.

This mark ⊤ is set by HENDRICK MARCELIS, aforenamed.

Philip Pieterse.
Richard Van Renselaer.

In my presence, D. V. SCHELLUYNE, Secretary, 1667.

We, the undersigned, commissaries of Albany, etc., testify and declare, by these presents, that on the date underwritten, before us appeared Hendrick Marcelis, who declares that in true rights, free ownership, he grants, transfers and makes over by these presents to and for the behoof of Volckie Jurriaense, widow of Jan Van Hoesen, in a lot lying here in Albany, adjoining to the east Robert Sandertse, to the south the street, to the west Andries de Vos and to the north Harmen Janse Ryckman, length ten rods breadth to the east four rods eight feet, and to the west four rods four feet, by virtue of a patent of a greater lot, of date the 24th of March, 1654; for which he, the grantor, acknowledges that he is fully paid and satisfied, the last penny with the first, and therefore giving *plenam actionem cessam* and full power to the aforenamed Volckie Jurrianse, her heirs and successors, or those who may hereafter receive title from her to do therewith as she might do with her patrimonial effects; promising to protect and free the aforesaid lot from all actions and claims as is right, and further, never more to do nor suffer anything to be done against the same, with or without law in any manner, on pledge of his person and estate, nothing excepted, subject to all laws and judges.

Done in Albany the $\frac{13}{23}$ of April, 1667.

This mark ⊤ is set by HENDRICK MARCELIS, aforenamed.

Abram Staes.
R. V Rensselaer.

In my presence,

D. V. SCHELLUYNE, Secretary, 1667.

---

[1] Jan Franse Van Hoesen was in Beverwyck in 1657.—*Dutch Manuscripts*, XVI 2, 64. Letters of administration were issued to his son, Jurriaen, 2 August 1703, and the following children were then living viz: Jurriaen, oldest son, Jacob, Volkert, Anna, wife of Luykas Gerritse, Styntiers, wife of Jan Tys Goes, Mary, wife of Hendrik Coenraetse Catharina, wife of Frank Hardingh, and Johannes; the latter was an aged man in 1724.—*Deeds*, VI, 199. Volkie Jurriaense, the widow of Jan Franse Van Hoesen, had a lot, in 1677, on the east side of North Pearl street north of Steuben street.—*Deeds*, I, 406.

Appeared before us, the undersigned commissaries, the said Volckie Jurraense, widow of the late Jan Franse Van Hoesen, who declares, by virtue and in consequence of the above standing conveyance by Hendrick Marcelis to her behoof passed, that she grants, transfers and in rights, free ownership makes over by these presents to and for the behoof of Andries de Vos, in the lot in said conveyance mentioned, in length and breadth so bounded, here in Albany as stands expressed and described therein, whereto reference is here made, without the grantor's making the least claim any more thereto; also acknowledging that she is fully paid and satisfied therefor by the hands of said de Vos, the last penny with the first, and therefore giving to him, his heirs and successors or assigns, such right and power as she received from the aforenamed Hendrick Marcelis, with a promise to protect and free the same from all actions, trouble and claims in her behalf as is right; and further, never more to do nor suffer anything to be done against the same, either with or without law, in any manner, on pledge of her person and estate, nothing excepted, subject to all laws and judges.

Done in Albany, the $\frac{13}{23}$ of April 1667.

This mark ∧ ∧ is set by VOLCKIE JURRIAENSE, aforenamed.

Richard Van Rensselaer.
Abram Staes.

In my presence, D. V. SCHELLUYNE, Secretary, 1667.

We, the undersigned, commissaries of Albany, etc., testify and declare, that on the date underwritten, appeared before us Mr. Cornelis Van Nes, old commissary of this jurisdiction, who declares that in true rights, free ownership, he grants, transfers and makes over by these presents, to and for the behoof of Jan Eps son (*Voor soon*) of his present wife, Maritie Damens, in a *bouwery* consisting of two parcels of land, together 21 morgens and 570 rods, lying at Schanechtade, according to patent of the Heer director general and council of New Netherland, of date the 16th of June, 1664, together with a house, lot and also a lot for a garden lying in the hamlet at Schanechtade aforesaid, being both bounded and in length and breadth according to the tenor of the deed of said Heer director general to the behoof of said Van Nes, of date the 20th of April, 1665, *stilo novo*, to which aforesaid patent and deed reference is here made; without the grantor's making the least claim thereto any more. also acknowledging that he is fully paid and satisfied therefor by the hands of said Jan Eps, the last penny with the first, and therefore giving *plenam actionem cessam*, and full power to the aforenamed Jan Van Eps, his heirs and successors or assigns to dispose of the aforesaid *bouwery*, house, lot and garden, as he might do with his own patrimonial lands and effects; promising to protect and free the same, from all actions, trouble and claims, of all persons as is right, and further never more to do, nor suffer anything to be done against the same, either with or without law, in any manner, on pledge of his person and estate, nothing excepted, subject to all laws and judges.

Done in Albany, the $\frac{15}{25}$ of April, 1667.

CORNELIS VAN NES.

Richard Van Rensselaer.
Abram Staes.

In my presence, D. V. SCHELLUYNE, Secretary, 1667.

We, the undersigned, commissaries of Albany, etc., testify and declare, that on the date underwritten, before us came and appeared Willem Janse Schut husbandman in the aforesaid colony, who declared that in true rights, free ownership, he grants, transfers and makes over by these presents, to and for the behoof of Jacob Loockermans, in all the right and action which he has had to the house and lot, at present occupied by him, Loockermans, here in Albany, by virtue of a patent for a greater lot, of date the 25th of October, granted by the Heer director general and council of New Netherland to the widow of the late Gysbert Cornelisse Van Wesop, at present wife of Francois Boon, who transferred her right therein to Andries Herbertse Constapel, of date the 22d of August, 1654, from whom [Andries Herbertse] the grantor received a part of the lot mentioned in the aforesaid patent by purchase and delivery, and by the regulation of the highway a part was taken from said Loockermans on the one side, and on the other side again, a portion was added by the aforementioned Heer director general and commissaries on the 6th of October, 1656, standing endorsed upon the patent so that the aforesaid house and lot stands free enclosed and fenced below the road two rods eight feet and a half, east of the road three rods, south a rod eleven feet, and west two rods seven feet, according to the survey bill of the surveyor Harmen Bastiaense [Visscher], of date the $\frac{13}{23}$ of this month of April; without the grantor's making the least claim to said house and lot any more; also acknowledging that he is fully paid and satisfied therefor by said Jacob Loockermans, and therefore giving to said Loockermans, or his assigns, *plenam actionem cessam*, and full power to dispose thereof as he might do with his patrimonial effects; promising to protect and free the same from all trouble, actions and claims of all persons as is right, and further, never more to do nor suffer anything to be done against the same, either with or without law, in any manner, on pledge of his person and estate, nothing excepted, subject to all laws and judges.

Done in Albany the $\frac{15}{25}$ of April, 1667.

WILLEM JANSEN SCHUDT.

Abram Staes.
Richard Van Rensselaer.

In my presence, D. V. SCHELLUYNE, Secretary, 1667.

We, the undersigned, commissaries of Albany, etc., testify and declare, that on the date underwritten, before us came and appeared Mr. Jan Hendrickse Van Bael, old commissary of this jurisdiction, who declares that in true rights, free ownership, he grants, transfers, and makes over by these presents, to and for the behoof of Gerrit Lansingh,[1] in a certain house and lot which was received by him by purchase at public sale, from Uldrich Cleyn, of date the 22d of July, 1658, and by virtue of a patent for a greater lot granted by the director general and council of New Netherland of date the 25th of October, 1653, and the first of November of the same year, to the aforenamed Uldrich Cleyn, standing and lying here in Albany, adjoining southerly on Symon Groot, northerly the road where Reyer Elbertse is at present, east and west the wagon road, now fenced and enclosed as the

[1] Gerrit Lansingh, late a citizen of Hasselt [*near Zwoll in Overyssell, Holland*] was deceased in 1679. He left the following children: Gerrit, Hendrik, Johannes, Aeltie wife of Gerrit Van Slichtenhorst, Guysbertie wife of Hendrik Rosenboom, and Hilletie wife of the late Storm Vanderzee, *alias* Bratt. – *Deeds*, III, 51.

same was surveyed, to the content of said Lansingh by the surveyor Harman Bastiaense [Visscher] on the $\frac{13}{23}$ of this month of April, according to the survey bill thereof; without the grantor's making the least claim thereto any more, also acknowledging that he is fully paid and satisfied therefor, the last penny with the first [* * * * * erased], therefore giving *plenam actionem cessam*, and full power to the aforenamed Gerrit Lansingh, his heirs and successors or assigns, to dispose of the aforesaid house and lot as he might do with his patrimonial lands and effects; promising to protect and free the same from all trouble, actions and claims of all persons, and further, never more to do nor suffer anything to be done against the same, either with or without law, in any manner, on pledge of his person and estate, nothing excepted, subject to all laws and judges.

Done in Albany, the $\frac{15}{25}$ of April, 1667

JAN H. VAN BAEL.

Richard Van Rensselaer.
Abram Staes.

In my presence,

D. V. SCHELLUYNE, Secretary, 1667.

Notwithstanding, Van Bael acknowledges, according to the above conveyance, that he is fully paid and satisfied, Gerrit Lansing remains indebted for the house and lot sixty-two guilders and thirteen stuivers in beavers, which he promises to pay at next business season [*handeltyt*], pledging therefor his person and estate, and especially the aforesaid house and lot to secure the payment thereof if need be.

Done in Albany, of date as above.

GERRIT LANSINCK.

In my presence,

D. V. SCHELLUYNE, Secretary, 1667.

Jan Van Bael acknowledges, that he is fully paid and satisfied for the above mentioned sum, and the foregoing mortgage deed is hereby cancelled and erased.

Done in Albany the $\frac{29}{8}$ August, September, 1667.

JAN VAN BAEL.

[The above mortgage is erased.]

We, the undersigned, commissaries of Albany, etc., testify and declare, that on the date underwritten, before us came and appeared Wouter Aertse, wheelwright here, as holding the right and claim of Pieter Meese Vrooman according to patent by the Heer director general and council of New Netherland, to him, Pieter Meese, granted, of date the 31st of October, 1658, who declares that in true rights, free ownership, he grants, transfers and by these presents makes over to and for the behoof of Geurt Hendrickse [Van Schoonhoven],[1] master carpenter here, in a lot for a house and a

[1] Guert Hendrik Van Schoonhoven had a farm on "Cahoos Island in 1681," and was of "*Halve Maen*" in 1675. He died the 12 Jan., 1702.—*Albany Church Records.* In his will, made 20 Aug., 1700, he speaks of his wife Maritie Cornelise and the following children: Jacobus eldest son, Hendrik, Margaret, Hendrikie, Geertruy, Jacomyntje.

garden lying here in Albany, at present occupied and possessed by the aforenamed Geurt Henderickse, in length, breadth and boundaries according to the tenor and purport of the aforesaid patent, without the grantor's having the least claim thereto any more, also acknowledging that he is fully paid and satisfied therefor by the hands of the aforenamed Geurt Henderickse, the last penny with the first, and therefore giving to said Geurt Hendrickse, his heirs and successors or assigns, *plenam actionem cessam*, and full power to dispose of said lot and garden, with the barn thereon standing, as he could do with his patrimonial land and effects; promising to protect and free the same from all trouble, claims and actions of all persons as is right, and further never more to do nor suffer anything to be done against the same either with or without law, in any manner, on pledge of his person and estate, nothing excepted, subject to all laws and judges.

Done in Albany, the $\frac{16}{26}$ of April, 1667.

PIETER MEESE VROOMAN.

This mark + is set by WOUTER AERTSE,[1] aforesaid.

Richard Van Rensselaer.

Philip Pieterse.

In my presence,

D. V. SCHELLUYNE, Secretary, 1667.

We, the undersigned, commissaries of Albany, etc., testify and declare, that on the date underwritten, before us came and appeared Captain Abram Staas, old commissary, who declares by virtue of a patent, of date the 25th of October 1653 by the Heer director general and council of New Netherland to him granted, that in true rights, free ownership, he grants transfers and makes over by these presents to Mr. Philip Pieterse Schuyler, also commissary of this jurisdiction, in a certain lot here in Albany, whereon said Schuyler has built his house, extending west to the lot of Ruth Jacobse, deceased, between which lots there is a path of five feet in breadth, from the path westward six rods and two feet, and southward twelve rods (besides which there was granted to said Schuyler by the Heeren commissaries in the year 1659, eight feet of ground westward on which his Indian house now stands); without the grantor's making the least claim thereto any more, also acknowledging that he is fully paid and satisfied therefor by the hands of said Schuyler, the last penny with the first, and therefore giving *plenam actionem cessam*, and full power to said Schuyler, his heirs and successors or assigns, to dispose thereof as he might do with his patrimonial lands and effects; promising to protect and free the aforesaid lot from all trouble, claims and actions of all persons as is right, and further, never more to do nor suffer anything to be done against the same, either with or without law, in any manner, under pledge of his person and estate, nothing excepted, subject to all laws and judges.

Done in Albany, the $\frac{17}{27}$ of April, 1667.

ABRAM STAES.

Goosen Gerretsen.

R. V. Rensselaer.

In my presence,

D. V. SCHELLUYNE, Secretary, 1667.

---

[1] Wouter Aertse Van Nieukerck.

We, the undersigned, commissaries of Albany, etc., testify and declare. that on the date underwritten, came and appeared before us D°. Gideon Schaets,[1] minister of the gospel of this place, who declares that in true rights, free ownership, he grants, transfers and makes over by these presents, to and for the behoof of Philip Pieterse Schuyler, commissary of this jurisdiction, in a lot lying between the Heer Rensselaer's garden, and begins at the *clapborden* of Abram Pieterse [Vosburgh], adjoining to the east a cartway, south also a road, and west a low lot, south breadth four rods and length ten rods, according to patent, to him granted by the Heer director general and council of New Netherland, of date the 22d of September, 1653, without the grantor's making the least claim thereto any more, also acknowledging that he is fully paid and satisfied therefor by the hands of the aforenamed Schuyler, the last penny with the first, and therefore giving *plenam actionem cessam*, and full power to the aforesaid Schuyler, his heirs and successors or assigns, to dispose thereof as he might do with his patrimonial lands and effects; promising to protect and free the aforesaid lot in his behoof from all trouble, claims, and actions of each and every person, and further, never more to do nor suffer anything to be done against the same, either with or without law, in any manner, on pledge of his person and estate, nothing excepted, subject to all laws and judges.

Done in Albany this $\frac{14}{24}$ of April, 1667.

GIDEON SCHAETS.

Abram Staes.
Goosen Gerritsen.

In my presence,

D. V. SCHELLUYNE, Secretary, 1667.

We, the undersigned, commissaries of Albany, etc., testify and declare, that on the date underwritten, before us came and appeared Andries De Vos, father-in-law of Cornelis Vos, who declares that in true rights, free ownership, he grants, transfers and makes over by these presents, to and for the behoof of Jurriaen Theunisse Glacsemaecker, in a lot lying here in Albany, at present occupied and built upon by said Jurriaen Theunisse, adjoining to the east of Barent Van Marle, in length seven rods, and with the consent of the Heeren [commissaries,] one rod to the kil, along the kil breadth two rods five feet, along the street length eight rods, in front breadth as the house stands, according to the survey bill of the surveyor, Jan Roeloffse; by virtue of a patent of a greater lot granted to the aforenamed Cornelis Vos, by the Heer director general and council of New Netherland, of date the 23d of April, 1652, also according to bill of sale, by the aforenamed Cornelis Vos, and said Jurriaen Theunisse, subscribed of date the 10th of August, 1662; without the said Cornelis Vos, or the grantor's making the least claim thereto any more in their behalf, also the grantor acknowledges that Cornelis Vos, before his departure for Holland, was fully paid and satisfied therefor by the aforenamed Jurriaen Theunisse, and therefore promising to protect and free the said lot from all actions and claims of every person for said Cornelis Vos, as is right, to the behoof of said Jurriaen Theunisse, his heirs and succes-

[1] For an account see *Annals of Albany* 1, 87, 95, 104, etc.

sors or assigns, and further, never more to do, nor suffer anything to be done against the same, either with or without law, in any manner, on pledge of his person and estate, nothing excepted, subject to all laws and judges.

Done in Albany, the $\frac{18}{28}$ of April, 1667

ANDRYES DE VOS.

Abram Staes.
Philip Pieterse Schuyler.

In my presence,

D. V. SCHELLUYNE, Secretary, 1667

We, the undersigned, commissaries of Albany, etc testify and declare, that on the date underwritten, before us came and appeared Mr. Philip Pieterse Schuyler, commissary of the same jurisdiction, who declares that in true rights, free ownership, he grants, transfers and makes over by these presents to and for the behoof of Jan De Noorman, in a lot on which his house has stood, which house he has removed by virtue of a conveyance, of date the 11th of September, 1664, by Pieter Adriaense [Soogemackelyck], to the behoof of said Schuyler passed; adjoining to the north, Adriaen Appel, and to the south Jan Barentse Poest, deceased, here in Albany, length ten rods and breadth four rods, without the grantor's making the least claim any more thereto, also acknowledging that he is fully paid and satisfied therefor through the hands of said Jan De Noorman, the last penny with the first, and therefore giving *plenam actionem cessam*, and full power to the aforenamed Jan De Noorman, his heirs and successors or assigns, to dispose thereof, as he might do with his own patrimonial effects; promising to protect and free the aforesaid lot in his behalf, from all trouble, actions and claims of each and every person as is right, and further, never more to do nor suffer any thing to be done against the same, either with or without law, in any manner, on pledge of his person and estate, nothing excepted, subject to all laws and judges.

Done in Albany the $\frac{18}{28}$ of April 1667.

PHILIP PIETERSE SCHUYLER.

Goosen Gerritse.
Abram Staes.

In my presence,

D. V. SCHELLUYNE, Secretary, 1667.

We, the undersigned, commissaries of Albany, etc., testify and declare, by these presents that on the date underwritten before us came and appeared Femmetie Alberts, widow of of Hendrick Janse Westercamp, dwelling in the Esopus, but now being at this place, who declares that in true rights, free ownership, she grants, transfers, and makes over by these presents to and for the behoof of Daniel Rinchout, baker, in her certain house and lot standing and lying here in Albany, at present occupied by the said Rinchout, being the same house and lot, in length, breadth, and boundaries according to the tenor and purport of the survey bill of the surveyor, and by virtue of a patent of a greater lot granted by the Heeren director general and council of New Netherland of date the 23d of April, 1652, to which reference is herein made, without the grantor's making the least claim any more to the same, also acknowledging that she is fully paid and satisfied therefor by the hands of said Rinchout, the last penny with the first, according to the bill of sale passed before the secretary Dirk Van Hamel,[1] deceased, of date the 8th of March, 1660, and therefore giving to the aforenamed Rinchout, his heirs and successors or assigns, full right and power to dispose of the aforesaid house and lot, as he might do with his own patrimonial lands and effects; promising to protect and free the aforesaid house and lot from all trouble, actions and claims of each and every person as is right, and further, never more to do nor suffer anything to be done against the same, either with or without law, in any manner, on pledge of his person and estate, nothing excepted, subject to all laws and judges.

Done in Albany the $\frac{1}{2}\frac{2}{3}$ of April, 1667.

This + mark is set by FEMMETIE ALBERTS, aforenamed.

Philip Pieterse.
R. V. Rensselaer.

In my presence,

D. V. SCHELLUYNE, Secretary, 1667

We, the undersigned, commissaries of Albany, etc., testify and declare, by these presents, that on the date underwritten, before us came and appeared Mr. Adriaen Van Ilpendam, attorney for Albert Gerritse, dwelling in the Esopus, who declares in his aforesaid character that in true rights, free ownership, he grants, transfers, and makes over by these presents, to and for the behoof of Jan Janssen Van Eeckelen, in a certain house and lot standing and lying here in Albany, by virtue of a patent granted by the Heeren director general and council of New Netherland, of date the 23d of April, 1652, to the aforenamed Albert Gerritse, a part of which was transferred to Jan Van Aecken, and by said Van Aecken to Gerrit Baucker, with whom the survey bill of the surveyor remains; also according to bill of sale of date the 3d of March, 1660, passed between the aforenamed Albert Gerritse, and said Van Eeckelen; without the grantor's (in his aforesaid character) making the least claim any more to said house and lot, also acknowledging that he is fully paid and satisfied by the hands of said Van Eeckelen, the last penny with the first, and therefore giving to the aforenamed Van Eeckelen his heirs and successors and assigns *plenam actionem cessam*, and full power to dispose thereof as he might do with his patrimonial lands and effects; promising in his aforesaid character to protect and free the aforesaid house and lot from all trouble, claims and actions, as is right, and further, never more to do nor suffer anything to be done against the same, with or without law, in any manner, on pledge of his person (in his aforesaid character), and estate, nothing excepted, subject to all laws and judges.

Done in Albany, the $\frac{2}{3}\frac{9}{0}$ of April, 1667.

ADRIAEN VAN ILPENDAM.

R. V. Rensselaer.
Philip Pieterse Schuyler.

In my presence,

D. V. SCHELLUYNE, Secretary, 1667.

[1] Dirck Van Hamel was town clerk of Rensselaerwyck in 1656.

Notwithstanding the aforewritten conveyance before passed, Jan Van Eeckelen acknowledges *per resto* on the aforesaid house and lot, that he is indebted according to a settlement had with Mr. Adriaen Van Ilpendam in the sum or quantity of thirty good whole merchantable beaver skins, which he promises to pay punctually in the month of July, next coming, without longer delay, for which pledging his person and estate, personal and real, nothing excepted, and specially the aforesaid house and lot, to secure the payment if need be, without loss and cost.

Done in Albany, *datum ut supra.*

JAN JANSSEN VAN EECKEL.

In my presence,

D. V. SCHELLUYNE, Secretary, 1667.

We, the undersigned, commissaries of Albany, etc., testify and declare, that upon the date underwritten, before us came and appeared Huybert Janse [De Vroome],[1] dwelling here in Albany, who declares that in true rights, free ownership he grants, conveys and makes over by these presents, to and for the behoof of Cornelis Van Nes, husband and guardian of Maritie Damens, last widow of Hendrick Andriesse [Van Doesburgh], as holding the right and title of Philip Hendrickse Brouwer in a certain lot, length seventy-three wood feet, breadth on the east side thirty feet, and on the west side breadth between twenty-six and twenty-seven feet as it stands in fence, according to contract, of date the 6th of March, 1659, likewise according to deed of conveyance for the grantor, of date $\frac{9}{19}$ of April, of this year, to his behoof passed by Jurriaen Janse Groenewout, husband and guardian of Maritie Thomase, last widow of the late Cornelis Theunise Bos, to all of which reference is here made; without the grantor's making the least claim thereto any more, also acknowledging that he is paid and satisfied therefor by the hands of the aforenamed Philip Hendrickse, the last penny with the first, and therefore giving to the aforenamed Van Nes, his heirs and successors or assigns, such right and power to dispose thereof as he might do with his own patrimonial effects; promising to protect and free said lot from all trouble, claims and actions of each and every person as is right, and further, never more to do nor suffer anything to be done against the same, with or without law, in any manner, on pledge of his person and estate, nothing excepted, subject to all laws and judges.

Done in Albany the $\frac{23 \text{ April}}{2 \text{ May}}$ 1667.

This mark is set by HUYBERT JANSE, aforenamed.

R. V. Rensselaer.
Teunis Cornelisse.

In my presence,

D. V. SCHELLUYNE, Secretary, 1667.

Appeared likewise the aforenamed Cornelis Van Nes, who declares in his aforesaid character, that he grants and conveys the abovenamed lot in free ownership to and for the behoof of Henderick Gerritse Vermeulen,

---

[1] Huybert Janse in 1677 owned a lot in Maiden lane next east of Harmen Gansevoort's, where Stanwix Hall now stands.—*Deeds*, I, 355.

master tailor, with such right and title as the aforesaid Huybert Janse has conveyed to him, also acknowledging, that he is fully paid and satisfied therefor; and promising never more to do nor suffer anything to be done against the same, under a like pledge and subjection as above.

Done in Albany, *datum ut supra.*

CORNELIS VAN NES.

R. V. Rensselaer.
Teunis Cornelisse.

In my presence,

D. V. SCHELLUYNE, Secretary, 1667.

Henderick Gerritse Vermeulen declares, by these presents, and in accordance with the above standing conveyance, that he grants, and makes over to the behoof of Arent Janssen, carpenter, here in Albany, his heirs and successors or assigns, with such right and title as was conveyed by Huybert Janse, in the foregoing conveyance, to Cornelis Van Nes, and by said Van Nes, as having the right and title of Philip Hendrickse Brouwer, to the grantor; without the grantor's making the least claim thereto any more, also acknowledging that he is fully paid therefor, and moreover, promising never more to do, nor suffer anything to be done, against the same, under the like pledge and subjection, as is mentioned in the aforesaid conveyance.

Done in Albany, *datum ut supra.*

HENDRICK GERRITSE.

R. V. Rensselaer.
Teunis Cornelisse.

Although the foregoing conveyances were before delivered, yet Henderick Gerritse Vermeulen acknowledges that in respect to the remaining purchase money for the aforesaid lot, due to the aforesaid Philip Henderickse or now to said Van Nes, he is justly indebted one hundred and nine guilders in beavers; and Arent Janse, carpenter, in like manner to Hendrick Gerritse [Vermeulen is indebted] nine beavers; so he, Hendrick Gerritse, assigns over to said Van Nes, the said nine beavers due from said Arent Janse, which said Arent Janse not only assents to by these presents, and said nine beavers promises to pay within six months from this date, but especially pledges and mortgages, therefor, the aforesaid lot, and house thereon standing, and further, pledges generally his person and estate, nothing excepted, subject to all laws and judges, to secure the payment thereof if need be, without cost or loss; and for as much as Henderick Gerritse furthermore remains indebted also to Van Nes for a balance of eighty-seven guilders in beavers, he promises honestly and justly to pay him the same, also within the time of six months after this date, under pledge of his person and estate, nothing excepted, subject as before.

Done in Albany, of date as above.

HINDRICK GERRITSE.
ARENT JANSE.

R. V. Rensselaer.
Teunis Cornelisse.

In my presence.

D. V. SCHELLUYNE, Secretary, 1667.

[On the margin of the above mortgage is the following note by the hand of Dirk Van Schelluyne.]

It appears to me, by the acquittance of Cornelis Van Nes, that Arent Janse, the carpenter, paid the nine beavers, mentioned herein, on the 24th of July, 1668, whereby this mortgage is cancelled.

We, the undersigned, commissaries of Albany, etc., testify and declare, that before us came and appeared, Mr. Gerard Swart, *schout* of this court, for himself, and to relieve and herein to act for Captain Abram Staes both together attorneys for Mr. Pieter Hartgers, and declares in said character, that he grants, conveys, and in true rights, free ownership, makes over to and for the behoof of Hendrick Cuyler, in the aforesaid Hartger's house and lot, standing and lying here in Albany, in consequence and by virtue of a contract therefor, of date the 27th of February, 1664; as the same house and lot stands fenced, enclosed and bounded on the hill, according to the tenor of said contract to which reference is here made; without the grantor's (in his aforesaid character) making the least claim thereto any more, also acknowledging that he is fully paid and satisfied therefor, by the hands of Hendrick Cuyler, the last penny with the first, and therefore giving *plenam actionem cessam*, and full power to said Cuyler, his heirs, successors or assigns, to dispose thereof as he might do with his patrimonial effects; and promising in his said character, to protect and free the aforesaid house and lot from all trouble, claims and actions of each and every person, as is right and further, never more to do nor suffer anything to be done against the same, either with or without law, in any manner, on pledge of his person and estate, nothing excepted subject to all laws and judges.

Done in Albany, the 24 April / 2 May, 1667. G. SWART.

Philip Pieterse Schuyler.

Teunis Cornelisse.

In my presence, D. V. SCHELLUYNE, Secretary, 1667.

Notwithstanding the above standing conveyance to the behoof of Hendrick Cuyler passed, he yet acknowledges that he is justly indebted for the last two payments of purchase money, due for the above standing house and lot, amounting together to the sum of five hundred and sixty-six guilders, and to be paid in good whole beavers, which sum said Cuyler promises to pay to said attorney on the first occasion of a demand being made, pledging and especially mortgaging said house and lot therefor, that the payment thereof may be secured, if need be, without loss or cost, and on a further pledge of his person and estate, nothing excepted, subject to all laws and judges.

Done in Albany, of date as above.

HENDRICK CUYLER.

In my presence,

D. V. SCHELLUYNE, Secretary, 1667.

We, the undersigned, commissaries of Albany, etc., testify and declare, that on the date underwritten, the Heer Jeremias Van Rensselaer, director of said colony in true rights, free ownership, grants and conveys by these presents in a little strip (*stroockie*) of a lot and garden behind the lot on which the horse mill and mill house stood, to and for the behoof of Jan

Evertse, schoemaker as he received said lot by purchase and conveyance from Willem Bout, according to the deed thereof, of date, the 18th of November, 1662, lying here in Albany, next to the house and lot conveyed by Theunis Cornelisse to said Jan Evertse, without the grantor's making the least claim thereto; also acknowledging that he is fully paid and satisfied therefor and promising never more to do nor suffer any thing to be done against the same in any manner, on pledge according to law.

Done in Albany the $\frac{25}{5}$ $\frac{\text{Apr'l}}{\text{May}}$, 1667.

J. V. RENSSELAER.

R. V. Rensselaer.
Teunis Cornelisse.

In my presence, D. V. SCHELLUYNE, Secretary, 1667

Appeared before us, underwritten commissaries of Albany etc , Philip Pieterse Schuyler and Dirck Van Schelluyne, as trustees of the estate of the late Cornelis Bogardus who declare that in true rights, free ownership they grant, convey and make over, by these presents, to and for the behoof of Jan Vinhagen, in the house and lot of the aforesaid Bogardus, standing and lying here in Albany, at present occupied by said Vinhagen, by virtue and in consequence of the contract of date the $\frac{5}{15}$ September, 1666, and of further evidences thereof, without the grantors' (in their aforesaid character) making the least claim thereto any more, also acknowledging that they are fully paid and satisfied therefor (through Jan Janse Bleecker, which payment is made in part, and further the remainder (?) must be made to said Jan Janse Bleecker, according to the tenor and contents of the aforesaid contract by which according to sentence [of the court] Jan Janse Bleecker is preferred), and therefore giving *plenam actionem cessam*, and perfect power to said Vinhagen, his heirs and successors or assigns, to use and possess in full ownership, the aforesaid house and lot as he might do with his own patrimonial effects; promising to protect and free said house as is right, from all trouble, claims and actions. and further, never more to do nor suffer anything to be done against the same, in any manner, on pledge of their respective persons and estates in their aforesaid character.

Done in Albany the $\frac{27}{7}$ $\frac{\text{Apr'l}}{\text{May}}$, 1667.

PHILIP PIETERSE SCHUYLER.
D. V. SCHELLUYNE, 1667.

R. V. Rensselaer
A. Van Curler.

Acknowledged before me,

G. SWART, *schout* at Albany.

Pursuant to the aforesaid conveyance and contract, Jan Vinhagen also acknowledges that he is indebted *per resto* in the quantity of fifty beavers or their value, according to the contents of said contract, promising to pay said sum at the set time, as the contract mentions, therefor pledging as a special mortgage, the aforesaid house and lot, and further, generally his person and estate, nothing excepted, subject to all laws and judges, to secure the payment thereof, if need be, without loss and cost.

Done in Albany of date as above.

JAN VINHAEGHEN.

Acknowledged before me,

G. SWART, *schout* at Albany, etc.

Appeared before us, the underwritten commissaries of Albany, etc., Carsten Carstense Noorman, who declares by these presents that in true rights, free ownership, he grants, conveys, and makes over, to and for the behoof of Claes Theunisse [*alias* Uylenspiegel]; in a lot lying behind Fort Albany, west the aforenamed Claes Theunisse, length six rods, south breadth three rods, east a low lot length six rods, north the road breadth three rods, according to the survey bill thereof of the surveyor Jan Roeloffse; as the aforesaid lot has been possessed, by grant of the Heeren commissaries many years, but as it appears, not as yet found registered; without the grantor's making the least claim thereto any more, also acknowledging that he is fully paid and satisfied therefor by the hands of Claes Theunisse, the last penny with the first, and therefor giving *plenam actionem cessam*, and full power to the aforesaid Claes Theunisse, his heirs and successors or assigns, to dispose thereof as he might do with his patrimonial effects; promising to protect and free the said lot from all trouble, actions and claims of all persons, as is right, and further, never more to do, nor suffer anything to be done against the same, either with or without law, in any manner, on pledge according to law.

Done in Albany 27 April / 7 May, 1667.

This mark /\ /\ /\ is set by CARSTEN CARSTENSE NOORMAN, aforesaid.

R. V. Rensselaer.
Teunise Cornelisse.

In my presence,

D. V. SCHELLUYNE, Secretary, 1667.

We, the undersigned, commissaries of Albany, etc, testify and declare, that before us came and appeared the honorable Sander Leendertse Glen, dwelling at Schanectade, who deliberately declares that by donation *inter-vivos* and free gift among the living, in true rights, free ownership, he grants, conveys and makes over by these presents, to and for the behoof of his three sons, namely. Jacob, Sander, and Johannes Sandertse Glen, in a certain parcel [1] of land lying between the lake and the river, over against the village of Schanechtade, consisting of fifty morgens, according to patent thereof, of date .... and therefore releasing the same forever for the behoof as above, for good reasons, and good services received by the subscriber; promising never more to do nor suffer anything to be done against the same, with or without law, in any manner, on pledge of his person and estate, nothing excepted, subject to all laws and judges.

Done in Albany the 11/21 of May, 1667.

SANDER LENRES GLEN.

A. Van Curler.
R. V. Rensselaer.

We, the undersigned, commissaries of Albany, etc., declare that on the day underwritten, before us came and appeared Jacques Cornelisse Van Slyck, dwelling at Schanectade. who acknowledges that he is well

[1] This parcel of land lies in the town of Glenville on the north bank of the Mohawk river, between that and the Round or Sanders lake. A portion of this land belongs to the Sanders family, who are descendants from Sander Leendertse Glen on the female side.

and truly indebted to Mr. Jan Hendrickse Van Bael, old commissary, in the sum of four hundred and fifty five guilders and six stuivers, growing out of goods to his content received according to obligation by the subscriber passed the 3d of January, 1666, to be paid in beavers, reckoned at eight guilders a piece, which aforesaid sum of *f* 455.6 the subscriber shall pay with the consent of said Van Bael, within the time of four years next following, with interest on the same at ten to the hundred, to commence on this date and to run till the final payment, nor under the pretext of paying interest shall the aforesaid capital sum be kept longer than four years, except at the pleasure of Van Bael, or the lawful bearer of this paper; for which the subscriber specially pledges and mortgages his *bouwery* lying at Schanechtade aforesaid as the subscriber now possesses it, and also his person and estate, personal and real, present and future, nothing excepted, subject to all laws and judges, to secure the payment without cost or loss.

Done in Albany the $\frac{6}{16}$ of July, 1667.

ACKES.

R. V. Rensselaer.
Abram Staes.

Acknowledged before me,

D. V. SCHELLUYNE, Secretary, 1667.

Appeared before us, the undersigned, commissaries of Albany, etc., the Heer Jeremias Van Rensselaer, as trustee of the estate of the late Jan Bastiaense Van Gutsenhoven, who declares by these presents that in true rights, free ownership, he grants, conveys, and makes over to and for the behoof of Mr. Jan Hendrick Bruyns, in two certain gardens lying in fence behind Fort Albany, by virtue and in consequence of a deed of conveyence by Sander Leendertse Glen, to the behoof of the aforenamed Gutsenhoven, passed on the 25th of October 1662, before the late Heer vice director and *commys* La Montagne in the presence of two commissaries, without the grantor's (in his aforesaid character), making the least claim any more thereto, as it appears that on the 14th of December, 1665, said Gutsenhoven was fully paid therefor by the sum of one hundred and twenty guilders by said Bruyns, and therefore giving *plenam actionem cessam*, and full power to said Bruyns, his heirs and successors or assigns, to dispose of said two gardens as he might do with his own patrimonial lands and effects; promising in his aforesaid character [of trustee,] to protect and free said gardens from all actions and claims of every person, and never more to do nor suffer anything to be done against the same, either with or without law, in any manner, on pledge of his person and estate, nothing excepted subject to all laws and judges.

Done in Albany the $\frac{6}{16}$ of July, 1667.

JEREMIAS VAN RENSSELAER.

Abram Staes.
R. V. Rensselaer.

In my presence,

D. V. SCHELLUYNE, Secretary, 1667.

Appeared before us, the undersigned, commissaries of Albany, etc. Messrs. Pieter Bogardus and Jonas Bogardus, for themselves, and as attorneys for Pieter Hartgers, Mr. Johannes Van Brugh, Sara Roeloffse, widow of the late Mr. Hans Kierstede in his life time, chirurgeon, Jan Roeloffse, William Bogardus, and on the part of the widow of the late Cornelis Bogardus, all children and heirs of their mother, Annetie Bogardus,[1] who declare, by reason of the bill of sale, of date the 21st of June, 1663, passed before the clerk, Johannes Provoost and certain witnesses, and by virtue of a patent granted first by the Heer director general and council of New Netherland, of date the 23d of April, 1652, and again on the 10th of this month of July, by the right honorable, the governor general Richard Nicolls, that, in true rights, free ownership, they grant, convey, and make over by these presents to and for the behoof of Dirck Wesselse [Ten Broeck], in the aforenamed Annetie Bogardus's certain house and lot standing and lying here in Albany, and occupied by said Dirck Wesselse, bounded, built upon, and enclosed both in breadth and length according to the tenor and contents of said bill of sale to which reference is here made, without the grantors' having the least claim thereto any more, likewise acknowledging that they are fully paid and satisfied therefor, the last penny with the first, and therefore giving *plenam actionem cessam*, and full power to the aforesaid Dirck Wesselse, his heirs and successors or assigns, to dispose of the aforesaid house and lot as he could do with his patrimonial effects; promising to protect and free the same from all trouble, actions, liens, and claims of every person, as is right, and further, never more to do nor suffer anything to be done against the same, either with or without law, in any manner, on pledge of his person and estate, nothing excepted, subject to all laws and judges.

Done in Albany the $\frac{17}{27}$ of July, 1667.

PIETER BOGARDUS.
JONAS BOGARDUS.

Teunis Cornelisse.
Abram Staes.

In my presence,

D. V. SCHELLUYNE, Secretary, 1667.

Appeared before us, the undersigned, commissioners of Albany, etc., the honorable Dirck Hesselingh and Eytie Hendrickse, newly married folks, dwelling here in Albany, who declare in presence of Jan Coster Van Aecken (late guardian of said Eytie Hendrickse from the year 1655, the time when she with her three sisters were taken prisoners by the wild barbarians on the land of Van der Donck,[2] on the east side of the North river, until her marriage state), that they appoint and empower by these presents, Mr. Samuel Van Goedenhuysen, merchant at New Haven in New England, specially to ask and demand of Mr. Ling, also merchant there, a girl named Albrechie Hendrixe, sister of the aforesaid Ytie Hendrixs, about seventeen or eighteen years old, who, with her and her two other sisters, was also taken prisoner by the Indians, and for a long time has been kept there, and only through God's mercy has arrived among Christians at New Haven, as they, the subscribers, are certainly informed; the aforesaid Aelbrechie, having received from her present aforesaid master, the same very speedily to send up to Manhatans or New York by the bearer of this, Claes Lock, to the end that she may as soon as possible reach

[1] This is the celebrated Anneke Janse.

[2] Now Yonkers.—*O'Callaghan's History of New Netherland*, I, 382; II, 551.

her aforesaid sister, Ytie Hendrickse, here in Albany; and in case of unwillingness (without hope), to make the matter known to the judge there, and to seek for and solicit a favorable result; and further all things to do, act and perform in the matter which he may deem needful and proper; promising at all times with thankful hearts to hold good and true all that shall be done and performed in the matter aforesaid by the aforenamed Mr Goedenhuysen in virtue of this paper, without any opposition, on pledge according to law

Done in Albany $\frac{28}{7}$ $\frac{\text{Oct.}}{\text{Nov.}}$, 1667.

DIRCK HESSELINGH.
YTIE HENDERICKSE.
JAN COSTER.

R. V. Rensselaer.
J. Dehinsse.

Acknowledged before me,

D. V. SCHELLUYNE, Secretary, 1667.

Appeared before us, underwritten, commissaries of Albany, etc., Mr. Andries Teller, merchant here, who acknowledges, that he is well and truely indebted to Jurriaen Theunisse, glazier, in the quantity of ninety good merchantable beavers reckoned at eight guilders a piece, growing out of the matter of the last installment, for the purchase and payment of a certain house and lot bought from him by the subscriber, according to the contract therefor, of date the $\frac{7}{17}$ August last, which aforesaid sum of ninety beavers the subscriber [Teller] according to the tenor and contents thereof promises to pay punctually on the $\frac{7}{17}$ of August next coming, therefor pledging specially the aforesaid house and lot and generally his person and estate, personal and real, present and future, nothing excepted, subject to all laws and judges.

Done in Albany, the $\frac{12}{22}$ November, 1667.

A. TELLER.

Philip Pieterse Schuyler.
J. Dehinsse.

Acknowledged before me,

D. V. SCHELLUYNE, Secretary, 1667.

Appeared before us, underwritten, commissaries of Albany, etc., Jurriaen Theunisse Glasemaecker, who declares that in true rights, free ownership, he grants, conveys, and makes over by these presents, to and for the behoof of Andries Tailler,[1] merchant here, his heirs and successors or assigns, the grantor's certain lot and house and stable thereon built, standing and lying here in Albany (at present in possession of said Teller), by virtue of a conveyance by Andries de Vos, passed to his behoof, of date the $\frac{18}{28}$ of April, last, and the survey bill thereof by the surveyor, and according to the patent of the right honorable governor general, of date the 24th day of April, old style, given to him, the grantor, and further, in consequence of a contract for the aforesaid house and lot, of date the $\frac{7}{17}$ of August last,

---

[1] Andries Teller was the oldest child of William Teller. He was born in 1642, and on the 6th of May, 1671, married Sophia Van Cortland, daughter of Oloff Stevense Van Cortland of New York. For many years he was a merchant and magistrate in Albany, but about the year 1698, the whole family removed to New York, save his brother Johannes. He made his will 1702, and died the next year, leaving a son Andries, and daughter Margarita.

all of which are delivered over herewith to said Teller, and respecting the boundaries, length and breadth of said house and lot referring to the said deeds, acknowledging that he is fully paid and satisfied for the aforesaid house and lot through the hands of said Teller, with the sum of ninety beavers received by him to his content, and with a mortgage of like sum according to the tenor of the aforesaid contract; without the grantor's making the least claim any more on the same, and therefore giving *plenam actionem cessam*, and full power to said Teller, and his heirs, to dispose thereof as he might do with his own patrimonial effects; promising to protect and free said house and lot from all trouble, actions and claims of every person as is right, and further, never more to do nor suffer anything to be done against the same, either with or without law, in any manner, on pledge, according to law.

Done in Albany the $\frac{1}{2}\frac{2}{2}$ of November, 1667.

JUREJAN TUNSEN.

Philip Pieterse Schuyler.
J. Dehinsse.

Acknowledged before me,

D. V. SCHELLUYNE, Secretary, 1667.

Appeared before us, undersigned, commissaries of Albany, etc., Lodovicus Cobes, court messenger of the college of the aforesaid commissaries, who declares by these presents that in true rights, free ownership, he grants, conveys and makes over to and for the behoof of Jan Clute, in his certain lot, granted him by the above mentioned commissaries, being allotment No. 4, breadth in front on the street thirty-six and a half feet, length six rods westward, lying here in Albany on the hill, adjoining to the south the lot of Geertruy Vosburgh[1] being No. 3, and to the north the lot of Willem Bout, being No. 5, and easterly the street, and to the west the public lands; by virtue of the aforesaid grant and a patent from the right honorable the governor general, of date the 6th of September last, together with such rights and immunities as were before received by said grantor; acknowledging that he is fully paid and satisfied therefor by the exchange of a house and lot, lying here in Albany, for said lot, by said Jan Clute, passed in like manner on the date hereof; giving, therefore, *plenam actionem cessam*, and full power to the aforenamed Jan Clute, his heirs and successors or assigns, to dispose thereof as he might do with his own patrimonial effects; promising further to protect and free the aforesaid lot from all trouble, actions and claims of each and every person as is right, and never more to do, nor suffer any thing to be done, either with or without law, in any manner, on pledge of his person and estate, personal and real, nothing excepted, subject to all laws and judges.

Done in Albany the $\frac{23}{3}$ $\frac{\text{Nov.}}{\text{Dec.}}$, 1667.

LUDOVICUS COBES.

Goosen Gerritson.
R. V. Rensselaer.

Acknowledged before me,

D. V. SCHELLUYNE, Secretary, 1667.

---

[1] She was the widow of Abraham Pieterse Vosburgh deceased.

Appeared before us, undersigned, commissaries of Albany etc., Mr. Jan Clute, merchant here, who declares that in true rights, free ownership he grants, conveys and makes over by these presents, to and for the behoof of Ludovicus Cobes, court messenger, in his certain house and lot standing and lying here in Albany, in length, breadth and boundaries as he received it by conveyance from Willem Bout, of date the 27/6 Aug./Sept. 1666, to which reference is here made, and according to patent of the right honorable governor general of date the 1st of April, 1666, the grantor acknowledging that he is fully paid and satisfied therefor through the hands of said Ludovicus Cobes, with a lot to him conveyed, on the date hereof, lying here in Albany on the hill, being No. 4, according to the conveyance thereof, and therefore giving *plenam actionem cessam*, and full power to the aforesaid Ludovicus Cobes, his heirs and successors or assigns, to dispose thereof as he might do with his own patrimonial effects; promising to protect and free the aforesaid house and lot from all trouble, actions and claims of all persons as is right, and further, never more to do nor suffer anything to be done against the same, either with or without law, in any manner, on pledge of his person and estate, nothing excepted, subject to all laws and judges.

Done in Albany the 23/3 Nov./Dec., 1667.

JOHANNES CLUTE.

Goosen Gerritse.
R. V. Rensselaer.

Acknowledged before me,

D. V. SCHELLUYNE, Secretary, 1667.

We, the commissaries of Albany, etc., declare by these presents, that in true rights, free ownership, we grant, convey and make over by these presents, to and for the behoof of Jan Coster Van Aecken, in a certain lot lying here in Albany on the hill, adjoining to the east the lot of Jan Thomasse, to the south the highway, to the west the common fence, and to the north the lot of Capt. Backer, said lot being in breadth in front on the street to the south forty feet; [1] without our making any claim on the same any more, also acknowledging that they are fully paid and satisfied therefor, by the hands of the aforesaid Van Aecken, according to contract, of date 16/26 July last, and therefore giving *plenam actionem cessam*, and full power to the said Van Aecken, his heirs and successors or assigns, to dispose thereof as he might do with his patrimonial effects, but with his neighbors submitting to the public burdens; promising to protect and free the aforesaid lot from all actions of each and every person, and further, never more to do nor suffer anything to be done against the same.

Done at the session of the Heeren commissaries in Albany, the 28/8 Nov./Dec., 1667.

R. V. RENSSELAER
PHILIP PIETERSE SCHUYLER.

Acknowledged before me,

D. V. SCHELLUYNE, Secretary, 1667.

Copy of an obligation and mortgage registered at the request of Mr. J. V. Rensselaer.

---

[1] This lot seems to have been on the east corner of State and Chapel streets. Capt. Backer's lot was on the east side of Chapel street, immediately in the rear of the above lot.

Appeared before us, Jacob Burhans and Hendrick Aertsen, commissaries of the village of Wildwyck, the honorable Hendrick Jochemse, who acknowledges that he is well and truly indebted to Mr. Abraham Wesselse or his order in the sum of two hundred and twenty-one guilders, six stuivers, growing out of wares received from Mr. Jan Bastianse [Van Gutsenhoven], and the subscriber promises to pay said sum of *f* 221.6, in harvest time of the year 1668; for which the subscriber specially pledges his house and lot with the declaration that the same is free and unincumbered, which house and lot are standing at Fort Orange [Albany], over against the church, to the south of Jan Rinchout, and to the north Philip Pieterse [Schuyler], further, pledging his person and estate, present and to come, subject to all laws and judges. The mortgagor witnesses the above with his own hand, with Jacob Burhans and Hendrick Aertse.

Subscribed in Wildwyck, this $\frac{12}{22}$ of Febr, 1668.

Below stood "Agrees with the principal," which was subscribed by Wil. Beeckman, *schout* of Esopus, as witness, in the absence of the secretary.

After a collation with the authentic copy of date and subscription as above, this is found to agree therewith.

In Albany, the $\frac{5}{15}$ of March, $166\frac{7}{8}$.

In my presence,

D. V. SCHELLUYNE, Secretary, $166\frac{7}{8}$.

Appeared before us, undersigned, commissaries of Albany, etc., the honorable Gerrit Lansingh, who declares that in true rights, free ownership, he grants, conveys, and makes over by these presents to and for the behoof of Jan Bricker, in his certain house and lot as said Bricker has purchased from him and occupies the same, and as the same was received by the grantor by conveyance and delivery from Jan Van Bael, of date the $\frac{15}{25}$ April, 1667; standing and lying here in Albany, built upon, fenced, enclosed and bounded according to the tenor and contents of the aforesaid conveyance, by virtue of the same and of a patent and other proofs to which reference is herein made, and which with the delivery of this paper are to be made over to said Bricker; without the grantor's making any claim any more on said house and lot, also acknowledging that he is fully paid and satisfied therefor by the hand of said Bricker, the last penny with the first, and therefore, giving said Bricker, his heirs and successors or assigns, *plenam actionem cessam*, and full power to dispose of said house and lot as he might do with his own patrimonial effects; promising to protect and free said house and lot from all trouble, actions and claims of each and every person as is right, and further, never more to do nor suffer anything to be done against the same, either with or without law, in any manner, on pledge of his person and estate, personal and real, nothing excepted, subject to all laws and judges.

Done in Albany $\frac{6}{16}$ of March $166\frac{7}{8}$.

GERRIT LANSINCK.

Goosen Gerritse.

J. Dehinsse.

Acknowledged before me,

D. V. SCHELLUYNE, Secretary, $166\frac{7}{8}$.

Conditions and proposals according to which certain burghers of Albany are minded to employ a herder for their cattle. *Firstly*, The herder shall be holden to guard the cattle at his own expense, also to keep a proper youngster with him to watch the cattle, and shall begin to go out with them on the 20th of April, 1667, new style, and not leave off before the 16th of November. *Secondly*, The herder every morning before or with, the rising of the sun, shall blow three times with the horn, and then with the youngster and cattle go out where they can best get feed for the cattle, or where the masters (undersigned) shall order, and about a quarter of an hour before the sun goes down, he shall deliver the cattle at the church. *Thirdly*, If a beast or beasts receive injuries through the neglect of the herder, then the herder shall be holden to make full recompense for the beast or beasts (according to value). *Fourthly*, If the herder shall be found sitting and drinking in any tavern, he shall each time forfeit ten guilders seewant. If a beast or beasts happen to die or run away within the [first] half of the aforesaid time, then not more than half of the herder's recompense therefor, shall be paid, and that punctually at that time. In like manner also shall all those who have their cattle herded, be holden, as soon as the half of the aforesaid time for herding is out, to pay to the herder the half of the herder's recompense without any delay.

On the aforesaid conditions Uldrick Kleyn accepted the contract and for his pains is to receive twenty guilders in seewant, for every great beast, or for two heifers in place of a great beast, and shall acknowledge and obey Jurriaen Theunisse and Arnout Cornelisse [Viele,] as his superiors for his masters. Below all those who have their cattle herded, pledge their cattle, and the herder pledges his person and estate, nothing excepted, as well having and as to have, under obligation to all laws and judges, and for the confirmation of the same, they have subscribed with their own hands this paper, without craft or guile, this $\frac{2}{12}$ of April, 1667.

ULDERICK KLEIN.
JUREJAN TUNSEN.
ARNOUT CORNELISSE

On this $\frac{31st\ March,}{10th\ April,}$ 1668, Ulderick Cleyn, accepts the aforesaid *cowherdership* according to the aforesaid conditions, except the price for last year, but has now agreed for sixteen guilders in seewant for every great beast or for two heifers in place of one great beast, and he shall be holden to begin his driving on Friday the $\frac{3}{13}$ of April, of this year, and shall not stop before the $\frac{6}{16}$ of November, and shall acknowledge and obey as his superiors, for his masters, Jan Clute and Doctor (*Meester*) Cornelis Van Dyck. In acknowledgment of the truth of which, the aforesaid herder and the aforesaid masters with their own hands have subscribed this paper.

Done in Albany of date as above.

ULDERICK KLEIN.
JOHANNES CLUTE.
CORNELIS VAN DYCK.

On the aforesaid conditions of the year 1668, the aforesaid Uldrick Cleyn has again accepted the herdership, on condition that he shall begin to drive out the cattle on the $\frac{13}{23}$ of April, 1669, and not stop until the

$\frac{6}{16}$ of November of the same year. And he shall receive for each great beast fourteen guilders in seewant, or for two heifers as much as for one great beast, and shall acknowledge and obey as his superior, for his masters the Honorable Dirck Wesselse [Ten Broeck] and Hendrick Bries.

Done in Albany this $\frac{5}{15}$ of April, 1669

ULDERICK KLEIN.
DIERCK WESSELSE.
HENDRICK BRIES.

On this 8th of April, 1670, Sacharias Sickels accepted the aforesaid *cowherdership* on the conditions aforewritten and aforesaid, provided he with his youngster and the cattle shall begin to go out on the 12th of this month and shall not stop before the 6th of November, old style, and shall receive for his pains seventeen guilders in seewant, and shall acknowledge and obey as his superior, for his masters the Honorable Jan Vinhagen and Heyndrick Kuyler.

Done in Albany of date as above.

SACHARIAS SECKELS.
JAN VINHAEGHEN.
HENDRICK COYLER.

1671 the 27th of March, promises to herd [the cattle]:

Harman Gansevoort for .... *f* 23
Sacharias Sickles for .... *f* 20
Harman Gansevoort,... .... *f* 19
Sacharias Sickles,.. *f* 18
Jacobus Gerritse Van Vost,[1] .. .. *f* 17
Sacharias Sickles,.. *f* 16

1672 the 28th of March:

Jurriaen Janse Groonewout,.. *f* 25
Jacob Tyssen Van der Heyden, ... *f* 19
Jan Mangelse,. .... *f* 18
Sacharias Sickles,...... .... *f* 17

* * * * * * under subjection and authority as above.

Done in Albany the $\frac{14}{24}$ of August, 1667.

WILLEM TELLER.

Present with the *weesmeesters*,
Philip Pieterse Schuyler.
Goosen Gerritse and the officer
Gerard Swart.

Acknowledged before me,

D. V. SCHELLUYNE, Secretary, 1667.

[The above paper seems to be the closing sentence of a mortgage deed given to secure his infant children's inheritance from their mother.]

---

[1] Jacobus G. Van Vorst was born in 1612.—*Notarial Papers*, I. He was for a time public porter and carman.—*Albany Annals*, XI, 94–8. In 168½ he bound out his son Gillis, aged eleven years to Jeronimus Wendel for six years.—*Notarial Papers*, II. This son removed to Schenectady and became the ancestor of the Van Vorsts of that vicinity.

The above obligation being first read, Willem Tailler answers that he does not know what he subscribed to, but the orphan masters suggested that he should select out of his effects whatever he pleased, out of which payment can be made to his infant children according to the sentence [of court]; with respect to his grown up children, he said that he assented thereto for their portion (namely that he, Tailler, should deliver to the two grown up ones an obligation, and with the first opportunity make payment to Helena, which agreement was arranged between him and Andries Teller and Pieter Van Alen in the presence of the orphan masters; and regarding the portion of Helena he said that he would reduce what she is to have according to settlement, excepting what by the aforesaid sentence is not to be done), he said also that he would give the orphan masters security as they demanded anew. "I shall provide for the payment, provided I receive payment of ten per cent interest yearly until the infants shall come of age;" the orphan masters, on the contrary, maintained that he, Tailler, be holden to sign the aforesaid obligation; the disagreement about which was turned over to the right honorable, the governor general, for his honor's decision in the matter.

Done in Albany the 23/2 July/Aug., 1667.

Present, the Orphan Masters.
Willem Tailler and his wife.

23 July/2 Aug., 1667. I, the court messenger, with the Heer *schout* repaired to the house and dwelling of Willem Teller, and for the third time asked him whether he would sign the obligation shown him; if not, I was authorized by the honorable court to proceed to execution. Willem Teller answered that he could not see that the obligation was according to sentence, but was willing, as he before said, to give security on his estate according to the sentence of the court of assize given, again requesting his honor's decision thereon.

By me G. Swart, *Schout.*
Ludovicus Cobes, Court Messenger of Albany, etc.

On date as above, the Heer officer reported to Willem Teller, that he, Teller, should give satisfaction to his daughter Helena, and make payment according to sentence of the court of assize, abating what he was to have by settlement; with regard to the infant children that he point out his estate to the satisfaction of the same, according to sentence as above. Willem Teller answered that he had nothing against the same but it was indeed reasonable, and that he would perform the same whenever it pleased them according to sentance of the honorable court.

G. Swart, *Schout.*
By me Ludovicus Cobes, Court Messenger.

(The above registry was made by mistake, and is therefore wholly erased.)

On date as before, the officer by order of the magistrates, in presence of me, the secretary, asked William Teller if he pleased to sign the above-standing obligation, according to agreement made with Andries Teller and Peter Van Allen, and if he would pay the eighty-five beavers to

Helena Tailler according to sentence; thereupon he answered as in the above standing first statement of *schout* and *messenger*, and with respect to Helena, that in case the Heer [governor] general decides that what he is to have on settlement may not be abated (save the settlement which by sentence of the court of assize is not to be done), that he then will pay the full sum for or in behalf of Helena.

Done etc.

By me G. SWART, *Schout.*
D. V. SCHELLUYNE, Secretary, 1667.

On this $\frac{24 \text{ July}}{3 \text{ Aug.}}$, 1667, Willem Tailler acknowledges that he is well and truly indebted to his oldest son, Andries Tailler, and Pieter Van Alen, husband and guardian of Maria Tailler, to each, in the sum of five and eighty beavers, according to sentence by the honorable court of Assize, at New York pronounced on the 1st of October, A. D. 1666, abating the value of twenty beavers by the wife of Van Alen received, namely, a *toursse* gown, and a red cloth coat, being clothing of her late mother, promising to pay the aforesaid respective sums according to the tenor and import of the aforesaid sentence, therefor pledging his person and estate, personal and real, having and to have, nothing excepted, subject to all laws and judges.

Done in Albany on date as above.

WILLEM TELLER.

Present one magistrate and two orphan masters:
Philip Pieterse Schuyler.
Jan Verbeeck.
Evert Janse Wendel.

In my presence, D. V SCHELLUYNE, Secretary, 1667.

According to the order of the Heer [governor] general, of date the 30th July last, Willem Tailler. subscribed the above standing obligation to the behoof of his four infant children on the $\frac{14}{24}$ of August, 1667, with promise also to pay his daughter Helena her portion, of eighty-five beavers.

Present, the orphan masters and magistrates:
Philip Pieterse Schuyler and
Goosen Gerritse,
besides the Heer *Schout G. Swart.*

[Copy.]

I, the undersigned, Helena Tailler, acknowledge that I have received of my father, Willem Tailler, the quantity of eighty-five good beavers, as adjudged to me by the honorable court of assize at New York, on the 1st of October, 1666, and I release him from all claims. In witness of the truth of this I have written and subscribed this with my own hand, in Albany, the $\frac{7}{17}$ of September, 1667. Was subscribed, "Helena Tailler widow of Cornelis Bogardus," and, ' In my presence D. V. Schelluyne, Secretary," besides, "As trustees, Philip Pieterse, and D. V. Schelluyne."

* * * * * according to the survey and regulation of the surveyor, of date the $\frac{25 \text{ April,}}{5 \text{ May,}}$ last, which lot the aforesaid Helmer

Otten, at public vendue purchased and paid for according to the conditions [of sale]. free and unincumbered (saving the lord's right), and therefore giving to the aforesaid Helmert Otten, his heirs and successors or assigns. full power to dispose thereof, as he might do with his own patrimonial effects, and therefore permission to ask for a patent for the aforesaid lot of the right honorable the Heer [governor] general.

Done in Albany the 29/8 May/June, 1668.

R. V. RENSSELAER.

Acknowledged before me,

D. V. SCHELLUYNE, Secretary, 1668.

[A portion of the above deed is wanting.]

The magistrates of Albany, colony of Rensselaerwyck and Schanechtade, declare by these presents that in true rights, free ownership, they grant, convey and make over to and for the behoof of Jan Clute, in lot No. 11, lying on the hill here in Albany. breadth in front two rods nine feet, in rear two rods ten feet four inches, on the east side two rods eleven feet and nine inches, adjoining on the west Helmer Otten, on the north the public street, on the east Jan Clute himself, and on the south Jacob Loockermans. according to the survey and regulation of the surveyor, of date the 25/5 April/May, last, which lot the aforesaid Jan Clute, at public vendue purchased and paid for according to conditions of sale; free and unincumbered (excepting the lord's right), and therefore giving full power to the afcrenamed Jan Clute, his heirs and successors or assigns. to dispose thereof as he might do with his patrimonial effects; and therefore permission to ask of the right honorable the Heer general, a patent for the aforesaid lot.

Done in Albany the 29/8 May/June, 1668.

R. V. RENSSELAER.

Acknowledged before me,

D. V. SCHELLUYNE, Secretary, 1668.

The commissaries of Albany, etc., declare by these presents, that in true rights, free ownership, they grant, convey and make over to Mr. Goosen Gerritse [Van Schaick] in a lot, No. 12, lying on the hill here in Albany (to and for the behoof his son-in-law, Hendrick Coster), breadth in front two rods seven feet and two inches, in rear two rods five and a half feet, length on the west side four rods and four feet, on the east side three rods and eleven feet, adjoining on the east Barent Reyndertse, on the south and west the public streets, and on the north Domine Schaets; according to the survey and regulation of the surveyor, of date the 25/5 April/May, last, which lot the said Goosen Gerritse purchased and paid for at public vendue according to conditions of sale; free and unincumbered. save the the lord's right, and therefore giving full power to the aforesaid Goosen Gerritse (to the behoof as before), his heirs and successors or assigns. * * * *

[The remainder of this deed is wanting.]

Appeared before me, Ludovicus Cobes, secretary of Albany, colony Rensselaerswyck and Schaenhechtade. in the presence of the right honorable the Heeren magistrates of said jurisdiction, Mons. Ryckart Van Rensselaer and Mr. Jan Verbeeck. Jan Lewis, soldier in the service of his majesty, king of England, who acknowledges that he is well and truly indebted to Jurriaen Janse Groenewout, in the quantity of one hundred and two good whole and merchantable beaver skins, reckoned at eight guilders a piece, growing out of the matter of three remaining installments, for the purchase and payment of a certain house and lot, by the said Lewis, of him bought, according to contract thereof, of date the 8th of Sept., *anno* 1669, which aforesaid sum of one hundred and two beaver skins, said Lewis promises to pay according to the tenor and contents of the same, in three installments, of a third part of said sum each, the first on the first of August, 1670, the second and third each a year thereafter, therefor pledging specially the aforesaid house and lot, and further, generally, his person and estate, personal and real present and future, nothing excepted, subject to all laws and judges, to secure the payment, if necessary, without cost and loss.

Done in Albany, in the 22d year of his majesty's reign, the 9th of Feb., *annoque Domini*, 1669.

JOHN LEWIS.

R. V. Rensselaer.
Jan Verbeeck.

In my presence,

LUDOVICUS COBES, Secretary.

Appeared before me, Ludovicus Cobes, secretary of Albany, etc., in the presence of the right honorable the Heeren magistrates of the same jurisdiction, Mr. Jan Verbeeck and Mr. Philip Pieterse Schuyler, Pieter Adriaense [Soegemackelyck], who declares that in true rights, free ownership, he grants, conveys and makes over, by these presents, to and for the behoof of his son Pieter Pieterse, his heirs and successors or assigns, the grantor's certain lot, with a part of a garden, and the fruit trees, standing and lying on Lubbede's land in the colony Rensselaerswyck, according to the proofs of his title existing, stretching along and adjoining the lot of Berent Pieterse [Coeymans], the same in length and breadth, as it lies in fence, free and unincumbered with no claim standing or issuing against the same, except the right of the Heer patroon of the colony, without the grantor's making the least pretensions thereto any more; also acknowledging that he is fully paid therefor, the last penny with the first and therefore giving *plenam actionem cessam*, and full power to the aforenamed Pieter Pieterse, his heirs and successors or assigns, to dispose thereof, as he might do his own patrimonial estate and effects; promising to protect and free the aforesaid lot, and part of the garden and fruit trees, from all trouble, claims or actions, of each and every person as is right, and never more to do nor suffer anything to be done against the same, either with or without law, in any manner, on pledge according to law.

Done in Albany, the 11th of Feb., 1669.

PIETER ADRIAENS.

Philip Pieterse.
Jan Verbeeck.

In my presence

LUDOVICUS COBES, Secretary.

N. B. This conveyance is made with this reserve, that the grantor shall receive a half of the stones which lie by the house and yearly two skipples of apples from the fruit trees.

Appeared before me, Ludovicus Cobes, secretary of Albany, etc., in the presence of the right honorable Heeren commissaries, etc., Mr. Jan Verbeeck and Mr Philip Pieterse Schuyler, Pieter Van Olinda,[1] inhabitant of Schaenhechtade, who declares that in true rights, free ownership, he grants, conveys and makes over by these presents, to and for the behoof of Mr. Jan Clute, his heirs and successors or assigns, the grantor's certain great island lying on the *Maaquaas kil* (Mohawk river) at Canastagioené (*Niskayuna*) to his wife Hilleken Cornelise [Van Slyck], given by the sachems of the Mohawks, the lawful owners, of date the 11th of June, 1667, with such title as the grantor has therein, lying and bounded according to the contents of the patent thereof to him, the grantor, given by the right honorable the Heer governor general of New York, Richard Nicoll, on the 8th of May, 1668, to which reference is herein made; free and unincumbered, without any claim standing or lying against the same, excepting the lord's right, without the grantor's making the least claim thereto any more, also acknowledging that he is fully satisfied and paid therefor, the last penny with the first, and therefore giving *plenam actionem cessam*, and full power to the aforesaid Mr. Jan Clute, his heirs and successors or assigns, to do with and dispose of the same as he might do with his patrimonial estate and effects; promising to protect and free the aforesaid island and the title thereof from all trouble, claims and liens of each and every person as is right, and further, never more to do nor suffer anything to be done against the same, either with or without law, in any manner, on pledge according to law.

Done in Albany the 4th of March, 1669.

PIETER DANIELSE VAN OLINDA.

Jan Verbeeck.
Philip Pieterse.

In my presence,

LUDOVICUS COBES, Secretary.

Appeared before me, Ludovicus Cobes, secretary of Albany, etc., in the presence of the right honorable Heeren commissaries, Mons. Ryckart Van Rensselaer and Mr. Jan Verbeeck, Sander Leendersen Glen dwelling at Schaenhechtade, who declares that in true rights, free ownership, he grants, conveys and makes over, by these presents to and for the behoof of his three sons, Jacob, Sander and Johannes Sanderse Glen, in a certain parcel of land lying between the [Round] lake and the [Mohawk] river over against the village of Schaenhechtade, consisting of fifty morgens, according to patent thereof from the right honorable heer governor general of New York, of date the 3rd of November, 1665, to which reference is herein made; free and unincumbered, with no claim standing or issuing

[1] Pieter Van Olinda's wife, Hilletie, was a half-breed, her mother being a Mohawk woman and her father Cornelis Antonissen Van Slyck. Her brother, Jacques Cornelise Van Slyck, settled at Schenectady. Hilletie for many years was employed as one of the provincial interpreters, and seems greatly to have interested Messrs. Dancker and Sluyter in their visit to Schenectady in 1680. She died the 10th of Feb, 1707. Peter Van Olinda made his will 1st of Aug., 1715, and speaks of sons Daniel, Jacob, and Matthys who was *non compos mentis*. He had land at the Willow Flat below Port Jackson, and at the Boght in Watervliet.

against the same, saving the lord's right, without the grantor's making the least pretension any more to the same, also acknowledging that he is fully paid and satisfied therefor, the last penny with the first, by the hands of his three sons, shown by an honest statement, and therefore giving *plenam actionem cessam*, and full power to his aforesaid sons, their heirs and successors or assigns, to do with and dispose of the same as they might do with their patrimonial estate and effects; promising to protect and free the aforesaid land from all trouble, claims and liens of every person as is right, and further, never more to do nor suffer anything to be done, either with or without law, in any manner, on pledge according to law.

Done in Albany the 9th of March, 1669.

SANDER LENRSE GLEN.

R. V. Rensselaer.
Jan Verbeeck.

In my presence,

LUDOVICUS COBES, Secretary.

Appeared before us, undersigned, commissaries of Albany, etc., the honorable Cornelis Theunisse VanVechten,[1] husbandman in the aforesaid colony, and Sara Salomonse [Goewey], his wife, daughter of Salomon Abelse, deceased, in his lifetime carpenter here, born in Amsterdam, Holland, give notice that Sara Salomonse and her four brothers and sister, namely, Philip, Jacob, Jan, David and Lysbet (of whom are still living, besides Sara, the aforesaid Jacob, Jan and Lysbet Salomonse), that by the will of her uncle, Poppe Abelse, deceased at Amsterdam aforenamed, each inherited the sum of one hundred guilders capital, which capital was put out at interest there, the interest to accumulate until it amounted to at least fifty guilders, for each of the aforesaid hundred guilders capital, and of which their guardians, named Cornelis Brantse and Benningh Weyman, dwelling at Amsterdam aforenamed, have the disposition and management; and as they, the subscribers, the value of the aforesaid hundred and fifty guilders, Holland money, acknowledge that they have received to their good content and satisfaction, in diverse goods and commodities, by the hands of Myndert Frederickse, smith, in Albany aforesaid, therefore the subscribers, by these presents, declare that they grant, convey and make over to the aforenamed Myndert Frederickse, smith, his attorney or the lawful bearer of this, their aforesaid right and hereditary portion, in said inheritance by the will of her uncle, Poppen Abelse, aforenamed, to the sum of one hundred guilders capital, abovementioned, with the aforesaid interest (accumulated to the full and complete sum according to said will), whom they authorize and fully empower, to demand, collect and receive said hundred guilders, capital and interest, in Holland, from the aforesaid guardians, or from whom it may concern, as his own estate, without the subscribers' making the least pretensions thereto any more, also acknowledging that they are well satisfied and paid therefor as above, and therefore releasing all their rights and title to the aforesaid inheritance, to the behoof as above, promising never more to do, nor suffer anything to be done against the same, either with or without law, in any manner,

[1] Cornelis Teunise Van Vechten, *alias* Keesoom, lived upon the island below Albany, called Paapsknee. *Annals of Albany*, VII, 102. He had three wives, first, Sara Salomonse [Goewey]; second, Annatie Leendertse [Conyn]; and third, Maria Lucasse, widow of Jacob Claas, whom he married 3d July, 1689. He had six children, perhaps more, of whom were Salomon, Dirk, Leendert, Lucas, Anna and Jannetie, the last three by the last wife.

on pledge of their persons and estates, nothing excepted, subject to all laws and judges.

Done in Albany, the $\frac{27 \text{ June}}{7 \text{ July}}$, 1668.

CORNELIS TEUNISSE.

This mark [mark] is set by SARA SALOMONSE.[1]

Philip Pieterse Schuyler.
J. Dehinsse

Acknowledged before me,

D. V. SCHELLUYNE, Secretary, 1668.

Appeared before us, undersigned, commissaries of Albany, etc., Mr. Gerrit Slichtenhorst, who declares that in true rights, free ownership, he grants, convey and makes over by these presents, to and for the behoof of Hendrick Bries,[2] a lot, in breadth twenty-three feet, breadth and boundaries according to the contract, of date the $\frac{19}{29}$ September, 1666, lying here in Albany, by virtue of the patent for a greater lot to the grantor given by the right honorable Heer general Richard Nicolls, of date the 27th of April, 1667, and therefore giving full *actionem cessam*, and power to the aforenamed Bries, his heirs and successors or assigns, to dispose thereof, as he might do with his own patrimonial effects; without the grantor's making the least pretension thereto any more, also acknowledging that he is fully paid and satisfied therefor by the hands of said Bries; and therefore promising to protect and free the same from all trouble and claims of each and every person, and further, never more to do nor suffer anything to be done against the same, either with or without law, in any manner, on pledge of his person and estate, nothing excepted, subject to all laws and judges.

Done in Albany, the $\frac{2}{12}$ July, 1668.

GERRIT SLICHTENHORST.

Philip Pieterse Schuyler.
Goosen Gerritse.

In my presence,

D. V. SCHELLUYNE, Secretary, 1668.

Appeared before us, undersigned, commissaries of Albany, Mr. Gerrit Slichtenhorst, who declares that in true rights, free ownership, he grants, conveys and makes over by these presents, to and for the behoof of Frans Janse Pruyn,[3] in a certain lot lying here in Albany, in breadth, length

---

[1] At least two of Sara S. Goewey's brothers settled in Albany: Jacob, who owned a house and lot, which he contracted to sell to Sara Van Borsum, in 1675 (*Deeds*, I, 260), and perhaps left the village; and Jan, who married Caatje Loockermans, and had a family of ten children, all baptized here. The latter was naturalized the 13th of March, 1716 (*Annals of Albany*, VIII, 50), and died 28th September, 1731.—*Ibid.*, I. In 1786, his house and lot were on the east side of Broadway, next south of Bleecker Hall.—*Ibid.*, I, 106.

[2] Hendrik Brice had one son, Antony, who married Catryn Ryckman, by whom he had five daughters and a son Hendrik.

[3] Frans Janse Pruyn was in Albany as early as 1665 (*Deeds*, I, 200); being a papist he could not take the oath of allegiance in 1699.—*Albany Annals*, III, 290. In 1703, he had a lot on the east corner of Maiden Lane and James street.—*Ibid.*, IV, 183. By his wife Alida or Aeltie, who died in 1704, he had eight children, Helena, wife of Jacob Lansing, Samuel, Johannes, Maria, wife of Elbert Gerritse, Christina, Frans, Barentje, and Arent.—*Church Records*.

and boundaries according to the tenor and contents of the contract of the $\frac{19}{29}$ of September, 1666, and by virtue of a patent for a greater lot, of date the 27th of April, 1667, to him granted by the right honorable Heer general Richard Nicolls, and therefore giving full power to said Frans Janse Pruyn, his heirs and successors or assigns, to dispose of the aforesaid lot as he might do with his patrimonial effects; also acknowledging that he is fully paid and satisfied therefor by the hands of said Frans Janse Pruyn; therefore promising to protect and free said lot from all trouble and claims of every person as is right, and further, never more to do nor suffer anything to be done against the same, either with or without law, in any manner, on pledge of his person and estate, nothing excepted, subject to all laws and judges.

Done in Albany of date as above.

GERRIT SLICHTENHORST.

Philip Pieterse Schuyler.
Goosen Gerritse.

In my presence,

D. V. SCHELLUYNE, Secretary, 1668.

Appeared before us, undersigned, commissaries of Albany, etc., Mr. Gerrit Slichtenhorst, who declares that in true rights, free ownership, he grants, conveys and makes over by these presents, to and for the behoof of Gerrit Lansingh, in a certain lot breadth five and twenty feet, length to the lot of Robert Sandertse, adjoining on the east side Hendrick Bries, on the south side the public street, on the west side the grantor, and on the north the aforesaid Robert Sandertse, by virtue of a patent of date the 27th of April, 1667, given him by the right honorable Heer general Richard Nicolls, and therefore giving to the aforenamed Gerrit Larsingh, his heirs and successors or assigns *plenam actionem cessam*, and full power to dispose thereof as he might do with his patrimonial effects, also acknowledging that he is fully paid and satisfied therefor by the hands of said Gerrit Lansingh; and therefore promising to protect and free said lot from all trouble and claims of every person as is right, and further, never more to do nor suffer anything to be done against the same, either with or without law, in any manner, on pledge of his person and estate, nothing excepted, subject to all laws, and judges.

Done in Albany the $\frac{2}{12}$ July, 1668.

GERRIT SLICHTENHORST.

Philip Pieterse Schuyler.
Goosen Gerritse.

In my presence,

D. V. SCHELLUYNE, Secretary, 1668.

By virtue and in consequence of the conveyance by Mr. Gerrit Slichtenhorst, passed of this date to the behoof of Gerrit Lansingh, of a lot lying here in Albany, of breadth, length, and boundaries according to the tenor and contents of the same, Gerrit Lansingh declares that in true rights, free ownership, he grants, conveys and makes over in said lot with the house and barn thereon standing to Barent Albertse [Bratt],[1] his heirs and successors

[1] Barent Albertse Bratt lived in 1700 without the north gate just west of the main guard, near or on the east corner of Steuben street and Broadway; he had frequent warnings from the common council not to fence in certain grounds there belonging to the city.—*Annals of Albany*, IV, 109, 127, X, 60; *Deeds*, I, 343. In 1710 he had a lot on Fox creek.—*Ibid.*, X, 92.

or assigns, also acknowledging that he is fully paid and satisfied therefor by the hand of said Barent Albertse, and therefore giving and conveying to said Barent Albertse such title in said lot as he received from Gerrit Slichtenhorst, acknowledging also that he is fully paid and satisfied by said Barent Albertse for the house and barn standing thereon, promising never more to do nor suffer anything to be done against the same, either with or without law, in any manner, on pledge of his person and estate, nothing excepted, subject to all laws and judges.

Done in Albany the $\frac{3}{13}$ of July, 1668.

GERRIT LANSINCK.

Philip Pieterse Schuyler.
Goosen Gerritse.

In my presence,

D. V. SCHELLUYNE, Secretary, 1668.

Appeared before us, undersigned, commissaries of Albany, etc., Mr. Adriaen Gerritse [Papendorp], burgher and inhabitant here in Albany, who declares that in true rights, free ownership, he grants, conveys and makes over to and for the behoof of Carsten Fredericksе, master smith, in a garden, allotment No. 5, lying in Albany, as it lies enclosed and fenced, adjoining on the east side the Heer director Jeremias Van Rensselaer, on the south side the burial ground (*kerckhoff*), on the west side the public street and on the north side Mr. Abraham Staets, by virtue and in consequence of a deed of conveyance of date the 28th of October A. D. 1656, from Adriaen Janse Van Ilpendam to his behoof passed; therefore giving *plenam actionem cessam*, and full power to said Carsten Fredericksе, smith, his heirs and successors or assigns, to dispose of the same as he might do with his own patrimonial effects, also acknowledging that he is fully paid and satisfied therefor; promising said garden to protect and free from all trouble and claims as is right, and further, never more to do nor to suffer anything to be done against the same, either with or without law, in any manner, on pledge of his person and estate, nothing excepted, subject to all laws and judges.

Done in Albany the $\frac{3}{13}$ of July, 1668.

ADRIAEN GERRITSEN

Goosen Gerritse.
Philip Pieterse Schuyler.

In my presence,

D. V. SCHELLUYNE, Secretary, 1668.

Appeared before us, undersigned, commissaries of Albany, etc., Myndert and Carsten Fredericksе, brothers, dwelling here in Albany, who declare that in true rights, free ownership, they grant, convey and make over by these presents, to and for the behoof of Jan Clute, in a garden lot lying here in Albany, breadth four and a half rods, length seven and a half rods, adjoining on the south Thomas Sandertse, to the east Jacob Clomp, to the north the road and to the west a low plain, by virtue and in consequence of a deed of conveyance of the 30th of July, 1655, by Cornelis Steenwyck, as attorney for Gabriel Leendertse to their behoof passed; therefore giving *plenam actionem cessam*, and full power to the aforesaid Jan Clute, his heirs and successors or assigns, to dispose of the aforesaid lot as he might do with his patrimonial effects; also acknowledging that he is fully paid and satisfied therefor: and therefore promising the aforesaid lot to protect and free from all trouble and claims of every person as is right, and further, never more to do, nor suffer anything to be done, against the same, either with or without law, in any manner, on pledge of his person and estate, nothing excepted, subject to all laws and judges.

Done in Albany, the 3/13 of July, 1668.

This mark + is set by MYNDERT FREDERICKSE.
KARSTEN FREDERICKSE.

Philip Pieterse Schuyler.
Goosen Gerritse.

In my presence, D. V. SCHELLUYNE, Secretary, 1668.

Appeared before us, undersigned, commissaries, of Albany etc., Mr. Philip Pieterse Schuyler, our *raedsvrunt*, and Margareta Slichtenhorst, his wife, dwelling here at Albany in America, who declare that they have appointed and fully empowered by these presents the Heer Johan Baptist Van Renssalaer merchant at Amsterdam, Holland, with his brother-in-law, Mr. Gerrit Slichtenhorst (who is proposing to depart for Holland) to inquire after the condition and inventory of the estate or a copy of the will which may have been made by the Heer Brant Van Slichtenhorst deceased, father of the aforenamed Margareta and Gerrit Slichtenhorst, (deceased at Nieukerck in Gelderland), and furthermore, their (subscriber's) contingent and hereditary portion in the aforesaid inheritance, to demand, collect, and receive; acquittance for receipts to pass, if need be and the matter demands it, with his aforenamed brother-in-law, to examine, seek out and approve of the condition and inventory of the estate; to compromise compound and arrange the real estate, lands, houses, and lots, as also the movables which may fall to the subscribers as a part of their inheritance to sell; the aforesaid real estate to establish and vest in the purchaser, the subscribers to disestablish and disinherit from the same, the stipulated purchase money to receive, of the receipts acquittance to pass, and if necessary (there being no hope) their aforesaid rights and claims, in their said inheritance, by justice to demand, collect and receive from those who have the care of the same, to that end all the terms of the laws to observe to sentence and extreme execution of the same *incluys*, with power also one or more persons in his place to substitute, having the like or limited power; and further all things to do, transact and perform, either with or without law, as he may think needful and reasonable; promising at all times to hold as true all that by the aforenamed Heer attorney and substitutes of the same by virtue hereof shall be done and performed without any gainsaying, on pledge according to the laws for that case made, provided that the attorney be holden, when requested, properly to answer for his transactions and receipts.

Done in Albany the 3/13 July, 1668.

PHILIP PIETERSE SCHUYLER
MARGARETA VAN SLICHTENHORST

Goosen Gerritse.
Jan Thomas.

In my presence,

D. V. SCHELLUYNE, Secretary, 1668.

Appeared before us, undersigned, commissaries of Albany, etc., Mr Goosen Gerritse [Van Schaick], and Jan Coster Van Aecken as attorneys for Anthony Janse, who declare in said character, that in true rights, free ownership, they grant, convey, and make over by these presents to and for the behoof of Mr. Jan Hendrickse Bruyns, in a certain house and lot and garden at present occupied by Jurriaen Theunisse Glaesmaker, belonging to said Anthony Janse, as he purchased the same from said Jurriaen Theunisse, and by the same was conveyed and made over to him according to the proof thereof existing, delivered over to said Bruyns as the aforesaid house, lot and garden are built upon, fenced, enclosed, standing and lying here in Albany, and bounded according to the tenor and contents of the contract, and further aforesaid evidences, to which reference is herein made, and according to conditions on which the same were offered at public sale and maintained to the last bid, viz: that Bruyns is to receive the rent of the house, lot and garden which Jurriaen Theunisse was to pay therefor to be reckoned from the day of sale, until the end of the lease; without the grantor's (in character as above) making the least pretension thereto any more, also acknowledging that he is fully paid and satisfied therefor by the hands of said Bruyns with the value of the sum of 695 guilders in beavers by exchange on Holland (provided that if there be no hope of the bill of exchange on Holland being paid, then the grantors maintain their right and action, specially to said house, lot, and garden, and further, generally against his person and estate), therefore giving *plenam actionem cessam*, and full power to the aforenamed Jan Hendrickse Bruyns, his heirs and successors or assigns, to dispose of the said house, lot and garden, as he might do with his patrimonial effects; promising to defend and free the same from all trouble, actions and claims of every person, and further, never more to do nor to suffer anything to be done against the same, either with or without law, in any manner, on pledge of their persons and estates, nothing excepted, subject to all laws and judges.

Done in Albany the $\frac{5}{15}$ of July, 1668.

JAN KOSTER.
GOOSEN GERRITSEN.

Philip Pieterse Schuyler.
Jan Thomase.

In my presence,

D. V. SCHELLUYNE, Secretary, 1668.

Appeared before us, undersigned, commissaries of Albany, etc., the honorable Cornelis Van Nes, old commissary, and Maritie Damen, last widow of Henderick Andriesse [Van Doesburgh], deceased, now his wife dwelling here in Albany, who declare that they have appointed and fully empowered by these presents, Lysbet Dirckse Van Eps,[1] daughter of said Maritie Damen, and wife of Gerrit Bancker, proposing to return to Holland. Firstly, for said Cornelis Van Nes, especially to demand, collect and receive from Joost Aertse Vanden Burgh Graefl, his cousin, dwelling at Gornichem in Holland, the yearly rent for three morgens of land lying at Laeckervell, or from those who have occupied the same, due since the 1st of May, A.D.

[1] Lysbet Dirkse Van Eps, was daughter of Dirk Van Eps, first husband of Maritie Damen. Her brother, Jan Baptist Van Eps, settled at Schenectady.

1661, till now, amounting yearly to the sum of forty-eight guilders; and for the receipt of the same acquittance to pass; secondly, in the name and for the sake of said Maritie Damen to demand and receive out of the hands of S. H. Sybingh, merchant at Amsterdam in Holland, a certain instrument sealed with the mark [mark] which she left in his hands at Amsterdam aforenamed on the 23d day of August, 1662, according to the receipt thereof from said Sybingh, which by these presents is placed in the hands of the aforesaid Lysbet Dirckse Van Eps, to be delivered over to said Sijbingh with the delivery of the aforesaid sealed instrument, with the commission then to acquit said Sybingh of all claims therefor; and having received said sealed instrument, the same to open and in accordance with the contents of the same, to demand, collect and receive the capital sum of 3,500 guilders with the accrued interest on the same, according to the tenor of said sealed instrument until now, from the honorable Jo^r Schaep, or if deceased from his heirs or those who are his administrators, dwelling at Doesburgh, for the receipts acquittance to pass; but in case Jo^r Schaep, or his heirs are pleased to retain the aforesaid capital, this may be done provided sufficient security be offered and an exemplified copy thereof be brought to these subscribers, otherwise the aforesaid capital to take and receive with the aforesaid accrued interest, the capital securely to invest on interest at the *comptoir generael*, in Holland or at Amsterdam or elsewhere; the evidences of the same, likewise to bring or send over and the remainder, the accrued interest, to employ and lay out in such wares and merchandise as the attorney is ordered by the subscribers, to be brought or sent hither; and in case of refusal in either case in regard to the matters aforesaid to further the respective rights and claims of the subscribers by means of justice, to which end all terms of the laws to observe to sentence and extreme execution of the same *in cluys*, with power also one or more persons in her place to substitute having like or limited power, and further all things to do, transact and perform, with or without law, which she may judge needful or proper; promising at all times to hold as true all that by the aforesaid attorney, our daughter Lysabet, or by her substitute shall be done and performed in the matters aforesaid by virtue of these presents, without any gainsaying, on pledge according to law therefor provided, provided the attorney remain holden when requested a proper answer to make of her aforesaid transactions and receipts.

Done in Albany the $\frac{5}{15}$ of July, 1668.

CORNELLIS VAN NES.
MARRIEN DAEMEN.

As witness G. Swart, schout.
Goosen Gerritse.
Philip Pieterse Schuyler.

In my presence,

D. V SCHELLUYNE, Secretary, 1668.

Appeared before us, undersigned, commissaries of Albany, etc., Jan Coster Van Aecken, who declares that in true rights, free ownership, he grants conveys, and makes over by these presents, to and for the behoof of Willem Teller, in a lot lying here in Albany on the hill, breadth in front on the street 21 feet, length to the lot of Capt. Backer, and breadth in the rear 20 feet Rynland measure together with an alley on the west side of said Van Aecken of 3 feet in breadth, which shall remain as a common alley, so far as the alley extends both in length and breadth must be comprehended, adjoining on the east the grantor, on the south the said street, on the west Jan Van Bael, and on the north Capt. Banker aforesaid; by virtue of a conveyance, of date the $\frac{28}{8}$ November/December, 1667, by the Heeren commissaries to his behoof granted, and therefore giving full power to said Willem Teller, his heirs and successors or assigns, to dispose thereof as he might do with his patrimonial effects, without the grantor's making the least pretension thereto any more, also acknowledging that he is fully paid and satisfied therefor by the hands of Willem Teller, and therefore promising to protect and free the aforesaid lot from all trouble and claims of every person as is right, and further, never more to do nor suffer anything to be done against the same, in any manner, on pledge of his person and estate, nothing excepted, subject to all laws and judges.

Done in Albany the $\frac{6}{16}$ of July, 1668.

JAN KOSTER.

Teunis Cornelisse.
Goosen Gerritse.

In my presence,

D. V. SCHELLUYNE, Secretary, 1668.

Appeared before us, undersigned, commissaries of Albany, etc., Madame Anthonia Slachboom,[1] widow of the late Heer Arent Van Curlar in his life time commissary the colony Rensselaerswyck and our late *raetsvrunt*, who declares that she appoints and fully empowers by these presents Mr. Gerrit Slichtenhorst proposing to depart for Holland specially to demand, collect and receive from the Saelevecr and Olderdom of Huselman's estate, lying in the jurisdiction of Nykerck (in Gelderland) in the district of Nautena, the right and title to the portion of the same, being a free estate (*gevreyt goot*) of the jurisdiction of Paterborn, coming to her, the subscriber, by virtue of the deed of usufruct (*acte van lyfftocht*), which her aforenamed husband, deceased, and she, the subscriber, executed with each other before the Heeren director Diderick Van de Sande and Everard Everroyn, aldermen of the city of Arnherm, of date the 30th of September, 1646, which deed for this purpose was originally delivered over to this attorney by these presents; also from the other lands and effects therein mentioned, alienated and sold by her aforesaid husband during his lifetime; and after the receipt of her over due claims, with the heirs of the aforenamed Huselmans or with those who have the management thereof, to arrange for a full release and acquittal for the further rights which she has therein, or may lay claim to at any future time; and therefore in her name and for her sake fully to release and yield the same and all her actions and claims in respect thereto, and acquittance in the matter aforesaid to pass; all for the recovery of the sum of 1,159 guilders, according to obligation, of date the 9th of October, 1655, by the said Curler passed to the behoof of the honorable Brandt Van Slichtenhorst, deceased, late father of the aforenamed Gerrit Van Slichtenhorst, and also the sum of 27 guilders by settlement, received from this attorney in goods, all to be received in current silver

[1] Antonia Slaghboom was the widow of Jonas Brouck in 1643, when she was betrothed to Arent Van Curler. She resided in Schenectady from the first settlement of that place in 1662 till her death in 1681. In 1672 she was licensed to trade at Schenectady in consideration of the loss of her husband in 1667 in public service, and of her house, barns, and corn by fire. It was thought also that her license would stop the quarrels of the other two tapsters, Cornelis Corn. Viele and Akes Corn. Gnatsh [Van Slyck] the Indian—*Order in Council*, p. 127.

money: and further in the matter aforesaid all things to do, transact and perform which he may deem necessary and reasonable; promising at all times to hold true all that shall be done and performed in the matter aforesaid by this attorney without any gainsaying, on pledge, according to law.

Done in Albany the $\frac{6}{16}$ of July, 1668.

This mark is + set by MADAME ANTHONIA SLACHBOOM, aforesaid.

Goosen Gerritsc.

Richard Van Rensselaer.

In my presence,

D. V. SCHELLUYNE, Secretary, 1668.

Appeared before us, undersigned commissaries of Albany, etc., Willem Janse Schut, *alias* Dommelaer, dwelling in the aforesaid colony, who declares that he has appointed and fully empowered by these presents, Stoffel Janse Abeel, master carpenter here, proposing to depart for Holland, together with his niece Eyttie Meyndertse, dwelling at Amsterdam in Holland, according to her advise, of date the 12th of April, 1666, specially to demand, collect, and receive, from Symon Jansse, his uncle, dwelling at Wieringer, all that was bequeathed to him by his deceased grandmother, with the accumulated rents on the same, in the custody of his aforesaid uncle; and therefore of the receipts acquittance to pass, and further, all things to do, transact and perform which he may deem needful and reasonable; promising at all times to hold for true all that shall be done and performed by the aforesaid attorney without any gainsaying, on pledge according to laws therefor provided, provided the attorney, when requested, remain holden a proper statement to make of his transactions and receipts.

Done in Albany, the $\frac{6}{16}$ of July, 1668.

WILLEM JANSEN SCHUT.

Goosen Gerretse.

R. V. Rensselaer.

In my presence,

D. V. SCHELLUYNE, Secretary, 1668.

Appeared before us, undersigned, commissaries of Albany, etc., the honorable Jan Vinhagen, master tailor here, born in Geemen in the province of Munster, who declares that he appoints and fully empowers by these presents Mr. Herman Vedder, merchant here, proposing to depart for Holland, specially to demand, collect, and receive from his brother, Willem Vinhagen, dwelling at Geemen aforesaid, what was inherited by him, Willem, and Anthony Vinhagen, his youngest brother, by the decease of their father, Dirck Vinhagen, in the year 1659, and their late mother, Aeltie, deceased, in the year aforesaid at Geemen, in the custody of his said brother, Willem Vinhagen, therefore the condition and inventory of the estate to examine, or the will, if one was made; the subscriber's just portion of the aforesaid inheritance having received acquittance therefor to pass, with power also to compromise by selling out or otherwise; and in case of refusal (without hope) his aforesaid portion by means of justice to obtain, to which end all terms of the laws to observe, to sentence and extreme execution of the same *incluys*, with power one or more persons in his place to substitute, having like or limited power; and further, all things to do, transact, and perform which he may deem needful and reasonable; promising at all times to hold true all that shall be done and performed in the matter aforesaid by said attorney or his substitutes, without any guinsaying, provided that this attorney be holden, when required, a proper statement to make of his transactions and receipts.

Done in Albany, the $\frac{6}{16}$ July, 1668.

JAN VINHAEGEN.

Goosen Gerritse.
R. V. Rensselaer.

In my presence, D. V. SCHELLUYNE, Secretary, 1668.

Appeared before us, undersigned, commissaries of Albany, etc., Adriaen Van Ilpendam, who declares that in true rights, free ownership, he grants, conveys and makes over to Pieter Quackenbos in the brickyard according to the fence thereabout set, lying here in the colony and by said Pieter Quackenbos occupied according to the right and ownership of the ground which he bought and paid for, of madame, the widow of the late Johan de Hulter, now wife of Jeronimus Ebbinck, according to release, of date the 20th of Aug., 1664, on condition that said Quackenbos pay yearly a rent of two Carolus guilders to the Heer director of the colony according to the tenor of the contract therefor, of date the 11th of November, 1657, to which reference is herein made; and therefore giving said Quackenbos, his heirs and successors or assigns, full power to dispose thereof as he might do with his patrimonial effects; also acknowledging that he is fully paid and satisfied therefor, and therefore promising to protect and free the same from all trouble and claims as is right, and never more to do nor suffer anything to be done against the same, in any manner, on pledge of his person and estate, nothing excepted, subject to all laws and judges.

Done in Albany the $\frac{11}{21}$ of July, 1668.

ADRIAEN VAN ILPENDAM.

Goosen Gerritse.
Philip Pieterse Schuyler.

In my presence,

D. V. SCHELLUYNE, Secretary, 1668.

Appeared before us, undersigned, commissaries of Albany, etc., Arent Janse, master carpenter here, proposing to return to Holland, who declares, that in consequence of the sentence of the court, of date the $\frac{18th}{28th}$ June and $\frac{25}{5}$ $\frac{June}{July}$ of this year, by the honorable court here, he gives a special mortgage bond on his house and lot standing and lying here in Albany as the lot was received by him by conveyance from Hendrick Gerritse Vermeulen, of date the $\frac{23}{3}$ $\frac{April}{May}$ 1667; free and unincumbered, save the lord's right, together with what was bequeathed to him on the death of his godmother, Lysbet Willemse, in the custody of his brother, Willem Janse, mason, at Amsterdam in Holland; and furthermore, generally his person and estate, personal and real, nothing excepted, subject to all laws and judges; to recover therein without loss or cost, in case it be found at Amsterdam aforesaid that he, the subscriber, is obliged to distribute [pay out] the two hundred and three hundred guilders in the sentence mentioned with the interest thereon, to the estate of the father of Gerritie Gerritse, wife of Arnout Cornelisse [Viele] also dwelling here; but if the contrary be true, according the allegations of the subscriber, then according to the tenor of the aforesaid sentence this mortgage deed is to be void and of no effect.

Done in Albany the $\frac{13}{23}$ July, 1668.

ARENT JANSE.

J. Dehinsse.
Goosen Gerritse.

In my presence, D. V. SCHELLUYNE, Secretary, 1668.

The commissaries of Albany, etc., declare, by these presents, that in true rights, free ownership. they grant, convey and make over by these presents, to and for the behoof of Stoffel Janse [Abeel], master carpenter here, in a lot lying here on the hill, breadth two and thirty Rynland feet, length back to the lot of Capt. Abraham Staets, adjoining on the east side the plant cellar, on the south side Capt. Staets, on the west side David Schuyler, and on the north the street; free and unincumbered, excepting the lord's right, which lot said Stoffel Janse has bought and paid for, and therefore giving him, his heirs and successors or assigns, full power to dispose thereof, as he might do with his patrimonial effects; and promising therefore to apply to the right honorable the Heer general for a patent for said lot.

Done in Albany, the $\frac{13}{23}$ of July, 1668.

PHILIP PIETERSE SCHUYLER,

Acknowledged before me, D. V. SCHELLUYNE, Secretary, 1668.

Appeared before us, undersigned, commissaries of Albany, etc., Cornelis Teunise Van Slyck, born at Breuckelen, in the province of Utrecht, late *ractsperson* of the aforesaid colony, making known that it is certainly reported to him, that his brother Cornelis Theunisse Van Slyck is deceased, in his lifetime having dwelt at Breuckelen aforesaid at the brewery of the Vyffhoeck, also that he has had no tidings for four or five years from his aforesaid brother and other friends and relations, therefore he, the subscriber, appoints and fully empowers by these presents, the honorable Johannes Vander Bogart, alderman of Breuckelen aforenamed, and dependencies of the same, or in case of his honor's decease, whoever may have succeeded to his place, especially in his name and for his sake to find out what has fallen to him by the death of his aforenamed brother or other of his friends by will or *ab intestato*; his rights and claims with respect to the same, as well effects personal as real, actions and credits to receive, the same to his advantage to administer upon, acquittance for receipts to pass, and in case of refusal by means of justice to proceed, with power to substitute another person in his place having like or limited power, and further, all things to do, transact or perform, which he may deem needful or reasonable; promising at all times to hold true all that shall be done and performed in the matter aforesaid by virtue of these presents, by the aforesaid attorney or his substitute, without any gainsaying, on pledge according to laws, provided that the attorney be holden a proper statement to make when requested, of his aforesaid transactions and receipts

Done in Albany, the $\frac{21}{31}$ July, 1668.

KORNELIS VAN SLICK.

Philip Pieterse Schuyler.
R. V. Rensselaer.

In my presence, D. V. SCHELLUYNE, Secretary, 1668.

Appeared before us, undersigned, commissaries of Albany, etc., Jacob Tyssen Vander Heyden, and John Coneall, who declare that by exchange made with each other, in true rights, free ownership, they grant, convey, and make over by these presents, namely, Jacob Tyssen Vander Heyden to said Coneall in his house and lot, standing and lying here in Albany, by virtue of a deed of conveyance, of date $\frac{10}{20}$ October, 1665, as the same stands fenced and enclosed, excepting a small parcel of ground for an alley lying without the fence, bounded according to the tenor and contents of the aforesaid conveyance; and John Coneal conveys and makes over by these presents, to the behoof of the aforenamed Vander Heyden, his house and lot standing and lying here in Albany on the hill, breadth in front on the street twenty-two feet, and in length six rods, by virtue of patent and contract, of date the 21st of January, 1667, as the lot came to him by purchase from Sergeant Percker; respectively free and unincumbered, with no claims standing or issuing against the same, excepting the lord's right, without either of the parties making the least claims thereto any more; also acknowledging mutually that they are fully paid and satisfied therefor the last penny with the first, and therefore giving the one to the other respectively for their heirs and successors or assigns. *plenam actionem cessam*, and full power each to dispose of his own as they respectively might do with their patrimonial effects; promising the one to the other as before to protect and free the aforesaid houses and lots from all trouble and claims as is right, and further, never more to do nor suffer anything to be done against the same, in any manner, on pledge of their respective persons and estate, nothing excepted, subject to all laws and judges.

Done in Albany the $\frac{29}{8}$ $\frac{\text{July}}{\text{Aug.}}$, A.D. 1668.

JACOB TEYSSEN.
JOHN CONELL.

R. V. Rensselaer.
Philip Pieterse Schuyler.

In my presence,

D. V. SCHELLUYNE, Secretary

Appeared before us, undersigned, commissaries of Albany, etc., Mr. Johannes Provoost, dwelling here in Albany, who declares that he grants, conveys, and makes over by these presents, to and for the behoof of Harmen Vedder, his brother-in-law, who proposes to return to Holland, a certain sum of eight hundred and thirty guilders, fifteen stuivers and twelve pence, coming to him *per resto* from a settlement, A D. 1664, from the right honorable the directors of the privileged West India Company at the Chamber of Amsterdam in Holland, earned here in the character of assistant in their honors' service, according to the tenor and contents of said settlement placed in the hands of the assignees with the original of this, also acknowledging that he has been fully paid and satisfied therefor in goods received to his satisfaction; therefore giving full power to his aforenamed brother-in-law, Harmen Vedder, or the lawful bearer of this to demand, collect and receive the payment of said sum of *f*. 830. 15. 12. from the aforenamed Heeren directors, acquittance for the receipts to pass, which shall be valid as if granted by the subscriber himself; furthermore all things to do and perform to col ect the said sum, which the subscriber could or might do if himself present even though the matter should demand greater and more special authority than is herein expressed; promising at all times to hold good and true whatever may be done by virtue hereof, on pledge according to law.

Done in Albany in America the $\frac{30}{9}$ $\frac{\text{July}}{\text{Aug.}}$, 1668.

JOHANNES PROVOOST.

Philip Pieterse Schuyler.
Goosen Gerritse.

In my presence,

D. V. SCHELLUYNE, Secretary, 1668.

Appeared before us, undersigned, commissaries of Albany, etc., Philip Pieterse Schuyler, who declares that in true rights, free ownership, he grants, conveys and makes over by these presents, to and for the behoof of Mr. Abraham Staets, in a house and lot,[1] with a garden over the back [Dean] street, by virtue of a patent and conveyance, of date the 24th of April, 1667, and $\frac{9}{19}$ of June, 1666, respectively, also according to contract, of date $\frac{10}{20}$ of February, of the year 1666, the lot extending along the street, in breadth thirty wood feet, in length back to the fence of the brewery of Herman Rutgers, where it is of like breadth; the little alley[2] that runs to the garden, is included herein, the said part lot, house and garden lies here in Albany, and is bounded according to the description and contents of the contract therefor; to which reference is herein made, received by said grantor, from Volckert Janse [Douw], attorney for Hendrick Jochimse, without the grantor's making the least claim thereto any more, also acknowledging that he is fully paid and satisfied therefor, the last penny with the first, by the hands of the aforenamed Mr. Abraham Staats, and therefore giving *plenam actionem cessam*, and full power to the aforesaid Mr. Abraham Staats, his heirs and successors or assigns, to do with and dispose thereof as he might do with his patrimonial estate and effects; promising to protect and free the said house, lot and garden from all trouble, claims and liens of every person as is right, and further, never more to do nor suffer anything to be done against the same, either with or without law, in any manner, on pledge according to law.

Done in Albany the $\frac{5}{15}$ September, 1668.

PHILIP PIETERSE SCHUYLER.

R. V. Rensselaer
J. Dehinsse.

In my presence, LUDOVICUS COBES, Secretary.

Appeared before us, undersigned, commissaries of Albany, etc., Claes Fredrickse Van Petten,[3] and Cornelis Cornelise Viele,[4] husbandmen dwell-

---

[1] This lot was a part of the lot fronting on Broadway, on which the Exchange now stands.

[2] This little alley widened, is now contained in that part of State street, between Broadway and the river.

[3] Claes Fredrickse Van Petten was in Schenectady as early as 1664, when with Isaac Corn. Swits, he hired Willem Teller's *bouwery*, No. 5, on the Great Flat. Subsequently he purchased Sander Leendertse Glen's *bouwery*, No. 3. By his wife, Aeffie Arentse Bratt, he had three daughters and two sons, Andries and Claas, both of whom lived in Schenectady and left families. He died Oct. 3, 1728, aged 87 years 5 months. His wife died January 23d, 1728, aged 78.

[4] Cornelis Cornelise Viele, one of the early settlers of Schenectady, left a numerous family, six of whom were sons and left families, save perhaps, the last. They were: Arnout who was an Indian interpreter and lived in Albany, Cornelis, Pieter, and Teunis who settled in Schenectady Lewis who removed to Schaghticoke, and Volkert; besides daughters. The lands early belonging to this family were on the Mohawk river, three miles west of Schenectady.

ing at Schaenhechtade, who acknowledge that they are well and truly indebted to Marten Cornelise [Van Ysselstein[1]] in the quantity of two hundred and twenty beavers reckoned at eight guilders a piece, growing out of a matter of two remaining installments for the purchase and payment for a certain *bouwery*, dwelling house, barn and three ricks, with four horses, five milch cows, eight hogs, cart, plough and harrow purchased by the subscribers from him according to contract thereof, of date the $\frac{4}{14}$ July, 1667, which aforesaid sum of two hundred and twenty beavers, the subscribers, according to the tenor and contents thereof, promise to pay, to wit, one hundred and ten beavers in the month of February, 1669, and the remaining one hundred and ten beavers in the month of February, 1670, punctually; pledging specially the aforesaid *bouwery* and effects, and further, generally, their persons and estates, personal and real, having and to come, nothing excepted, subject to all laws.

Done in Albany, the 23d October, 1668.

CLAES FREDRICKSE.
CORNELIS CORNELISE VIELE.

R. V. Rensselaer.
Abram Staes.

This mortgage is satisfied as it respects the payment of Cornelis Cornelise Viele, but of Claes Van Petten not yet. Albany, 17 Sept., 1670.

Appeared before us, undersigned, commissaries of Albany, etc., Marten Cornelise [Van Ysselstein] husbandman, who declares that in true rights, free ownership, he grants, conveys and makes over by these presents to and for the behoof of Claes Fredericksе Van Petten and Cornelis Cornelise Veilen, husbandmen at Schaenectade, their heirs and successors or assigns, in the grantor's certain *bouwery*, with dwelling house, barn, three ricks, four horses, five milch cows, eight hogs, cart, plough and harrow, standing and lying at Schaenectade, at present in possession of said Claes Fredericksе and Cornelis Cornelisse, and according to patent of the right honorable Heer general, of date the 13 April, 1668, to the grantor given, and to the contract for the aforesaid *bouwery* and effects passed, of date $\frac{4}{14}$ July, 1667, all of which are by these presents delivered to the aforenamed Claes Fredericksе and Cornelis Cornelise, and regarding the boundaries, length and breadth of the aforesaid *bouwery* the grantor refers to the aforesaid four documents, acknowledging that he is fully paid and satisfied for the aforesaid *bouwery* and effects by the hands of said Claes Fredericksе and Cornelis Cornelise, namely with the sum of one hundred and ten beavers by him to his content received and with a mortgage for two hundred and twenty beavers according to the tenor of the aforesaid contract, without the grantor's hereafter making the least claim any more thereto, and therefore giving *plenam actionem cessam*, and full power to said Claes Fredericksе and Cornelis Cornelise, and their heirs, to dispose thereof as they might do with their patrimonial effects ;

[1] Marten Cornelisse Van Ysselstein or Esselstyn, was one of the fourteen first proprietors of Schenectady. After the sale of his *bouwery* there he removed to Claverack, where his descendants are still found. He was born in the city of Ysselstein, his wife Mayke Cornelise in Berrevelt; they made a joint will in 1677. He was not living in 1705, when his eldest son and heir, Cornelis Martense [Van Ysselstein] confirmed the conveyance to Van Petten of the Schenectady property.

promising to protect and free the aforesaid *bouwery* and effects from all trouble, actions and claims of every person as is right, and further, never more to do nor suffer anything to be done against the same, either with or without law, in any manner, on pledge according to law.

Done in Albany, 23d of October, 1668.

The mark of + MARTEN CORNELISE,
with his own hand set.

R. V. Rensselaer.
Abram Staes.

In my presence,

LUDOVICUS COBES, Secretary.

Appeared before us, undersigned, commissaries of Albany, etc., Rhynier Vander Coelen, dwelling in the Esopus, at present here in Albany, who acknowledges that he is well and truly indebted to Skipper Lucas Andriesse and Jan Joosten, dwelling at New York, in the sum of three hundred and forty-one guilders and eighteen stuivers in good strung seewant, growing out of freight due, and goods received at various times since the year 1666, from them received to his content, which aforesaid sum of three hundred and forty-one guilders and eighteen stuivers said Vander Coelen promises to pay at the farthest, by the first of the month of November next coming, whenever they, the creditors or the lawful holders of this obligation, shall come to Esopus; therefor pledging specially his distiller's kettle, helmet and worm, which he is now carrying from hence to the Esopus, and furthermore, generally, his person and estate, nothing excepted, to recover the aforesaid sum without loss and cost, and for the greater security of the above special bond in the matter aforenamed, the same shall be registered, if need be, by the secretary in the Esopus.

Done in Albany, the 24th of September, 1668.

REYNIER VANDER COELE.

J. Dehinsse.
Jan Verbeeck.

In my presence,

LUDOVICUS COBES, Secretary.

Appeared before us, undersigned, commissaries of Albany, etc., Willem Martense Huis, seaman, at present here in Albany, who acknowledges that he is well and truly indebted to Eldert Gerbertse Cruiff, in the sum of seven hundred guilders in good seewant, growing out of and for the matter of a great boat with sail and rigging (*seyl en treyl*), anchor and cable, bought of him on New Year's, 1668, with some other wares also to his full content received, which aforesaid sum of seven hundred guilders in seewant, said Willem Martense promises to pay as follows, when he next comes to New York, one hundred guilders in seewant to Aeltie Van Bremen, also a hundred guilders in seewant, when he comes up from thence, and the remaining five hundred guilders next April, or forepart of May of the year 1669, therefor pledging specially his half ferry boat (*schouw*) or the portion which he owns in company with Evert Lucasse [Backer], and furthermore generally his person and estate, nothing excepted, subject to all laws and judges, for the recovery of said sum, without cost or loss.

Done in Albany, the 29th of September, *Anno* 1668.

WILLEM MARTENSE HUES.

J. Dehinsse.
Jan Thomase.

In my presence,

LUDOVICUS COBES, Secretary.

This is canceled in presence of Volckert Janse [Douw] and Jan Bruyn this 27th May, 1669.

Appeared before us, undersigned, commissaries of Albany, etc., Davidt Pieterse Schuyler, who declares, that in true rights, free ownership, he grants, conveys and makes over by these presents, to and for the behoof of Claes Locq, his heirs and successors or assigns, in the grantor's certain half sloop *(jacht)* owned in company by him and said Lock and now in possession of the same, according to contract therefor, acknowledging that he is fully paid and satisfied for said half sloop by the hands of said Claes Locq, the last penny with the first, without the grantor's making the least claim any more thereto, and therefore giving *plenam actionem cessam*, and full power to Claes Lock and his heirs to dispose thereof as he might do with his patrimonial effects, promising to protect and free said half sloop from all trouble, actions and claims of every person as is right, and never more to do nor suffer anything to be done against the same, either with or without law, in any manner, on pledge, according to law.

Done in Albany, the 29th of October, 1668.

DAVYET SCHUYLER.

R. V. Rensselaer.
Abram Staes.

Appeared before us, undersigned, commissaries of Albany, etc. John Corneel, and Johannes De Wandelaer,[1] who declare that in exchange with each other in true rights, free ownership, they grant, convey and make over by these presents, namely, Jan Cornell to said Wandelaer his house and lot standing and lying here in Albany, in accordance with a deed of conveyance, of date $\frac{10}{20}$ October, 1665, as the same stands in fence and enclosure excepting a small parcel of ground for an alley without the fence, bounded according to the description and contents of the aforesaid conveyance; and Johannes De Wandelaer conveys and makes over by these presents to and for the behoof of the aforesaid John Corneel, his house and lot standing and lying also here in Albany on the hill, breadth in front on the street eighteen and a half wood feet, and length according to the evidence of the vendue book, being the just half bought in company with Omy La Grand; respectively free and unincumbered, with no claim standing or issuing against the same, excepting the lord's right, without either party's making the least claim in the matter aforesaid, and moreover, also

[1] Johannes De Wandelaer, of Leyden, Holland, married Sara Schepmoes, of New York, 17 March, 1672, and of ten children the fruit of this marriage eight were living at the date of his will, the 20th of June, 1705. In 1678 he bought of Jan Thomase the lot on the east corner of State and Chapel streets. His son, Johannes, settled in Albany, and for many years occupied the west corner of Maiden lane and Broadway. He married Lysbeth Gansevoort and had ten children.

acknowledging that they are mutually fully paid and satisfied therefor, but Johannes De Wandelaer in the exchange must contribute twenty-two whole good and merchantable beaver skins to be paid on the first of July, A. D. 1669, for which a mortgage shall be passed; and therefore giving respectively to each other, their heirs and successors or assigns, *plenam actionem cessam*, and full power to dispose thereof as they respectively might do with their patrimonial effects; promising to protect and free the aforesaid houses and lots, each as before, from all trouble and claims as is right, and further, never more to do nor suffer anything to be done against the same, in any manner, on pledge their respective persons and estates, nothing excepted, subject to all laws and judges.

Done in Albany, the 3d of December, 1668.

JOHN CONELL.
JOHANNES DE WANDELAER.

Abram Staes.
R. V. Rensselaer.

In my presence,

LUDOVICUS COBES, Secretary.

Appeared before us, undersigned, commissaries of Albany, etc., Johannes De Wandelaer, young man, dwelling here in Albany, who acknowledges that he is well and truly indebted to Corneel, in the quantity of twenty-two whole merchantable beaver skins, reckoned at eight guilders a piece, growing out of the matter of a remaining installment for the purchase and payment of a certain house and lot by the subscriber bought or exchanged, which aforesaid sum of twenty-two whole beavers the subscriber promises to pay on the first of July, of the year 1669, punctually, therefore pledging specially the aforesaid house and lot, and furthermore generally his person and estate, personal and real, having and to have, nothing excepted, subject to all the duke's (*Heeren*) laws and judges, to recover in time, if need be, the payment thereof without cost and loss.

Done in Albany, this 3d of December, 1668.

JOHANNES DE WANDELAER.

Abram Staes.
R. V. Rensselaer.

In my presence,

LUDOVICUS COBES, Secretary.

Appeared before us, undersigned, commissaries of Albany, etc., Frans Janse Pruyn, acting for Aekes Cornelise [Van Slyck], who declares that in true rights, free ownership, he grants, conveys, and makes over by these presents, to and for the behoof of Jan Labatie, his heirs and successors or assigns, in the grantor's certain house, lot, barn, garden and fruit trees, standing and lying in colony Rensselaerswyck, according to the evidence of the vendue book of said colony bid off by said Labatie at public sale, of date the 16 of January, 1664, extending and bounding on the westerly side the Heer *patroon* of the colony, northerly *corst kouts* easterly and southerly the public road, as the same lies in length, breadth and fence, free and unincumbered, with no claim standing or issuing against the same, excepting the right of the patroon of the colony, according to the description and contents of the conditions and proposals of said vendue book, and by virtue of a conveyance, of date the 5th of May, new style, 1666, in the Esopus; without the grantor's making the least claim thereto, also acknowledging that he is fully paid and satisfied therefor, the last penny with the first, therefore giving *plenam actionem cessam*, and full power to the aforesaid Labatie, his heirs and successors or assigns, to do with and dispose thereof as he might do with his patrimonial estate and effects; promising to protect and free the aforesaid house, lot, barn, garden and fruit trees, from all trouble, actions and liens of every person as is right, and further, never more to do nor suffer anything to be done against the same, with or without law, in any manner, on pledge according to law.

Done in Albany, the 7th of January, 166 8/9.

FFRANS JANSEN PRUEN.

Jan Verbeeck.
Jan Thomase.

In my presence.

LUDOVICUS COBES, Secretary.

Appeared before me, Ludovicus Cobes, secretary of Albany, etc., in the presence of the honourable Heeren commissaries, etc., Mr. Jacob De Hinsse, and Mr. Jan Verbeeck, Jan Labatie, who declares that in true rights, free ownership, he grants, conveys and by these presents, makes over to and for the behoof of Barent Pieterse [Coeymans], his heirs and successors or assigns, in the grantor's certain house, lot, barn, garden and fruit trees standing and lying in the colony Rensselaerswyck, according to the proofs of the vendue book of said colony, bid off at public sale by said Labatie, of date the 16th of January, 1664, extending and bounding on the westerly side the Heer patroon of the colony, northerly *corst couts*, easterly and southerly the public road as the same lies in length, breadth and fence, free and unincumbered, with no claim standing or issuing against the same, excepting the right of the Heeren patroon of the colony, according to the description and contents of the conditions and proposals of said vendue book, also by virtue of conveyance passed, of date the 5th of May, new style, 1666, in the Esopus, whereto reference is herein made, received by said grantor from Frans Janse [Pruyn] and Aques Cornelise [Van Slyck], without the grantor's making the least claim any more against the same; also acknowledging that he is fully paid and satisfied therefor, the last penny with the first, and therefore giving *plenam actionem cessam*, and full power to said Barent Pieterse, his heirs and successors or assigns, to do with and dispose thereof as he might do with his patrimonial effects; promising to protect and free said house, lot, barn, garden and fruit trees from all trouble, claims and liens of every person as is right, and further, never more to do nor suffer anything to be done, either with or without law, in any manner, on pledge according to law.

Done in Albany, the 12th of January, 166 8/9.

JAN LABATIE.

J. Dehinsse,
Jan Verbeeck.

In my presence,

LUDOVICUS COBES, Secretary.

Appeared before me, Ludovicus Cobes, secretary of Albany, etc., in the presence of the honorable Heeren commissaries of the same jurisdiction, Mr. Jacob Dehinsse, and Mr. Jan Verbeeck, Jan Bronck in character of attorney for his mother, Hilletie Bronex, who declares, that in true rights, free ownership, he grants, conveys and by these presents makes over to and for the behoof of Johannes Provoost vendue master, and trustee for the estate of the late Jan Adriessen, the Irishman, assisted by the Heer officer Gerard Swart, who by this conveyance makes over the same to Marten Gerritse [Van Bergen, his heirs and successors or assigns], in a certain pa[illegible] of land sold to said Jan Andriessen, containing about 69 morgens and a [illegible]t for a homestead (*hoftstede*) in breadth 20 rods and length 30 rods, bounded according to the descriptions of the patent to which reference is herein made; the grantor Jan Bronck, so also Provoost acknowledging that he is fully paid and satisfied for said lands, the first penny with the last, without the grantor's [Bronck] making the least pretension thereto any more, and therefore giving *plenum actionem cessam*, and full power to said Marten Gerritse and his heirs to dispose thereof as he might do with his patrimonial effects; promising the aforesaid piece or parcel of land to protect and free from all trouble, actions and claims as is right, and further, never more to do nor suffer anything to be done against the same, either with or without law, in any manner, on pledge according to law.

Done in Albany, the 8th of March, 166$\frac{8}{9}$.

JAN PIETERSEN BRONCK.
JOHANNES PROOVOST.
G. SWART.

J. Dehinsse.
Jan Verbeeck.

In my presence,

LUDOVICUS COBES, Secretary.

Appeared before me, Ludovicus Cobes, secretary of Albany, etc., in the presence of the honorable Heeren commissaries of the same jurisdiction, the Heer Ryckert Van Rensselaer and Mr. Jacob De Hinsse, Dirckie Hermes, wife of Jan Martense [De Wever], who acknowledges that she is well and truly indebted to the Heer Jeremias Van Rensselaer and Jacob Sanderse Glen, attorneys for Messrs. Mommaes, merchants at Amsterdam, in the sum of ..... in beavers according to obligation passed in the year 1661, of date ...... which aforesaid sum of ...... in beavers she, the subscriber, promises to pay to the aforementioned Mr. Rensselaer and Jacob Sanderse Glen,[1] or their order, to wit, twenty beavers every following year until full payment is made, therefor pledging her person and estate, personal and real, present and future, and specially three horses, to wit, an old mare and two young mare colts in their second year, also three oxen of one year, with a heifer of one year, also a milch

[1] Jacob Sanderse Glen was the eldest son of Sander Leenderse Glen, of Schenectady. He settled in Albany, his house lot being on the south side of State street, second west of Pearl street, which lot afterwards passed to his son-in-law, Harmanus Wendel, who married his daughter, Anna *Albany Annals*, I, 124. His wife was Catharina Van Whitbeck, who after his death in 1663, married again Jonas Volkertse Douw, 24th of April, 1669. Of his children, only the following were living in 1707; Anna wife of Harmanus Wendel, Helena, Jacob, Johannes; the latter also settled in Albany, married Janneite Bleecker, and died 1707 leaving three children.

cow of three years, which is a good one; to recover the payment thereof, if need be without cost or loss. (The milch cow of three years must be delivered next May).

Done in Albany, 13th of March, 166$\frac{8}{9}$.

DERCKIEN HERMES.

Appeared before me, Ludovicus Cobes, secretary of Albany, etc., in presence of the honorable Heeren commissaries, etc., the Heer Ryckart Van Rensselaer and Mr Jacob De Hinsse, Sweer Theunisse [Van Velsen],[1] husbandman, dwelling in the Colonie Rensselaerswyck, who acknowledges that he is well and truly indebted to Geertruyt Barents, wife of Jacob Heven, in the number of fourteen whole and merchantable beaver skins, for money disbursed, and merchandise received to his full content, according to obligation therefor, which aforesaid beavers, he, the subscriber, promises to pay with interest on the same since the receipt thereof until the final payment, therefor specially pledging his two lots lying at Lubberde land, in occupation of Jacob Heven, and generally his person and estate, personal and real, present and future, nothing excepted, for the recovery of the payment thereof, if need be, without loss or cost.

Done in Albany, the 27th of May, 1669.

SWEER THOONUSSEN.

R. V. Rensselaer.

Appeared before me, Ludovicus Cobes, secretary of Albany, etc., in the presence of the honorable Heeren commissaries, Mons. Ryckart Van Rensselaer and Mr. Jacob De Hinsse, Madame Johanna Ebbinck, empowered and commissioned by her husband Mr. Jeronimus Ebbinck, who declares, that in true rights, free ownership, she grants, conveys and makes over by these presents, to and for the behoof of Sweer Theunisse [Van Velsen], his heirs and successors or assigns, in the grantor's certain lot,[2] to the west the [North] river, lying between Hendrick Reur and said Sweer Theunisse at Lubberde land in the colony Rensselaerswyck, according to the description thereof made in the contract with his predecessor *(voorsaet)* Jan Barentse Wemp, deceased,[3] and of such length and breadth as the buyer has taken possession of; free and unincumbered with no claim standing or issuing against the same, excepting the right of the Heer patroon of the colony, without the grantor's making the least pretension thereto, any more, also acknowledging that she is fully paid and satisfied therefor, the last penny with the first, and therefore giving *plenam actionem cessam*, and full power to said Sweer Theunisse, his heirs and successors or assigns, to do with and dispose thereof as he might do with his patrimonial estate and effects; promising to protect and free said lot from all trouble, actions or liens of every person as is right, and further, never more to do nor suffer

[1] Sweer Theunisse Van Velsen the first miller at Schenectady, was killed at the massacre, February 9, 1690.

[2] This lot of land was near the mouth of the Poestenkil. In 1667 April, 13, Van Velsen obtained a patent for three morgens of *bouw* land and a mill-site there, which in 1675 he sold to Jan Corn. Vyselaer and Lucas Pieterse Coeymans.— *Deeds*, I, 271. The lot conveyed to him above by Mad. Ebbinck formed an addition to his former grant, on which he subsequently built a saw mill.

[3] Van Velsen married Maritie Myndertse, widow of Jan Barentse Wemp, his *voorsaet*; having no children of his own, on his death in 1690, his large property in Schenectady passed to the church and to the children of his wife by Wemp.

anything to be done against the same, with or without law, in any manner, under pledge according to law.

Done in Albany, the 13th of June, 1669.

JOHANNA EBBINCK.

R. V. Rensselaer.
J. De Hinsse.

Appeared before me, Ludovicus Cobes, secretary of Albany, etc., in the presence of the honorable Heeren commissaries, etc., Mr. Jan Verbeeck and Mr. Jacob De Hinsse, Volckert Janse [Douw], attorney for Hendrick Jochemse, who declares that in true rights, free ownership, he grants, conveys, and by these presents makes over, to and for the behoof of Abraham Staas, his heirs and successors or assigns, in a certain house and lot standing and lying in Albany, being the lot extending to the brewery of the grantor, in length ....and in breadth........., adjoining to the south, said Mr. Abraham, to the north Jan Vinhagen, to the west the street, to the east the brewery,[1] by virtue of a patent, of date 23d of April, 1652, to which reference is herein made, received by him from Hendrick Westerkamp, without the grantor's making the least pretension thereto any more, also acknowledging that he is fully paid and satisfied therefor the last penny with the first, by the hands of said Mr. Abraham Staas, and therefore giving *plenam actionem cessam*, and full power to said Mr. Abraham, his heirs and successors or assigns, to do with and dispose of the same, as he might do with his patrimonial estate and effects; promising to protect and free said house and lot from all trouble, actions, and liens of every person as is right, and further, never more to do nor suffer anything to be done against the same, with or without law, in any manner, on pledge according to law.

Done in Albany, the 12th of July, 1669.

VOLCKART JANSE.

Appeared before me, Ludovicus Cobes, secretary of Albany, etc., in the presence of the honorable Heeren commissaries, Mr. Jan Verbeeck and Mr. Jacob De Hinsse, Johannes De Wandelaer, who declares that in true rights, free ownership, he grants, conveys and makes over by these presents, to and for the behoof of Mr. William Paterson, his heirs and successors or assigns, in a certain house and lot, standing and lying here in Albany, in accordance with a deed of conveyance of date the 3d of December, 1668, received by the grantor from Jan Corneel, by way of exchange, and as the same stands fenced and enclosed, to which reference is herein made, without the grantor's making the least pretension any more thereto, also acknowledging that he is fully paid and satisfied therefor, the last penny with the first, by the hands of the aforesaid Mr. William Paterson, and therefore giving *plenam actionem cessam*, and full power to said Mr. William Paterson, his heirs and successors or assigns, to do with and dispose of the same, as he might do with his patrimonial estate and effects; promising to protect and free said house and lot from all trouble, actions and liens of every person as is right, and further, never more

[1] This lot was a part of the present Exchange lot fronting on Broadway.

to do nor suffer anything to be done against the same, with or without law, in any manner, on pledge according to law.

Done in Albany, the 21st of July, 1669.

JOHANNES DE WANDELAER.

Jan Verbeeck.
J. De Hinsse.

In my presence,

LUDOVICUS COBES, Secretary.

Appeared before me, Ludovicus Cobes, secretary of Albany, etc., in the presence of the honorable Heeren commissaries, Mr. Jan Verbeeck and Mr. Jacob De Hins e, Jacob Janse Flodder [*alias* Gardenier],[1] who acknowledges that he is well and truly indebted and in arrears to Eldert Gerbertsen Cruiff for a settlement with Lambert Albertse Van Neck, by him assumed, in the sum of one hundred and fourteen guilders in beavers for goods to his full content received, which said sum of *f* 114 in beavers the subscriber promises to pay to Eldert Gerbertse or the lawful holder of this in boards, three and twenty per beaver, punctually on the first of November next, therefor pledging specially his negro youngster, named Bockie, and furthermore generally his person and estate, nothing excepted, subject to all laws for the recovery of the aforesaid sum, without loss or cost.

Done in Albany, the 4th of August, A.D. 1669.

JACOB JANSE GERDENYER.

Jan Verbeeck.
J De Hinsse.

In my presence,

LUDOVICUS COBES, Secretary.

Appeared before me, Ludovicus Cobes, secretary of Albany, etc., in the presence of the honorable Heeren commissaries, Mons. R. V. Rensselaer and Mr. Jan Verbeeck, Jacob Janse Gardenier, who acknowledges that he is well and truly indebted to Heer Jeremias Van Rensselaer and Jacob Sanderse Glen, attorneys for Messrs. Mommaes, in regard to the estate of the late Jan Bastiaense Van Gutsenhoven, in the sum of two hundred and twenty-five guilders and seventeen stuivers in beavers for merchandise and wares to his full content received, which aforesaid sum of *f*. 225-17 in beavers the subscriber promises to pay said Messrs. or to the lawful holder of this, in the month of June, 1670, punctually and without farther extension. therefor specially pledging his mill and effects lying on the kill, his *bouwery*, horses and cattle at Kinderhoeck, the negress with a negro youngster named Christiaen, and further, generally, his person and estate, having and to have, nothing excepted, subject to all the lord's laws and judges, for securing the payment of the same, if need be, without loss or cost.

Done in Albany, the 5th of August, 1669.

JACOB JANSE GERDENYER.

R. V. Rensselaer.

In my presence,

LUDOVICUS COBES, Secretary.

---

[1] The Gardeniers, children of Jacob Janse Flodder, ten in number, settled chiefly in and about Kinderhook.

Appeared before me, Ludovicus Cobes, secretary of Albany, etc., in the presence of the honorable Heeren commissaries, etc., Mons. R. V. Rensselaer and Mr. Jacob De Hinsse, Jacob Loockermans, who declares that in true rights, free ownership, he grants, conveys, and makes over by these presents, to and for the behoof of Hans Hendrickse and Helmer Otten, their heirs and successors or assigns, in the grantor's certain lot lying on the hill here in Albany, breadth in front two rods eleven inches, in the rear two rods, length on the south side six rods one foot and nine inches, on the north side five rods ten feet and eight inches, adjoining on the north side Helmer Otten and Jan Clute, on the east side Geertruyt Vosburgh, on the south side Omy La Grand, on the west side the public street, by the grantor received from the Heeren commissaries of Albany, and by virtue of a conveyance, of date the $\frac{29}{8}$ $\frac{\text{May}}{\text{June}}$, of the year 1668, to which reference is herein made, free and unincumbered, without any claim standing or issuing against the same, save the lord's right, and therefore giving to the aforesaid Hans Hendrickse and Helmer Otten, their heirs and successors or assigns, *plenam actionem cessam*, and full power to dispose thereof, as they might do with their own patrimonial effects; promising to protect and free the aforesaid lot from all trouble, actions and liens of every person as is right, and further, never more to do nor suffer anything to be done against the same, with or without law, in any manner, on pledge according to law.

Done in Albany, the 15th of August, 1669.

JACOB LOKERMANS.

R. V. Rensselaer.
J. De Hinsse.

In my presence,

LUDOVICUS COBES, Secretary.

Appeared before me, Ludovicus Cobes, secretary of Albany, etc., in the presence of the honorable Heeren commissaries, Mr. Jan Verbeeck and Jacob De Hinsse, Jan Labatie, who declares that in true rights, free ownership, he grants, conveys and makes over by these presents, to and for the behoof of Pieter Jacobse Borsboom, his heirs and successors or assigns, in the grantor's certain house and lot lying here in Albany, breadth in front on the street forty wood feet and three and one-half inches, and in the rear on the end of Jacob Joosten's [Van Covelen's] lot, breadth thirty wood feet, and in the rear on the bank, breadth eight and twenty wood feet, and length to the [river] bank, which aforesaid house and lot is bounded northerly by the king's [court] house,[1] and south by the house of Jacob Joosten, by virtue of patent in the care of Mr. Jacob De Hinsse, of date the 3d of May, 1667, to which reference is herein made, under condition that the grantor also has purchased some feet of the lot from Sander Leendertse [Glen], the conveyance of which is also made, and which extends to the king's house, with a garden also, behind the fort, bounded on the one side by Herman Vedder, and on the other by Mr. Willet; free and unincumbered, with no claim standing or issuing against the same, excepting the lord's right; therefore giving to the aforesaid Jacob Borsboom, his heirs and successors or assigns, *plenam actionem cessam*, and full power to dispose thereof, as he might do with

---

[1] The Court House stood on the east corner of Broadway and Hudson street.

his own patrimonial effects; promising to protect and free the aforesaid lot from all trouble, actions and liens of every person as is right, and further, never more to do nor suffer anything to be done against the same, with or without law, in any manner, on pledge according to law.

Done in Albany, the 17th of September, 1669.

JAN LABATIE.

Jan Verbeeck.
J. De Hinsse.

Appeared before me, Ludovicus Cobes, secretary of Albany, etc., in the presence of the honorable Heeren commissaries, Mr. Jan Verbeeck and Mr. Jacob De Hinsse, Pieter Jacobse Borsboom, who declares, that in true rights, free ownership, he grants, conveys and makes over by these presents, to and for the behoof of Jan Labatie, his heirs and successors or assigns, in the grantor's certain *first* lot of land lying at Schaenhechtade bounding upon the land of Gerrit Bancker and the land of Claes Van Petten, containing eleven morgens and two hundred and sixty-three rods,[1] by virtue of a patent from the right honorable Heer general, Richard Nicolls, of date the 9th of May, 1668, to which reference is herein made, free and unincumbered, with no claim standing or issuing against the same, excepting the lord's right, and therefore giving to the aforenamed Jan Labatie, his heirs and successors or assigns, *plenam actionem cessam*, and full power to dispose thereof, as he might do with his patrimonial effects; promising to protect and free the aforesaid lot of land from all trouble, actions and liens of every person as is right, and further, nevermore to do nor suffer anything to be done against the same, with or without law, in any manner, on pledge according to law.

Done in Albany, the 17th of September, 1669.

PIETER YACOPSEN BORSBOOM.

Jan Verbeeck.
J. De Hinsse.

Appeared before me, Ludovicus Cobes, secretary of Albany, etc., in the presence of the honorable Heeren Mr. Jan Verbeeck and Mr. Jacob De Hinsse, Rhynier Vander Koelen, dwelling in the Esopus, who declares that he is well and honestly indebted and in arrears to Mr. Helmer Otten, in the quantity of one hundred and ninety whole and merchantable beaver skins to be paid in two installments, for a house and lot bought from him, according to contract therefor, and which lies here in Albany, which aforesaid sum the subscriber promises to pay punctually at the set time, therefor pledging specially the aforesaid house and lot, and generally his person and estate, nothing excepted, subject to all laws and judges, for the recovery of the aforesaid sum, without cost and loss.

Done in Albany, the 6th of October, 1669.

REYNIER VANDAER COELE.

Jan Verbeeck.
J. De Hinsse.

In my presence, LUDOVICUS COBES, Secretary.

---

[1] The land on the *Groote Vlachte*, at Schenectady, was divided into twenty lots numbered in two series from 1 to 10, commencing at each end of the Flat, and ten of the proprietors had each two of these allotments bearing the same number. P. J. Borsboom drew the two lots numbered seven, the first of which nearest the village he conveyed to Jan Labatie, but the *hindermost* lot being the one farthest off was inherited by his four daughters.

Appeared before me, Ludovicus Cobes, secretary of Albany, etc., in the presence of the honorable Heeren commissaries, Mr. Jan Verbeeck and Mr. Jacob De Hinsse, Capt. Thomas Willet, who acknowledges that he is well and honestly indebted and in arrears to Mr. Philip Pieterse Schuyler, in the quantity of four hundred ells of the best English cloth (*dosynties*), to his full content, and in payment for beavers received, which aforesaid four hundred ells of cloth the subscriber promises to pay to Mr. Philip Pieterse Schuyler, or his order, at the farthest, next May, in the year 1670, half blue and half red, like the samples exhibited, therefor pledging specially his house and lot lying here in Albany, and generally his person and estate, nothing excepted, subject to all laws and judges, for the recovery of said four hundred ells of cloth, without cost or loss.

Done in Albany, the 7th of October, 1669.

THO. WILLET.[1]

Jan Verbeeck.
J. De Hinsse.

In my presence, LUDOVICUS COBES, Secretary.

Appeared before me, Ludovicus Cobes, secretary of Albany, etc., in presence of the honorable Heeren commissaries, Jan Verbeeck and Mr. Jacob De Hinsse, Mr. Hendrick Koster, who declares by these presents that in true rights, free ownership, he grants, conveys and makes over by these presents, to Mr. Robert Sanders, in part of lot No. 12, lying on the hill here in Albany, breadth in front on the street fourteen feet one inch, and on the rear, twelve feet and three inches, Rynland measure, length three rods eleven feet, received by him, the grantor, from the Heeren commissaries, the same bounded and lying, according to the description in the patent from the right honorable governor general, Francis Lovelace, of date the 24th of May, A. D. 1669, to which reference is herein made, free and unincumbered, with no claim standing or issuing against the same, excepting the lord's right, without the grantor's making the least pretension thereto any more, also acknowledging that he is therefor fully paid and satisfied, the last penny with the first, by the hands of Robert Sanders[2] aforesaid; giving therefor *plenam actionem cessam*, and full power to said Robert Sanders, his heirs and successors or assigns, to dispose of and do therewith as he might do with his patrimonial possessions and effects; promising to protect and free said part lot from all claims, actions and liens of every person as is right, and never more to do nor suffer anything to be done against the same, either with or without law, in any manner, on pledge according to law.

Done in Albany, the 11th of October, 1669.

HENDERECK KOSTER.

Jan Verbeeck.
J. DeHinsse.

In my presence, LUDOVICUS COBES, Secretary.

[1] Thomas Willet came to New Amsterdam from New England at the capture of the province by the English in 1664. He was made the first mayor of the city under English rule, and for several years was a trader. Subsequently he returned to Massachusetts; and died in 1674.—*Valentine's Manual*, 1864, 622: *Savage's Genealogical Dictionary*.

[2] Robert Sanders was the eldest child of Thomas Sanders and his wife Sarah Van Gorcum, and was baptized in New Amsterdam the 10th of Nov., 1642. By trade he was a smith, but later became a trader. His wife was Elsie Barentse; they had one son, Barent, and daughters Maria, who married Gerrit Rosenboom, Elsie, who died in 1732, aged 48 years, and Sara, wife of Henrich Greefraat.

Appeared before me, Ludovicus Cobes, secretary of Albany, etc., in the presence of the honorable Heeren commissaries, Mr. Jan Verbeeck and Mr. Ryckart Van Rensselaer, Mr. Philip Pieterse Schuyler, who declares by these presents that in true rights, free ownership, he grants, conveys and makes over by these presents, to Mr. Thomas De Lavall,[1] merchant, dwelling at new York, in a certain parcel of land lying in the Esopus, bounded according to the description in the patent thereof from the right honorable governor general, Richard Nicolls, of date the 23d of April, 1667, to which reference is herein made, free and unincumbered, with no claims standing or issuing against the same, except the lord's right, without the grantor's making the least pretension thereto any more, also acknowledging that he is fully paid and satisfied therefor, the last penny with the first, by the hands of Mr. Delavall aforenamed, and therefore giving *plenam actionem cessam*, and full power to said Mr. DeLavall, his heirs and successors or assigns, to do with and dispose thereof as he might do with his patrimonial estate and effects; promising to protect and free said parcel of land from all trouble, actions and liens of every person as is right, and further, never more to do nor suffer anything to be done against the same, with or without law, in any manner, on pledge according to law.

Done in Albany, the 2d of November, 1669.

PHILIP PIETERSE SCHUYLER.

Jan Verbeeck.
R. V. Rensselaer.

Appeared before me, Ludovicus Cobes, secretary of Albany. etc., in presence of the honorable Heeren commissaries, Mr. Jan Verbeeck and Mr. Philip Pieterse Schuyler, Goosen Gerritse [Van Schaick], trader, who declares that in true rights, free ownership, he grants, conveys, and makes over by these presents, to Mr. Thomas De Lavall, trader, dwelling at New York, in certain parcels of land lying in the Esopus, bounded according to evidence of the patent thereof from the right honorable governor general, Richard Nicolls, of date the 25th of April, 1667, to which reference is herein made, free and unincumbered, with no claim standing or issuing against the same, except the lord's right, without the grantor's making the least claim against the same any more; also acknowledging that he is fully said and satisfied therefor, the last penny with the first, by the hands of Mr. De Lavall, aforesaid, and therefore giving *plenam actionem cessam*, and full power to said Mr. De Lavall, his heirs, and successors or assigns, to do with and dispose thereof, as he might do with his patrimonial estate and effects; promising to protect and free said parcels of land from all trouble, claims and liens of every person as is right, and further, never more to do nor suffer anything to be done against the same, either with or without law, in any manner, on pledge according to law.

Done in Albany, the 5th of November, A.D. 1669.

Note.—This conveyance is made with this reservation: as Goosen Gerritse has sold said land to Claes Teunisse, for three hundred and

---

[1] Thomas Delavall came to New York with the English expedition in 1664, and settled there as a merchant. He prospered, held many important civil offices, and died in 1682.—*Valentine's Manual*, 1864, 577.

fifty skipples of wheat, which sale begins now, and as said Claes Theunisse is to pay the aforesaid three hundred and fifty skipples of grain, within the time of four years, every year a fourth part, the first installment next year, and so on every year, until payment is completed, which payment shall be made to Mr. De Lavall; failing of said payment, said Claes Theunisse shall lose the purchase of the land. *Actum ut supra.*

GOOSEN GERRETSEN.

Jan Verbeeck.
Philip Pieterse Schuyler.

In my presence,

LUDOVICUS COBES, Secretary.

Appeared before me, Ludovicus Cobes, secretary of Albany, etc., in the presence of the honorable Heeren commissaries, Mons. Ryckart Van Rensselaer, and Mr. Jan Verbeeck, Mr. Goosen Gerritse [Van Schaick], trader, dwelling here in Albany, who declares by these presents that in true rights, free ownership, he grants, conveys and makes over to Mr. Philip Pieterse Schuyler, also trader, dwelling here, in the half of his *bouwery* with all the appurtenances as well of lands, as cattle and horses, which are lawfully coming to him in company with said Mr Schuyler, together with the lands lying in the Halfmoon, set forth in three patents thereof, in the custody of said Schuyler, to which reference is herein made, free and unincumbered, with no claim standing or issuing against the same, save the lord's right, without the grantor's making the least pretension thereto any more, also acknowledging that he is fully paid and satisfied therefor, by a bill of exchange of fifteen hundred guilders, Holland money, by the hands of Mr. Schuyler, aforenamed, and therefore giving *plenam actionem cessam*, and full power to the aforesaid Philip Schuyler, his heirs and successors or assigns, to do with and dispose thereof, as he might do with his patrimonial estate and effects, promising to protect and free said half *bouwery*, and the appurtenances of the same, from all trouble, actions and liens of every person as is right, and further, never more to do nor suffer anything to be done against the same, either with or without law, in any manner, on pledge according to laws, therefor provided.

Done in Albany, the 23d of November, 1669.

GOOSEN GERRITSEN.

R. V. Rensselaer.
Jan Verbeeck.

In my presence,

LUDOVICUS COBES, Secretary.

This conveyance is canceled this 8th of March, 1669.

Appeared before me, Ludovicus Cobes, secretary of Albany, etc., in presence of the honorable Heeren commissaries, Mr. Ryckart Van Rensselaer and Mr. Jan Verbeeck, Mr. Philip Pieterse Schuyler, trader and commissary of Albany, who acknowledges that he is well, truly and honestly indebted and in arrears to Mr. Goosen Gerritse [Van Schaick], in the sum of fifteen hundred Carolus guilders, to be paid in Holland, by exchange, in the month of November next, in the year 1670, growing out of the matter of the purchase and consideration money for the half of a *bouwery* and lands with their appurtenances, bought by the subscriber from him, according to the descriptions of three patents thereof; which 1500 guilders, Holland money, the subscriber promises to pay, according to the tenor and contents of the bill of exchange, to Mr. Goosen Gerritse, aforesaid, therefor pledging specially said half of the *bouwery* and appurtenances of the same, and furthermore, generally, his person and estate, personal and real, having and to have, nothing excepted, subject to all laws, to recover said payment if need be, without loss or cost.

Done in Albany, the 23d of November, 1669.

PHILIP PIETERSE SCHUYLER.

R. V. Rensselaer.
Jan Verbeeck.

In my presence,

LUDOVICUS COBES, Secretary.

This mortgage is canceled this 8th of March, 1669.

Appeared before me, Ludovicus Cobes, secretary of Albany, etc., in the presence of the honorable Heeren commissaries, Mons. Ryckart Van Rensselaer and Mr. Philip Pieterse Schuyler, Jan Janse Bleecker, burgher and inhabitant here, dwelling in Albany, who acknowledges that he is well, truly and honestly indebted and in arrears to Mr. Jan Clute, in the quantity of eighty-five whole and good merchantable beaver skins, reckoned at eight guilders a piece, growing out of the matter of two remaining installments on the purchase and payment of a certain house and lot, by the subscriber of him, bought according to contract thereof, dated 5th of January, 1669, which aforesaid sum of eighty-five whole beavers, the subscriber promises to pay according to the tenor and contents of the same, in two installments of a half each, in the year 1670 and 1671, on the first of July; therefor pledging specially the aforesaid house and lot, and further, generally, his person and estate, personal and real, having and to have, nothing excepted, subject to all laws and judges, to recover the payment thereof, if need be, without loss or cost.

Done in Albany, the 5th of January, 1669.

JAN JANSE BLEECKER.

R. V. Rensselaer.
Philip Pieterse Schuyler.

In my presence,

LUDOVICUS COBES, Secretary.

Appeared before me, Ludovicus Cobes, secretary of Albany, etc., in the presence of the honorable Heeren commissaries, Mons. Ryckart Van Rensselaer and Mr. Jan Verbeeck, Jurriaen Janse Groenewout, who declares by these presents that in true rights, free ownership, he grants, conveys and makes over to Jan Conneel, in a certain house and lot, lying here in Albany, with all that is fast by earth and nailed, and in breadth and length as it lies in fence, adjoining on the north the *dwars* house, and south the house of Paulus Martense [Van Benthuysen], on condition that the *dwars* house shall retain a foot of land running in a straight line to a point on the northeast side, and a free drip between him and Paulus Martense; by virtue of a patent from the right honorable general, Richard Nicolls, dated the 11th of May, 1667, to which reference is herein made, free and unincumbered, with no claim standing or issuing against the same, except the lord's right, without the grantor's making the least pretension thereto any more; also acknowledging that he has received a mortgage therefor by the hands of said John Conneel, for the sum of sixty-five beavers, to be paid in two installments, and therefore giving *plenam actionem cessam*, and full power to the aforenamed Jan Conneel, his heirs and successors or assigns, to do with and dispose of the same, as he might do with his patrimonial estate and effects; promising to protect and free said house and lot from all such trouble, actions and liens of every person as are lawful, and further, never more to do nor suffer anything be done against the same, either with or without law, in any manner, on pledge according to laws therefor provided.

Done in Albany, the 8th of February, 1669.

The mark of ⋎⋏ JURRIAEN JANSE GROENEWOUT, with his own hand set.

R. V. Rensselaer.
Jan Verbeeck.

In my presence,

LUDOVICUS COBES, Secretary.

Appeared before me, Ludovicus Cobes, secretary of Albany, etc., in the presence of the honorable Heeren commissaries, etc., Mons. Ryckart Van Rensselaer and Mr. Jan Verbeeck, Jan Conneel, burgher here in Albany, who acknowledges that he is well and honestly indebted to Jurriaen Janse Groenewout, in the quantity of sixty-five whole, good and merchantable beaver skins, growing out of the matter of two remaining installments for the purchase and consideration money of a certain house and lot, purchased of him by the subscriber, which aforesaid sum of sixty-five whole and good merchantable beaver skins, the subscriber promises to pay, according to the tenor and contents of the same [contract], in two installments, to wit, thirty beavers the last of July, 1670, and thirty-five beavers the year following, therefor specially pledging said house and lot, and further, generally, his person and estate, personal and real, having and to have, nothing excepted, subject to all laws, to recover in due time (if need be) the payment without loss or cost.

Done in Albany, the 8th of February, 1669.

JOHN CONELL.

R. V. Rensselaer.
Jan Verbeeck.

In my presence,

LUDOVICUS COBES, Secretary.

Appeared before me, Ludovicus Cobes, secretary of Albany, etc., in the presence of the honorable Heeren commissaries, etc., Mr. Abraham Staas and Mr Jan Verbeeck, Pieter Adriaense [Soogemakelyk *alias* Van Woggelum] who declares that he grants, conveys, and by these presents makes over to and for the behoof of Helmer Otten, a barn and rick lying at Schaenhechtede, and a garden in the valley (*leeghte*), together with twenty-six morgens and a hundred and sixty-four rods of land,[1] in two lots, fenced and bounded according to description in the patent thereof,

[1] Helmer Otten died soon after this conveyance, and his widow married Ryer Schermerhorn, some of whose descendants occupy this farm to this day.

from the right honorable general, Nicolls, dated the 5th of June, 1667, to which reference is herein made; free and unincumbered, with no claims standing or issuing against the same, excepting the lord's right, without the grantor's making the least pretension thereto any more, also acknowledging that he is fully paid and satisfied therefor by an obligation for the sum of thirty-five beavers, and therefore giving *plenam actionem cessam*, and full power to said Helmer Otten, his heirs and successors or assigns, to do with and dispose of said barn, rick, garden and lots of land as he might do with his patrimonial estate and effects; promising to protect and free the same from all such troubles, actions and liens of every person as are lawful, and further, never more to do nor suffer anything to be done against the same, with or without law, in any manner, on pledge according to laws therefor provided.

Done in Albany, the 13th of August, 1670.

PIETER ADRIAENSE.

In my presence,

LUDOVICUS COBES, Secretary.

Appeared before me, Ludovicus Cobes, secretary of Albany, etc., in the presence of the right honorable Heeren commissaries, etc., Mr. Abraham Staas and Mr. Jan Verbeeck, Domine Gideon Schaets, preacher here, who declares that in true rights, free ownership, he grants, conveys and by these presents, makes over to and for the behoof of the honorable Mr. Thomas De Lavall, in his house and lot lying here in Albany on the hill, with all that is fast by earth and nailed, and the lot is in breadth front and rear, twenty-five feet, length on the south side, four rods six feet and three inches, on the north side four rods three feet three inches, adjoining on the east side Claes Van Rotterdam, on the south side, Barent Rhynderse, smith, on the west and north side the highway, according to survey and regulation of the surveyor, of date the 5th of May, 1668, and by virtue of a conveyance to him, the grantor, given, to which reference is herein made, free and unincumbered, with no claims standing or issuing against the same, excepting the lord's right, without the grantor's making the least pretension against the same any more, also acknowledging that he is fully paid and satisfied therefor, the first penny with the last, and therefore giving *plenum actionem cessam*, and full power to *Mynheer* De Laval, his heirs and successors or assigns, to do with and dispose of the aforesaid house and lot, as he might do with his patrimonial estate and effects; promising to protect and free the same from all such trouble, claims and liens, as are lawful, and further, never more to do nor suffer anything to be done against the same with or without law, in any manner, on pledge according to laws provided therefor.

Done in Albany, the 17th of August, 1670.

This conveyance is made with the reservation that the honorable Heer De Laval shall furnish sureties and security for the remaining payments, to give satisfaction to Domine Schaets or his order according to the conditions of the sale.

GIDEON SCHAETS, P: in N. Albany.

Abram Staes.
Jan Verbeeck.

Acknowledged before me,

LUDOVICUS COBES, Secretary.

By virtue of the conveyance by Domine Gideon Schaets, passed for the behoof of the honorable Heer De Laval, of a house and lot lying on the hill, here in Albany, in breadth, length and boundaries, according to the tenor and contents of the same, *Mynheer* Thomas De Laval, declares that in true rights, free ownership, he grants, conveys and by these presents, makes over in said house and lot, to Jan Conneel, his heirs and successors or assigns, also acknowledging that he is fully paid and satisfied therefor, by the hands of said Jan Conneel by the half of the promised purchase money and a mortgage deed for the other half, and therefore giving *plenam actionem cessam*, to the aforenamed Jan Conneel, or his assigns, to do with and dispose of said house and lot, as he might do with his patrimonial estate and effects; promising to free and protect the same from all such troubles, claims and liens, as are lawful, and further, never more to do nor to suffer anything to be done against the same, with or without law, in any manner, on pledge according to laws therefor provided.

Done in Albany, the 17th of August, 1670.

THO: DE LAVALL.

Abram Staes.
Jan Verbeeck.

Acknowledged before me,

LUDOVICUS COBES, Secretary.

Appeared before me, Ludovicus Cobes, secretary of Albany, etc., in the presence of the right honorable Heeren commissaries, etc., Mr. Jan Verbeeck and Mr. Abraham Staas, Jan Conneel, burgher here, who acknowledges that he is well and honestly indebted to the right honorable Mr. De Laval, in the sum of two hundred and seven guilders in whole, good and merchantable beaver skins, growing out of the matter of a payment, remaining due for the purchase and consideration money of a certain house and lot bought of him, by the subscriber, according to the tenor and contents of the contract therefor, which aforesaid sum of two hundred and seven guilders, in whole, good and merchantable beaver skins, the subscriber promises to pay on the set day of payment, therefor pledging specially the aforesaid house and lot, and generally his person and estate, personal and real, present and future, nothing excepted, and putting the same in subjection to the lord's laws and judges, for the recovery of the payment in due time, if need be, without loss and cost.

Done in Albany, the 17th of August, 1670.

JOHN CONELL.

Abram Staes.
Jan Verbeeck.

Acknowledged before me,

LUDOVICUS COBES, Secretary.

Appeared before me, Ludovicus Cobes, secretary of Albany, etc., in the presence of the honorable Heeren commissaries, etc., Mr. Jan Verbeeck and Mr. Abraham Staas, Jan Conneel, who declares that in true rights, free ownership, he grants, conveys, and by these presents, makes over, to and for the behoof of Mr. John Stuart,[1] a shanty (*loodts wooning*), with the lot of the same, lying on the hill between Evert Janse

[1] John Stuart was deceased in 1675, when his administrators sell his house and lot on the hill to Lourens Van Alen.— *Deeds*, I, 276.

[Wendel], and Wynant Gerritse [Vander Poel],[2] the lot is twelve feet, seven and one-half inches, Rynland measure in breadth, and in length, back six rods and five feet; free and unincumbered, with no claims standing or issuing against the same, excepting the lord's right, without the grantor's making the least pretension any more thereto, also acknowledging that he is fully paid and satisfied therefor, the first penny with the last, by the hands of said Stuart, and therefore giving *plenam actionem cessum*, and full power to Mr. Stuart, his heirs and successors or assigns, to do with and dispose of said shanty and lot, as he might do with his patrimonial estate and effects; promising to protect and free the same from all such troubles, claims and liens as are lawful, and further, never more to do nor suffer anything to be done against the same, with or without law, in any manner, on pledge according to laws, therefor provided.

Done in Albany, the 20th of August, 1670.

JOHN CONELL.

Abram Staes.
Jan Verbeeck.

Acknowledged before me,

LUDOVICUS COBES, Secretary.

Appeared before me, Ludovicus Cobes, secretary of Albany, etc., in the presence of the honorable Heeren commissaries, etc., Mr Jan Verbeeck and Mr. Abraham Staas, Herman Vedder, who declares, that in true rights, free ownership, he grants, conveys and by these presents makes over, to and for the behoof of Robert Sanders, the half of the land called Stone Arabia with all his title thereto, free and unincumbered, with no claims standing or issuing against the same, save the lord's right, without the grantor's making the least pretension thereto any more, also acknowledging that he is fully paid and satisfied therefor, the first penny with the last, by the hands of Robert Sanders, and therefore giving *plenam actionem cessam*, and full power to said Robert Sanders, his heirs and successors or assigns, to do with and dispose of said portion of land, as he might do with his patrimonial estate and effects; promising to protect and free the same from all such trouble, actions and liens as are lawful, and further never more to do nor suffer anything to be done against the same, either with or without law, in any manner, on pledge according to laws therefor provided.

Done in Albany, the 21st of August, 1670.

HARMEN VEDDER.

Abram Staes.
Jan Verbeeck.

Acknowledged before me,

LUDOVICUS COBES, Secretary.

Appeared before me, Ludovicus Cobes, secretary of Albany, etc., in presence of the honorable Heeren commissaries, etc, Mr. Jan Verbeeck and Mr. Philip Pieterse Schuyler, Mr. Jurriaen Theunisse, tapster [*alias* glazier] who declares, that in true rights, free ownership, he grants, con-

[1] Evert Janse Wendel owned the lot on the west corner of State and James streets; Wynant Gerritse Vander Poel, on the east corner of State and North Pearl streets.

veys and makes over by these presents, to and for the behoof of Mr. Abraham Staes and Mr. Johannes Provoost, his just third part of land belonging to him in partnership with Jan Bruyns and Jan Clute, with the barn and his right thereto appertaining, according to contract for the same, and in virtue of a patent thereof given by the right honorable general, Nicolls, now in custody of Jan Bruyns, to which reference is herein made, free and unincumbered, with no claims standing or issuing against the same, excepting the lord's right, and without the grantor's making the least pretension any more against the same, acknowledging that he is fully paid and satisfied therefor, the first penny with the last, by the hands of said Mr. Abraham Staes and Johannes Provoost, and therefore giving *plenam actionem cessam*, and full power to the aforesaid Mr. Abraham Staes and Johannes Provoost, their heirs and successors or assigns, to do with and dispose of said third part of the land, barn and appurtenances of the same, as they might do with their patrimonial estate and effects; promising to protect and free said third part of the land, barn and appurtenances of the same from all such troubles, claims and liens of every person as are lawful, and further, never more to do nor suffer anything to be done against the same, with or without law, in any manner, on pledge according to laws therefor provided.

Done in Albany, the 24th of Aug., 1670

JURREJAN TUNSEN.

Jan Verbeeck
Philip Pieterse Schuyler.

Acknowledged before me,

LUDOVICUS COBES, Secretary.

Appeared before me, Ludovicus Cobes, secretary of Albany, etc., in presence of the honorable commissaries, etc., Mr. Jan Verbeeck and Mr. Abraham Staas, Cornelis Cornelisse Viele who declares that in true rights, free ownership, he grants, conveys and by these presents makes over to and for the behoof of Jurriaen Theunisse [Glasemacker], in a house and barn with two ricks and also one on the land, with a garden behind the house, together with twelve morgens and one hundred and thirty rods of land lying at Schaenhechtede,[1] being lot No. 8, fenced and bounded according to the description of the patent thereof, to which reference is herein made, free and unincumbered, with no claims standing or issuing against the same, excepting the lord's right, and without the grantor's making the least pretension any more against the same, also acknowledging that he is fully paid and satisfied therefor, the first penny with the last, through the hands of the aforenamed Jurriaen Theunisse, and therefore giving *plenam actionem cessam*, and full power to the aforesaid Jurriaen Theunisse, his heirs and successors or assigns, to do with and dispose of the said house, lot, garden, ricks and lands, as he might do with his patrimonial estate and effects; promising to protect and free the same from all such troubles, claims and liens, of every person as are lawful, and further, never more to do nor suffer anything to be done against

[1] This lot No. 8, lies on the Groote Vlachte and was originally patented to Marten Cornelise Van Ysselsteyn by whom it was conveyed to C. V. Petten and C. C. Viele. From Theunisse it passed to Dirk Hesselingh who sold it to Harmen Vedder in 1672, in which family it remained many years. This lot is now included in the homestead of Col. Daniel D. Campbell of Rotterdam.

the same, with or without law, in any manner, on pledge according to laws therefor provided.

Done in Albany, the 25th of August, 1670.

CORNELIS CORNELISSE VIELE.

Abram Staes
Jan Verbeeck.

Acknowledged before me,

LUDOVICUS COBES, Secretary.

Appeared before me, Ludovicus Cobes, secretary of Albany, etc., in the presence of the honorable Heeren commissaries, etc., Mr. Jan Verbeeck and Mr. Abram Staes, Jurriaen Theunisse Tappen, who declares that in true rights, free ownership, he grants, conveys and makes over by these presents, to and for the behoof of Cornelis Cornelisse Viele, in a house and lot lying in Albany on the south side of Pieter Hartgers, to the west the first kil, on the north side the great street, breadth in front on the street one rod three feet, eleven inches, and in the rear on the kil one rod one foot and four inches, length on the east side five rods one foot ten inches, on the west side five rods five feet and two inches, Rynland measure, by virtue of the patent thereof from the right honorable general. Nicolls, dated the 2d of May, 1668, to which reference is herein made, free and unincumbered, with no claims standing or issuing against the same, excepting the lord's right and without the grantor's making the least pretension thereto any more, also acknowledging that he is fully paid and satisfied therefor, the first penny with the last, and therefore giving *plenum actionem cessam*, and full power to the aforenamed Cornelis Cornelisse Viele, his heirs and successors or assigns, to do with and dispose of said house and lot, as he might do with his patrimonial estate and effects; promising to protect and free the same from all such troubles, claims and liens, as are right, and further, never more to do nor suffer anything to be done against the same, with or without law, in any manner, on pledge according to laws therefor provided.

Done in Albany, the 26th of August, 1670.

JUREJAN TUNSE.

Abram Staes.
Jan Verbeeck.

Acknowledged before me,

LUDOVICUS COBES, Secretary.

Appeared before me, Ludovicus Cobes, secretary of Albany, etc., in the presence of the right honorable Heeren commissaries, etc., Mr. Ryckard Van Rensselaer and Mr. Jan Verbeeck, Capt. Thomas Willet, trader, who declares that in true rights free ownership, he grants, conveys and makes over by these presents, to and for the behoof of Jan Byvanck[1] in a garden lying behind Fort Albany, before this belonging to Gerrit the cooper as the same now lies in fence between the garden of Jan Hermense, baker, and Pieter Jacobse Borsboom, free and unincumbered, with no claims standing or issuing against the same, except the lord's right, and without

---

[1] Jan Byvanck, from Olderzee in Holland, was in Albany, as early as 1665. — *Deeds*, I, 206. In 1666, he married Belitje Evertse Duycking, of New York; several of their children were baptized in Albany as late as 1688, soon after which he appears to have returned to New York, where he married again, Sara Fraus, widow, Nov. 3, 1692.— *Valentine's Manual*, 1862. He was born in 1634.

the grantor's making the least pretension any more against the same, acknowledging that he is fully paid and satisfied therefor, the first penny with the last, by the hands of Jan Byvanck, and therefore giving *plenam actionem cessam*, and full power to said Jan Byvanck, his heirs and successors or assigns, to do with and dispose of the aforesaid garden, as he might do with patrimonial estate and effects; promising to protect and free the same from all such troubles, claims and liens as are lawful, and further, never more to do nor suffer anything to be done against the same, with or without law, in any manner, on pledge according to laws therefor provided.

Done in Albany, the 29th of August, 1670.

Jan Verbeeck. THO. WILLET.
R. V. Rensselaer.

Acknowledged before me,

LUDOVICUS COBES, Secretary.

Appeared before me, Ludovicus Cobes, secretary of Albany, etc., in the presence of the right honorable Heeren commissaries, etc., Mr. Abraham Staes and Mr. Jan Verbeeck, Barent Albertse Brat, burgher here, who acknowledges that he is well and honestly indebted and in arrears to Mr. Daniel Hondecoutre, in the sum of three hundred and seventy-eight guilders and nine stuivers in beavers, for merchandise to his full content received, which aforesaid *f* 378–9 the subscriber promises to pay to Mr. Hondecoutre, or his order, in good whole and merchantable beaver skins, reckoned at eight guilders a piece in the month of June next, of the year 1671, with interest on the same at eight per cent, but if he pay the half he shall be free from interest; therefor pledging specially his house and lot standing and lying here in Albany, next the house of Hendrick Bries, and further more generally, his person and estate, personal and real, present and future, nothing excepted, to recover the payment in due time, if need be, without cost or loss.

Done in Albany, the 6th of September, 1670.

The mark of BARENT + ALBERTSE BRAT,
Abram Staes. with his own hand set.
Jan Verbeeck.

Acknowledged before me,

LUDOVICUS COBES, Secretary.

Appeared before me, Ludovicus Cobes, secretary of Albany, etc., in the presence of the honorable Heeren commissaries, etc., Mr. Jan Verbeeck and Mr. Philip Pieterse Schuyler, Mr. Jan Clute, Jurriaen Theunisse [Tapster] and Meyndert Fredericksе, smith, who declare that in true rights, free ownership, they grant, convey, and make over by these presents, to and for the behoof of Marten Gerritse [Van Bergen] in a certain parcel of land lying at Coxhaxki, adjoining southerly the land of Hilleken Bronex,[1] and taking its beginning from the Stone creek extending south along the Katskil path to the woods or the hill *Styftsinck*, and east to the river, and again north to the land of Hilleken Bronex, abovenamed.

* * * [The remainder is wanting.]

---

[1] Hilleke was the wife of Pieter Brouck, who was perhaps deceased in 1670.

Appeared before me, Ludovicus Cobes, secretary of Albany, etc., in the presence of the honorable Heeren commissaries, etc., Mr Philip Schuyler and Mr. Jan Van Bael, Mr. Jan Bruyns, who declares that in true rights, free ownership, he grants, conveys and makes over by these presents, to and for the behoof of Mr. Helmer Otten, in a certain house, lot and garden at present occupied by Pieter Adriaense [Sogemakelyck, *alias* Van Woggelum] as the same is built, enclosed and fenced, standing and lying here in Albany, bounded according to the tenor and contents of the contract, and other proofs, to which reference is made, free and unincumbered, with no claims standing or issuing against the same, save the lord's right, and without the grantor's making the least pretension thereto any more, acknowledging that he is fully paid and satisfied therefor with an obligation and mortgage, from the hands of said Helmer Otten, and therefore giving *plenam actionem cessam*, and full power to said Helmer Otten, his heirs and successors or assigns, to do with and dispose of said house, lot, and garden as he might do with his patrimonial possessions and effects; promising to protect and free the same from all such trouble, claims and liens of every person as are lawful, and further, never more to do nor suffer anything to be done against the same, with or without law, in any manner, on pledge according to laws therefor provided.

Done in Albany, the 8th of Oct., 1670.

JAN HENERCK BRUYNS.

Philip Pieterse Schuyler.
Jan Hend. Van Bael.

Acknowledged before me,

LUDOVICUS COBES, Secretary.

Appeared before me, Ludovicus Cobes, secretary of Albany, etc., in the presence of the afternamed witnesses, Mr. Helmer Otten, who acknowledges that he is well and honestly indebted and in arrears to Mr. Jan Bruyns, in the quantity of one hundred whole, good and merchantable beaver skins, growing out of the purchase of a house, lot and garden, which said hundred beavers the subscriber promises to pay to said Mr. Bruyns, or to the lawful holder of this in the month of June, 1671, with proper interest at ten *per cent*, therefor pledging his person and estate, personal and real, present and future, nothing excepted, putting the same in subjection to the lord's laws and judges.

In witness of the truth the same is subscribed by his own hand on this 8th of October, 1670, in Albany.

HELMERIN OTTEN.

Acknowledged before me,

LUDOVICUS COBES, Secretary.

On this 1st of April, 1687, Ryer Schermerhoorn appeared before the secretary with the authentic copy of the foregoing obligation, and on the back of the same was written by Jan Hendr: Bruyns:

" Albany, the 22d of July, 1679, I acknowledge, that I have received full satisfaction for this obligation on the above date.

" JAN HENDRICK BRUYNS."

Was subscribed, *quod attestor.*

ROBERT LIVINGSTON.

Appeared before me, Ludovicus Cobes, secretary of Albany, etc., on the date underwritten, in the presence of the honorable Heeren commissaries, etc., Mr Philip Schuyler and Mr. Jan Hendrickse Van Bael, Helmer Otten, who declares that in true rights, free ownership, he grants, conveys and makes over, by these presents, to and for the behoof of Pieter Adriaense [Sougemakelyck], in a certain house, lot and garden, as the same is built, fenced and enclosed, standing and lying here in Albany, received by the grantor from Jan Bruyns, bounded according to the tenor and contents of the contract and other evidences thereof, to which reference is herein made, free and unincumbered, with no claims standing or issuing against the same, excepting the lord's right, and without the grantor's making the least pretension thereto, any more, acknowledging that he is fully paid and satisfied therefor, the first penny with the last, by the hands of said Pieter Adriaense, and therefore giving *plenam actionem cessam*, and full power to said Pieter Adriaense, his heirs and successors or assigns, to do with and dispose of the aforesaid house, lot, and garden, as he might do with his patrimonial estate and effects; promising to protect and free the same from all such trouble, claims and liens as are right, and further, never more to do nor suffer anything to be done against the same, with or without law, in any manner, on pledge according to laws therefor provided.

Done in Albany, the 12th of October, 1670.

HELMERIN OTTEN.

Philip Pieterse Schuyler.
Jan Hend: Van Bael.

Acknowledged before me,

LUDOVICUS COBES, Secretary.

Appeared before me, Ludovicus Cobes, secretary of Albany, etc., present the afternamed witness, Helmer Otten, who declares that he is well and honestly indebted to Pieter Adriaense, in the quantity of five and thirty whole, good and merchantable beaver skins, in the matter of the exchange and boot for the house and lot, conveyed to him to-day, which thirty-five beavers, the subscriber promises to pay to Pieter Adriaense, or his order on the *Vernal* day, according to the tenor of the contract; therefor pledging his person and estate, personal and real, present and future, nothing excepted, putting the same in subjection to all the lord's laws and judges.

In witness of the truth, of which he subscribes this, in presence of Mr. Philip Schuyler, as witness, hereto invited, on this 12th of Oct., 1670.

HELMER OTTEN.

Philip Pieterse Schuyler.

Acknowledged before me,

LUDOVICUS COBES, Secretary.

Appeared before me, Ludovicus Cobes, secretary of Albany, etc., on the date underwritten, in the presence of the honorable Heeren commissaries, etc., Mr. Philip Pieterse Schuyler and Mr. Jan Van Bael, Claes Keener, dwelling behind Kinderhoeck, who acknowledges that he is well and honestly indebted, and in arrears to Jan Cornelisse Root, in the sum of one hundred and sixty guilders in good seawant, and ten skipples of good winter wheat, in the matter of a cow and a heifer, by the subscriber, to his content received, which said one hundred and sixty guilders seewant, and ten skipples of wheat, the subscriber promises to pay to Jan Cornelisse Ioot, or his order, within the time of three months, therefor pledging specially the aforesaid cow and heifer, and generally his person and estate, personal and real, present and future, nothing excepted, for the recovery of the payment, in due time, if need be, without loss or cost, submitting the same to the authority of all the lord's laws and judges.

Done in Albany, this 15th of November, 1670.

KLESE KENER.

Philip Pieterse Schuyler.
Jan Hend: Van Bael.

Acknowledged before me, LUDOVICUS COBES, Secretary.

Appeared before me, Ludovicus Cobes, secretary of Albany, etc., on the date underwritten, in the presence of the honorable Heeren commissaries, etc., Mr. Philip Pieterse Schuyler and Jan Hendrickse Van Bael, Bastiaen De Winter, who declares that in true rights, free ownership, he grants, conveys and makes over by these presents to Jan Labatie, in a lot, in breadth one hundred feet, or four or five feet more of ground, as shall appear by a just survey, lying at Schaenhechtade, bounded on the east by Pieter [Van] Olinda,[1] on the south side Theunis Cornelisse [Swart],[2] on the north side Joris Arisse [Vander Baast], and on the west side the highway [Church street], by virtue of a patent thereof from the right honorable general, Francis Lovelace, of date the 21st of October, 1670, to which reference is herein made.[3] free and unincumbered, with no claims standing or issuing against the same, excepting the lord's right, and without the grantor's making the least pretension to the same any more, acknowledging that he is fully paid and satisfied therefor, the first penny with the last, by the hands of the said Labatie, and therefore giving *plenam actionem cessam*, and full power to said Jan Labatie, his heirs and successors or assigns, to do with or dispose of said lot,[4] as he might do with his patrimonial estate and effects; promising to protect and free the same from all such trouble, claims and liens as are right, and further, never more to do nor to suffer anything to be done against the same, with or without law, in any manner, on pledge according to laws therefor provided.

Done in Albany, the 21st of November, 1670.

BASTIAEN DE WINTER.

Philip Pieterse Schuyler.
Jan Hend: Van Bael.

In my presence, LUDOVICUS COBES, Secretary.

---

[1] Pieter Van Olinda's house lot in Schenectady fronted on Union street, two hundred feet east of Church street, and is now occupied by the Court House.

[2] Theunis Cornelisse Swart was one of the original settlers of Schenectady. By his wife Elizabeth Lendt or Vander Linde, he had four sons, of whom Cornelis, the eldest, settled in Ulster county, and Esaias in Schenectady. His house lot was on the east corner of State and Church streets.

[3] Bastiaan De Winter's house lot in Schenectady was on the south corner of Union and Church streets, two hundred feet square; the northerly half he conveyed to Joris Arissen Vander Baast (now occupied by James R. Craig, Esq.), and the southerly half as above. The later lot is now occupied by Volney Freeman, Esq. In the massacre of 1690, Vander Baast was killed by the Indians.

[4] This lot was sold subsequently to Davidt Christoffelse, who, with his children, was massacred by the Indians on the 9th of February, 1690. It was still owned by his heirs in 1699.

Appeared before me, Ludovicus Cobes, secretary of Albany, etc., in the presence of the honorable Heeren commissaries, etc., Mr. Philip Pieterse Schuyler and Mr. Jan Van Bael, Bastiaen De Winter, who declares, that in true rights, free ownership, he grants, conveys and makes over by these presents, to and for the behoof of Elias [Van] Gyselingh and Pieter Cornelisse Viele, in a certain plantation [1] lying at Schaenhechtede, in breadth on the west side 350 rods and length on the north side 60 rods, lying by the first land of Willem Teller and Maritie Damen, by virtue of a patent thereof from the right honorable general, Francis Lovelace, of date the 21st of Oct., 1670, to which reference is herein made; free and unincumbered, with no claims standing or issuing against the same, and without the grantor's making the least pretension thereto any more, acknowledging that he is fully paid and satisfied therefor, the first penny with the last, by the hands of said Elias Gyselingh and Pieter Cornelisse Viele, and therefore giving *plenam actionem cessam*, and full power to the aforesaid Elias Gyselingh and Pieter Cornelisse Viele to do with and dispose of said plantation, as they might do with their patrimonial estate and effects; promising to protect and free said plantation from all such trouble, claims and liens of every person as are lawful, and further, never more to do nor suffer any thing to be done against the same, either with or without law, in any manner, on pledge according to law therefor provided.

Done in Albany, the 22d of November, 1670.

BASTIAEN DE WINTER.

Philip Pieterse Schuyler.
Jan Hend : Van Bael.

In my presence,

LUDOVICUS COBES, Secretary.

Appeared before me, Ludovicus Cobes, secretary of Albany, etc., on the date underwritten, in the presence of the honorable Heeren commissaries, etc., Mr. Philip Pieterse Schuyler and Mr. Jan Van Bael, Bastiaen De Winter, who declares that in true rights, free ownership, he grants, conveys and makes over by these presents, to and for the behoof of Joris Arissen [Van der Baast], in a cellar, dwelling, barn, rick and lot lying at Schaenhechtade, the lot being in breadth one hundred feet and in length two hundred feet,[2] by virtue of the patent thereof from the right honorable general, Lovelace, dated the 21st of October, 1670, to which reference is herein made; free and unincumbered, with no claims standing or issuing against the same, excepting the lord's right, and without the grantor's making the least pretension thereto any more, acknowledging that he is fully paid and satisfied therefor, the first penny with the last, by the hands of the aforenamed Joris Arissen and therefore giving *plenam actionem cessam*, and full power to the aforenamed Joris Arissen, his heirs and successors or assigns, to do with and dispose of said cellar, dwelling, barn, rick and lot, as he might do with his patrimonial estate and effects; promising to protect and free the same from all such trouble, claims and liens of every person as are lawful, and never

---

[1] "Elias' *Plantatie*" lies in the Groote Vlachte on the east side of Willem Teller's (now Poenties) kil. It remained in the Van Guysling family until 1865. The ancient house built by the first settler is still standing there, and occupied by the present owner of the farm.

[2] This lot, lying on the south corner of Union and Church streets, is now occupied by James R. Craig, Esq. Vander Baast was a surveyor and lived here twenty years, until the massacre in 1690, when he was killed by the Indians. It is not known that he left any family.

more to do nor suffer anything to be done against the same, with or without law, in any manner, on pledge according to laws therefor provided.

Done in Albany the 22d of November, 1670

BASTEIAEN DE WINTER.

Philip Pieterse Schuyler.
Jan Hend: Van Bael.

In my presence,

LUDOVICUS COBES, Secretary.

Appeared before me, Ludovicus Cobes, secretary of Albany, etc., in the presence of the honorable Heeren commissaries, etc., Mr. Philip Pieterse Schuyler and Mr. Jan Van Bael, Bastiaen De Winter, who declares that in true rights, free ownership, he grants, conveys and makes over by these presents, to and for the behoof of Gerrit Clacse Kulernan, in a garden lying at Schaenhechtede, in length, breadth and boundaries according to the tenor and contents of the patent thereof, to which reference is herein made; free and unincumbered, with no claims standing or issuing against the same, save the lord's right, and without the grantor's making the least pretension thereto any more, acknowledging that he is fully paid and satisfied therefor, the first penny with the last, and therefore giving *plenam actionem cessam*, and full power to said Gerrit Claese, his heirs and successors or assigns, to do with and dispose of said garden, as he might do with his patrimonial estate and effects; promising to protect and free the same from all such claims, troubles and liens of every person as are lawful, and further, never more to do nor suffer anything to be done against the same, with or without law, in any manner, on pledge according to laws therefor provided.

BASTEIAEN DE WINTER.

Philip Pieterse Schuyler.
Jan Hend: Van Bael.

In my presence,

LUDOVICUS COBES, Secretary.

Appeared before me, Ludovicus Cobes, secretary of Albany, etc., in the presence of the honorable Heeren commissaries, etc., Mr. Philip Pieterse Schuyler and Mr. Jan Hendrickse Van Bael, the honorable Volkert Janse [Douw], and Jan Thomase, who declare that in true rights, free ownership, they grant, convey and make over by these presents, to and for the behoof of Jan Laurense [Van Alen], in a certain parcel of land or plantation, as the same lies in fence and formerly occupied by Adriaen Dirruxse De Vries, lying on the fast bank [of the North river], at Schotack, with a little piece outside the fence formerly planted by the Indians; free and unincumbered, with no claims standing or issuing against the same, excepting the lord's right, and without the grantors' making the least pretension thereto any more, acknowledging that they are fully paid and satisfied therefor, the first penny with the last, and therefore giving *plenam actionem cessam*, and full power to said Jan Laurense, his heirs and successors or assigns, to do with or dispose of said land, as he might do with his patrimonial estate and effects; promising to protect and free the same from all such trouble, claims and liens of every person as are lawful, and further, never more to do nor suffer anything to be done against the same, with or without law, in any manner, on pledge according to laws therefor provided.

Done in Albany, the 29th of December, 1670.

VOLKERT JANSE.
JAN THOMAS.

Philip Pieterse Schuyler.
Jan Hend: Van Bael.

In my presence,

LUDOVICUS COBES, Secretary.

Appeared before me, Ludovicus Cobes, secretary of Albany, etc., in the presence of the honorable Heeren commissaries, etc., Mr. Philip Pieterse Schuyler and Mr. Jan Hendrickse Van Bael, the honorable sergeant William Parker, who declares that in true rights, free ownership, he grants, conveys and makes over by these presents, to and for the behoof of Dirck Albertse Bratt, in his certain lot lying on the hill to the north of Ryck Claese [Van Vranken], breadth twenty feet, and length four rods, by virtue of the patent thereof, dated the 2d of June, 1669, to which reference is herein made, free and unincumbered, with no claims standing or issuing against the same, saving the lord's right, and without the grantor's making the least pretension thereto any more, acknowledging that he is fully paid and satisfied therefor, the first penny with the last, and therefore giving *plenam actionem cessam*, and full power to the aforesaid Dirck Albertse, his heirs and successors or assigns, to do with and dispose of said lot, as he might do with his patrimonial estate and effects; promising to protect and free the same from all such trouble, claims and liens of every person as are lawful, and further, never more to do nor suffer anything to be done against the same, with or without law, in any manner, on pledge according to laws therefor provided.

Done in Albany, the 11th of February, 167$\frac{0}{1}$.

WM. PARKER.

Philip Pieterse Schuyler.
Jan Hend: Van Bael.

In my presence,

LUDOVICUS COBES, Secretary.

Appeared before me, Ludovicus Cobes, secretary of Albany, etc., in the presence of the honorable Heeren commissaries, etc., Mr. Philip Pieterse Schuyler, and Theunis Cornelise Vander Poel, Dirckie Hermense, empowered by her husband Jan Martense [De Wever], who acknowledges that she is well and honestly indebted and in arrears to Mr. Goosen Gerritse [Van Schaick], in the sum of three hundred and eighteen guilders, in good, whole and merchantable beaver skins for wares and merchandise to her full content received, which aforesaid sum of three hundred and eighteen guilders in beavers she, the subscriber, promises to pay to the aforesaid Goosen Gerritse in the following manner. *Firstly*, twenty-five skipples of winter wheat next spring, or other wares at market and beaver prices, and the remainder in the three following years also in wheat and grain, therefor pledging specially her house, barn, ricks, land and soil, behind Kinderhoeck, together with all her horses and cattle, and generally her person and estate, personal and real, present and future, nothing excepted, placing the same in subjection to all the lord's law and judges.

Signed with her own hand in witness of the truth of the same this 21st of February. 167$\frac{0}{1}$ in Albany.

The mark + of JAN MARTENSE, with his own hand set.
DERCKIEN HERMENSE.

Philip Pieterse Schuyler.
Teunis Cornelisse.

In my presence,

LUDOVICUS COBES, Secretary.

Appeared before me, Ludovicus Cobes, secretary of Albany, etc., in the presence of the honorable Heeren commissaries, etc., Philip Pieterse Schuyler and Theunise Cornelisse Van der Poel, Symon Volckertse [Veeder, *alias* de Backer], husbandman dwelling at Schaenhechtede, who declares, that in true rights, free ownership, he grants, conveys and makes over by these presents, to and for the behoof of Joris Arissen [Vander Baast] in his certain lot of pasture land [1] lying at Schaenhechtede, in length 75 rods, adjoining to the east of Gerrit Bancker, on the north side the [Mohawk] river, breadth 15 rods, on the west side [of] the common pasture ground, and on the south side the wood road [Front street]; free and unincumbered, with no claims standing or issuing against the same, except the lord's right, and without the grantor's making the least pretension any more thereto, acknowledging that he is fully paid and satisfied therefor, the first penny with the last, by the hands of the said Joris Arissen, and therefore giving *plenum actionem cessam*, and full power to said Arissen, his heirs and successors or assigns, to do with and dispose thereof, as he might do with his patrimonial estate and effects; promising to protect and free the same from all such troubles, claims and liens of every person as are lawful, and further never more to do nor suffer anything to be done against the same, with or without law, in any manner, on pledge according to laws therefor provided.

Done in Albany the 27th of Feb., 167$\frac{0}{1}$.

The mark of ⊥⊥⊥/ SYMON VOLCKERTS, with his own hand set.

Philip Pieterse.
Teunisse Cornelisse.

In my presence,

LUDOVICUS COBES, Secretary.

Appeared before me Ludovicus Cobes, secretary of Albany, etc., in the presence of the honorable Heeren commissaries, etc.. Theunisse Cornelisse Vander Poel and Pieter Meese Vrooman, Dirck Hesselingh, who acknowledges, that he is well and honestly indebted to Juriaen Theunisse Tappen in the quantity of a hundred and five good whole and merchantable beaver skins according to the contract, of date the 21st of March, therefor passed for a *bouwery*, [2] house, barn, and ricks lying at Schaenhechtede, to his content received, which aforesaid 105 beavers the subscriber promises to pay at the stipulated time, therefor pledging specially his house and

---

[1] The *weyland!* allotted to the first settlers lay between Front street and the Mohawk river. These lots contained from four to five acres each; the one above described was the easternmost lot next to the *arme wey* or poor pasture.

[2] This *bouwery*, being the hindermost lot number eight of the *Groote Valckte*, Hesselingh sold to Harmen Albertse Vedder in 1672, in whose family it remained many years. It forms now a part of the homestead of Col. Daniel D. Campbell of Rotterdam.

lot lying here in Albany and the aforesaid land or *bouwery* with house, barn, and ricks, and generally his person and estate, personal and real, present and future, to recover in due time, if need be, the payment without cost or loss.

Done in Albany, the 21st of March 167$\frac{0}{1}$.

DIRCK HESSELINGH.

Teunisse Cornelissen.
Pieterse Meese Vrooman.

In my presence,

LUDOVICUS COBES, Secretary.

For this special obligation Jurriaen Theunisse acknowledges that he is honestly satisfied.

Albany, the 21st of Oct. 1672.

JUREJAN TUNSEN.

Appeared before me, Ludovicus Cobes, secretary of Albany, etc., in the presence of the honorable Heeren commissaries, etc., Messrs. Goosen Gerritse [Van Schaick] and Jan Hendrickse Van Bael, Jan Timmel, who declares that in true rights, free ownership, he grants, conveys and makes over by these presents, to and for the behoof of Theunis Dirrixse [Van Vechten], in his house, barn, rick and stable, standing in Greenbush, formerly belonging to Thomas Koningh, except some boards, according to stipulations made, free and unincumbered, with no claims standing or issuing against the same, excepting the right of the Heer patroon of the colony, without the grantor's making the least pretension thereto any more, acknowledging that he is fully paid and satisfied therefor, the first penny with the last, by the hands of said Theunis Dirrixse, and therefore giving *plenam actionem cessam*, and full power to said Theunis Dirrixse, his heirs and successors or assigns, to do with and dispose of said house, barn, rick and stable, as he might do with his patrimonial estate and effects; promising to protect and free the same from all such trouble, claims and liens of every person as are lawful, and further, never more to do nor suffer anything to be done against the same, with or without law, in any manner, on pledge according to laws therefor provided.

Done in Albany, the 30th of March, 1671.

The mark of + JAN TIMMEL, with his own hand set.

Jan Hend: Van Bael.
Goosen Gerritse.

In my presence,

LUDOVICUS COBES, Secretary.

Appeared before me, Ludovicus Cobes, secretary of Albany, etc., in the presence of the honorable Heeren commissaries, etc., Philip Pieterse Schuyler and Jan Hendrickse Van Bael, Mr. Jan Clute, Jurriaen Theunisse [Tappen] and Meyndert Fredrickse [smith], who declare that in true rights, free ownership, they grant, convey and make over, by these presents, to and for the behoof of Marten Gerritse [Van Bergen], in a certain parcel of land, lying at Kocxhaxki, adjoining on the south side of the land of Hilleken Bronck, beginning at the stone kil and extending south along the Katskil path to the spring (*fonteyn*) or the hill *styftsinck*, east to the river, and north again to the land of Hilleken

Bronck, by virtue of a patent thereof, to which reference is herein made; free and unincumbered, with no claims standing or issuing against the same, excepting the lord's right, without the grantors' making the least claim thereto any more, acknowledging that they are fully paid and satisfied therefor, the first penny with the last, and therefore giving *plenam actionem cessam*. and full power to said Marten Gerritsen, his heirs and successors or assigns, to do with and dispose of said parcel of land, as they might do with their patrimonial estate and effects, promising to protect and free the same from all such troubles, claims and liens of every person as are lawful, and further, never more to do nor suffer anything to be done against the same, with or without law, in any manner, on pledge according to laws therefor provided.

Done in Albany, the 26th of April, 1671.

JOHANNES CLUTE.
JUREJAN TUNSEN.
The mark of + MEYNDERT FREDERICKSE.
with his own hand set.

Philip Pieterse Schuyler.
Jan Hend: Van Bael.

In my presence,

LUDOVICUS COBES, Secretary

Appeared before me, Ludovicus Cobes, secretary of Albany, etc., in the presence of the honorable Heeren commissaries, etc., Mr. Philip Schuyler and Theunis Cornelise Vander Poel, Mr. John Stuart, who acknowledges that he is well and honestly indebted and in arrears to Mr. Goosen Gerritse [Van Schaick], trader, dwelling here in the quantity of thirty whole and good beaver skins, every piece of which shall weigh one and a half pounds, for two pieces of duffels, to his content received; likewise twenty-seven whole good and merchantable beaver skins for two pieces of blankets (*deeckens*), also to the content of the subscriber received; which aforesaid beavers, as well the heavy as the common, the subscriber promises to pay to the aforesaid Mr. Gerritse, to begin with the next business season, and, according to opportunity, to end with the same, therefor pledging specially his shanty (*loodtswooninge*), with the lot of the same lying on the hill, according to conveyance of date the 20th of August, 1670, received by him from Jan Conneel, and further, generally, his person and estate, personal and real, present and future, nothing excepted, putting the same in subjection to all the lord's laws and judges for the recovery of the payment in due time, if need be, without cost or loss.

Done in Albany, the 27th of May, 1671.

JOHN STEWART.

In my presence,

LUDOVICUS COBES, Secretary.

Copia Vera.

Appeared before me, Nicholaes Bayard, admitted secretary of the honorable mayor's court of the city of New York, on the island of Manhatan and before the afternamed witnesses, the honorable Adriaen Appel, inhabitant here, being about to depart for Albany, who acknowledges that he is well and honestly indebted to Mr. Petrus Stuyvesant, in the net sum of five hundred and fifteen guilders eighteen stuivers in seewant growing out of house hire due according to sentence of the honorable mayor's court, of date the 2d of March, A. D. 166$\frac{8}{9}$, which aforesaid sum of ƒ 515–18 the subscriber promises to pay to said Heer Stuyvesant, or his lawful order, in good current strung seewant in the time of the three following years, every year a just third part of the said sum, and for the accomplishment of which and the full payment of said sum, offers as a special pledge and mortgage his house and lot standing and lying in the village of New Albany aforesaid, to the north the house and lot of David Schuyler, and at present leased and occupied by Johannes Dyckman, and further more, generally, his person and estate, personal and real, putting the same in subjection to all laws and judges, requesting moreover my secretary here to pass this deed *in communi forma* to the end that the same may be recorded in the register of the village of Albany aforesaid, to be used when proper.

Signed in witness of the truth of the same by the principal and underwritten witnesses with their own hands in New York, this 3d of May, A. D. 1671.

Was subscribed A. APPEL.

Symon Romeyn.
Cornelis Vanden Burch.

Acknowledged before me, N. BAYARD, Secretary.
Collated by me, LUDOVICUS COBES, Secretary.

Appeared before me, Ludovicus Cobes, secretary of Albany, etc., in the presence of the honorable Heeren commissaries, etc. Mr. Philip Pieterse Schuyler and Jan Hendrickse Van Bael, Mr. Robert Orteers, master hatter, and Jannetie Donckertse, widow of the late Thomas Paulus [Powell] who declare that in true rights, free ownership, they grant, convey and make over by these presents, to and for the behoof of Hendrick Coenraets [Van Bon], in a certain lot of ground to the west of the kil behind the Kinderhoeck, extending inland along a brook, and bounded to the south by Lourens Van Alen, free and unincumbered, with no claims standing or issuing against the same, excepting the lord's right, without the grantor's making the least pretension thereto any more, acknowledging that they are fully paid and satisfied therefor, the first penny with the last, and therefore giving *plenam actionem cessam*, and full power to said Hendrick Coenraets, his heirs and successors or assigns, to do with and dispose of the aforesaid lot of land, as he might do with his patrimonial estate and effects; promising to protect and free the same, from all such trouble, claims and liens of every person as are lawful, and further, nevermore to do nor suffer anything to be done against the same, with or without law, in any manner, on pledge according to laws therefor provided.

Done in Albany, the 31st of May, 1671.

ROBERT ORCHARD.

The mark of JENNEKEN X DONCKERTS, with her own hand set.

Philip Pieterse.
Jan Hend: Van Bael.

In my presence, LUDOVICUS COBES, Secretary.

Appeared before me, Ludovicus Cobes, secretary of Albany, etc., in the presence of the right honorable Heeren commissaries, etc., Mr. Philip Schuyler and Jan Hendrickse Van Bael, Mr. Robbert Ortiers and Janneken Donckertse, widow of the late Thomas Paulus [*Powell*], who declares, that in true rights, free ownership, they grant, convey and make over, by these presents, to and for the behoof of Laurens Van Alen, in a certain lot and land lying behind the Kinderhoeck to the west of the kil, to the south of Hendrick Coenraets, to the east of Jacob Janse Flodder; free and unincumbered, with no claims standing or issuing against the same, excepting the lord's right, without the grantor's making the least pretension thereto any more, and acknowledging that they are fully paid and satisfied therefore, the first penny with the last, and therefor giving *plenam actionem cessam*, and full power to said Loureus Van Alen, his heirs and successors or assigns, to do with and dispose of said lot and land, as he might do with his patrimonial estate and effects; promising to protect and free the same from all such troubles, claims and liens of every person as are lawful, and further, never more to do nor suffer anything to be done against the same, with or without law, in any manner, on pledge according to laws, therefor provided.

Done in Albany, the 31st of May, 1671.

ROBERT ORCHARD.

The mark of × JENNEKEN DONCKERTSE, with her own hand set.

Philip Pieterse.

Jan Hend: Van Bael.

In my presence, LUDOVICUS COBES, Secretary.

Appeared before me, Ludovicus Cobes, secretary of Albany, etc., in the presence of the honorable Heeren commissaries, etc., Philip Pieterse Schuyler and Jan Hendrickse Van Bael, Mr. Robert Ortier and Janneken Donckerts, widow of the late Thomas Paulus [*Powell*], who declare, that in true rights, free ownership, they grant, convey and make over by these presents, to and for the behoof of Jacob Martense in a certain lot lying behind the Kinderhoeck to the west of the kil, breadth on the kil 3 rods, on the road five rods, also a parcel of land there to the east of Jan Martense [De Wever] to the west of the kil, free and unincumbered, with no claims standing or issuing against the same, except the lord's right, without the grantor's making the least claim any more against the same, acknowledging that they are fully paid and satisfied therefor, the first penny with the last, and therefore giving *plenam actionem cessam* and full power to said Jacob Martense, his heirs and successors or assigns, to do with and dispose of the same, as he might do with his patrimonial estate and effects; promising to protect and free the same from all such claims, troubles and liens of every person as are lawful, and further, never more to do nor suffer anything to be done, with or without law, in any manner, on pledge according to laws therefor provided.

Done in Albany, the 31st of May, 1671.

ROBERT ORCHARD.

The mark of × JANNEKEN DONCKERTS, with her own hand set.

Philip Pieterse.

J. Hend: Van Bael.

In my presence, LUDOVICUS COBES, Secretary

Appeared before me, Ludovicus Cobes, secretary of Albany, etc., in the presence of the honorable Heeren commissaries, etc., Mr Philip Pieterse Schuyler and Jan Hendrickse Van Bael, Mr. Robbert Ortiers and Janneken Donckerts, widow of the late Thomas Paulus [Powell], who declare that in true rights, free ownership, they grant, convey and make over, by these presents, to and for the behoof of Direk Hendricxse Sweed [*alias* Bye[1]], in a certain lot lying behind Kinderhoeck, to the west of the kil, to the south of Jacob Martense, to the east of Jan Martense [De Wever], free and unincumbered, with no claim standing or issuing against the same, excepting the lord's right, without the grantors' making the least pretension thereto any more, also acknowledging that they are fully paid and satisfied therefor, the first penny with the last, and therefore giving *plenam actionem cessam*, and full power to the said Dirck Hendricxse Sweed, his heirs and successors or assigns, to do with and dispose of said lot, as he might do with his patrimonial estate and effects; promising to protect and free the same from all such trouble, claims and liens of every person as are lawful, and further, never more to do nor suffer anything to be done against the same. with or without law, in any manner, on pledge according to laws therefor provided.

Done in Albany, the 31st of May, 1671. ROBERT ORCHARD.

This is the mark of × JENNEKEN DONCKERTS,
with her own hand set.

Philip Pieterse.
Jan Hend: Van Bael.

In my presence, LUDOVICUS COBES, Secretary.

Appeared before me, Ludovicus Cobes, secretary of Albany, etc., in the presence of the honorable Heeren commissaries, etc., Mr. Philip Schuyler and Jan Hendricxse Van Bael, Mr Robbert Ortiers and Janneken Donckerts, widow of the late Thomas Paulus [Powell], who declare that in true rights, free ownership, they grant, convey and make over, by these presents, to and for the behoof of Andries Hanse [Sharp], in a certain parcel of land, lying behind Kinderhoeck, separated from Jan Martense [De Wever's] land by a little brook; free and unincumbered, with no claims standing or issuing against the same, excepting the lord's right, without the grantors' making the least pretension thereto any more, also acknowledging that they are fully paid and satisfied therefor by a mortgage for the sum of *f* 64 in beavers and *f* 7 in seewant, and therefore giving *plenam actionem cessam*, and full power to said Andries Hanse,[2] his heirs and successors or assigns, to do with and dispose of said parcel of land, as he might do with his patrimonial possessions and effects; promising to protect and free the same from all such troubles, claims and liens of every person as are lawful, and further, never more to do nor suffer anything to be done against the same with or without law, in any manner, on pledge according to laws therefor provided.

Done in Albany, the 31st of May, 1671.

ROBERT ORCHARD.

This is the mark of × JENNEKEN DONCKERTS,
with her own hand set.

Philip Pieterse.
Jan Hend: Van Bael

In my presence, LUDOVICUS COBES, Secretary.

---

[1] He conveyed this or another lot to Pieter Du Moree, in 1676.—*Deeds*, I. 286.

[2] The surname of Andries Hanse is variously spelled Sharp, Scharp, Scherp and Schaap. He early settled at Kinderhook, where his two sons, Johannes and Gysbert also settled, and had large families.

Appeared before me, Ludovicus Cobes, secretary of Albany, etc., in the presence of the honorable Heeren commissaries, etc,, Mr Philip Schuyler and Jan Hendrixse Van Bael, Mr. Robbert Ortiers and Janneken Donckerts who declare, that in true rights, free ownership, they grant, convey and make over by these presents, to and for the behoof of Jan Martense [De Wever], in a certain parcel of land lying behind Kinderhoeck, adjoining to the south Dirck [Hendrickse Bye *alias*] De Sweed, to the west Jacob Martense and the kil, easterly a little brook dividing the same from the land of Andries Hanse [Sharp]; free and unincumbered. with no claims standing or issuing against the same, save the lord's right, without the grantors' making the least claim any more thereto, also acknowledging that they are fully paid and satisfied therefor by a mortgage for the sum of seventy whole and good merchantable beaver skins, and therefore giving *plenam actionem cessam*. and full power to said Jan Martense, his heirs and successors or assigns, to do with and dispose of said land, as he might do with his patrimonial estate and effects; promising to protect and free the same from all such troubles, claims and liens of every person, as are lawful, and further, never more to do nor suffer anything to be done against the same. with or without law, in any manner, on pledge according to laws therefor provided.

Done in Albany, the 31st of May, 1671.

ROBERT ORCHARD.

The mark of × JENNEKEN DONCKERTS, with her own hand set.

Philip Pieterse.

Jan Hend: Van Bael.

In my presence,

LUDOVICUS COBES, Secretary.

Appeared before me, Ludovicus Cobes, secretary of Albany, etc., in the presence of the honorable Heeren commissaries, etc., Mr. Philip Schuyler and Jan Hendricxse Van Bael, Dirckie Hermens, empowered by her husband Jan Martense [De Wever] dwelling behind Kinderhoeck, who acknowledges that she is well and honestly indebted and in arrears to Mr. Jan Bruyns in the quantity of seventy whole, good and merchantable beaver skins, growing out of the matter of the purchase, and consideration of a parcel of land by her, the subscriber, purchased, lying behind Kinderhoeck, which aforesaid seventy whole beavers, she promises to pay to said Mr. Bruyns or his order, to wit, thirty next spring, 1672, and the remaining forty beavers also in the spring, and in default of payment of the forty beavers promises to pay as interest four beavers a year, but if she cannot make the payment in beavers then she promises to give good winter wheat at beaver and market price; therefor pledging specially her land and *bouwery* behind Kinderhoeck, and generally her person and estate, personal and real, present and future, nothing excepted, placing the same in subjection to all the lord's laws and judges, for the recovery in due time, if necessary, of said payment, without loss or cost.

Done in Albany, this 31st of May, 1671.

DERCKIEN HERMENS.

Philip Pieterse.

Jan Hend: Van Bael.

In my presence,

LUDOVICUS COBES, Secretary.

Appeared before me, Ludovicus Cobes, secretary of Albany etc., in the presence of the honorable Heeren commissaries, etc., Philip Pieterse Schuyler and Jan Hendrickse Van Bael, Eldert Gerbertse Cruiff who acknowledges that he is well and honestly indebted and in arrears to Messieurs Jan Hendrick Bruyns and Hans Hendrickse, in the net sum of *f* 350 in beavers and *f* 48 in seewant together with seventy-five boards, growing out of the matter of security, as principals bound for said Cruiff, in consequence of a certain sentence, dated the 5th of January, 1670, which aforesaid money the subscriber promises to pay to said Jan Hendrick Bruyns and Hans Hendricxse punctually in the time of six weeks, without any longer delay, therefor pledging specially his distilling kettle, worm and dome, his saw mill at Bethlehem and all his lands in Catskil together with all his title to his house, brewery and lot lying here in Albany, likewise two cows here, four cattle with Gerrit Theunisse [Van Vechten,] two cattle with Melgert Abrahamse [Van Deusen] at Schotack, three head of cattle with Jan Helmerse [*alias* de Boek] the half of which is coming to him, three heifers with Hendrick Maersen and a bull; and further more generally his person and estate, personal and real, present and future, nothing excepted, putting the same in subjection to all the lord's laws and judges, for the recovery of said payment in due time, if need be, without loss or cost.

Done in Albany, the 21st of June, 1671.

Philip Pieterse. ELDERT GERBERTSE CRUYFF.
Jan Hend: Van Bael.

Acknowledged before me, LUDOVICUS COBES, Secretary.

Appeared before me, Ludovicus Cobes, secretary of Albany, etc., in the presence of the honorable Heeren commissaries, etc., Philip Pieterse Schuyler and Jan Hendricxse Van Bael, Paulus Janse, who declares that in true rights, free ownership, he grants, conveys and makes over by these presents to and for the behoof of Christiaen Christiaense,[1] dwelling at Schaenhechtede, in his plantation lying there, consisting of one and a half morgens and bounded according to the patent thereof from the right honorable general of New York, Francis Lovelace, dated the 24th of May, 1669, to which reference is herein made; free and unincumbered, with no claims standing or issuing against the same, excepting the lord's right, without the grantor's making the least claim thereto any more, acknowledging that he is fully paid and satisfied therefor, the first penny with the last, and therefore giving *plenam actionem cessam*, and full power to the aforenamed Christiaen Christiaense, his heirs and successors or assigns, to do with and dispose of said plantation, as he might do with his patrimonial estate and effects; promising to protect and free the same from all such troubles, claims and liens of every person as are lawful, and further, never more to do nor suffer anything to be done, with or without law, in any manner, on pledge according to law therefor provided.

Done in Albany, the 23d of June, 1671.

Philip Pieterse. POULYS JANSEN.
Jan Hend: Van Bael.

In my presence, LUDOVICUS COBES, Secretary.

[1] Christiaen Christiaense's house lot in Schenectady had a front of 100 feet on Union street, one-half being now included in the lot of the First Reformed church, and the remainder owned and occupied by Aaron Barringer, Esq. He sold this lot in 1694, to Neeltie Claese, widow of Hendrik Gardenier.

Appeared before me, Ludovicus Cobes, secretary of Albany, etc., in the presence of the honorable Heeren commissaries, etc., Philip Pieterse Schuyler and Jan Hendricxse Van Bael, Mr. Jan [Hendrick] Bruyns, who declares, that in true rights, free ownership, he grants, conveys and makes over by these presents, to and for the behoof of Hendrick Gerritse Vermeulen in certain two gardens lying near the others behind Fort Albany, by virtue of a deed of conveyance given by the Heer Jeremias Van Rensselaer to the behoof of the grantor, of date the $\frac{8}{18}$ July, 1667, without the grantor's making the least pretension thereto any more, acknowledging that he is fully paid and satisfied therefor, the first penny with the last, and therefore giving *plenam actionem cessam*, and full power to Hendrick Gerritse, his heirs and successors or assigns, to do with and dispose of said two gardens, as he might do with his patrimonial lands and effects; promising to protect and free said gardens from all such troubles, claims and liens of every person as are lawful, and further, never more to do nor suffer anything to be done against the same, with or without law, in any manner, on pledge according to laws, therefor provided.

Done in Albany, the 18th of June, 1671.

JAN HENDERICK BRUYNS.

Philip Pieterse.
Jan Hend: Van Bael.

In my presence, LUDOVICUS COBES Secretary.

Note.—In accordance with the above conveyance the two gardens were again made over to Herman Vedder.

Appeared before me, Ludovicus Cobes, secretary of Albany, etc., in the presence of the honorable Heeren commissaries, etc., Philip Pieterse Schuyler and Jan Hend. Van Bael, Mr. Jan [Hendricxse] Bruyns, who declares that in true rights, free ownership, he grants, conveys and makes over by these presents, to and for the behoof of Ruth Arissen, master shoemaker, in a little barn, with a lot lying here in Albany, on the plain, to the east of the road, length six rods; to the north, the road, breadth three rods; to the west, Thomas Paulus [Powell], length six rods; to the south, the plain, breadth three rods, by virtue of the patent thereof from the right honorable general Nicolls, of date the 20th of April, 1667, to which reference is herein made; free and unincumbered, with no claims standing or issuing against the same, excepting the lord's right, without the grantor's making the least pretension thereto any more, acknowledging that he is fully paid and satisfied therefor, the first penny with the last, and therefore giving *plenam actionem cessam*, and full power to said Ruth Arissen, his heirs and successors or assigns, to do with and dispose of said barn and lot, as he might do with his patrimonial estate and effects; promising to protect and free the same from all such troubles, claims and liens of every person as are lawful, and further, never more to do nor suffer anything to be done against the same, with or without law, in any manner, on pledge according to laws therefor provided.

Done in Albany, the 18th of July, 1671.

JAN HENDERCK BRUYNS.

Jan Hend: Van Bael.
Philip Pieterse.

In my presence, LUDOVICUS COBES, Secretary.

Appeared before me, Ludovicus Cobes, secretary of Albany, etc., in the presence of the honorable Heeren commissaries, etc., Messrs. Goosen Gerritse [Van Schaick] and Jan Hendricxse Van Bael, Capt. Thomas Willet, who declares that in true rights, free ownership, he grants, conveys and makes over by these presents, to and for the behoof of Mr. Philip Pieterse Schuyler, in a certain house and lot standing and lying here in Albany, bounded and enclosed according to patent thereof, of date the 13th of August, 1668, from the right honorable Heer general, Richard Nicolls; free and unincumbered with no claims standing or issuing against the same, excepting the lord's right, without the grantor's making the least pretension thereto any more, acknowledging that he is fully paid and satisfied therefor, the first penny with the last, and therefore giving *plenam actionem cessam*, and full power to said Philip Pieterse Schuyler, his heirs and successors or assigns, to do with and dispose of said house and lot, as he might do with his patrimonial estate and effects, promising to protect and free the same from all such troubles, claims and liens of every person as are lawful, and further, never more to do nor suffer anything to be done against the same, with or without law, in any manner, on pledge according to laws therefor provided.

Done in Albany, the 2d of Sept. 1671.

THO: WILLET.

Goosen Gerritse.
Jan Hend: Van Bael.

In my presence,

LUDOVICUS COBES, Secretary.

Appeared before me, Ludovicus Cobes, secretary of Albany, etc., and in the presence of the honorable Heeren commissaries, etc., Messrs. Philip Pieterse Schuyler and Jan Hendricxse Van Bael, Mr. Hendrick Koster, who declares that in true rights, free ownership, he grants, conveys and makes over by these presents, to and for the behoof of Gerrit Reyerse, in a certain parcel of land, lying on the hill here, length to the south fifteen feet and eight and a half inches, wood feet, length to the north sixteen feet one inch, wood feet, and breadth fifteen feet, Rynland measure, by virtue of a patent to him, the grantor, given; free and unincumbered, with no claims standing nor issuing against the same, excepting the lord's right, without the grantor's making the least pretension thereto any more, also acknowledging that he is fully paid and satisfied therefor, the first penny with the last, and therefore giving *plenum actionem cessam*, and full power to Gerrit Reyerson, his heirs and successors or assigns, to do with and dispose of said lot, as he might do with his patrimonial estate and effects; promising to protect and free the same from all such trouble, claims and liens of every person as are lawful, and further, never more to do nor suffer anything to be done against the same, with or without law in any manner, on pledge according to laws therefor provided.

Done in Albany, the 13th of September, 1671.

HENDFRECK KOSTER.

Philip Pieterse.
Jan Hend: Van Bael.

Appeared before me, Ludovicus Cobes, secretary of Albany, etc., in the presence of the honorable Heeren commissaries etc., Messrs. Philip

Pieterse Schuyler, and Jan Hendricxse Van Bael, Andries De Vos, who declares that in true rights, free ownership, he grants, conveys and makes over by these presents, to and for the behoof of Jan Andriesse [Kuyper], in a certain parcel of land lying here on the hill, bounded on the north side by the road, on the east side also by the road, to the south the lot of Edward Schot, to the west the lot of Jacob Thyssen [Vander Heyden], in breadth and length according to the fence; free and unincumbered, with no claims standing or issuing against the same, excepting the lord's right, without the grantor's making the least pretension thereto any more, also acknowledging that he is fully paid and satisfied therefor, the first penny with the last, and therefor giving *plenam actionem cessam*, and full power to the aforesaid Jan Andriesse, his heirs and successors or assigns, to do with and dispose of the aforesaid lot, as he might do with his patrimonial estate and effects; promising to protect and free the same from all such trouble, claims and liens of every person as are lawful, and further, never more to do nor suffer anything to be done against the same, with or without law, in any manner, on pledge according to laws therefor provided.

Done in Albany, the 13th of September, 1671.

ANDRYES DE VOS.

Philip Pieterse.
Jan Hend: Van Bael.

In my presence,

LUDOVICUS COBES, Secretary

Appeared before me, Ludovicus Cobes, secretary of Albany, etc., in the presence of Messrs. Philip Pieterse Schuyler, and Jan Hendricxse Van Bael, commissaries, Johannes De Wandelaer, who declares that in true rights, free ownership, he grants, conveys and makes over by these presents, to and for the behoof of Evert Janse [Wendel], in his house and lot lying on the hill here in Albany, and the lot is fifteen feet in breadth in front according to the patent thereof in the custody of Omy La Grand; free and unincumbered, with no claims standing or issuing against the same, excepting the lord's right, without the grantor's making the least pretension thereto any more, also acknowledging that he is fully paid and satisfied therefor, the first penny with the last, and therefore giving *plenam actionem cessam*, and full power to the aforenamed Evert Janse, his heirs and successors or assigns, to do with and dispose of said house, as he might do with his patrimonial estate and effects; promising to protect and free the same from all such troubles, claims and liens of every person as are lawful, and further, never more to do nor suffer anything to be done against the same, either with or without laws, in any manner, on pledge according to laws therefor provided.

Done in Albany, the 22d of September, 1671.

JONANNES DE WANDELAER.

Philip Pieterse.
Jan Hend: Van Bael.

In my presence,

LUDOVICUS COBES, Secretary.

Appeared before me, Ludovicus Cobes, secretary of Albany, etc., in the presence of the honourable Heeren commissaries, etc., Messrs. Philip

Pieterse Schuyler and Jan Hendricxse Van Bael, Pieter Jacobse Borsboom, who declares, that in true rights, free ownership, he grants, conveys and makes over by these presents, to and for the behoof of Mr. William Loveridge, his heirs and successors, in a certain house and lot here in Albany, breadth in front on the street forty wood feet 3½ inches, and in the rear on the end of Jacob Joosten [Van Covelen's] lot breadth thirty wood feet, and in the rear on the river bank (*strant*) breadth twenty-eight wood feet, length to the river bank, which said house and lot is bounded north by the King's [court] house [1] and south by the house of Jacob Joosten [Van Covelen]; by virtue of a patent in the custody of the widow of the late Mr. Jacob De Hinsse, dated the 3d of May, 1667, to which reference is herein made, on condition that the grantor has purchased some feet of land from Sander Leendertse [Glen], which is also comprehended herein, extending also to the King's house; all free and unincumbered, with no claims standing or issuing against the same, excepting the lord's right, without the grantor's making the least claim thereto any more, also acknowledging that he is fully paid and satisfied therefor in a sum of nineteen beavers in wares, together with a mortgage on said house and lot for the sum of five and thirty whole and merchantable beaver skins, and therefore giving *plenam actionem cessam*, and full power to said Mr. William Loveridge, his heirs and successors or assigns, to do with and dispose of said house and lot, as he might do with his patrimonial estate and effects; promising to protect and free the same from all such trouble and liens of every person as are lawful and further, never more to do nor suffer anything to be done against the same, with or without law in any manner, on pledge according to laws therefor provided.

Done in Albany, the 30th September, 1671.

PIETER YACOBSE BORSBOOM

Jan Hend: Van Bael.
Philip Pieterse.

In my presence, LUDOVICUS COBES, Secretary.

Appeared before me, Ludovicus Cobes, secretary of Albany, etc., in the presence of the honorable Heeren commissaries, etc., Messrs. Philip Pieterse Schuyler, and Jan Hendricxse Van Bael, Mr William Loveridge, master hatter, who acknowledges that he is well and honestly indebted and in arrears to Pieter Jacobse Borsboom in the quantity of five and thirty whole, good and merchantable beaver skins growing out of the matter of the purchase and consideration of a certain house and lot received from him, which said thirty-five beavers the subscriber promises to pay to said Pieter Jacobse or his order in two installments of the half each, the first in the business season of 1673 and the second the year following, therefor pledging specially the aforesaid house and lot, and generally, his person and estate, personal and real present and future, nothing excepted placing the same in subjection to all the lord's laws and judges for the recovery of said payment in due time, if need be, without cost and loss.

Albany, the 30th of September, 1671. WILLIEM LOVERIDGE.

Jan Hend: Van Bael.
Philip Pieterse

In my presence, LUDOVICUS COBES, Secretary,

[1] The King's [court] house was on the east corner of Broadway and Hudson street, the above lot extended south forty feet along Broadway and in the rear to the river.

Appeared before me, Ludovicus Cobes, secretary of Albany, etc., in the presence of the honorable Heeren commissaries, etc., Messrs. Philip Pieterse Schuyler and Jan Hendricxse Van Bael, sergeant William Parker, who declares that in true rights, free ownership, he grants, conveys and makes over by these presents, to and for the behoof of Ryck Claese [Van Vranken] [1] in his certain lot lying on the hill, breadth twenty feet and length about three and a half rods, south of the lot of Dirck Alberse Brat, by virtue of the patent thereof, dated the 2d of June, 1669, to which reference is herein made; free and unincumbered, with no claims standing or issuing against the same, excepting the lord's right, without the grantor's making the least pretension thereto any more, also acknowledging that he is fully paid and satisfied therefor, the first penny with the last, and therefore giving *plenam actionem cessum*, and full power to the aforesaid Ryck Claese, his heirs and successors or assigns, to do with and dispose of said lot, as he might do with his patrimonial estate and effects; promising to protect and free the same from all such troubles, claims and liens of every person as are lawful, and further never more to do nor suffer anything to be done against the same, with or without law, in any manner, on pledge according to laws therefor provided.

Done in Albany, the 13th of Oct., 1671.

WM. PARKER.

Philip Pieterse.
Jan Hend: Van Bael.

In my presence, LUDOVICUS COBES, Secretary.

Appeared before me, Ludovicus Cobes, secretary of Albany, etc., in the presence of the honorable Heeren commissaries, etc., Messrs. Philip Pieterse Schuyler and Jan Hendricxse Van Bael, Adriaentie Cornelise Van Velpen, wife and attorney of Jacob Joosten [Van Covelens], who declares that in true rights, free ownership, she grants, conveys and makes over by these presents, to and for the behoof of Jan Conneel, in her house and lot lying here in Albany, in breadth, length and boundaries, according to the showing of the contract thereof to which reference is herein made; free and unincumbered, with no claims standing or issuing against the same, except the lord's right, without the grantor's making the least pretensions any more thereto, also acknowledging that she is fully paid and satisfied therefor, the first penny with the last, and therefore giving *plenam actionem cessam*, and full power to said Jan Conneel, his heirs and successors or assigns, to do with and dispose of said house and lot, as he might do with his patrimonial estate and effects; promising to protect and free the same from all such trouble, claims and liens of every person as are lawful, and further, never more to do nor suffer any thing to be done against the same, with or without law, in any manner, on pledge according to laws therefor provided.

Done in Albany, the 13th of Oct., 1671.

ADRIANA CORNELIS VAN VELPEN.

Philip Pieterse.
Jan Hend: Van Bael.

In my presence, LUDOVICUS COBES, Secretary.

---

[1] Ryckert Claese Van Vranken was in Albany as early as 1665.—*Deeds*, I, 198. In 1672 and 1677 in company with Claes Janse Van Boeckhoven, he bought land over the river at Niskayuna.—*Deeds*, I, 393, and *Notarial Papers*. He probably had sons, Maas, Gerrit and Evert.

Appeared before me, Ludovicus Cobes, secretary of Albany, etc., in the presence of the honorable Heeren commissaries, etc., Mr. Gerrit Van Slichtenhorst and Jan Hendricxse Van Bael, Mr. Marten Cregier, [Junior],[1] who, by warrant and power from the right honorable Heer general, Francis Lovelace, declares that in true rights, free ownership, he grants, conveys and makes over by these presents, to and for the behoof of Jurriaen Theunisse Tappen, two houses, both of which, with their lots, formerly belonged to Dirck Janse Croon, standing and lying-here in Albany, of such size and boundaries as the same lies in fence on the little brook; free and unincumbered, with no claims standing or issuing against the same, save the lord's right, without the grantor's making the least pretension any more thereto, also acknowledging that he is fully paid and satisfied therefor, the first penny with the last, and therefore giving *plenam actionem cessam*, and full power to said Jurriaen Theunisse, his heirs and successors or assigns, to do with and dispose of said two houses and lots, as he might do with his patrimonial estate and effects (*nota bene* that the Heer De Laval has received seventy beavers); promising to protect and free the same from all such troubles, claims and liens of every person as are lawful, and further, never more to do nor suffer anything to be done against the same with or without law, in any manner, on pledge according to laws therefor provided.

Albany, the 13th of September, 1672.

M. CREGIER, Junior.

Jan Hend: Van Bael.
Gerrit Van Slichtenhorst.

In my presence,

LUDOVICUS COBES, Secretary.

Appeared before me, Ludovicus Cobes, secretary of Albany, etc., in the presence of the honorable Heeren commissaries, Goosen Gerritse [Van Schaick] and Jan. Hend. Van Bael, Eldert Gerbertse Cruyff, who acknowledges that he is well and honestly indebted and in arrears to Heer Jeremias Van Rensselaer, director of the colony Renselaerswyck, in a sum of two thousand six hundred and seventy guilders in grain (*coren*), the wheat at ten guilders in beavers the mudde [four bushels], and the oats at four guilders in beavers the mudde; likewise the sum of two hundred and seventy-eight guilders in seewant; growing out of the rent of a water privilege, lands, etc., for which sum the subscriber conveys and makes over to said Heer Rensselaer, the quantity of fifty beavers, to be received from Hendrick Maerse, which remaining sum in beavers and seewant the subscriber promises to pay to said Heer Rensselaer or his order, in three installments of a third part each, the first on the first of November, 1672, the second in the month of August, 1673, the third a year following, all punctually, or failing the same, interest on the same at ten per cent., therefor pledging specially his saw mill at Bethlehem, and also his house there, together with his right and title to lands in Katskil, and generally his person and estate, personal and real, present

[1] Marten Cregier, Jr., was son of Capt. Marten Cregier of New Amsterdam. About the year 1686 both removed to Albany and received a grant of land on the Mohawk river at Niskayuna. In 1671 the son married Jannetie Hendrikse Van Doesburgh of Albany, daughter of Hendrik Van Doesburgh and Maritie Damen: seven of their children were living at the death of their father in 1702, viz: Marten, Elizabeth wife of Daniel Van Olinda, Maria wife of Johannes Vreelandt, Annatie wife of Victor Becker, Samuel, Johanna, and Geertruy wife of Ulderick Van Vranken. At the death of their mother in 1731 all these children were living except Johanna.

and future, nothing excepted, for the recovery of said payment in due time, if need be, without cost or loss.

Done in Albany, the 15th of November, 1671

Note.—In this special bond is not included a certain obligation of the subscriber in favor of Jan Baptist Van Rensselaer.

ELDERT GERBERTSE CRUIF.

Jan Hend: Van Bael.
Gerrit Van Slichtenhorst.

In my presence,

LUDOVICUS COBES, Secretary.

Appeared before me, Ludovicus Cobes, secretary of Albany, etc., in the presence of the honorable Heeren commissaries, etc., Jan Hendricxse Van Bael and Gerrit Van Slichtenhorst, Sander Leendertse Glen, who declares that in true rights, free ownership, he grants, conveys and makes over by these presents, to and for the behoof of Mr. Jurriaen Theunisse Tappen in his certain lot with a well lying right over against the king's [court] house,[1] formerly belonging to Jan Bastiaense [Van Gutsenhoven], deceased, being in breadth in front on street [Broadway] up to the city fence [palisadoes] and in the rear twenty-four feet broad; and along back to the eighth post of the former city fence; free and unincumbered, with no claims standing or issuing against the same, excepting the lord's right, without the grantor's making the least pretension thereto any more, also acknowledging that he is fully paid and satisfied therefor, the first penny with the last, and therefore giving *plenam actionem cessam*, and full power to said Jurriaen Theunisse, his heirs and successors or assigns, to do with and dispose of said lot and well, as he might do with his patrimonial estate and effects; promising to protect and free the same from all such trouble, claims, and liens of every person as are lawful, and further, never more to do nor suffer anything to be done against the same, with or without law, in any manner, on pledge according to laws therefor provided.

Done in Albany, the 10th of January, 167½.

SANDER LENRSEN GLEN.

Jan Hend: Van Bael.
Gerrit Van Slichtenhorst.

In my presence,

LUDOVICUS COBES, Secretary.

Appeared before me, Ludovicus Cobes, secretary of Albany, etc., in the presence of the honorable Heeren commissaries, etc., Jan Hendricxse Van Bael, and Gerrit Van Slichtenhorst, Pieter Pieterse Van Woggelum, who acknowledges that he is well and honestly indebted and in arrears to Meyndert Janse Wemp,[2] in the quantity of two hundred and fifty whole good beaver skins, to be paid in six installments, either in wheat or seewant, according to the market, at beavers' price at such times as are in accordance with the contract thereof, dated the 15th of January 167½, growing out of the matter of a *bouwery* and lands bought of him, therefor

[1] The court house being on the east corner of Broadway and Hudson street the above lot was on the opposite north corner of the same streets and bounded southerly by the city palisadoes

[2] Meyndert Janse Wemp, eldest son of Jan Barentse Wemp, early settled at Schenectady. He married Diewer Wendell and had a son Johannes, and daughter Susanna. In the massacre of Feb. 9, 1690, he was slain, and his son was carried away captive to Canada, but was afterwards redeemed and returned to Schenectady.

specially pledging the aforesaid *bouw ry*, lands, horses, and cattle, and generally his person and estate, personal and real present and future, nothing excepted, subject to all the lord's laws and judges, for the recovery of said payment in due time, if need be, without cost or loss.

Albany, the 15th of January, 167½.

PIETER PIETERSE

Jan Hend: Van Bael.
Gerrit Van Slichtenhorst.

In my presence,

LUDOVICUS COBES, Secretary.

On this 16th day of April, 1672, appeared before me, Ludovicus Cobes, secretary of Albany, etc., in the presence of the honorable Heeren commissaries, etc., Messrs. Gerrart Van Slichtenhorst and Jacob Schermerhoren, Volckert Janse [Douw], who declares that in true rights, free ownership, he grants, conveys and makes over by these presents, to and for the behoof of Barent Pieterse [Coeymans], in his island named *Schutters* island lying below the *Beeren* island, in this [North] river, by virtue of the patent thereof, dated the 14th of August, 1671, to which reference is herein made; free and unincumbered, with no claims standing or issuing against the same, excepting the lord's right, without the grantor's making the least pretension thereto any more, also acknowledging that he is fully paid and satisfied therefor, the first penny with the last, and therefore giving *plenam actionem cessam*, and full power to said Barent Pieterse, his heirs and successors or assigns, to do with and dispose of the same, as he might do with his patrimonial estate and effects; promising to protect and free the same from all such troubles, claims and liens of every person as are lawful, and further, never more to do nor suffer anything to be done against the same, with or without law, in any manner, on pledge according to laws therefor provided

Done in Albany.

VOLCKART JANSE.

Gerrit Van Slichtenhorst.
Jacob Schermerhooren.

In my presence,

LUDOVICUS COBES, Secretary.

On this 14th day of May, 1672, appeared before me, Ludovicus Cobes, secretary of Albany, etc., in the presence of the honorable Heeren commissaries, etc., Messrs. Jan Hendricxse Van Bael and Gerrit Van Slichtenhorst, Mr. Siston, who declares, that in true rights free ownership, he grants, conveys and makes over by these presents, to and for the behoof of Pieter Adriaense Soo Machelyck, in a certain lot lying here in Albany on the hill, to the south of Wynant Gerritse [Vander Poel] to the north of Jochem Backer, breadth in front and rear 22½ feet and length two rods and eleven feet as well on the south as on the north sides all Rynland measure, free and unincumbered, with no claims standing or issuing against the same, save the lord's right, without the grantor's making the least pretension thereto any more, also acknowledging that he is fully paid and satisfied therefor, the first penny with the last and therefore giving *plenam actionem cessam*, and full power to said Pieter Adriaense, his heirs and successors or assigns, to do with and dispose of said lot as he might do with his patrimonial estate and effects; promising to protect and free the same from all such troubles, claims and liens of every person as are lawful, and further, never more to do nor suffer anything to be done against the same, with or without law, in any manner, on pledge according to laws therefor provided.

Done in Albany.

MICH: SISTON.

Jan Hend: Van Bael.
Gerrit Van Slichtenhorst.

In my presence,

LUDOVICUS COBES, Secretary.

On this 18th day of June, 1672, appeared before me, Ludovicus Cobes, secretary of Albany, etc., in the presence of the honorable Heeren commissaries, etc, Jan Hendricxse Van Bael and Gerrit Van Slichtenhorst, Andries de Vos, who declares that in true rights, free ownership, he grants, conveys and makes over by these presents, to and for the behoof of Jan Conneel in a certain lot No. 1, lying on the hill, bounded westerly by Jan [De la] Wardt,[1] easterly by the public road, northerly by Pieter Winne, breadth on the south side four rods and westerly three rods and six feet, free and unincumbered, with no claims standing or issuing against the same, save the lord's right, without the grantor's making the least pretension against the same any more, also acknowledging that he is fully paid and satisfied therefor, the first penny with the last, and therefore giving *plenam actionem cessam*, and full power to said Jan Conneel, his heirs and successors or assigns, to do with and dispose of said lot, as he might do with his patrimonial estate and effects; promising to protect and free the same from all such troubles, claims and liens of every person as are lawful, and further, never more to do nor suffer anything to be done, with or without law, in any manner, on pledge according to laws therefor provided.

Albany.

ANDRYES DE VOS.

Jan Hend: Van Bael.
Gerrit Van Slichtenhorst.

In my presence,

LUDOVICUS COBES, Secretary.

On this 18th day of June, 1672, appeared before me, Ludovicus Cobes, secretary of Albany, etc., in the presence of the honorable Heeren commissaries, etc., J. H. Van Bael and Gerrart Van Slichtenhorst, Jochim Wesselse Backer, who declares that in true rights, free ownership, he grants, conveys and makes over by these presents, to and for the behoof of Jacob Abrahamse [Vosburgh], in his house and lot standing and lying on the High street in New York, bounded by the house of Abel Hardenbroeck on the one side and Adriaen Van Laer on the other, by virtue of a patent thereof to which reference is herein made, free and unincumbered, with no claims standing or issuing against the same, excepting the lord's right, without the grantor's making the least pretension any more thereto,

[1] Jan De La Ward came over in 1662 from Antwerp. Besides a lot in Albany he owned land at Niskayuna and an island in the Mohawk river above Schenectady, which he sold to Joris Aertse Vander Baast. He died 28th of January, 1702.

also acknowledging that he is fully paid and satisfied therefor, the first penny with the last, and therefore giving *plenum actionem cessam*, and full power to said Jacob Abrahamse, his heirs and successors or assigns, to do with and dispose of said house and lot, as he might do with his patrimonial estate and effects; promising to protect and free the same from all such trouble, claims and liens of every person as are lawful, and further, never more to do nor suffer anything to be done against the same, with or without law, in any manner, on pledge according to laws therefor provided.

Done in Albany.

JOCHEM BACKER.

Jan Hend: Van Bael
Gerrit Van Slichtenhorst.

In my presence,

LUDOVICUS COBES, Secretary.

Appeared before me, Ludovicus Cobes, secretary of Albany, etc., in the presence of the honorable Heeren commissaries, etc., Messrs. Jan Hend. Van Bael and Gerrit Van Slichtenhorst, Mr. Philip Pieterse Schuyler, who declares that in true rights, free ownership, he grants, conveys and makes over by these presents, to and for the behoof of Heer Jeremias Van Rensselaer, in a certain house and lot standing and lying here in Albany, received by him from Capt. Thomas Willet, by conveyance and patent to which reference is herein made; free and unincumbered, with no claim standing or issuing against the same, excepting the lord's right, also acknowledging that he is fully paid and satisfied therefor, the first penny with the last, and therefore giving *plenum actionem cessam*, and full power to said Heer Jeremias Van Rensselaer, his heirs and successors or assigns, to do with and dispose of said house and lot, as he might do with his patrimonial estate and effects; promising to protect and free the same from all such troubles, claims and liens of every person as are lawful, and further, never more to do nor suffer anything to be done against the same, with or without law, in any manner, on pledge according to laws therefor provided.

Done in Albany, the 3d of July, 1672.

PHILIP SCHUYLER.

Jan Hend: Van Bael.
Gerrit Van Slichtenhorst.

In my presence,

LUDOVICUS COBES, Secretary.

Appeared before me, Ludovicus Cobes, secretary of Albany, etc., in the presence of the honorable Heeren commissaries, etc., Messrs. Jan Hendricxse Van Bael and Gerrit Van Slichtenhorst, Jan Conneel, who declares that in true rights, free ownership, he grants, conveys and makes over by these presents, to and for the behoof of Marten Hoffman, in his house and lot standing and lying here in Albany, in length, breadth and boundaries according to the showing of the contract by him received from Jacob Joosten [Van Covelens] and by conveyance thereof, to which reference is herein made; free and unincumbered, with no claims standing or issuing against the same, save the lord's right, without the grantor's making the least pretension thereto any more, also acknowledging that he is fully paid and satisfied therefor, the first penny with the last, and therefore giving *plenam actionem cessam*, and full power to said Marten Hoffman, his heirs and successors or assigns, to do with and dispose of said house and lot, as he might do with his patrimonial estate and effects; promising to protect and free the same from all such trouble, claims and liens of every person as are lawful, and further, never more to do nor suffer anything to be done against the same, with or without law, in any manner, on pledge according to laws. therefor provided.

Done in Albany, the 3d of June, 1672.

JOHN CONELL.

Jan Hend: Van Bael.
Gerrit Van Slichtenhorst.

In my presence,

LUDOVICUS COBES, Secretary.

On this 3d day of July, 1672, appeared before me, Ludovicus Cobes, secretary of Albany, etc., in the presence of the honorable Heeren commissaries, etc., Jan Hend. Van Bael and Gerrit Van Slichtenhorst, Mr. Evert Wendell, who acknowledges, that he is well and honestly indebted and in arrears to Mr. Jan Verbeeck and Theunis Dirricxe [Van Vechten], in the character of guardians of Anna Thomase, young daughter of the late Thomas Janse [Mingael], in the quantity of nineteen whole, good and merchantable beaver skins, growing out of merchandise delivered and received by him to his content, which aforesaid nineteen beavers the subscriber promises to pay to said guardians or the lawful bearer of this paper when said daughter shall come to lawful age or marriage state or sooner, with proper interest at ten per cent yearly, pledging therefor specially his house and lot here in Albany, and generally his person and estate. personal and real, present and future, nothing excepted, submitting the same to the authority of all the lord's laws and judges for the recovery of said payment in due time, if need be, without loss or cost.

Albany, the 3d of July, 1672.

EVERT WENDEL.

Jan Hend: Van Bael.
Gerrit Van Slichtenhorst.

In my presence,

LUDOVICUS COBES, Secretary.

On this 12th day of August, 1672, appeared before me, Ludovicus Cobes, secretary of Albany, etc., in the presence of the honorable Heeren commissaries, etc., Messrs. Jan Hendricxse Van Bael and Gerrart Van Slichtenhorst, Madam Johanna De Hulter, attorney for her *vaeder* [husband ?] Mr. Jeronimus Ebbinck, who declares, that in true rights, free ownership, she grants, conveys and makes over to and for the behoof of Paulus Martense [Van Benthuysen], in her certain house and lot standing and lying here in Albany, bounded on the east side by the highway, on the south side by the house of Hendrick de Backer, on the west side by the garden of Hendrick Andriesse [Van Doesburgh] and Lambert Van Neck, and on the north side by the house of Lambert Van Neck, the lot being in breadth in front on the street thirty-two wood feet and four inches, and in length ten rods, as the said lot was received by him by conveyance from Tierck Claese De Wit, by virtue of a patent and deed thereof with whatsoever is thereon fast by earth and nailed; free and unincumbered, with no claims standing or issuing against the same, excepting the lord's right acknowledging that she is fully paid and satisfied therefor the first penny with the last, and therefore giving *plenam actionem cessam*, and full power to said Paulus Martense, his heirs and successors or assigns, to do with and dispose of said house and lot as he might do with his patrimonial estate and effects, promising to protect and free the same from all such troubles, claims and liens of every person as are lawful, and further, never more to do nor suffer anything to be done against the same, with or without law, in any manner, on pledge according to laws, therefor provided.

Done in Albany *datum ut supra.*

Jan Hend: Van Bael JOHANNA DE HULTER.
Gerrit Van Slichtenhorst.

In my presence, LUDOVICUS COBES, Secretary

On this 12th day of August, 1672, appeared before me, Ludovicus Cobes secretary of Albany etc., in the presence of the honorable Heeren commissaries, etc, Messrs. Jan Hendricxse Van Bael and Gerrart Van Slichtenhorst, Paulus Martense [Van Benthuysen], who declares that in true rights, free ownership, he grants, conveys and makes over by these presents, to and for the behoof of Arnhout Cornelisse [Viele] in a certain house and lot standing and lying here in Albany enclosed and bounded according to patent and conveyance thereof, by him received from Mr Jeronimus Ebbinck, free and unincumbered, with no claims standing or issuing against the same, save the lord's right, without the grantor's making the least pretension thereto any more, acknowledging that he is fully paid and satisfied therefor, the first penny with the last and therefore giving *plenam actionem cessam*, and full power to said Arnhout Cornelise, his heirs and successors or assigns, to do with and dispose of said house and lot, as he might do with his patrimonial estate and effects; promising to protect and free the same from all such troubles claims and liens of every person as are lawful, and further, never more to do nor suffer anything to be done against the same, with or without law, in any manner, on pledge according to laws therefor provided.

Albany, *dato ut supra.* POULUS MARTEN.

Jan Hend: Van Bael.
Gerrit Van Slichtenhorst.

In my presence, LUDOVICUS COBES, Secretary.

On this 13th day of August, 1672, appeared before me, Ludovicus Cobes, secretary of Albany, etc., in the presence of the honorable Heeren commissaries. etc., Mons Jan Hendricxse Van Bael and Gerrart Van Slichtenhorst, Arnhout Cornelisse Vielen, who declares that in true rights, free ownership, he grants, conveys and makes over by these presents, to and for the behoof of Jan Cornelisse Vyselaer, in his certain house and lot, standing and lying here in Albany, with all that is fast by earth and nailed, and as it lies fenced in a square, received by him from Jan Koster [Van Aecken]. and furthermore according to patent and contract thereof, dated 9th of August, 1670, to which reference is herein made, free and unincumbered with no claims standing or issuing against the same, save the lord's right without the grantor's making the least pretension thereto any more, acknowledging that he is fully paid and satisfied therefor, the first penny with the last, and therefore giving *plenam actionem cessam*, and full power to said Jan Cornelisse Vyselaer, his heirs and successors or assigns, to do with and dispose of the same, as he might do with his patrimonial estate and effects; promising to protect and free the same from all such trouble, claims and liens of every person as are lawful, and further, never more to do nor suffer anything to be done against the same, with or without law, in any manner, on pledge according to laws therefor provided.

Albany, *dato ut supra.* ARNOUT COR. VIELEN.

Jan Hend: Van Bael.

Gerrit Van Slichtenhorst.

In my presence, LUDOVICUS COBES, Secretary.

On this 23d day of August, 1672, appeared before me, Ludovicus Cobes, secretary of Albany etc., in the presence of the honorable Heeren commissaries, etc., Messrs Jan Hendricxse Van Bael, and Gerrart Van Slichtenhorst, Gysbert Gerritse [Van Brakel],[1] attorney for Mary Goossense [Van Schaick], who declares that in true rights, free ownership, he grants, conveys and makes over, to and for the behoof of Barent Pieterse [Cocymans] miller, in a certain house and lot, as the same lies in fence, with all that is fast by earth and nailed, lying in *colonie* Rensselaerswyck, next the house of said Barent Pieterse; free and unincumbered, with no claim standing or issuing against the same, save the lord's right, without the grantors' making the least claim any more thereto, acknowledging that he is fully paid and satisfied therefor, the first penny with the last, and therefore giving *plenam actionem cessam*, and full power to said Barent Pieterse, his heirs and successors or assigns, to do with and dispose of the same, as he might do with his patrimonial estate and effects; promising to protect and free the same from all such trouble, claims and liens of every person as are lawful, and further, never more to do, nor to suffer anything to be done against the same, with or without law, in any manner on pledge according to law, therefor provided.

Albany, *dato ut supra.*

The mark of × GYSBERT GERRITSE, with his own hand set.

Jan Hend. Van Bael.

Gerrit Van Slichtenhorst.

In my presence, LUDOVICUS COBES, Secretary.

* * * * * * The commissaries of Albany, *colonie* Rensselaerswyck and Schanechtade, declare by these presents, that in true rights, free ownership, they grant, convey and make over, to and for the behoof of Barent Ryndertse, smith, in a lot No 13, lying on the hill here in Albany, breadth in front, two rods five feet, in the rear two rods and nine inches, length on the east side, three rods seven feet, and on the west side three rods eleven feet, bounded on the west by Goosen Gerritse [Van Schaick], on the east by Willem Bout, on the south by the public street, and on the north by Domine Schaets, according to the survey and regulation of the surveyor, dated 25 Ap./5 May, last, which lot, the aforesaid

---

[1] Gysbert Gerritse Van Brokel was an early settler at Schenectady. His first wife was Reyntle Stephens. in 1693 he married Elizabeth Janse, "weduwe van Jan Van Eps, beide op Scheneghtade woonachtig." He had four sons and one daughter, of whom Sander was killed, and Stephen was carried away captive by the Indians, Feb. 9, 1690. He made his will Dec. 10. 1709, and left a good estate to his children.

Barent Reyndertse, bought and paid for at public sale, according to the conditions; free and unincumbered (save the lord's right), and therefor giving full power to said Barent Reyndertse, his heirs and successors or assigns, to dispose thereof, as he might do with his patrimonial effects, with authority to ask for a patent for said lot, of the right honorable Heer general.

Done in Albany, $\frac{29\ \text{May}}{8\ \text{June}}$, 1668. R V. RENSSELAER.

Acknowledged before me,

D. V. SCHELLUYNE, Secretary, 1668

The commissaries of Albany, etc , declare by these presents, that in true rights, free ownership. they give and grant to the minister Domine Gideon Schaets, in a lot No. 14, lying here in Albany on the hill, breadth in front and rear five and twenty feet, length on the south side four rods six feet and three inches, on the north side four rods three feet and three inches, bounded on the east side by Claes Van Rotterdam, on the south side by Barent Reyndertse, smith, on the west side and north side the public highway and grounds, according to the survey and regulation thereof, of the surveyor dated $\frac{25\ \text{April}}{5\ \text{May}}$, last; free and unincumbered, excepting the lord's right, and therefor giving full power to said Dominie Schaets, his heirs and successors or assigns, to dispose thereof, as he might do with his patrimonial possessions, with authority to ask for a patent for said lot of the right honorable Heer general.

Done in Albany, the $\frac{29\ \text{May}}{8\ \text{June}}$. 1668. R. V RENSSELAER.

Acknowledged before me, D. V. SCHELLUYNE, Secretary, 1668.

On this $\frac{3}{13}$ of July, 1668, Tys Evertse de Goyer, declares that he appoints and empowers by these presents, Mr. Jacob Schermerhoorn proposing to depart for Holland, specially to demand, collect and receive, of his brother, Evert Evertse, master carpenter, at Amsterdam, Holland, payment of the sum of one hundred and eighty guilders with the accrued interest on the same, which his late mother Grietie Janse, widow of his father, the late Evert Tyssen (deceased at Naerden), left for his hereditary portion, according to advices from his said brother, dated the 23d of September 1663, and of the 5th of April, 1666, for which the subscriber, on the 17th of June, 1664. gave his said brother a power of attorney; together with whatever was bequeathed to him by his aforesaid deceased father, therefore for the receipt of said capital and accrued interest, together with whatever is found to be coming to him from his late father, *ex testamento vel ab intestato*, to his said brother or whosoever has the direction thereof, acquittance to pass, and furthermore all things to do, transact, and perform which he shall think needful and proper ; promising at all times to hold true all that shall be done and performed by the said attorney in the matter aforesaid by virtue of this power, without any gainsaying, on pledge according to laws therefor made, provided this attorney be holden of his transactions and receipts, when requested, a proper statement to make.

Done in Albany in America, of date as above, in presence of Cornelis Cornelisse Van Voorhout and Barent Albertse [Bratt] as witnesses.

THYS EVERTSEN.

This mark is set by + Cornelis Cornelisse Van Voorhout.

This mark is set ∞ by Barent Albertse, aforenamed.

In my presence, D. V. SCHELLUYNE, Secretary, 1668.

Appeared before me, Ludovicus Cobes, secretary of Albany, etc., in the presence of the honorable Heeren commissaries, etc., Mons. Ryckart Van Rensselaer and Mr. Jan Verbeeck, Capt Backer, who declares that in true rights, free ownership, he grants, conveys and makes over by these presents, to and for the behoof of Wynant Gerritse Vander Poel, in lot No. 6 lying on the hill here in Albany, breadth in front two rods five inches, in the rear two rods, length on the south six rods eleven feet, on the north six rods and eight feet, bounded north by Gerrit Hardenberen, east by the grantor, south by Jacob Schermerhorn, Van Bael, and Jan Thomase [Mingal] and west by the public street, according to the survey and regulation of the surveyor, dated the 5th of May, 1668; free and unincumbered, with no claims standing or issuing against the same, save the lord's right, without the grantor's making the least pretension thereto any more, acknowledging that he is fully paid and satisfied therefor, the first penny with the last and therefore giving *plenam actionem cessam*, and full power to said Wynant Gerritse, his heirs and successors or assigns, to do with and dispose of the same, as he might do with his patrimonial estate and effects; promising to protect and free said lot from all such trouble, claims, and liens of every person as are lawful, and further, never more to do nor suffer anything to be done against the same, with or without law, in any manner, on pledge according to laws therefor provided.

Done in Albany, the 16th of March, 1669.

R. V. Rensselaer. JOHN BAKER.
Jan Verbeeck.

Appeared before me, Ludovicus Cobes, secretary of Albany, etc., in the presence of the honorable Heeren commissaries, etc., Mr. Jan Verbeeck and Mr. Philip Schuyler, Hendrick Meese Vrooman, husbandman, dwelling on the land behind Kinderhoeck, who acknowledges that he is well and honestly indebted and in arrears to Tryntje Claese, in the quantity of one hundred and twenty-five skipples of good winter wheat or in seewant, twenty-five guilders for every six skipples of wheat, to the full sum and supplementary to the same a further sum of *f* 3.5 in seewant, for goods to his full satisfaction and content received, which aforesaid sums the subscriber promises to pay in manner hereafter written; *Firstly*, in the month of May next three beavers each of which shall be worth nine guilders, and in the month of June following, *f* 100 in seewant, and in the fall also following one of his largest oxen on a valuation of indifferent persons, therefor specially pledging five *loop* hogs and a cart, and generally his person and estate, personal and real, having and to have, nothing excepted, submitting the same to the force of all laws and judges, for the recovery of said payment in due time, if need be, without cost or loss.

Done in Albany, the 6th of April, 1670.

Jan Verbeeck. HEINDERICK MEESEN.
Philip Pieterse Schuyler.

In my presence, LUDOVICUS COBES, Secretary.

Appeared before me, Ludovicus Cobes, secretary of Albany, etc., in the presence of the honorable Heeren commissaries, etc., Mr. Jan Verbeeck and Mr. Philip Pieterse Schuyler, Jan Thomase [Mingael], old commissary, who declares by these presents, that in true rights, free ownership, he grants, conveys and makes over, to and for the behoof of *Mynheer* Thomas

De Lavall, merchant in his certain claim upon some parcels of land lying in the Esopus, according to contract and patent thereof to which reference is herein made; free and unincumbered. with no claims standing or issuing against the same, save the lord's right, without the grantor's making the least pretension thereto any more, acknowledging that he is fully paid and satisfied therefor, the first penny with the last, by the hands of Heer De Lavall aforesaid, and therefore giving *plenum actionem cessam*, and full power to said Mynheer De Lavall, his heirs and successors or assigns, to do with and dispose of the aforesaid contract, claim and patent with the appurtenances of the same, as he might do with his patrimonial estate and effects; promising to warrant and defend against whatever may be brought against the same, if lawful, and further, never more to do nor suffer anything to be done against the same, with or without law, in any manner, on pledge according to law.

Done in Albany, the 30th of April, 1670.

Jan Verbeeck. JAN THOMASE.

Philip Pieterse Schuyler.

In my presence,

LUDOVICUS COBES, Secretary.

Appeared before me, Ludovicus Cobes, secretary of Albany, etc., in the presence of the honorable Heeren commissaries, etc., Messrs. Philip Pieterse Schuyler and Jan Verbeek, Volckert Janse [Douw], burgher and inhabitant here. who declares that in true rights, free ownership, he grants, conveys and makes over, to and for the behoof of *Mynheer* Thomas De Laval, merchant at New York, in his certain title to some parcels of land and buildings standing thereon, lying at the Esopus, according to patent thereof granted by the right honorable governor general, Richard Nicolls, to which reference is herein made, free and unincumbered, with no claims standing or issuing against the same, excepting the lord's right, without the grantor's making the least pretension thereto any more, also acknowledging that he is fully paid and satisfied therefor, the first penny with the last, by the hands of the Heer De Laval aforesaid, and therefore giving *plenum actionem cessam*, and full power to said *Mynheer* De Laval, his heirs and successors or assigns. to do with and dispose of said title to the aforesaid land, patent and the appendances and dependences of the same, as he might do with his patrimonial estate and effects; promising to protect and free the said parcels of land from all such trouble, claims and liens of every person as are lawful, and further, never more to do nor suffer anything to be done against the same, with or without law, in any manner, on pledge according to laws therefor provided.

Done in Albany, the 3d of May 1670. VOLCKART JANSE.

This conveyance is made with this reservation, that the grantor must pay the carpenters according to contract, but the victuals and drink which the carpenters shall receive after the date of this conveyance, are to be at the cost of the honorable Heer De Laval.

Jan Verbeeck.

Philip Pieterse Schuyler.

In my presence,

LUDOVICUS COBES, Secretary.

By the aforesaid conveyance, Volckert Janse promises to deliver to the honorable Heer De Laval, all the materials which the grantor has carried thither, as well as carts, ploughs, harrows and all that he has there.

Albany, the 3d of May, 1670.

The honorable Heeren commissaries of Albany, *colonie* Rensselaerswyck and Schaenhechtede, have granted a warrant (*acte van authorisatie*), on two certain sentences, the one of date the 17th of January, 1664, and the other of date the $\frac{16}{26}$ of January, 166$\frac{7}{8}$, against Dirk Van Schelluyne, late secretary here, and in favor of Jacob Vis, said execution being made effectual by the purchase of a lot of land lying at Lubberde's land[1] in the colony Rensselaerswyck, belonging to Dirck Van Schelluyne, and that at public sale to the highest bidder on the 26th of October, 1668, according to proofs and conditions thereof in the custody of Mr. Provoost, vendue master, according to which conditions the purchaser was promised his warrant, and for the aforesaid lot of land Dirck Hesselingh, remained the highest bidder for the sum of one hundred and twenty guilders in beavers, said Vis ordering said money to be paid at New York, to Mr. Withart, or his servant Jan Janse Bleecker, so it is that the aforesaid Hesselingh, payment having been made, demands said promised warrant, wherefore their honors [the commissaries etc.,] grant their warrant, and ownership, in said lot of land, as by these presents they do warrant and grant him ownership in said land, so as to do with and dispose of the same, as he might do with his patrimonial estate and effects; *et tanquam actor et procurator in rem suam ac propriam*; promising to free the same from all such claims and liens as are lawful, and further, never more to do nor suffer anything to be done against the same, with or without law.

Given in Albany, the 17th of June, 1670.

ABRAM STAAS.
JAN VERBEECK.

In my presence, LUDOVICUS COBES, Secretary.

Appeared before me, Ludovicus Cobes, secretary of Albany, etc., in the presence of the honorable Heeren commissaries, etc., Mr. Abraham Staes and Mr. Jan Verbeeck, Mr. Roeloff Swartwout, dwelling in the Esopus, who declares that in true rights, free ownership, he grants, conveys and makes over by these presents, to and for the behoof of Ryckie Dareth, widow of the late Jan Dareth,[2] dwelling in Albany, in a lot lying on the road to the south and east of the house of Volckert Janse [Douw], according to extract from the conditions of public sale, in length and breadth as the same lies in fence and at present occupied by Sturm Vanderzee; free and unincumbered, with no claims standing or issuing against the same, excepting the lord's right, etc. * * * *

[This conveyance is imperfect.]

Appeared before me, Ludovicus Cobes, secretary of Albany, etc., in the presence of the honorable Heeren commissaries, etc., Mr. Jan Verbeeck and Mr. Abraham Staes, Jan Clute, burgher and inhabitant here

[1] Lubberde's land lay on the east side of the Hudson river, in the neighborhood of the present city of Troy.

[2] Jan Dareth and wife, Ryckie Van Dyck, both from Utrecht, were married in New Amsterdam Nov. 1, 1654. He soon after removed to Beverwyck.

who declares by these presents, that in true rights, free ownership, he grants, conveys and makes over, to and for the behoof of Mr. Gabriel Thomase [Stridles] [1] in a certain house and lot standing here in Albany, in length on the east side of Evert Luycasse [Backer] five rods seven feet and two inches, on the south the public highway breadth two rods and one foot, on the north side breadth three rods, on the west side Ruth Arentse length five rods one foot and three inches, Rynland measure; by virtue of a patent thereof granted by the right honorable the late Heer general Nicolls, of date the 24th of May, 1667, to which reference is herein made, except that fifteen feet to be taken off from this lot, sold by the grantor to Myndert Fredervickse, and said house and lot shall be delivered to Gabriel Thomase, free and unincumbered, with no claims standing or issuing against the same, saving the lord's right, etc. * *

[This deed is imperfect, a part wanting.]

* * * * + [This conveyance is imperfect, wanting both the name of the grantee and description: it is subscribed by Robbert Sanders.]

On this the 25th day of August [1672], appeared before me, Ludovicus Cobes, secretary of Albany, etc., in the presence of the honorable Heeren commissaries, etc., Mons. Jan Hendricxse Van Bael and Gerrart Van Slichtenhorst, Pieter Meese Vrooman, who declares that in true rights, free ownership, he grants, conveys and makes over by these presents, to and for the behoof of Mons. Philip Pieterse Schuyler, in a certain house, barn and rick, with orchard and three morgens of land as the same lies in fence, (except the *Steenberch*), standing and lying here in the *colonie* Rensselaerswyck, by virtue of the contract thereof, dated the 22d of January, 167½, and the conveyance from Madam Ebbinck to the subscriber, of date the 28th of June, to which reference is herein made; free and unincumbered, with no claims standing or issuing against the same, save the lord's right, without the grantor's making the least pretension thereto any more, also acknowledging that he is fully paid and satisfied therefor, the first penny with the last, and therefore giving *plenam actionem cessam*, and full power to said Mons. Philip Pieterse, his heirs and successors or assigns, to do with and dispose of said house, barn, rick, orchard and land, as he might do with his patrimonial estate and effects; promising to protect and free the same from all such troubles, claims and liens of every person as are lawful, and further, never more to do nor suffer anything to be done against the same, with or without law, in any manner, on pledge according to laws therefor provided.

Albany.

Jan Hend: Van Bael PIETER MEESEN.
Gerrit Van Slichtenhorst.

In my presence, LUDOVICUS COBES, Secretary.

On this 9th day of September, 1672, appeared before me, Ludovicus Cobes, secretary of Albany, etc., in the presence of the honorable Heeren commissaries, etc., Mons. Jan Hendricxse Van Bael and Gerrart Van

[1] Gabriel Thomase Stridles came to Beverwyck about 1662, and hired himself to Thomas Powell as a baker for two years at twenty-two beavers ($70.40) a year. He remained here until about 1692, when he removed to New York, where he died about 1718. He had four children baptized in Albany, and two in New York.

Slichtenhorst, Hendrick Koster, who declares that in true rights, free ownership, he grants, conveys and makes over by these presents, to and for the behoof of Mr. Jan Clute, in his house and lot lying on the hill here in Albany, to the north Hendrick Roosenboom, to the south the widow of Hendrick Andriesse [Van Doesburgh], east and west the public highway, breadth five rods, and length eighteen rods as the same was purchased at public sale on the 7th of September, 1672, and by virtue of a patent and conveyance thereof, to which reference is herein made; free and unincumbered, with no claims standing or issuing against the same, excepting the lord's right, without the grantor's making the least pretension thereto any more, also acknowledging that he is fully paid and satisfied therefor, the first penny with the last, and therefore giving *plenam actionem cessam*, and full power to said Mr. Jan Clute, his heirs and successors or assigns, to do with and dispose of the same, as he might do with his patrimonial estate and effects, promising to protect and free the same from all such trouble, claims and liens of every person as are lawful, and further, never more to do nor to suffer anything to be done against the same, with or without law, in any manner, on pledge according to laws therefor provided.

Albany, *ut supra*

Jan Hend: Van Bael. HENDERICK KOSTER.

Gerrit Van Slichtenhorst.

In my presence, LUDOVICUS COBES, Secretary.

* * * * * * [This conveyance, dated 11th of Aug., 1670, is wanting save a few lines conveying no information, and the signature of the grantor, Geertruyt Vosburgh,[1] by her mark.]

Appeared before me, Ludovicus Cobes, secretary of Albany, etc., on the date underwritten, in the presence of the honorable Heeren commissaries, etc., Sander Leendertse Glen, old commissary, dwelling at Schaenhechtede, who acknowledges that he is well and honestly indebted to Mr. Abraham Staes in the sum of two hundred and eighty-eight guilders in beavers for wares and merchandise to his content received, which aforesaid *f*. 288 in beavers the subscriber promises to pay to Mr. Abraham or his order within the time of two years, therefor pledging specially his *bouwery* with land, house, barn and ricks lying at Schaenhechtede, and further more, generally his person and estate, personal and real, present and future, nothing excepted, for the recovery of said payment in due time, if need be, without loss or cost.

Done at Schaenhechtede, the 12th of August, 1670.

Jan Verbeeck. SANDER LENRSEN GLEN.

Philip Pieterse Schuyler.

Acknowledged before me,

LUDOVICUS COBES, Secretary.

On this 5th day of July, 1687, Maj. Abraham Staas appeared before the secretary, and declared that he had received full payment and satisfaction by the hands of Catharina [Van Witbeck] widow of the late Jacob Sanderse Glen, oldest son of Sander Leendertse Glen, for the above bond and mortgage executed for my behoof, the 12th of August, 1670, thereby releasing all the heirs and successors of said Sander Leendertse Glen from

[1] Geertruy Vosburgh was the wife of Pieterse Jacobse Vosburgh, the first of the name in Albany.

all actions and claims. In confirmation of which I have hereto set my hand and seal in Albany, on the above date.

[Seal][1]

ABRAM STAES.

Acknowledged before me, * * * * * *

Appeared before me, Ludovicus Cobes, secretary of Albany, etc., in the presence of the honorable Heeren commissaries, etc., Mr. Abraham Staas and Mr. Philip Schuyler, Sander Leendertse Glen, old commissary, dwelling at Schaenhechtede, who acknowledges that he is well and honestly indebted for arrears to the Heer Jeremias Van Rensselaer and Jacob Sanderse Glen, attorneys for the administrators of the late Jan Bastiaense [Van Gutsenhoven], in the sum of *f* 6000 in beavers, for wares and merchandise, to his content received, according to an obligation therefor, which sum of *f* 6000 in beavers, the subscriber promises to pay to said attorneys, or their order, therefor pledging specially his *bouwery*, land, house, barn and ricks, horses and cattle therein, lying at Schaenhechtede, and generally his person and estate, personal and real, present and future, nothing excepted, for the recovery of said sum, in due time, if need be, without loss and cost.

Done in Schaenhechtede, the 13th of August, 1670.

SANDER LENRSEN GLEN.

Acknowledged before me,

LUDOVICUS COBES, Secretary.

On this 9th day of September, 1672, appeared before me, Ludovicus Cobes, secretary of Albany, etc., in the presence of the honorable Heeren commissaries, etc., Mons. Jan Hendricxse Van Bael and Gerrart Van Slichtenhorst, Mr. Jan Clute, who declares that in true rights, free ownership, he grants, conveys and makes over, by these presents, to and for the behoof of Jan Janse Bleecker, in his house and lot, standing and lying in Albany, on the hill, on the west side Helmer Otten length two rods ten feet and three inches, in front on the highway one rod ten feet and six inches, length on the east side three rods, all Rynland measure, also a little corner of land that adjoins on said lot in the rear, in breadth, one rod ten feet six inches, on the south end one rod nine feet and two inches, length east and west six feet less three inches, also Ryuland measure; free and unincumbered, with no claims standing or issuing against the same, excepting the lord's right, without the grantor's making the least claim any more thereto, also acknowledging that he is fully paid and satisfied therefor, the first penny with the last, and therefore giving *plenam actionem cessam*, and full power to said Jan Janse Bleecker, his heirs, successors or assigns, to do with and dispose of said house and lot, as he might do with his patrimonial estate and effects; promising to protect and free the same from all such trouble, claims and liens of every person as are lawful, and further, never more to do nor suffer anything

[1] This is the only instance of a seal being attached to an instrument in the first two volumes of deeds.

to be done against the same, with or without law, in any manner, on pledge according to laws therefor provided.

Albany, of date *ut supra.*

JOHANNES CLUTE.

Jan Hend: Van Bael.
Gerrit Van Slichtenhorst.

On this 9th day of September, 1672, appeared before me, Ludovicus Cobes, secretary of Albany, etc., in the presence of the honorable Heeren commissaries, etc., Mons. Jan Hendricxse Van Bael and Gerrart Van Slichtenhorst, Mr. Jan Clute, who declares that in true rights, free ownership, he grants, conveys and makes over by these presents, to and for the behoof of Hendrick Lansinck [1] and Lucas Gerritse [Wyngaert],[2] in a certain lot lying on the hill, breadth in front on the street three rods one and one-sixth feet, and the same in the rear on the east side, on the west two rods and eleven feet, all Rynland measure; free and unincumbered, with no claims standing and issuing against the same, excepting the lord's right, without the grantor's making the least pretension thereto any more, also acknowledging that he is fully paid and satisfied therefor, the first penny with the last, and therefore giving *plenam actionem cessam*, and full power to said Hendrick Lansinck and Luycas Gerritse, their heirs and successors or assigns, to do with and dispose of said lot, as they might do with their patrimonial estates and effects; promising to protect and free the same from all such trouble, claims, and liens of every person as are lawful, and further, never more to do nor suffer anything to be done, with or without law, in any manner, on pledge according to laws therefor provided.

Albany, of date as above.

JOHANNES CLUTE.

Jan Hend: Van Bael.
Gerrit Van Slichtenhorst.

On this 9th day of September, 1672, appeared before me, Ludovicus Cobes, secretary of Albany, etc., in the presence of the honorable Heeren commissaries, etc., Mons. Jan Hendricxse Van Bael and Gerrart Van Slichtenhorst, Mr. Jan Clute, who declares that in true rights, free ownership, he grants, conveys and makes over by these presents, to and for the behoof of Jan Byvanck, in a certain lot lying on the hill, length on the east side, next to Hendrick Lansinck, two rods and eleven feet, in front on the street twenty-one feet and seven inches, in the rear two rods less a half foot, length on the west side, next to Gerret Hardenberch, thirty-four feet and one inch, all Rynland measure; free and unincumbered, with no claims standing or issuing against the same, excepting the lord's

[1] Hendrik Lansingh was son of Gerrit Lansingh, who came to Albany from Hassell near Swoll, in Overyssell, Holland. He had two children, Jacob and Alida. The date of his death in the church records, is the 11th of July 1709.

[2] Lucas Gerritse Wyngaert was a baker, and owned the lot on south corner of Broadway and State street, in 1715.—*Annals of Albany*, VII, 22, 72; X, 16. By his wife, Anna Janse Van Hoesen, he had three sons and one daughter. He made his will 30 Oct., 1709.

right, without the grantor's making the least pretension thereto any more, also acknowledging that he is fully paid and satisfied therefor, the first penny with the last, and therefore giving *plenam actionem cessam*, and full power to said Jan Byvanck, his heirs and successors or assigns, to do with and dispose of said lot, as he might do with his patrimonial estate and effects; promising to protect and free the same from all such trouble, claims and liens of every person as are lawful, and further, never more to do nor suffer anything to be done against the same, with or without law, in any manner, on pledge according to laws therefor provided.

JOHANNES CLUTE.

Jan Hend: Van Bael.
Gerrit Van Slichtenhorst.

On this 9th day of September, 1672, appeared before me, Ludovicus Cobes. secretary of Albany, etc., in the presence of the honorable Heeren commissaries, etc., Messrs. Jan Hendricxse Van Bael and Gerrart Van Slichtenhorst. Mr. Jan Clute, who declares that in true rights, free ownership, he grants, conveys and makes over by these presents. to and for the behoof of Gerrit Hardenberch, in a certain lot lying on the hill, length on the east side next to Jan Byvanck, thirty-four feet and one inch, Rynland measure, breadth front and rear, twenty-four wood feet, on the west side next to Jan Bleecker, thirty-two feet and eight inches, Rynland measure, also a little corner of land in the rear. breadth front and rear ten feet three and one-sixth inches, on the east side length two rods, and on the west side two rods and two inches; free and unincumbered, with no claims standing or issuing against the same, excepting the lord's right, without the grantor's making the least pretension thereto any more, also acknowledging that he is fully paid and satisfied therefor, the first penny with the last, and therefore giving *plenam actionem cessam*, and full power to said Gerrit Hardenberch, his heirs and successors or assigns, to do with and dispose of said lot, as he might do with his patrimonial estate and effects; promising to protect and free the same from all such trouble, claims and liens of every person, as are lawful, and further, never more to do nor suffer anything to be done against the same, with or without law, in any manner, on pledge according to laws therefor provided.

Albany, *dato ut supra.*

JOHANNES CLUTE.

Jan Hend: Van Bael.
Gerrit Van Slichtenhorst.

On this 17th day of September, 1672, appeared before me, Ludovicus Cobes, secretary of Albany, etc., in the presence of the honorable Heeren commissaries, etc., Mr. Jan Hendricxse Van Bael and Gerrart Van Slichtenhorst, Claes Ripse [Van Dam] who declares that in true rights, free ownership, he grants, conveys and makes over, by these presents, to and for the behoof of Gerrit Theunisse [Van Vechten], in his certain house and lot, which he received by conveyance from Marcelis Janse [Van Bommel] and Cornelis Wynkoop, and by virtue of the patent thereof, dated the 6th of June, 1667, to which reference is herein made; free and unincumbered, with no claims standing or issuing against the same, save the lord's right, without the grantor's making the least pretension thereto any more; also acknowledging that he is fully paid and satisfied therefor, the first penny with the last, and therefore giving *plenam actionem cessam*, and full power to said Gerrit Theunisse, his heirs and successors or assigns, to do with and dispose of said house and lot, as he might do with his patrimonial estate and effects; promising to protect and free the same from all such trouble, claims and liens of every person as are lawful, and further, never more to do nor suffer anything to be done against the same, with or without law, in any manner, on pledge according to laws therefor provided.

Albany *dato ut supra.*

CLAES RIPSE VAN DAM.

Jan Hend: Van Bael.
Gerrit Van Slichtenhorst.

In my presence,

LUDOVICUS COBES, Secretary.

On this 17th day of September, 1672, appeared before me, Ludovicus Cobes, secretary of Albany, etc., in the presence of the Heeren commissaries, Jan H. Van Bael and G. Van Slichtenhorst, Gerrit Theunisse [Van Vechten], who declares, that in true rights, free ownership, he grants, conveys and makes over by these presents, to and for the behoof of Ricchard Shisair, in his certain house and lot by him received from Claes Ripse [Van Dam], by virtue of the patent thereof, to which reference is herein made, free and unincumbered, with no claims standing or issuing against the same, excepting the lord's right, without the grantors' making the least pretension thereto any more, also acknowledging that he is fully paid and satisfied therefor, the first penny with the last, and therefore giving *plenam actionem cessam*, and full power to said Ricchard Srisair, his heirs and successors or assigns, to do with and dispose of said house and lot, as he might do with his patrimonial estate and effects; promising to protect and free the same from all such trouble, claims and liens of every person as are lawful, and further, never more to do, nor suffer anything to be done against the same, with or without law, in any manner, on pledge according to laws therefor provided.

Albany, *dato ut supra.*

The mark of ⊕ GERRIT THEUNISSE,
with his own hand set.

Jan Hend: Van Bael.
Gerrit Van Slichtenhorst.

In my presence,

LUDOVICUS COBES, Secretary.

On this 15th day of December, 1672, appeared before me, Ludovicus Cobes, secretary of Albany, etc., in the presence of the honorable Heeren commissaries, etc., Mons^rs. Andries Teller and Adriaen Gerritse [Papendorp], Jurriaen Theunisse Tappen, who declares that in true rights, free ownership, he grants, conveys and makes over by these presents, to and for the behoof of Herman Vedder, in a house, barn and ricks, also a garden in the rear on the land, together with twelve morgens and one hundred and thirty rods of land lying at Schaenhechtede, being allotment No. 8, enclosed and bounded according to the description of the patent to which reference is herein made; free and unincumbered, with no claims standing or issuing against the same, excepting the lord's right, without the grantor's making the least pretension thereto any more, also acknowledging that he is fully paid and satisfied therefor, the first penny with the last, by the hands of said Harmen Vedder, and therefore giving *plenam actionem cessam*, and full power to Herman Vedder, his heirs and successors or assigns, to do with and dispose of said house, lot, garden and lands, as he might do with his patrimonial estate and effects; promising to protect and free the same from all such trouble, claims and liens of every person as are lawful, and further, never more to do nor suffer anything to be done against the same, with or without law, in any manner, on pledge according to laws therefor provided.

Albany, *dato ut supra.* JUREJAN TUNSEN TAPPEN.

Adriaen Gerritsen.

A^s Teller.

In my presence,

LUDOVICUS COBES, Secretary.

Appeared before me, Ro^t. Livingston, secretary of Albany, colony Rensselaerswyck, Schaenhectady, etc., in the presence of the honorable Heeren Mr. Dirk Wessells [Ten Broeck] and Mr. Cornelis Van Dyk, commissaries of the same jurisdiction, Pieter Janse Lokermans, who declares that in true rights, free ownership, he grants, conveys and makes over, to and for the behoof of Jan Andriese de Cuyper, in a certain lot lying here in Albany, whereon said Jan Andriese's house stands, bounded south by the lot of Wynant Gerritse Van der Poel, north by the house of the grantor, Pieter Lokermans, east by the highway, and west by the cart way, in breadth in front on the street twenty wood feet and six inches and in the rear twenty wood feet, length south and north seven and a half rods, which the grantor does by virtue of a patent to him from the late governor Rich: Nicolls, of date the 14th of May, 1667, to which reference is herein made; free and unincumbered, with no claim standing or issuing against the same (excepting the lord's right), without the grantor's making the least pretension thereto any more, also acknowledging that he is fully paid and satisfied therefor, the first penny with the last, and therefore giving *plenam actionem cessam*, and full power to do with and dispose of the same as he might do with his patrimonial estate and effects; promising never more to do nor suffer anything to be done against the same, with or without law, in any manner, on pledge according to laws therefor provided.

Done in Albany, the 3d of March, 1679.

PIETER LOOCKERMANS.

Acknowledged before me,

RO: LIVINGSTON, Secretary.

Appeared before me, Ro[t] Livingston, secretary of Albany, etc., in the presence of Arnont Cornelise Viele, and William Parker, Ryckie Staes, wife of Jacob Staes,[1] who declared that she has sold, and that Philip Schuyler has purchased her house and lot with barn, with all that is fast by earth and nailed, standing and lying here in Albany, bounded north by the first *killetie* and Jochem Wessells [De Backer], west by the highway, south by the house of William Loveridge, hatter, and east by the river, breadth in front on the street nine rods, and in the rear four rods and nine feet, length on the south side thirteen rods, and north seventeen rods, from which lot forty feet in breadth in front on the street, and twenty feet in the rear, must be deducted for the public street; with all the appurtenances according to patent thereof from governor R: Nicolls, dated the 3d of May, (?) 1667, (except the lord's right), in consideration of which the purchaser is obligated and promises to pay said Ryckie Staes, her order or assigns, the quantity of one hundred and fifty good whole merchantable beaver skins, to be paid in two installments, to wit, the first next July, a just half, being seventy-five beavers, and the last installment in July, 1680, the remaining half. The buyer shall have the privilege of occupying and using said house and lot immediately, and a conveyance shall be made on full payment for the same. In witness of which the parties hereto have subscribed their names, in presence of the aforesaid witnesses.

Done in Albany, the......

[The above paper was not executed.]

---

[1] Jacob Staes, "chirurgeon," was the eldest son of Maj. Abram Staes. He settled in Albany, but there is no mention in the records of any descendants. His brothers, Samuel and Abraham, left large families.

INDEX.

Auringer families, 94
Aurora, extraordinary, 56
Austin Elsie, 94
William, 130
families, 94

Baast, family, 94
Madalena, 181
Margarita, 182
Babbington family, 94
Babcock, Abel S., died, 49
Mary J. died, 76
Bacheller, Kitty, died, 28
Bachus, Backis (Bockes), family, 94
Backer, Capt. John, 428; sells his house, 500
Coenradtsen, 322
Evert Luycasse, 89 451, 503; see Luykasse family, 94
Hans Coenraetse, 85
Hendrik, 2 1, 286
Hendrick Willemse 91; his lot, 203
Jan Claessen, 380, 386, 387
Jan Harmense, 87
Jochem, 229, 262, 493 495
Jochem Wesselse, 91 228, 290, 298, 315, 316, 340, 343, 351, 355, 372, 389, 398 399, 494; see Becker Jochem Wesselse
Simon Volkertse, 408; see Veeder de Backer; also Bakker and Baker
Willem, Jurriaense, 89
Woutert, 250
Backes, Eva, 165
Bacon Hannah, 147
Badt family, 94
Baehtgen, 225
Bailey family, 94
W. H. H., 46
Bain, Wm. died, 33
Bake, Mrs Catharine, died, 40
Baker, Barnard, died, 31
Capt. John, lot, 215, 217
for Christians and savages, 385; in Beverwyck, 307, 308
Baking, Margaret, 96
Bakker, family, 94
Jochem Janse, 88
Bal, Barent Janse, 88, 167
Baldwin, Maria, 133
Mrs. Clarissa, died, 37
Ball, Jas., 16
Mary, died, 13
Bambus family, 94
Harmen Jacobse, 84, 194
Bamnitz family, 94
Bank, Rachel, 158
Banken, Gerrit, lot, 202
Jane, 131
Banker (Baker), Catharine, 156
Captain, 444
Elizabeth, 140, 156
Evert, 184z; his lot 186
families, 94
Gerrit, 112, 184a, 250, 281, 369, 382, 383, 389 407, 418, 412, 460, 478; witness, 292; his lots, 186, 190, 202, 223
Jannetie, 163, 184w
Bankly family, 95
Orsel, 95
Banks, alderman, 35
Robert Lenox, 46
Bantic, Jannetie, 184w
Baptist cemetery, 35
Baquena (?) Catrina, 107

Barbara, Maria, 111
Barber Anna, died, 64
Fletcher, 5
Lena (Magdalena), 157
Barclay, John, 109, 184z
Rev. Thomas, lot, 209, 221
Barent, Margarita, 112
the smith, 352
Barents, Elizabeth, 106
Barentse, Ariaantje, 177
Elsie, 160
family, 95
Jannetje, 184q
Judikje, 177
Maritie, 125, 147
Barentsen, Elsie, 352, 461
Foh, 246
Frans, 209; see Pastoor
Geertruyt, 365, 409, 456
Jan, 354; see Wemp, and Poest
Barheit, Alida, 124, 145
(Bareith), Barentje 125
Catalyna, 95
Christina, 134
Dirkje (Gerritje), 184l
families, 95
Jan Hanse, 87
Jeronimus Hanse, 87
Johanna, 184g
Johanna Hanse 87
Margarita, 184h
Rebecca, 148
Rachel, 95
Theuntje, 184h
Tyrie, 148
Wouter Jeronimus, 89
family, 95
Barhydt, or Barheit, Andries Hanse, 87
Barkhuff, Mrs. Hannah (Van Schaack), died, 15
Barkley, Haccost, 184n
Barnard, Frances, died, 11
Barnes, Mrs. George M., died, 12
Wm., 38
Barney, Paul C., died, 21
Barnham, Hannah, 137
Barnton, Sarah, 132
Baroquier, Jacob Clomp, 244
Reyntyen Pieterse, 276
Barret, Barrentje, lot, 206, 207
(Berrit), families, 95
(Bergen), Maria, 167
Willem, 102
Barreth, Mary, 184z
Barreith (see Barret), 95
Barrith, Margarita, 184m
Barrett, John, died 60
Barringer, Aaron (see Berringer), 95, 485
Barrington (Barlington), Elsie, 116
family, 95
Sara 133
Barrois Barroa, Barroway, Bewar, Benvee), families, 95
(Barreway) Maria, 132
Catharine, 101
Barroquier, Jacob Symonse Clomp, 91
Reyntjen Pieterse, 90
Barrows, Mrs. Ephriam, died, 80
Barry, Elizabeth, 184q
Bartay, Harriet, 184y
Bartel, Annatie, 101
family, 95
Barth family, 95
Bartlett Thirza, died, 67
Bartow, Theodosia, 106

Bas (Janse) Lysbeth, 118
Baschasche, family, 95
Bastiaense Harmen, 273, 306, 366; his lot, 214; see Vischer
(Visscher) Harmen, lot, 197
Jan 352
Bassett, Daniel E, 15
(Bussel), Elizabeth, 184w
(Bessidt) families, 95
Marytje, 160
Bat, see Boer
Batchelder, Mr., 55
Mrs. Sarah L., died, 8
Bates family, 95
Harriet A., died, 10
Bath family, 95
Sara, 95
Batlolado, family, 95
Batt, Cornelia, 129
Baxter (see De Baxter) family, 95
John S., died, 56
Martha, 95
Susanna, 170
Bayard, Ariaantje, 184n
Father, 38
(Basert) Judith, 184d
Miss, 20
Nicholaes, 480, 481
Sara, 107
Baylie (Malbary) Mary, 150
Beach, Wm. M., died, 60
Beardsley, Mrs. Henry, died, 77
Bears, Margarita, 106
Beasely family, 95
Beaufils (see Bovie family, 95
Beaumont, Mrs. Jane, died, 47
Beaver, 249, 435; at 8 guilders, 369; at 12 guilders, 252; 16 guilders, 370; to be rated at par 20 stuyvers to the guilder, 365; ship, 376; shipped 1657, 244
block, 12
Beck, Dennis, died, 45
Dr. T. R., 68
Elizabeth, 184a
Becker, Anna, 135
Annatie, 184w
(Bekker) families, 95
Cornelia, 184b
Elizabeth, 101, 184l
Eva, 137
Fytje, 114
Hilletje, 184k
Jan Juriaense, 89
Maritie, 121, 180, 182
Marytje (Mary Baker), 184w
Victor, 111, 491
Beckker, Maria, 131
Beckett, Thomas S., 15
Bedell, Richard, died, 39
Beebe family, 96
Beecraft (Bickroft), family, 96
Beekman, Alida, 124
Anna (Johanna), 146
Ariaantje, 140
Barber, 148
Catharine, 137
Christina, 104
Debora, 118, 168
Effie, 124
Elizabeth, 184r
Engeltie, 119
Eva, 145, 163
families, 96
Gerard, 160
Helena, 159
Hendrick Jacobse, 88
Hendrick Martense, 89

Beekman, Hester, 163
Jeannetie, 112, 139
Johannes, 160, 161
Johannes, Jr. lot, 211
Johannes Martense, 89
John, Ja., 184z
Lena, 136
Maria, 133
Maritie, 122
Matilda, 123
Marten Hendrickse, 87
Metie, 181
Neeltie, 186
Willem, 191, 429
Beeley (see Bailey), 96
Beem, Elizabeth, 97
family, 96
Beemus Cath., 147
Beer, excise on, 315, 316, 389
Beeren island, 493
Beers, A. S. 16
family, 96
Beesinger (see Besinger) family, 96
Beesley, Ann, 107
Beever, Caroline 156
Beint family, 96
Bekker, Catharine, 122
Martena (Anna), 133
(see Becker) family, 96
Bel, Hannah, 167
Belgian pavement, 33, 35, 36
pavement laid, 74
Bell, families, 96
Mrs. Flora, died, 10
Belvil (Belleville), family, 96
Bembo, family, 96
Bement, Caleb N., died, 41
Bemis, Henrietta Josephine, died, 41
Ida, Marietta, died, 49
Ben family, 96
Bender, C. W., 16, 53
family, 97
Margaret, died, 15
(Reisdorp), Margarita, 175
W. M., & Co., 42
Bendingh (see Bordingh), family, 97
Bendon, Thomas, pedestrian, 30
Benedict, J. & Son, 42
Lewis, 12
Mrs. Lewis, died, 82
Bengburn (see Pangburn) family, 97
Benjamin, Sarah, 2
Benne, Stafford Spencer, died, 40
Bennet family 97
Mrs. William C., died, 47
Thomas D., died, 40
Benneway (Benoit), Maritie, 128
(Benoit), Martha, 151
Bennewe (Benoit), Eva, 128
Hendricks, 112
Margarita, 110
(Bennoit), Marie (Molly), 132
Martha, 150, 156
Bennington, 45
Benoit (Bennaway, Bennewe), families, 97
Bensen (Benson, Bensingh, Bensinck), families, 97
Bensinck, Dirk, 194
Bensing, Catalyntie, 104
Caturina, 160
Dirck, 322, 323, 395, 401; deceased, 278; widow of married Hun, 394; written also Bensingh and Bensick
Bensing, Maritje, 184a
Bent (see Bout), family, 97
Benthuysen, P. M. V., lot, 194
Bentley, Sarah Emily, died, 10
Benton, Nathaniel S., died, 64
Nathaniel S., Jr., died, 27
Berex, Catalyn, 97
Catalyntie, 135, 278
Catrina, 322, 323
Berdan's sharpshooters, 58
Bergen, N. J., 35
Sara, 180
Berher family 97
Berkhoven (Barko, Beekhoven), Anna, 132
Berkley family, 97
Bernard, Catharina, 117
families, 97
Bernhard family, 97
Bernhart (Bernard), family, 97
Berns, James died, 49
Beronger Marytje, 110
Berringer, Catharina, 165
Christina, 184f
(Barringer), families, 97
Berrit families, 95
(Bareuth), Judith, 133
(see Barrit), family, 97
Berry Elizabeth, 184f
families, 97
Mr., 20
Bertley, Elizabeth, 152
Berwee, Berwey (see Barrois), family 97
Berx, see Berex
Bessidt (see Bassett), family, 97
Best, Mrs. David, died, 16
Bet Adriaen Symonse, 10, 387
or Bats (see Boer), family, 97
Beth (see Badt and Barth) family, 97
Bevee (see Bovee), family, 97
Beveers, Marytje, 161
Bever, see Beaver
Bevier family, 97
Beving (Bevens), Antje, 184b
Beverkil, or first kil, 380
Beverwyck, 260, 502
Bierdriger, Teunis Jacobse, 88
Bierman, Hendrick, 223, 224, 257
Bigelow, Francis, died, 67
John B., died, 12
Mrs. Edward, died, 67
Biggam, Mrs. Andrew S., died, 69
Bigham, Mrs. John, died, 76
Bigley, Michael A., 1
Billson, Mrs. Abram, died, 26
Binghamton, rail road opened to, 43
telegraph completed, 38
Birch, Mrs. Sylvanus, died, 48
S. M., 81
Birds, early, 55
Birdsall, Fassett & Co., 42
Birmingham, Mrs. Edward, died, 75
Black Elizabeth, 133, 184v
Neeltie, 332
Blackfield, Hester, 148
Blackney family, 97
Blanchard family 97
Blass, Jonas, died, 32
Blatner, H. M., died, 61
Blecker, Barent, 111
Caatje, 112
Cathalina, 160, 161
Charles E., 184z
Elizabeth, died, 27
Eliza Margaret, died, 8
Bleeker, families, 97
Geertruy, 184t
Hall, 438
Harms, 6; his lot, 216
Henry I., 8
Jacob, lot, 216
Jan Jans, 184z
Jan Janse, 88, 159, 350, 422, 464, 502, 505, 507; his lots, 201, 217
Jannetie, 126, 455
Janneke, 173
Johannes, 110, 172; lot, 216
Johannes Rutse, 90
John R., 27
Margarita, 109, 146, 172
Mrs. Charles E., died, 28
Rutger, 184z; his lot, 213
Bligh, Ann, died, 30
Blockhouse built, 239; church, 240; sold, 301
Bloemendaal, Alida, 100
families, 98
Jacomyntie 111
Judith Maas., 115
Engeltie (Amilia), 184q
Geertruy, 97
Johannes, 115
Lea, 120
Maria, 113
Marytje, 135
Sarah, 144
Bloom Engeltje, 184q
Bloomingdale, Ann, 103
W. H., 43
Bloomendall, 185
Blom, Antje, 150
family, 99
Bloodgood families, 99
Francis, 184z
Maria, 142
Mary, 122
Boardman, Rev. William J., 52
Board of Trade election, 5
Bockes, Elizabeth, 137
(Backis, Bacchis), families, 99
(Bakkes, Bacches), Christina, 122
Boehm, Peter Joseph, died, 77
Boer, Adriaen Symonse, 90, 295, 381
Boeringley family, 99
Boets (see Bots), 99
Boffe, or Boffy (see Bovie), 99
Bogaard family, 100
Jannetje, 128
Cornelis, 151
Isaac 151
Magdalena, 177, see Bogart
Bogardus (or Bogart), Domine Everhardus, 99
Anneatie, 184j
Annetie Janse, 183, 271, 27 , 289, 319, 324, 333, 356, 357 392, 425; her lot, 189, 190; deceased, 323; see Anneke Janse
Antje (Hanna), 104
Catharina, 184o
Cornelia, 184n
Cornelis, 170, 324, 333, 351, 352, 398, 422, 425; widow of, 453
families, 99
Jonas, 324, 424, 425; his lots, 189, 190
Maria, 128, 184i
Marytje, 180
Pieter, 128, 321, 424, 425; his lots, 190, 200
Shibboleth, lot, 210
Willem, 111, 321

Bratt, Jesie, 390
Johannes Barentse, 85
Johannes Dirkse, 86
Margaret, 145 156
Maria, 131, 184, 184j
Maria Dirkse, 86
Mettie, 158, 184w
Mary, 100, 144, 181
Neeltie 138
Pieterje, 113
Rebecca, 109, 114, 150
Saartje 149
Samuelse, 84, 391
Samuel Arentse, 85
Storm Albertse, 84
Susanna, 130, 153, 164, 184r, 184g
Trytje, 113
or Van Der Zee, Wouter Storm 90
Willempie, 100, 103, 184e
Willempie Teunise, 91, 102
Wyntie, 104; see Bradt
Ytje, 131
Brawley Mrs J. N., died, 69
Bray, Mrs. Agnes, died, 59
Francis, died 28
Brayton, Albert S., died, 72
Brazee, family, 104
Breckenbridge Robert, died, 13
Breem family, 104
Breen, Elizabeth, died, 55
Breeze, see Bries, 104
Brennan, Margaret, died, 56
Brennock Patrick, died, 28
Brewster, see Bruster, 104
Bresser Geertje, 175
Bressie, and Bresie; (see Brussey, 104
Bressy (Brussy) Claartje, 184q
Brett, Margaret, 105
Brewery and mill house 300, 304, sold, 304, 346
Brewslin (Brewster), Lidia, 184
Briant, Mrs. J. P. S. died, 65
Brice family, 104
Brick kiln, sold, 344
manufacture, 55
point, 54
Bricker, Jan, 429; lot, 200
Bridge at Maiden lane, 59
Bride, Elizabeth, 145
Bridgen Eliza 98
Bridgford, John, 46
Bries, Anthony 159, 184y
Antony, married C. Ryckman, 438
Christina (Catharina), 158
Elizabeth, 94
(Briesch, Breeze), families, 104
Hendrick 388 418, 439, 471; the order to obey, 431
Hendrick, lot 211
Jennetje, 126
Maj. Hendrick 184
Maria, 94, 184a
Margaret 43
Rosina, 93
Briesch, Marytje 178
Briety, Mrs. James H., died, 40
Brikkers (Bekkers) Hester, 166
Brinckerhoff families 104
Pieter, 98
Mrs. Peter, died, 27
Brinckhout, Daul., lot, 194
Brissy, Jenny, 170
Britton, Lucy 104
Britton, Margaret, 147
Broadhurst family, 104
Jonathan 160
Broadway, 390, 438, 449, 506; repaving of, 38
Brockhols family, 104
Broadin, Annatie, 109
Brodhead, Rev. Jacob, 98
family, 104
Broeck, Nicholaes, 280
Broecks, Anna, 133
Molly (Maria) 184m
Broedts, Annatie, 145
Broeckhuysen, Michael Janse, 249; see Janse
Broer, Cornelis (Van Slyck so called), 254
Brogdon family, 104
Brokus, Caty, 117
Bromley, Lary (Lena), 127
family, 104
Brommily family, 104
Bronck, Agnietje, 184x
Casparus Janse, 88
Commertje, 110
families, 104
Jan, 455
Jan Pieterse, 90
Johannes, 109
John L. 184f
Jonas Janse, 88
Hanna, 179, 180
Hilleken, 455, 471, 479, 480
Hilletie (Helena), 184n
Leonard Janse, 89
Peter, 245, 246, 249, 261, 263, 276, 297, 298, 299, 304, 305, 309, 310, 321, 332; sells his brewhouse, 266
Philip Janse, 89
Pieter 99; lot, 194, 197, 211
Pieter, Janse 89
R., 104
Sara, 97, 177
W. F., died, 11
Bronk, Marrietje, 184v
Brook, Sara, 164
Brooklyn military visit, 30
Brooks, Angelica, 105
(Broecks), Catharina, 120
Elizabeth, 133
(Brocks, Broecks), families, 105
Jonathan, lot, 206
Marietta H., died, 41
Rebecca, 184p
Broom (Groen), Annatie, 184r
Brophy, Patrick, died, 77
Brouwer, —— 184n
Anna, 184q
Annatie, 100, 101
Catarina, 184p
Cornelia Pieterse, 101
families, 105
Jacob, 99
Jan de, 246
Jane 109
Lea, 181
Lysbet Willemse, 114
Maria, 108, 142, 184m
Maria Willemse, 173
Nelletje, 137
Philip Hendrickse, 87, 263, 284, 299, 301, 328, 346, 347 348, 384, 419, 420; account of, 228; lot, 193
William, 251, 351, 356, 357, 390; his descendants, 228
Willem, lot, 187
Brown, Albert H., died, 74
Mrs. Almon, died, 26
Catrina, 181
Brown, Charity, 154
Edward, died, 76
Esther, 144
families, 105
Francis P., died, 18
Gen., 14
John, died, 76, 81
Margaret, 157
Maggie J., died, 13
Mary, died, 32
Michael, died, 28
Patrick, died, 64
Rev. J. H., 30
Robert, 4
Mrs. S. D., 7
Samuel, died, 67
Thomas, died, 21
William G., died, 49
Brownlow families, 105
(Bremlee), 105
Bruce families, 105
William, died, 76
Brumaghim, David H., died, 76
Estelle, died, 33
Brunt family, 105
Brun Louis Francois Alphonse, died, 38
Brussin, Anna Barbara, 112
Brussey (Bressi, Bressy), Jannetie, 113
families, 105
Bruster family, 105
Bryan family, 105
Barentje, 120
Hage, 260
Jan, 152, 469, 472, 482
Jan Hendricks, 330, 351, 352, 357, 358, 359, 367, 410, 421, 442, 472, 473, 485, 486; lot, 187, 196; see Hendrickse
Bruyns families, 105
Jan Hendrickse, 87
Bruynsen, Hage, lot, 201
Buckbee, Isaac, died, 11
Buckhout family, 105
Buckley, Cornelius, died, 27
family, 105
Buel, Jesse, 3
Building in winter, 40
Buisscher (Butcher ?), family, 105
Bulman, Margaret, died, 27
Bullock, Wm., secretary, 82
Bullocks, Anna, 157
Bulsen (Bulsing, Bunsing) families, 106
Hannah (Alida), 157
Rachel, 184m
Bulsing, Alida, 167
Annatie, 139
Saartje, 184q
Bulson, Caroline, died, 49
Mrs. D. A., 1
Sarah, died, 77
Bunt, Mary, 96
Bunting, Rebecca, died, 45
Burch, Lydia, 106, see Bots, 106
Burcharts (Burger) Cathryn, 149
Burchgraeff, Mayken Hendricks, 184b
Burden, Henry, 20
portrait of, 29
Burdick, James D., died, 41
Burgaart Burger, Burghart, Burgaat Borgat), family, 106
Burger, Ann, 106
Cataryna, 321
Catharine, 107
Coenraet Hendrickse, 87
Engeltie, 138

Burger excise, 338
 (Borgaart), families, 106
 Jan, 211
 lieutenant of, 372
 Isaac Hendrikse 87, 126
Burgert family, 106
Burgess Bortjes, Elizabeth, 133
 Susanna, 184r
Burgess, Caroline M., died, 40
 (Burghess, Burses), Margarita (Maria) 184m
Burgess Corps, 21, 47; visit Washington, 48
Burghart (Burger), families, 106
Burghes family, 106
Burhans, Aaltie (Alida) 161
 Catharyntje 141
 (Borhans), families, 106
 Jacob 429
 Jacomyntje, 184k
 Jane, 135
Burk families, 106
 Father, 38
 Michael, died, 65
 Mrs. James, died, 74
 Thomas J., died, 17
Burnham Mary, 96
Burn (Bruyn), families, 106
 Helena, 169
Burns, Elizabeth, 147
 family, 106
 Jacomyntje 184h
 James, died, 69
 Michael, died, 21
 Mrs. Catharine, died, 79
 Mrs. Mary, 4
 Wm. died, 45
Burnside families, 106
 Margarite 184r
Burnside, Mary, 184r
Burr, Aaron, 7
 family 106
Burt family, 106
Burton, Elizabeth, 129
 families, 106
 Mary, 134
 Matthew, died, 21
 Mrs. Isaac, died, 51
Buscher, Cornelia, 111
Bush family, 106
Bussing, Elizabeth, 173
 families, 106
 Hannah, 124
Butler, Amos, 76
 family 106
 Mary 95
Butter, price of, 12
Buys, Antje, 135
 families, 106
 Jan Cornelise, 86
 Buis), Rebecca, 184x
Buyse family, 106
By, Cornelis Jacobsen, 380
 see Jacobsen
 Cornelis Jacobse 88
 Dirk Hendrickse 87
 Lena Dirkse, 86
 see Swed
Byvanck (Byvang), 106
 Byvanck, Jan, 245, 350, 470, 506, 507; account of, 471
 Jan, lot, 215

Caarn family, 106
Cadagan, Mrs. Daniel, died, 69
Cadogan, Mary, 105
Cadoghan, Nancy, 129
Cadwees, Marytje, 118
Cady, D. P., died, 37
Cafferty, James Henry, died, 68
Cagger, Michael, 24
 Peter, killed, 23
 William, 24
Caghill family, 106
 Daniel died, 40
Cahoen, Francyntie, 94
Cahoos island, 414
Caillier (see Collier), 106
Cain, Mrs. James, died, 67
Caldwell, Elizabeth, 150
 (Colwell) family, 106
 Mrs. Wm J., died, 33
 & Solomons, 43
Calff, Claas, 153
Callen, Peter, died, 33
Callingon, Eleanora, 157
Cameron, Margaret, died, 45
 Mary, 148
Cambefort (Comfort), families, 107
 Geraldus, 184j
Campbell, Col. Daniel D., 469, 478
 Charles H., 1, 2
 families, 107
 Isabella, 147
 Jane 169
 Margaret, 145
 Rev John N., 7
 Susan G. died, 28
Campion, Margaret, died, 29
Canada family, 107
Canals, table of opening and closing, 78
Canary Mrs. John, died, 39
Cane family, 107
Canker family, 107
 Anna Johanna 184p
Cannel (Connor), Catharine, 149
 Maria, 165
Canner, Dorothea, 169
 family, 107
Cannum, Mary, 145
Canton family, 107
Cautuquo, sachem, 373
Cantwell, Thomas Joseph, died, 36
Capitol, excavations for, 40
 foundation stone laid, 64
 houses demolished to give room for, 32
Capron, Mrs. Benjamin, died, 70
 John D., 5
Captain free from burger excise, 367
Cardenwright, Margaret, 184z
Cardiff giant, 77
Cardigan family, 107
Carel, Anna, 163
Carew Patrick, died, 60
Carey, Mrs. Jane, 48
 Thomas, died, 28
Carich (Carik), Tanneke, 184e
Carkner (see Kirchner), 107
Carlan, Manas, lot, 207
Carles, Susanna, 124
Carlin, Elizabeth, 156
 Mrs. Henry died, 76
 James, died, 57
 Mary, died, 36
 Philip, died, 26
Carmody, Patrick E., died, 49
Carnin, Maria, 133
Carolan, Mary, died, 69
Carpenter, Cynthia, 163
 E. M., 5
Carr family, 107
 Rachel, 136
Carroll, Edward, died, 59
 John, died, 59
 Mrs. Margaret, died, 81
 Mrs. Patrick, died, 65
 William, died, 22
Carson, Thomas, died, 28
Carstense, Anna Maria, lot, 203
Carstense, Lysbeth, 126
Carstensen, Dirk, 2 1
Carter, Catarina, 184x
 family, 107
Cartridge family, 107
Cartwright family, 107
Casemay family, 107
Casparus Annatie, 94
 Annatie Andriesse, 85
 families, 107
Casper family 107
Casperse (Carstense) family, 107
Cass, Mrs. Horatio G., died, 76
Casselman, family, 107
Cassiday, family, 107
Cassidy, Margaret, died, 57
 William, 79
Cate (Kerk), Catharine, 106
Catholic church, first, 49
 Easter services, 51
Cavel, Elizabeth, 101
Cavert Mr, 38
Cayuga lake steamers, 6
Cemetery removals expense of, 35
Centre Market lot to be built upon, 23; demolished, 25
Cetin family, 107
Chace family, 107
Chambers Annatie, 184w
 Elizabeth, 103, 145
 families, 107
 Thomas, 236, 281, 335; see Clabbort
Chamberlain, Frank, president, 5, 12
Chamberlain's report, 17, 83
Chandler, Sarah, 169
Chapin, Cornelia, 7
Chapman family, 107
 Mrs. Judge, died, 8
 William, 55
Charles family, 107
Chasley Eleanor, 145
Chatterly James, 15
Cheese, large export, 28
Cherbonneau, Mrs. Anthony, 4
 Louisa, died, 21
Chesney family, 107
Chimney tax, 262
Chipman, James H., died, 45
Chisholm family, 107
Chisson, Tabitha, 106
Christianse, Christiaen, 485
 families, 107
 Maria, 101
 Neeltie, 184m
Christian, negro, 458
Christman families, 107
 Maria, 107
Chrysler (Schuyler), Jane, 151
 John, 61
Chun family, 108
Church, assistance asked to build, 239; 1656, designed also for a block house, 240; sends alms to the New Amsterdam poor, 236; sued for the cost of a doophuysje 382
 of Holy Innocents, election, 16, 53
 of the Assumption of the Blessed Virgin, 79
 Eva, 153
 Sarah, 147
 Walter S., 20
Cider, excise of, 315, 366, 367
Cincinnati society, 6
Cittene, see Kidney, 107
City Building on Pearl st., 74; to be built on Pearl st., 23

City finances 17 33
salaries 17, 83
Claerbos, families, 107
Pieter, 249, 256, 329, 330; his lot, 180
Wouraeff, Pieterse, 90, 256
Claese, Aagje, 153
, Adrian 341; see Vryman
Catryn, 181
Christina, 105
Cornelia, 95
Elizabeth, 211, 152
Ennetie, 100
families, 107
Geerti, 176
Jacob, 427
Lysbet 131
Neeltje, 125, 152, 485
Pieter, 184c
Rycke, lot, 214; see Van Vrank
(Svits, Jillesje, 139
Tryntje, 184a, 398, 500
Claessen, Carsten, 306; lot,197
Catharine, 148
Jan (Backer van Oranen), 340
Susanna, 156
Clapp, Mary E., died, 79
Clapper, Barber, 167
family, 107
Clark Ann, 166
(Klerk), families, 107
Francis, 72
Margaret 107
Maria, died, 27
Mathew C., 12
Neeltie, 139
Peter V., died, 47
Rev. Dr. R. W. 24, 21, 48, 59
Sumner & Co., 42
Clarke, Elizabeth, died, 48
Clarkson David, 124
Matthew, died, 53
Mrs. Matthew, died, 56
Claus see Claes
Clauw, Engeltie, 105
(Klau), families, 107
Frans Pieterse, 90
Judik France, 184a
Jurriaen, 129
or Klauw, Elsie Franse, 86
Hendrick Franse, 86
Jannetie Franse, 86, 184h
Jurrian Franse, 86
Wyntie Franse, 86
Maria Franse, 86
Claver families, 108
Claverack, 13, bouwery at, mortgaged, 379, purchased of the Indians, 302; sloop from, 247; see Ysselstein, 450
Clay, Henry 26
Cleary, Joshua, died, 13
Thomas, died, 12
Clement families, 108
Clem rger (Clemison, Clemisher, Clemisham), family, 108
Clemons, George, died, 40
Clerk, Elizabeth, 188
Josina, 157
Cleyn, Lmerhu sen, 259
Uldrich, 413; see Kleyn
Clietman, Mrs. John, died, 77
Clinton, DeWitt, 6, 14, 41, 77; his cemetery, 77
Elizabeth, 123
family 108
Cline Margaret, 156; see Cleyn
Clockluyer, Pieter Jacobse, 88
Clomb, Franz 109
Clomp, Jacob 440; see Baroquier
Clute, Alida, 113, 152
Anna, 152 155
Anna Barber, 123
Ariaantje, 184k
Bata, 129, 155 181
Capt Jan, lot, 189, 217
Claartje, 10, 166, 170
Elizabeth, 96, 152, 155, 157, 184g, 184j
Engeltie, 184w
(Cloet) families, 108
Francyntje, 153, 167, 180, 184v
Geertruy 106, 184v
Hannah, 180
Jan, 262, 288, 336, 386, 405, 406, 407, 427, 428, 430, 440, 459, 464, 469, 471, 479, 502, 504, 505, 506; bestows an island upon his daughter, 436; buys a lot, 433; see Kloet; his lot, 190, 193, 203, 211, 215 217
Johannes, 262, 428, 488, 507
Judge, 38
Margarita, 102
Mary, 157
Neeltie, 136, 152
Saartje, 166
Sara, 136, 184w
Wyntje, 184l
Clyne, 109; see Cline and Klein
Congler, Anna, 97
Coal by Susquehannna road, 48
Coan, Peter died, 70
Cobb, Mrs. James N., 56
Cobes family, 109
Ludovicus, lot 189, 193, 215
see Cobussen
Cobble stone superseded, 31, 36
Colburn Peter, died, 65
Cobussen, Ludovicus, 249, 256, 261, 267, 268, 271, 330 366, 374, 382, 427, 428, 432, 435, 454, 459, 477 506; secretary, 434, 449, 505; tipstaff, 2?5
Cochrane Maj. James, 163
Cock Koch), Anna, 135
Cocks, Annatie, 121
Coddington, Catarina, 184o
Sara, 127
Codman, Elizabeth, 184a
Coen, Anna Elizabeth, 144
Barber, 99
Barbara 127
Jannetie, 172
Coens, Christina, 131
(Coons or Koonz), Hannah, 168
Coenraads, family, 109
Coenraadtse, Hendrick, 411, 481, 182
Matthys, 146
Hendrick, 184a
Coeny family, 109
Coeymans, Anna Margar'ta, 172
Arent Pieterse, 90
Ariaantje 184n
Ariaentie Barentse, 85
Andries Barentse, 85
Barent Pieterse, 90, 116, 191, 230, 250, 264, 388 455, 454, 493
David Pieterse, 90
Dirckie Pieterse, 116
families, 109
Geertje, 172
Geertruy Pieterse, 184q
Jacob Pieterse, 90
Jannetie Barentse, 85
Coeymans, Lucas Pieterse, 90, 268, purchases mill on Poesten kil, 456; see Pieterse.
Pieter Luykase, 89
Samuel, 184f
Samuel Barentse, 85
see De Molenaer
Cogswell, Mrs. William, died, 64
Cohen, Isaac, suicide, 18
Coit, Rev. Dr. 39
Colbern, Sarah, died, 33
Colbrecht, family, 109
Cold, 1, 4, 7, 11, 46, 48, 49, 59
Coldin family, 109
Cole, Col. John O., 20, 30
Mary, 115
(Cool, Rachel, 168
Collier (Caillier, Caljer), families, 109
Collen family, 109
Collins, Bridget, died, 31
Dennis, died, 11
Edward, 98
families, 109
Coleman, Mrs. Mary, died, 45
Colligan, Ellen, died, 64
Collins, Johanna, died, 16
John, 2
Margarita, 134
Mary, died 56
Mary E., 64
Mrs. James, died, 37
Collinson family, 109
Colwell, Elizabeth, 113
family, 109; see Caldwell, 109
Combes, Elizabeth, 107
James M., died, 59
Commissaris, terms expire, 225
Compston family, 109
Conchlin family, 109
Conchron (Cochron), Elizabeth, 147
Conckkel family, 109
Concklin family, 109; see Coucklin
Conceel (Conel family, 109
J. lot, 215
Jan, lot, 194, 196, 214, 215, 217
John, 448, 461, 468, 480, 490, 494, 496; sells his house, 495; exchanges his house, 452; see Corneel
Confiscation for error in invoice, 336
Congel family, 109
Conger, Anna (Any), 165
family, 109
Sofia, 136
Congregational church, last sermon in, 7, 10; ground broken for new, 16; dedicated, 71; spire, 58
Coninck, Catalyntje, 154
Steven Janse, 228, 224, 230, 231 233; sells his goods, 225; fight of, 232; see Janse
Conjunction Moon and Jupiter, 4
Conklin (Cochran), Margarita, 176
Conkling, Alfred, 2
Conlan, Mrs., died, 45
Conlon, Michael, died, 45
Connally, Mrs. Charles H., died 77
Mrs. William, died, 58
Connecticut, steam boat, 55
Connel family, 109

D'Honneur, Lysbeth, 340
De Hooren [Hooges] Catharina, 182
(Hooges) Marytje, 184c
De Hooges, Anthony, 102, 226, 231; schout and secretary, 233; decease of, 271; his lot, 214, 224
family, 114
De Hulter Johan, 226, 234; widow of, 416
Johanna, 496, 497; see Ebbingh, and De Laet
family 114
De Jongh, Pieter Cornelise, 86
De Karreman, Michiel, 244
De Kay, Katarina, 184e
Teunis, 99, 184m
De Koning family, 115
De Kuyper Jan, 244, 249, 349
De Laet, Johanna, 114, 285, 286, 287, 401; see De Hulter and Ebbingh
(De) La Grange, Annatie, 115
Christiaen, 405
Christina, 98, 103
Isaac 105
Omy, Jr., 405; see La Grange
families, 115
De La Montagne, Johannes, the heer officer, 248; see La Montagne
De Lange, Maria, 106
De Laval, Heer, 502
Thomas, 466, 467, 491, 501; account of, 462; see Laval
Capt Thomas, lot, 204
family 115
De Lavil (perhaps De Lave); see Donnowa, 115
De La Ward, Janse, lot 217
family 115
De La Wardt, Jan, account of, 494
De Long family, 115
De Looper, Jacobse Tennise, 91, 218; see Looper
family, 116
De Maecker, Pieter, 242, 269, 320 379, 385, his lot, 187; see Maecker
family, 116
De Manse, family, 116
De Marchal family 116
De Mes, Hester, 148
De Mese family, 116
De Metselaer; see Metselaer, 116
De Meyer, Elizabeth, 162
Lydia, 118
Nicolaas, 184a; lot, 188, 194
De Milt, Antony, 328
De Moer family, 116
De Necker, Gillis, 279
De Noorman, Poulus, 350; see Noorman and Bratt, 116
Jan, 417
De Paep, Jan Teunise, 91
De Peyster, Anna, 118
Cornelia, 171
Isaac, 176
Johannes, 94, 162, 279
John, 184z
Margaret, 97
Maria, 95
Mrs. Angustus D. died, 56
Mrs. Frederick, died, 75
family, 118
De Poolt, Dirkse Teunis; see Van Vechten
De Bruyn, see Bruyn, 113
De Rademaker, Albert Gysbertse, lot, 190
De Remer family, 116
De Reus, Gerrit Teunise, 91
De Rham; see Rham, 116
De Ridder, Annatje, 96 184c
Autje, 184y
Ariaantje, 108
Catarina, 179
Geertie, 184f
Maria, 108, 180
Marytje, 183
Rachel, 179
Santje, 184w
(Ridder) families, 116
De Ryk, Jannetie Janse, 184a
De Sille, Walburga, 99, 111
De Sweed, Dirk, 484
De Tiere, Mrs P F., died, 16
De Truwe [Trieux], Abraham, 384
Susanna, 327; see Truax, also De Trueux
De Visser family, 184; see Visscher
De Voe (Anna), 119
Catharina (Maria), 155, 160
Elizabeth, 150
Lena, 118
Margarita, 181
(De Vooer), Maritie Janse, 182
Marytje, 118, 183
(Vous) family, 116
(Voy) families, 116; see De Voy
De Vos, Andries, 282, 292, 311, 411, 412, 416, 417, 426, 488, 494; deputy, 390; director of Rensselaerswyck, 391; his lot, 210, 213, 215
Catalyntje, 177
Cataryn Andriese, 85; account of, 390
Catryna Andriesee 85
Cornelia, 112
Cornelis, 391, 416
Cornelis Cornelise, 85
Hans, 245
Mattheus, notary, 369
families, 116
De Vous family, 116
De Voy (Voe?) Catharina, 155
Jannatie, 116
DeVries, Adriaen Dirkse, 86, 218
Adriaen Janse (Dirkse), 88; lot, 201
Annetie, 115, 405
Dirn xse, 476
Johannes, lot, 211
family, 117
DeVroome, Huybert Janse, 419; his lot, 194; see Janse
DeVyselaer, see Visscher, 116
De Wandelaer, Agnietje, 128
Alida, 110
Anna, 104
Catrine, 124
Elizabeth, 184j
Johannes, 202, 457, 458, 488; account of, 452, 453; exchanges his house, 452; lot, 188
Maria, 184v
Rebecca, 138
Sara, 123, 149
families, 117
DeWarran, Maria, 164
De Weever (Weever) 117
Anna, 144
Catharina, 169
Jan, 247; see Wever
De Weever (Weever), Jan Martense, 267, 269, 274, 455, 482, 484, 485, sells his house, 320; see Wever, and Martense
Marytje, 105
(Wever) family, 117
De Willeger family, 117
De Winter Bastiaen, 306, 401, 475, 476 account of, 402, location of house, 474
family 117
De Wit, Jacob Bastiaense, 85
Rachel, 99
Ragel Tjerckse, 99
families, 117
De Witt, Alice J., died, 56
Clinton, steamboat, 14
Dr. Thomas, 51
Elizabeth, died, 73
Ephraim, 184b
John, 6
Richard Varick, died, 5
Simeon, 5, 6
Tjerck Claessen, 85, 285, 286, 322, 323, 496; see Claessen
William H., 16, 53
family, 117
De Witte Emmerentje, 133
Deal, Jane, died, 33
family, 113
Dealy (Daily Lidia, 176
Dean, Amos, died, 2
Maria, 163
family, 113
Deane family, 113
Death record unprecedented, 27
Debrouwer, Martin, 246
Debt, Christina, 124
Decket (Dekker) families, 113
family 115
Decrstyne, Catharine, 110
Mary, 167
Defrieze, family, 114
Degraaf, Jesse Claese, 85
Dehm, Very Rev. Father Fidelis, 38
Dekker, Heyltie, 158
family 115, see De Decker,
Delamont, families, 115
Delarey John, died, 73
Michael, died, 37
Mrs. Capt. John, died, 30
Delaval, Thomas, 216
Thomas, lot, 187
Delavan, Edward C., 43
Delehanty, Catharine, died, 49
John, died, 69
M., 75
Martin, 34
Dellius, family, 115
Delmont, Maria, 134
Demarest, Harriet, 115
Democratic triumph, 76
Demoer, Philip Philipse, 90
Dempsey, Mrs. Bridget, died, 59
Denison, Candice, died, 46
Denker, Mary, 181
Denison families, 116
Denniston families, 116
Dennstedt, Mrs. Charles, died, 77
Denny family, 116
Denys, Sara, 184l
Deppe, Christine, 184r
Deppen, Christina, 124
Derham family, 116
Derick Elizabeth, 184r
Derrith, see Dret, 116
Davenant, Mary, 169

Dev.ne, Daniel, died, 65
Mrs. George, died, 64
Devlin, Mrs. Mary, died, 66
Devoe, Eva, 137
Devol, Mrs. Dr. C., died, 15
Dext r, George, 53
Mary L., died, 28
Diaconate, 289
Diamond, Mary, 174
family 117
Dickson, Walter, 36
Dickinson family, 117
Diel family, 117
Dienmaker (Denemark), Antje, 151
Dieppendorp, Barbara, 184v
Dillon, John, died, 18
family, 117
Dingman, Aaltie Adamse, 84
Adam, 125
Josina, 174
Maria, 125
Rachel, 151, 184c
Sara, 174
families, 117
Dingmanse, Alida, 110
Diocese Northern New York, met, 39
Dirkse, Margaret, 133
Jan, widow of, lot, 200
(Hendrickse) Helena, 125
Osseltie, 136
Theunise, lot, 198
Wyntie, 109
Dirksen, Lucas, 254
Pieter, 331
Disle, Catharina, 135
Ditmarse, Cornelis Barentse, 85
Doane, Wm. Croswell, 39, 52; introduces high church ceremonies, 15; consecrated, 46; resigned rectorship, 59
Dobbler, Mrs. George 2
Dobbs, Mrs. John, died, 76
Dobel family, 117
Dochsteder, Cath., 107
Catharina, 173
Dochter, Geertruy Andriesse, 85
Geertruy Andriese, 184w
Wybrecht Jacobse, 88, 170
Dody (Doty ?) Any, 131
Doesburgh, in Holland, 443
Doff, Anna, 126
Doherty, Mrs. Ann, died, 36
Dohey, Thomas, died, 11
Doksi, Thomas, 127
Dole families, 117
Don, Mrs. Mary, died, 10
William, died, 49
Donahoe, Michael, died, 28
Donahue, Mrs. John, died, 30
Donaldson family, 117
Donavan, Elizabeth, died, 64
Margaret Ann, died, 30
Doncassen [or Dongan] Catalyn, 126, 346
Donchesen, Margaret, 170
Donckertse, Jannetie, 152, 154, 481, 482, 483, 484
Donkesen, Margariet, 345
Donlan, Mrs. Patrick, died, 64
Donnan, Lydia, 118
Donnelly, Edward, died, 28
Mrs. Edward, died, 27
John, died, 56
Capt. John M., died, 47
Mrs. Richard, died, 31
Donneway, Mary, 165
family, 117
Donnowa family, 117
Donovan, Mrs. William, died, 75
Dool family, 117
Dooland, Mrs. John died, 64
Dooner, Eliza, died, 68
Doophuysje, suit for making, 382
Doorethe, 226
Doorn, Aert Martense, 89
Dooth (Doth Staats) Rebecca, 159
Dorsey, Mrs. Elizabeth, died, 17
Doran, Father, 38
John, died, 40
Mrs. Wm. died, 32
Dorsche family, 117
Dorson, Anna, 115
Doth, Elizabeth, 161
Doughney, John, died, 27
Douglass, Catharine, 165
J. & Sons, 42
Dowland, Christina, 101
Douw, Andries Volkertse, 91
Anna, 96
Annatje, 171
Caatje Volkertse, 151
Catharina, 133
Catryntie Volkertse, 91
Dorothea, 184x
Dorothea Volkertse, 91
Elizabeth, 96, 184u
Engeltie Volkertse, 184w
Grietie Volkertse, 91
Hendrick, 149, 176
Hendrick Volkertse, 91
Jan Andriese, 85; lot, 201
Johannes Volkertse, 91
John D. P., 61
Jonas Volkertse, 91, 126, 185w, 455
Lydia, 151
Magdalena, 124, 169
Margarita, 172, 184a
Maria, 124, 172
Rachel, 184d
Volkert Janse, 9, 150, 223, 231, 237, 238, 293, 325, 334, 342, 347, 351, 352, 353, 396, 399, 449, 452, 476, 493, 502; sells land at Esopus, 501; purchases whole of island, 397; trustee of estate of Andries Herbertsen, 365; office of commissaris expires, 240; nominated for commissaris, 235; attorney for Hend. Jochemse, 457; lot, 187, 195, 198, 204, 221; see Janse
Volkert P., 116, 184z; died, 61
families, 117
Douwe, Alida, 142
Elsie, 122
Douwes, Hester, 347, see Fonda
Douw's Building, 61
Dow, Pietertje, 133
Dowel, Catharine, died, 43
Dower, Mrs. Maurice died, 17
Dowey, Rhoda, 158
Downal family, 118
Downey, Ann, 5
Downs, Mrs. Thomas, died, 15
Downing family, 118
Dox, Elizabeth, 107, 184w
Jane Jennet Dunse), 165
Maria, 151
families, 118
Doxat, Alida, 148
Doxie, (Dox, Dauchsi) families, 118
Doyle & Dugan, 72
Drake, Sara, 105
Drayer, Capt. Andries, 184f
Dreeper, Hendrikie Hanse, 87, 184v
Dreper, Hans, 202
Dressans, Elizabeth, 137
Dret (Dareth, Derith, Droit, Duret), families, 119
Drew, Daniel, steamboat, 28
Mary, 166
Dries, Geertruy, 93
Driesbach, Kathinka, died, 49
family, 119
Drinckvelt, Elizabeth, 157, 385
Drinkwater, Hester, 184y
Driscol, Mrs. Timothy, died, 27
Droit, see Dareth, and Dret, 119
Drue, James, died, 72
Drummer, Elizabeth, 127
Dubois, Mrs. Augustus, died, 58
families, 119
Dudley, Charles E., 98, 184z
Mrs., 27
Duer family, 119
Duff, Eliza, died, 14
Duffy, Barney, killed, 66
Du Fou, Geertruy, 118
Du Four families, 116
Du Fou; Du Foy; see De Voe, 119
Duicher, Caty V., 184m
Duischer, Sara, 165
Duitscher, Lydia, 139
Duivebach family, 119
Dulleman, Jan Barentse, 85, 307
family, 119
Du Mon Walleron, 370, 384
Du Mond, Tempie (Temperance), 106
Du Mont, Francyntje, 108
Maria, 168
Susanna, 184p
Du Moree, Pieter, 483
family, 119
Dunagoe, Judith, 117
Dunbar, Cataline, 184y
Catharina, 184k
Cornelia, 155, 184x
Ellie, 133
Margarita, 164
Maria, 175
(Tumbart) family, 119
Duncan & Brother, 67
James, 36
Dunham, Green & Co., 42
Dunkin, Ann, 184e
Dunlop, Mrs. A. A., died, 79
Robert, 55
Dunn, Bernard, died, 70
Dunn, Henry M., died, 77
Mrs. W. J., died, 27
Dunne, John F., died, 27
Dunnevan, see Donnowa, 119
Dunning, Elizabeth, 116
Dunphy, Andrew, died, 45
Dunscomb, E. 42
Durant, Clark, 55
Edward P., 5
William, 55
Durck, or Turk, Catharina, 184h
Duret, Cath., 132
Jannetie, 113
Nelly, 119
see Dret, 119
Duryea, Jane, 137
Dutch church statistics, 59
claimed Bastian De Winter's property, 402
Ref. cemetery, 35
Dutchmen not slaughtered, 238
Du Trieux, Sara, 113
Susanna, 184s

Ferguson, R. H., pedestrian, 30
Fer), Annatie, 152
family, 121
Rosino, 169
Ferrel, Hanna, 124
Ferris, Rev. I. N., 50
Ferry expenses, 18, 83
Fester family, 121
Fetter, Margaret, 120
Fetterly family, 12?
Fierse, family, 121
Filden, Debora, 140
File (Viele?) Elizabeth, 124
Magdalena, 116
Filkins, I. J., 82
Filman, family, 121
Finch, Mrs. Wm. H., died, 61
Fine family, 121
Finger, Helena, 121
Finke family, 121
Finky family, 121
Finklebach family, 121
Finn, Thomas A., died, 28
Finnegan, Mrs. H. C., died, 13
Finnerty, Mr., 30
Fire alarm telegraph introduced, 21; department, 17 83
Fires, losses by, 83
First African Baptist Society, 80
Bap. church collection, 69; corner stone laid, 65 original member died, 13
Congregational church, corner stone laid, 31
Lutheran church, corner stone laid, 65
Presbyterian church, 12; pastor retired, 37; cemetery 35
Fish, Gov. Hamilton, 6
Isaac, died, 69
Fisher (see Visscher), 121
Mrs. Moses, died, 45
Fitzgerald, Mrs. C. C., 2
Mrs. Martin, died, 41
Fitzpatrick, Mrs. Julia, died, 58
Peter, died, 82
Flagler, F. W., 16
Flamisham family, 121
Flannary, Timothy, died, 21
Flansburgh (Flansborough) family, 121
Mattheus, lot, 220; see Flensburgh
Flat family, 121
Flatbush, schoolmaster at, 355
Flatterly, John, died, 37
Fleegring (Fliegery) Catharina, 164
Fleetwood, Burdett, 111
Fleming, Annie E., died, 56
Margarette L., died, 59
Mrs. Martin, died, 11
Flemming family 121
James, 2
Maggie, died, 77
Flensburgh (see Flansburgh), 122
Annatie, 147, 184a
Lena, 184w
Margarita, 180
Fletcher family, 122
Flinn families, 122
Flint family, 122
Flipse family, 122
Flipsen; see Phillipse
Flodder Jacob Jansen, 321, 353, 482, children of, settled at Kinderhook, 458
Flodder, Jan Jacobse, 267
or Gardenier, Jan Janse 88
see Gardenier, 122
Flood, James, died, 12, 67
Mrs. John, died, 36
Flora, Agneta, 154
Florid (Floyd) family, 122
Flynn, Catharine, died, 66
Fogarty, Mrs. John, died, 15
Folent, Elizabeth, 93
Folger, John B., died, 18
Folin, Anna Maria, 150
Folksby, Margarita, 161
Follansbee (Volansby) family, 122
Foller, Elizabeth, 103
Follett family, 122
Follevin, Margarita, 184u
Follewyzer, Mary, 124
Fonda, Abraham Isaackse, 87
Agnietje, 184t
Alida, 118, 141, 184i, 184p
Antje, 161
Barbara, 184p
Catharina, 103
Catharine (Helena), 184z
Douwe, 104; lot, 210
Douwe Gillis, 89, 347
Douwe Isaacse, 88, 152
Elizabeth, 138, 184l, 184n
Eva, 184y
families, 122
Geertie, 166
Geertien Gillis, 347
Geertje, 181k
Geertruy, 183
Gillis Douwese, 86, 246
Helena, 152
(Van Buren) Hendrikje, 175
Hester, 175
Hester Douwese, 347
Jan Douwese, 86
Lyntje, 144
Maacke, 103
Maria, 110, 111, 117, 143, 159, 184o
Rachel, 131
Rebecca, 98, 99, 134, 138, 180, 184v
Santje, 184x
Susanna, 114, 141
Willem, 130
Fondey, T., 16
Foot, Hon. Alfred, 19
family, 123
Footman, Jeremiah, died, 11
Forbeliot family, 123
Forbes, Anna, 121
Ford, James, died, 27
Mary, died, 13
Sweton Grant, died, 45
William, died, 2
Wm. R., 15
Foreest, see De Forest, 123
Isaac, 327
Susannah, 157
Forer, Anna Maria, 142
Forest, Thomas, died, 26
Forgess, Rebecca, 124
Forry, Maria, 125
Forseight (Forsyth?) 123
Forster, family, 123
Forsyth, Mrs. John, died, 65
Fort, Anna, 97
Ariaantie, 184m
Catrine, 123
Elizabeth, 138, 184l
Eva, 184o
families, 123
Francina, 184o
Jan, 84
Johannes Danielse, 86
Maria, 97, 184k, 184m
Fort Orange, 249, 293; houses in, 291; gardens sold, 356, 357, 360; collector at, 245; fortifications, building of, 239
Fortune, Edward, died, 60
Foss, Rev. Cyrus D., 22
Sara, 163
Foster family, 123
John N., 12
Mary, 154
Fourth of July, hot day, 23
Presbyterian Easter services, 52
Fowler, Sarah, died, 12
Fox, Thomas, died, 45
Frame, Mrs. George M., died, 43
Frances Anna, died, 41
Francisco, Jane, 126
Frank families, 123
Frankheid, Jannetie, 138
Franklin, Carrie S., died, 59
Frans, Sara, 106, 470
Frause, Jodik, 136
Fraser family, 123
Mary, 123
Frasier (Frazer), Margaret (Majory), 127
Richard, lot, 211
Frederick family, 123
Fredrickse, C. and M., lot, 203
Carsten, 260, 261, 441; his lot, 203
Claes, 450
Cornelia, 184g
family, 123
Myndert, 184i, 260, 321, 407, 441, 471, 479, 480, 503; his lot, 202, 203; see Myndertse
Neeltie, 166
Selytien, 339
William, see Bout
Fredricx, Seletie, 339
Free Academy established, 30
Freehold family, 123
Freelich, Anna B., 139
Annatie, 100
family, 123
Freelig, Elizabeth, 132
Freeman, Dr. Samuel, 184x
Elizabeth, 115
family, 123
Mrs. Henry, died, 56
Robert, 66
Volney, Esq., 474
Freer, Catharina, 104
Maria, 184o
Neeltje, 162
Sara (Elizabeth), 162
Freerman family, 124
Rev. Barnbardus, 184f
Freet family, 124
French, Mary, 143
Freshet 18, 36, 43, 53, 56, 70; extraordinary, 58
Frets family, 124
Margarita, 137
Frey family, 124
Freydach families, 124
Friday family, 124
Friedlander, Mrs. Col. David, died, 70
Frieer, Catharina, 96
Frielinghuysen family, 124
Friends cemetery, 35
Froment, Theodore, died, 28
Fry family, 124
Margarita, 103
Fryer, Caty, 133
Elizabeth, 141, 176
families, 124

Fryer, Isaac, lot, 206, 210, 221
June C. Jeranah, Libanah, 157
Lydia, 184p
Maria, 127
Mrs. Martin died, 17
Sara, 184u
William, lot, 206
Fuller, Clark, died, 28
families, 124
Sarah Ann, died, 46
Fulsom, family, 124
Funeral of Stephen Van Rensselaer, 29
Furrie, Maria, 124
Furlong, Patrick H., died, 18
Furt Flur family, 124
Furtle, family, 124
Fyle; see Fell, 124
Fynhout, Neeltie 165

Gaaf family, 124
Gansbeck, Maria, 160
Gabel, Barbara, died, 49
Gaffers family, 124
Gaffney Peter J., died, 47
Thomas M., died, 77
Gaguier, Rev. Father, 80
Gaignen, family, 124
Gale, Jacob, died, 32
Gallagher, Jeannie A., died, 13
Henry, died, 28
Neil, died, 21
Rose, died, 56
Gannon, Richard, died, 27
Gano, John died, 45
Gansevoort, Agnietje, 184u
Annatie, 184y
Catharine D., 118
Catryna, 154
cemetery removed, 77
Elizabeth, 116
Elsje, 184v
families, 124
General Peter 9
Gerritje, 117
Harme, proposes to herd cattle, 431
Harmen, 419
Harmen Harmense, 348
Hilletie, 183
H., lot, 194
Johannes, 118
Leendert, 184d
Lysbeth, 117, 452
Magdalena, 172
Pieter, 172
Rachel, 143, 184z
Sara, 171
Gantz family, 125
Gardner family, 125
John, died, 8
R., lot, 214
Samuel, died, 40
Gardens, near fort Orange sold, 356, 357, 369
Gardenier, Aeltie Jacobse, 88, 117
Albert Jacobse, 88
Alida Janse, 121
Andries Andriesse, 85
Andries Jacobse, 88
Annatie, 173
Ariaantje, 184x
Arien Andriesse, 85
Catarina, 184x
Cathalina, 149
Catharina (Althumne ?), 156
Cornelia, 110, 117
Cornelia Janse, 88
Elizabeth, 99, 153
Gardenier (alias Flodder), families, 125
or Flodder, Jacob Janse 88
or Flodder, Jan Jacobse, 88
Geertruy, 157
Henderick, 485
Hester 136
Jacob Andriesse, 85
Jacob Janse, 458
Jan Jacobse, 267
Johanna, 184k
John, died, 26
Josine, 184u
Josine Jacobse, 88
Josina (Jacomyntje) Janse, 177
Josyna, 125
Lena Janse, 89
Magdalena, 121
Neeltie, 139, 146, 184i
Rachel, 148, 155, 173
Rebecca, 173
Sara, 98, 114
Samuel Jacobse, 88
Garner, Annatie, 96
Garretson M E. cemetery 35
Garret, Annie C., died, 76
Garrison, Andrew, died, 82
Garritson family, 126
Gasley Ann, 107
Gates, Albert W., died, 33
families, 125
Gautsch, see Van Slyck
Gavit, Alice M., died 13
Gay, Richard, died, 32
Geary, George N., 66
Gebhard Gibhart, Geefhart family, 125
Gebbns (Gibbs ?) family, 125
Gebertsen (Cruiff) family, 125
Geer, Mrs. Robert, died, 22
Gellise, Douwe, 347; see Fonda
Genet, Laure, died, 15
Gentry, Mrs. John S., died, 41
Geon, Mary died, 28
George, Thomas, died, 59
Gerbertse, Albert, lot, 201
Gerbertsen, Eldert, 267, 268, 287; see Cruif
Gerdenyer, see Gardenier
German catholic church, 38
Germond, Morris, died, 47
Gerrit, the cooper, 470
Gerritse (Gerritie Geeritje), 249, 250, 446
Adrien, lot, 220
Albert, lot, 202
Anna, 184y
Annatie, 146
Ariaantie, 120, 177
Barent, 122
Claas, 210
Elbert, 154, 438
families, 125
Gerritje, 184o
Goossen, 261, 312, 322, 331, 339, 341, 342, 343, 352, 362, 438, 449; see Van Schaick
(Van Schaick) Goosen, lot, 198, 223
Hendrick, 174, 190
Hilletje, 184y
Huybert, 139
Lucas, lot, 215, 411
Maria, 184f
(Reyertse), Maritie, 184
Reyer, lot, 195
(Van der Werken) Roeloff, lot, 193
Tryntje, 119
Wynant, lots, 201 214, 217
Gerritsen, Adriaen, 228, 249, 290, 295, 301, 312, 314, 351,
Gerritsen, Adriaen, continued.—
352, 379, 391, 408, see Papendorp
Albert, 335, 356, 357, 407, 418
Alida, 127, 129
Annatje, 184q
Catharina, 145
Eefie 169
families, 126
Hendrick, 264, 379 420, 466
Hester, 184c
Luykas, 184a
Maritie, 134
(Van Bergen), Marten Herbertsen, lot, 212
Marytje, 121
Geveck, Jacob, 297, 300, 305, 310, 311; see Hevick (see Hevick and Heven), 126
Jacob, 153
Geyel Mary ?), 106
Gibbert see Gebhard), 126
Gibbons, George W., 15
Hogan, died, 38
Gibbs, Abigail, 120
John E., died, 59
Gibson family, 126
John, died, 26
Margaret, 131
Gifford, Anson E., 5
Isaac, died 29
Mrs. Philip H., died, 41
Gilbert, Catharina, 95
families, 126
John, 132, 158, 214, 215
Maria, 184u
Mary, 167
Gilchrist family, 126
Robert, died, 58
Gill, Carolina, died, 18
Charles H., died, 77
Mary, died, 76
Patrick, died, 28
Peter, suicide, 11
Gillespie (Gillaspy), family, 126
Michael, died, 36
Gillig, John, died, 70
Gilliland (Gillilon), family, 126
Jane, 98
Gillise, Eva, 130
Pieter, lot, 201
Gillisen (Meyer) Pieter, 280, 281
Gilroy, California, 48
Ginn, John, died, 15
Ginning family, 126
Gisbert, Gerbert, arrested, 246
Giver family, 126
Gladding, Mrs. Joseph, died, 15
Glasemacker, Jurriaen Theunisse, 248, 257, 262, 295, 315, 316, 341, 351, 356, 359, 368, 370, 393, 416, 426, 442, 469; sells his house, 263; see Tappen
Jurriaen Teunise, 91
Glazier, D. N., 5
Gleason, Patrick, died, 67
Glen, Alexander Leendertse, 369; his lot, 196
Anna, 184s
Anna, marries Harmanus Wendell, 455
Capt. Sander, 184s
Catharina, 184e
Catryntje Sanderse, 90, 139
Debora, 160
Elizabeth Sanderse, 184o
families, 126
Helena, 455
Helena Sanderse, 184a

Glen, Jacob, 423, 436, 455; his lot, 218
Jacob Sanderse, 90, 184w, 214, 458, 504; account of, 455; his lot, 185
Jacomyntje, 184a
Jannetie, 112
Jno. Sanderse, 160
Johannes, 455
Johannes Jacobse, 88
Johannes Sanderse, 90, 436
Maria, 184m
Robert, died, 30
Sander, 436
Sander, Jr., 420
Sander Leendertsen, 89, 236, 239, 250, 251, 252, 261, 263, 264, 265, 268, 270, 271, 272, 273 275, 277, 289, 293, 300, 301, 313, 319, 341, 342, 346, 392 424, 436, 437, 455, 459, 489, 492, 505, 594; sells his house, 336, 358, 314, 391; sells his bouwery 449; buys a house, 390; account of, 423; term of office expires, 240; divides his land among his sons, 423; his lots, 190, 197, 198, 204, 212
Sander Sanderse, 90
Glenosing, Dennis, died, 36
Glennville, divided by Glen, 423
Glevin, Catharine died, 40
Glover, Charlotte, 136
Goarley (Gourley ?), 126
Godenhuysen, Mr., 426
Goeldin, Elizabeth, 116
Goes, Anna, 177
Anna Dirkse, 86
Anna Janse, 88, 184q
Cornelia Tyssen, 91
Dirk Janse, 88
(Hoes) families, 126
Jan Janse, 88
Jan Tys, 184a, 287, 411
Jan Tyssen, 91
Johannes Dirkse, 86
Judick, Janse, 89
Lena, 184q
Luykas Dirkse, 86
Matthys, Janse, 89
(Hoes), Mayke, 136
Mayke, Janse, 89
Teuntie Janse, 89, 184v
Tys Janse, 89
Goewey (Hovey), Alida, 141
Barbar Janse, 88, 118
Cathalyna, 105, 184h, 184y
David, 437
Elizabeth, 121, 164
families, 127
Geertruy, 149
Jacob 437, 438
Jacob Salomanse, 90
Jan, 437, 438
Jan Salomonse, 90
Lysbet 437
Lysbet Janse, 89, 164
(Houwy) Margarita, 125
Maria 125, 156, 175
Maria Janse, 157
Philip, 437
Sara, 184f
Sara Salomonse, 184i, 437, 438
Goeweys settled in Albany, 438
Goe (Goewey), Alida, 184r
(Goewey), Cornelia, 149
(Goewey), Jannetie, 155
Gojer's kil, 334, 353
Gold, Mary, 154
Gonsaulus families, 127
Goodair family, 127
Goodbrood family, 127
Goodenough, Mrs. M. J., died, 49
Goods, 75 per cent advance on, 376
Goodwin, Albert, died, 47
Gordon, Agnes 146
family, 127
Kate M. J., died, 32
Samuel J., died, 82
Gorman, Eliza, died, 10
Mary, died, 29
Mrs. Thomas, died, 66
Gornichem, in Holland, 442
Gould, William, president, 11, 48
Gourlay, Elizabeth, died, 39
family, 127
Gouverneur, Nicolaes, 357, 358, 359
Gouw, Jan, 201, 202, 245, 246, 247; see Vyselaer
Gow, see Visclaer, 127
Goyer, Gerber de, 246
Goyer, Albert, 246
Goyert, Klaes, 247
Grace church election, 15
M. E. church dedicated, 81
Grady, Margaret, died, 79
Graeff, Joost Aertse Vandenburgh, 442
Elizabeth, 129
Graham, Elizabeth, died, 45
families, 127
Maria, 124
Mary 173
Granger, Wm., 16
Grant, Elizabeth (Abigail), 111
families, 127
Nancy, 107
Nelly, 172
Gratwick, W. H. & Co., 42
Grauw family, 127
Graw, Leendert, Arentse, 85
Gray families, 127
Mary A., died, 54
Mrs. Wm. died, 60
Stephen R., 11, 48
Grazing refused, 231
Great, Eva, 184s
Flat at Schenectady purchased, 373, 449, 460; account of, 301; see Groote Vlachte
Vly in Kingston, 264
Western turnpike, 54
Greedy family, 127
Greeff, Cornelis Geeritse, 87
Greefraadt (see Greveraad), 127
Hendrick, 160
Henrick, 461
Green (Groen) families, 127
Nancy, died, 43
Greenwout, Jurrian Janse, lot, 200
Greer, Sarah M., died, 67
Gregory, Charles, died, 17
family, 128
Oscar V., 2
Wm. H., died, 68
Gregri (Gregory) family, 128
Grelle (Grennell) Susanna, 184z
Gremmer family, 128
Grennel (see Crannel), 128
Gresham, Christopher, died, 64
Grevenraet, Andries, 90
Elizabeth, 109
(Greefraadt families, 128
family, 128
Grevenraedt Andries, 184u
Grevenraedt, Isaac, lot, 192
Grewell, see Cribel, 129
Grey, Ann, died, 70
Maggie M., died, 65
Mrs. William, 14
Griffen, Mrs. Elias N., died, 59
Griffith family, 128
Mrs. John, died, 47
Groen, Jacob Marius, 89
see Green, 128
Groenendyk families, 128
Sara, 169
Groenwout family 128
Juriaen Janse, 89, 90, 101, 317, 333, 399, 408, 409, 410, 419, 435, 464, 465; proposes to herd cattle, 131; butcher, 400; see Janse his lots, 190, 191, 193, 194, 199, 212, 217
Groesbeek, Alida, 131
Barber Claese, 85, 146
Catalyntie, 184c
Cathalina, 184t
Catharina, 154, 163
Catharine, 105, 122, 184e
Catharine V. D., 121
Claartje, 148
Claas Jacobse Van Rotterdam, 88; lot, 214
David, lot, 210
Elizabeth, 184d
families, 128
Geertruy, 94, 104, 172, 184w
Gerrit Willemse, 91
Jacob Claese, 85
Johannes, lot, 214
Johannes Claese, 85
Margarita, 146
Maria, 128; died, 49
Maritie Willemse, 91
Mrs. Jacob, died, 11
Neeltie, 102, 144
Nicolaas Willemse, 91
Rachel, 184e
Rebecca, 123, 184f
Rebecca Claese, 85
Stephanus, 139
Willem Claese, 85
Grogan James, died, 56
Groom, see Green, 129
Groot, Elizabeth, 165, 184p
families, 129
Maria, 175, 184k
Mary, wife of D. J. Van Antwerpen, 401
Neeltie, 184k
Rebecca, 184d
Sara, 184m
Susanna, 170
Symon, 268, 282, 413
Symon Symonsen, 91, 274, 327; his lot, 200
Groote Vlachte, 402, 475, 478; how divided, 460; account of, 469; see Great Flat
Grunm family, 129
Guatsh, see Akes Corn. Van Slyck
Gudsenhoven, see Van Gudsenhoven
Guest families, 129
Sidney, died, 48
Gui, see Goewey, 129
Guiton, Mary, died, 77
Gunn, Rosanna, died, 45
Gunner family, 129
Gunpowder, given to Indians, 237
Gunsaulus, see Gonsaulus, 129
Gutter, right to, 269
Guy, Mrs. T. J., died, 59
Guyer, see Goewey, 129

Schuyler, Geertruy, 161, 128, 140, 161
Gen. Philip, 14, 20
Gertrude, 129
Jacob Abrahamse, 84
Jacobus, lot, 193
Johannis, 184z
John, 184z
Margarita, 109, 143, 150, 184n, 184d
Magdalena, 168
Maria, 112, 184a
Myndert, 111, 184z; lot, 186
Neeltje 184n
Philip, 81, 90, 168, 472, 473, 483, 484, 500, 505, 509
Philip Pietersen, 90, 237, 247, 256, 257, 271, 290, 296, 297, 300, 301, 306, 308, 313, 314, 316, 319, 331, 345, 350, 360, 363, 364, 368, 371, 382, 383, 384, 387, 392, 396, 399, 406, 407, 408, 409, 415, 416, 417, 421, 422, 426, 427, 428, 429, 431, 433, 436, 439, 440, 441, 442, 446, 448, 449, 461, 462, 463, 464, 468, 469, 471, 474, 475, 476, 477, 478, 480, 481, 482, 485, 486, 488, 498, 490, 501, 503, 504; nominated for commissaris, 225, 240; makes over land to his son, 435, sells his house, 495; lot, 190, 195, 196, 211, 223
Pieter, 84, 189; lot, 189; mayor, 184z
Pieter Davidtse, 86, 184f, 184g
Pieter Pieterse, 435
Pieter, Jr., 163
widow Catharine, lot, 193
Schworer, Mrs. John, 21
Schyarch family, 164
Scobie, Amy, died, 65
Scott families, 164
Mary, 152, 151
Scovel, Charles, died, 33
Scovil, Mrs. Nelson R., 33
Scranton, Margaret, died, 82
Scully, Michael, died, 81
Scutt, Jan Willemse, 91
Seabury, Elizabeth, 145
J. F., 82
Mrs. Isaac C., died, 16
Sealey, Mrs. Isaac died, 44
Seaman family, 164
Lottie V. S., died, 69
Searle, Rev. J., installed, 18
Searls, John, died, 28
Seate, Mrs. Catharine, died, 47
Seaton family 164
Seckel-e; see Sickels
Second Dutch Church, 6
Presb. Church, 19; cemetery, 135; mission chapel corner stone laid, 22
See family, 164
Seewant, at twelve guilders to the beaver, 267; value of, 296, 315, 316, 378
Seger, Annatie, 132
Antje, 105
Catharine, 117
Elizabeth, 125
Johannes, lot, 209
Maria, 164
Margarita, 122
Sarah, 152
Susanna, 156
Syntje, 122
Segers, Bregje, 110
Segers, Jannetie, 160
families, 164
Jno., lot, 221
Lydia, 103
Maria, 103
Susanna, 102, 103
Segerse (Van Voorhoudt), Cornelis, lot, 192
Cornelis, lot, 211
Segersen, Cornelis, 288
Sehly, Jenny, 134
Seits, John, 1
Sellers, Hugh, died, 75
Seqna family, 164
Sevenbergen, 332
Seymour, Gov., signs rail road bill, 41; portrait of, 29; Mrs. Gov., 27
Wm. R., died, 28
Shafer, Joseph, killed, 66
Shaffer, Ira, 73
Mrs. William H., died, 76
Shafner, Lena, 101
Shallow, John, died, 58
Shaughnessy, Julia, died, 10
Shankland, Peter V., 115
Shanklin, Anna (Nancy), 184l
Shanks, D. W., 72
Sharp, Andres Hanse, 483, 484
Barbara, 99
Catharina, 99
Cornelia Andriesse, 107
Eva, 101
families, 165
Johannes, 483
Gysbert, 483
Hilletje, 130
Maritie, 181
see Scharp, Scherp, Schaap, &c., 164
Shaw, Mrs. Christopher, died, 47
families, 165
Mary, 142
Shea, Mrs. Thomas, 2
Shear, Mrs. Wm. H., died, 77
Sheer, Catharina, 180
Christina, 94
Sheers (Cheir, Sheerum), Catharina, 165
Sheffer, Eleanor, 132
Shehan, Rev. Mr., 80
Mrs. Mary, died, 59
Sheldrick, Edward G., died, 57
Shelly, Christina, 184c
Shepard, A. K., 46
Alexander Brown, died, 36
Alfred D., died, 53
Jane Maria, died, 26
Robert, 37
Sheppard, William, died, 30
Sheridan, John, 16; died, 15
Mary, died, 67
Mrs. William, died, 75
Sherman, Capt., steamboat pioneer, 57
John W., died, 33
Capt. Richard W., died, 14
(Shariman) family, 165
Mrs. Horace A., died, 59
Sherwood, Mrs. Lemuel, died, 77
Shever family, 165
Shewdy (Shoudy) family, 165
Shields, Bernard, died, 68
Bridget, died, 47
Ellen C., died, 15
Shipboy, Rosanna, 184p
Shisair, Richard, 508
Shisley Maria 156
Shockat (Chucat, Shoccat, Joucat), Rosina, 147
Shoemaker, Julia B. died, 58
Shram, Maria, 111
Shrovetide irregularities, 245
Shuckburgh family, 165
Shutt, Maria, 130
Shutter (Poel), Dorothea, 178, 182
Elizabeth, 154
family, 165
Hilletje, 178
Siachemoes, Indian, 299
Sibinck, Jacob Hendrickse, 87
Jan, 86
Sibry (Sibree) family, 165
Sickaseeck, 302
Sickel, Lysbeth, 153
Sickels, Anna, 184n
Hannah, 157
(Zikkels, Zichelson), family, 165
Lysbeth, 95
Mary, 152
Zecharias 253, 254, 274, 280, 356, 386, 387; cowherder, 481
Sickelsen: see Sickels
Sicker, Mary, 184c
Sickket family, 165
Sickles, Mrs. Daniel, died, 21
Sill family, 165
Silliman & Co., 42
Silman, John, died, 13
Silvercssen family, 165
Simmons, Anna Maria, 136
family, 165
& Griswold, 42
Simons, Mrs. John, died, 31
Simonse, Pieter, 245
Simpson, Elizabeth, 153
family, 165
Francis W., died, 21
Moses, 59
Sims, Elizabeth, 124
Simson, Caty, 167
Simssin, Antje, 152
Singer, Maria, 167
Sinhoo family, 165
Sinnot, Patrick, died, 49
Sioketas, Indian, 298, 299
Siston, Michael, 214
Sitzer family, 165
Siverse family, 165
Sixberry, Billy, 136
families, 165
Maritie, 150
Sixby, Annatie, 150
Catharina, 184i
Maria, 152
family, 166
Skidmore family, 166
Skinner, Eleanor M., died, 43
family 166
Skipper, ancient, died, 12
Pieter, 345
Slaghboom, Antonia; widow of A. Van Curler, 178, 444
Slane, Mrs. Daniel, died, 27
Slatterly, Mrs. Bridget, died, 17
Slaughter duty, 239; excise, 258, 312, 334; lot, 287; farming of, 364; sold, 388
Slawson, Josephine, died, 31
Slecht, Cornelis, 350
Slichtenhorst, Bata, 108
Gerard, 245
Gerrit, 251, 255, 264, 287, 288, 289, 302, 311, 312, 318, 319, 323, 329, 331, 332, 341, 342, 351, 356, 358, 359, 372, 374, 375, 388, 389, 438, 441, 444; lot, 211, 220; commissaris, 355, conveys lot, 440; see Van Slichtenhorst

Staes, Ryckie, 509
Stafford, Anna, 139
Annie, died, 61
Spencer, 130
Susan, died, 82
Mrs. Wm. J., died, 32
Stage bus'ness, 46
Stake, John Martin, died. 15
Stalker family, 169
St. Andrew's Society election, 36
Stanwix Hall, 419
St. Anne's church dedicated, 40
State Street Presb. Sunday School anniversary, 56
Starenberg, Christina, 107
Staring Eva, 157
family, 169
Starke Mrs. Catharine J., died, 48
Stater family, 169
Stavast, Claas Janse, 88; lot, 194, 197
family, 169
Gerrit Janse, 88, 187, 211
Steam boat, first up, 55; hindered by freshet, 58
Steel, Catharine, 107
family 169
James, died at sea, 66
Steely, Mary, 169
Steen family, 169
Steenberg, Catharina, 98
Steenbergen, Janneke, 108
Steenwyck, Cornelis, lot, 186, 189, 203, 223; see Steinwyck
Steer & Turner, 71
Stein, Philip, died, 38
Steinwyck Abraham, 246
Cornelis, 279, 305, 364, 440; attorney, 357
Stenekil, 298
Stenhouse (Steenhuysen), family, 169
Stephens, Reyntie, 498
Sterling, Gen. Lord, 113
Sterrevelt, Cornelis Cornelisse, 248, 282; sells his house and lot, 199, 200, 283
family, 169
Stetson, Mrs. Hannah H., died, 64
Steur, Catarina, 121
Stevens & Cagger, 24
Jonathan, 178, 184g
Mary, died, 65
Oscar F., died, 56
Samuel, 19, 24
Mrs. Wm. M., died, 13
Stevense, Oloff, see Van Cortlandt
Pieter, 245, 247; the wicked domine, 246, 247
Stevenson Stevens) family, 169
James, 184z
John, 185
Sarah, 107
Stewart, Mrs. James, died, 77
Jennet, 93, 179
Stierbrander Sarah, 184o
Still family, 169
Stillman, Rev. S. L., 55
Stimson & Henry, 43
Sting, Lena, 93
St. Jacob, ship, 340
St. Joseph's church members die of sunstroke 27, repairs, 54
St. Mary's cemetery, 35; dedicated, 49
Stol family, 169
Stoll, Jacob Jansen, 184, 271
William Jansen, 80, 184g, 367, 368; sells his house and lot, 293, 294
Stone Arabia by H Vedder, 468
Mary, 107
Stoone family, 169
Stoppelbean family, 169
Storey, Catharine, died, 56
Story, Ellen, 126
family, 169
Henry, died, 59
Joseph D., died, 31
R. J., 16
Robert 216; lot, 217
Storm, Mary, 98
Stoutenburgh, Engeltie, 184r
Jacob Janse, 88
Stover family, 169
St. Patrick's church dedicated, 30
St. Paul's church election, 16; statistics, 21; election, 1869, 53; rectorship, 60
St. Peter's church cemetery 35; centennial, 58; high church ceremonies introduced, 15; election, 16; election, 1869, 53
Strain, James, died, 27
Mrs. Joseph, died, 65
Strauss, Mrs. S., died, 56
Strat mans, Barentje, 125
Stratton, S. A., 82
Streel family, 169
Street fountains introduced, 21; car, new style, 59
Elizabeth, died, 41
Streets, change of name reprehended, 11
Streler family, 169
Strickland, Volkert J., died, 15
Strioles family, 169
Gabriel Tomassen; account of, 91, 503; lot, 220; see Thomase
Stringer family, 169
Gertrude, 173
Lydia, 141
Strobel family, 169
Strong, Anna, 110
Anna Margarita, 110
Joseph, 15
Maria, 149, 150
Stroop, Annatie, 161
(Strook) family, 169
Strother, John, died, 35
Strounk (Strunck, Strong) family, 169
Strover, Grace, died, 28
Strunk, Catharine, 149
(Strong), Elsie, 165
family 169
Stuart, (Swart), Eve, 184t
(Stewart), family, 169
John, 480; died, 467, 468; lot, 217
Studevant family, 169
Stuip family, 169
Stulversand, Cornelia, 171
Sturges family, 169
Stuyvesant, Petrus, 223, 242, 480
Styfsinck hill, 471, 479
Swartwout, Eva, 117
families, 170
Rachel, 438
Suatt, Elizabeth, 157
Suidam family, 169
Tennis Picterse, 90
Sulliman (Sullivan?), family, 169
Sullivan, Eleanor, 93
family, 169
Sumner & Hasey, 42
William A., died, 30
Sunday schools, first, 6
Sunderland, Margaret, 147
Sun stroke, 23, 27
Susquehanna rail road completed, 42; opened, 43; seizure, 66; election, 68
Sutherland, Cornelia L. died, 31
family 169
Mrs. I. P., died, 49
Judge Jacob, 16
Suydam (Zerdam Neeltie, 165
Swain, Martin, died, 31
Patrick, 4
Swart, Catharina, 141
Cornelis Teunise, 91
Elizabeth, 184q
Esaias Teunise, 91, 184l
families, 170
Gerrit, 253, 318, 353, 358, 394, 395, 421, 422, 431 432, 433, 443, 455; schout or sheriff of Rensselaerswyck, 246
Jannetje, 183
Jaquimina, 184a
Marytje, 182
Neeltje, 173
Theunis Cornelise, 86; location of his house, 474
Swarts, Mrs. Charles, died, 66
Swartwout, Roeloff 102, 114, 214, 267, 271, 273 274, 502
Swartz, Nathan, 12
Sweed [alias Bye] Dirck Hendricxe, 483
Sweeney, Bridget, died, 27
Swift, Hugh, died, 61
Kate Helena, died, 65
Swits, Annatie, 96
Claes Cornelise, 85
Cornelis Cornelisse, accidentally shot, 228
families, 170
Geertruy, 158
Hannah, 184w
Helena A., 115
Isaac Corn., 86, 449; see Cornelise
Rebecca, 126
Susanna, 184c
Sybingh, S. H., 443
Sybrantse, Wyntie, 99,
Syckelse, Sacharyas, 260; see Sickels
Symense, Ariaantje, 127
Aryaen, 295
Symes family, 170
Symonse family, 170
Symonsen, Adriaen, 382, 388
Jan, 299
Willem, 258
Syphes (Seckels, Seckens), Annatie, 184z
Taafe, Mrs. Wm. O., died, 27
Taber, Azor, 2
Tack, Aert Pieterse, 90, 276, 286
family, 170
Tailler, see Teller
Talbot (Tarbird) family, 170
Talcott, Gen. S. V. R., 20
Mrs. Col. George H., died, 48
Tannson family, 170
Tappen family, 170
Jurriaen Teunisse, 470, 478, 479, 491, 492, 508; lot, 185, 186; see Glasemaker, and Theunisse

Tapster, 468, 471
excise 228, 229, 240, 366, willing to fight against the collector, 236, 237
Tarrant, Catharina, 137
Tassanas, Moeset, 101
Tataukenat, 302
Tattem (Tatton) Rebecca, 105
Taxes, 1868, 18; 1880, 83
Taylor, Celia 108
families, 170
Gen., 26
John, 55, 184z; propeller, 14
John & Sons 1
Joseph B, died, 1
Richard, died, 79
William H., 1
Teabear (Taber?) family, 170
Tebt(?)s, Gertrude died, 45
Teel(?)n, Charles William, 1
Teitz, aged voter, 36
Teller, Andries, 345, 432, 433, 508; account of, 426, buys house and stable, 426 his lots, 185, 195
David A. 12
Dr. James V. C., died, 67
Elizabeth, 182, 345
families, 170
Helena 99
Helena (Martjen, 345, 432, 433
Jacob, 345
Janneke, 162
Johannes, 346
Lysbeth, 184h
Maria, 174, 433
Willem, 345, 346, 426, 433, 442, 443, 444, 475; his bouwery at Schenectady, 449; his lots, 187, 198
William, lot, 188
Telyer, Dirk, nominated for commissaris, 235
Willem, 293; see Teller
Tempoier or Temper, Teunis Pietersen, 281
Temper, Teunis Pieterse, 90
Temperature, 1-83, extraordinary 23, 26, 27; see Hot day
Temple, Gen., 41
Ten Broeck, Abraham, 184z
Albertina, 160
Anna Catharina, 184f
Catalyntie Dirkse, 86
Catharina, 100, 123, 130, 140, 143, 184j
Christina, 143, 163, 174, 184a
Christina Dirkse, 86
Christina Wesselse, 91
Cornelia Dirkse, 86
Cornelis Wesselse, 91
Dirck, 184z
Dirck Wessels, 91, 177, 189, 190, 224, 352, 425, 509; ships beaver, 244; the herder to obey, 431; his lot, 214; see Wesselse
Elizabeth 86, 110, 112
families, 171
Geertruy, 86, 102
Jacob Wesselse, 91
Johannes Dirckse, 86
Judikje, 184i
Lydia, 184i
Lydia Dirkse, 86
Maria, 186, 184f
Samuel Dirkse, 86
Samuel, 184d
Sarah, 172
Seth, died, 61
Tobias Dirkse, 86
Ten Broeck, Wessel, lot, 201, see Dirk Wesselse
Ten Eyck, Alida, 130
Annatie, 146, 180
Ariaantie, 108
Barent, 129, 161, 172
Catharina, 141, 142
Charlotte, 172
Coenraet, 184f
families, 171
Gerritje, 124
Harmanus, 98
Jacob, 109, 124, 184o; his lots, 191, 201
Jacob C, 184z; his lot, 207
Jacob H., 20, 67, 125
Janneke, 98
Johannes Hendrickse, 87
Lena, 163
Lyntje, 118
Margaret, 98
Maria, 103, 147, 158, 184c
Mayke, 184d
Neeltie, 154
P. 16
Pieter, 109
Sarah, 173
Schuyler, 160
Tobias, 116
V., 53
Ter Bush (Ter Boss), Mary, 184z
Terhune, Magdalena, 184p
Terwillegen family, 172
Tennis, Gerritje, 95
Indian 302
Tennise, Anna, 102
Dirkje, 184o
Elizabeth, 148
Maritje, 143
Philip, 115
Sweer, 84
Teunis, lot, 201
Tennissen, Barent, 402
Claes, 246, 462, 463
Cornelisse, 245, 247, 273; see Van Vechten; see also Westbroeck
family, 172
Gerrit, 507, see Van Vechten
Jacobus de Looper, 246
Jan, 247, 288
Jurriaen, 296, 352, 403, 426, 430, 468, 470, 471, 479; guardian, 391; see Glasemaker and Tappen
Pietertie, 321
Sweer, 456; see Van Velsen, see also Tunsen, same name
Theunis, 398
see Vylenspiegel, and Thennise
(Teuwisse) Lysbeth Matheuse, 97
Thacher, George H., 55, 184z
Thaner, Anna Margaret, died, 13
Thaw, 40, 48, 47
Thayer, Mrs. Nathaniel, 20
Theatre opened, 70
Theter, Catharina, 192
Jacob, lots, 179, 202
Jan, lot, 198
Jurriaen, lots, 187, 196, 204; lot, 191
Gysbert 109
see Teunisse
Theyssen, Jacob, 336
Thiel, family, 172
Thiff (Kief), Fanny, 107
Thing (Tinny, Tingley), family, 172
Third Presb. cemetery, 35; church, 10
Dutch church, new pastor, 18
flat, 401
This, Klaes, see Thys
Thomas, Annatie, 133
family, 172
Gabriel, lot, 220
George L, died, 21
John, died, 77
Sara, 133
& Haytt, 42
Thomase, Anna, 148, 496
Gabriel, 503, his lot, 203; see Stridles
Jan, 305, 307, 328, 354, 442, 452, 454, 476, 477; his lots, 188, 189, 190, 194, 195, 211, 212
Maritie, 408, 409 419
Thomason Maria, 96; see Tomasson
Thompson, Catharina, 145
Catharine, 118
families, 172
John Sealy, died, 59
Margaret, 145
Thomson family, 173
L. & Co., 42
Thong, Maria, 143
Sara, 130
Thonissen, Thonissen; see Teunissen
Thorn family, 173
Mrs. William, died, 22
Thorne, Elizabeth, died, 66
Thorndike, Mrs. A., died, 73
Thornton, Mrs. Abraham S., died, 11
Philip drowned, 36
Thorp & Sprague, stage owners, 46
Thousek family, 173
Thunder storm in winter, 46
Thunissen; see Teunissen
Thys, Claes, 244
Jan, 246
Tibbets, Mrs., 27
Tice, Mrs. George, died, 15
Mrs. Simon, died, 67
Tiel, Anna, 150
Tiets family, 173
Tietsoort family, 173
Willem Abrahamse, 84
Tile baker, 317
making, set up in New York, 264
Tilman family 173
Tilson Nancy, 106
Tilton family, 173
Tillery Margarita, 161
Tillman Elizabeth, 173
Timmel family, 173
Jan, 479
Timmer Jan Ysbrantse, 91
Timmerman, Albert, 245
Carsten Claes, 85
Carsten Claessen, 302
Gillis Pieterse, 260, 322, 355; see Meyer
Harme, 245
Jan Barentse, 85
Jan Cornelise, 86
Steven Janse, 246 see Van Schoonhoven
Tingue, Caty, 184i
Tipball, Frank, 9
Tippen, Anna (Johanna), 125
Tittle, Mrs. Christopher, died, 31

TJaus; see Jones, 173
Tjerk, Elsie, 105
Tjerkse, Elsie, 228
family, 173
Hester, 184o
Tobey, Edward M., died, 40
Todd, Hibbard, died, 83
Toeper, Margarita, 158
Toinel, Anthony, 345, 376
family, 173
Tolhammer, Hannah, 138
Tolk, Lourens Claese, 85
Toll, Carel Hanse, 87
Eva, 103, 184a
families, 173
Neeltie, 184a
or Van Toll, Rachel Hanse, 87
Sara, 184o
Tomasse family, 173
Tomassen, Harmen, 336; see Hun
Jan, 268, 277, 283, 293, 300, 302, 304, 307, 311, 314, 320, 322, 323, 325, 326, 327, 330, 333, 334, 336, 342, 353, 358, 365, 391, 392; see Hun, also Mingael, also Thomasse
Tompkins, Stephen A., died, 60
Toomey, wid. Jeremiah, died, 11
Tortler family, 173
Totems, 302, 342, 353
Tournours, Magdalena, 119
Tounsel family, 173
Towhay family, 173
Towner, B. A., & Son, 42
J. O., & Co., 42
Townsend, Amos B., died, 28
Franklin, 184z
I. & J., 12
John, 184z
Mary, died, 41
Mrs. Dr. Howard, 20
Townsley, Anna, 184v
Tracy, Ettie, died, 23
Kitty, died, 67
Lucy, 173
Michael, died, 33, 47
Treadwell, George C., 69
Mrs. Wm. P., died, 56
Treal family, 173
Treat family, 173
Richard S., 169
Tremain, Lyman, 53
G. A., 12
Tremper, Mrs. Charles W., died, 32
Trephagen family, 173
Rebecca, 184c
Trever (Dryver) Eva, 132
Hannah, 184r
Trimble, Miss A. G., 4
Trinity church, election, 16
M. E., church dedicated, 22
Trotter families, 173
Gen. Matthew, 184t
Maria, 184t
Sara, 184t
Trowbridge family, 173
John H 5
Troy and Burlington stages, 16
fire commission entertained, 21; see Lubberde's land
Truax, Abraham, 244
Annatje, 184k
Ariaantje, 115
family, 173
Isaac, 98
Susannah, 327; derived from De Trieux, q. v
Truex families, 173
Tryon, William, (?) lot, 206
Tuck (Tok, Toch, Dock), 126
family, 173; see Turk
L. Charles, died, 27
Tucker, F. G., 16
& Crawford, 72
Tunsen, Jurlaen, 270, 295, 341, 393, 479, 480
same as Teunissen
Turck, Symon Claese, 85
Annatje, 184h
families, 173
Simon Janse 89
Turkyen, Harmen Janse, 88
Turner family, 173
Mary, 14
Mrs. John, died, 14
Robert, died, 36
Tuttle family, 173
Martha, died, 11
Tweddle, John, 16
John, Jr., died, 8
Tyler, Mrs. Harvey H., died, 77
Tymesen, Annatie, 184p
Eldert Cornelise, 86
Marytje, 184p
Tymensen families 173
Tyser, Thomas, died, 56
Tyssen, Evert, 499
Jacob, 309, 318; his lot, 210; see Vanderheyden
Jacques, 265; his lot, 193
Lysbet, 147
Symon, 274
Tyssinck, Hilletie, 104
Tzelerin, Catharina, 138
Tzisesa, Regina, 158
Uldrick, Ariaantie, 107, 184j
Union bank, attempt to rob, 31
College, 14; alumni, 58; question of removal to Albany, 38
Unitarian church converted into a theatre, 46; edifice, 70; Sunday School, 56
United Presbyterian cemetery, 85
Universalist cemetery, 35
Upham, Amelia, 135
Magdalena, 172
Urlub family, 174
Usher, Mary, 142
Usile, Maria, 142
families, 174
Uylenspiegel, Claas Teunise, 91
see Vylenspiegel
Uytenbogart, Abigail, 184n
Uzil, Cornelia, 95
Lena, 135
family, 174
Valentine, Annatie, 97
Valk family, 174
Valkenaer, Justus, 131
Van Aalsteyn, Abigail, 113
Abraham Franse, 86
Barbara, 114
Catharina, 123
Cornelia, 149
Dirkje, 183
Elbertie, 114
Eva, 136
Jannetie, 154
Lysbetje, 184y
Marytje, 151
Van Abconde, Poulus Cornelise, 86
Van Aecken, Jan Coster, 86; his lots, 188, 190, 201, 202, 203
family, 174
Van Aecken, Jan Koster, 252, 261, 269, 275, 326, 353, 356, 360, 361, 362, 363, 365, 379, 407, 410, 425, 428, 434, 442, 449; see Koster
Van Aelst, Antony, 306
Van Aelsteyn, Abraham Janse, 88
Cornelis Martense, 89
Isaac Janse, 88
Cathalina, 141
Van Aerkar, Annatie, 103
Van Aernham, Maria, 142
Van Aernam, Mrs. Jacob, died, 26
Van Aken, 283, 307 347, 350, 352, 354, 403, 406, 413; his mark, 386
see Van Aecken
Van Ale: see Van Alen
Van Alen, Anna, 98
Catharina, 182, 184
Elbertje (Hendrikje), 122
families, 174
Heyltie, 184a
Jacob, 109
Jan Laurense, 476
Jan, lot, 187
Johannes, 171
Johannes Pieterse, 90
Johannes Laurense, 89
Laurens, 134, 282, 467, 481; lot, 201, 210, 215, 217; see Lourens
Maria, 175, 176
Pieter, 170, 190, 330, 331, 346, 348, 349, 410, 433
Pieter Lourense 89
Rachel, 184v
Styntje (Christina), 184
Willem, lots, 220, 222
Willem Pieterse, 90
Van Alkmaer, Adriaen Pieterse, 90
Van Alstein, Dirkje, 182
Van Alsteyn, Annatie, 137
Catharina, 184h
Cornelia, 166, 183, 184c
Dirkie, 184q
Dorothea, 103
Elizabeth, 145
Geertie, 184q
Helena, 174
Lydia, 103
Maria, 103, 165
Sara, 184y
The: 184
Volkie, 111
Van Alystyn, Cathalyna, 97
Cornelis, 178
Eva, 180
families, 174
Marten, 178
Jannetie, 94
Van Alystyne, Mrs. David, died, 65
Van Amersfort, Evert Brantse, 85
Harmen Tomase Hun, 84, 91, see Hun
Jan, 350
Jan Dirkse Engelsman, 86
Thomase Harmense Hun, 87
Van Amsterdam, Albert Janse, 88
Gysbert Claese 85
Jacob Janse Schermerhorn, 88
Jurriaen Tyssen, 91; see Ryckman
Van Autwerp, Annatie, 129
Cornelis, 133

Van Gorcum, Sarah, 352, 161
Sarah Cornelise, 160
Van Gottenburgh, Dirk Hendrickse, 87
Van Gudsenhoven family, 184a
Jan, 85; lot, 196, 204
Jan Sebastiansen, 85, 279, 313, 314, 319, 341, 352, 369, 374, 376, 377, 429, 458, 492, 505; trustee of his estate, 424; lot, 196, 204
Van Guysling, Elias, 402; his plantation, 475
family, 184a, 475
Van Haarlem, Jan Janse, 88
Van Hamel, Dirk, town clerk of Rensselaerswyck, 418
family, 184a
Van Hamelwart, Adam Bolantsen, 90
Van Harlingen, Jan Wybesse, 91
Van Harstenhorst, Hendrick Hendrickse, 87, 311, 330
Van Hemstraater, Sara, 146
see Heemstraat, 184a
Van Heerden, Roeloff Willemse, 91, 249, 320
Van Henson, Mrs. Harmon, died, 19
Heyltje, 134
Rebecca, died, 56
Mrs. Robert, died, 56
Van Hilleken, Cornelise, 436
Van Hoeck, Arent Isaacse, 88, 249, 328
Bennony Arentse, 85; account of, 249
family, 184a
Van Hoesen, Anna, 411
Anna Janse, 88, 184y, 506
Bregje, 131
Catharine, 411
Catrine Janse, 131
Engeltie, 136
(Hoesen) family, 184a
Fytie Jurriaense, 89, 109
Geesie, 149, 176
Gerritie, 116
Hendrick, 179
Jacob, 411
Jacob Janse, 88
Jan, 234; widow of, 411
Jan Cornelise, 86
Jan Frans, lot, 210
Jan Fransen, 86, 298, 302, 358, 359; account of him, 411; see Franse
Jan Jacobse, 120
Johannes, 411
Johannes Janse, 88
Judic Janse, 89
Juriaen, 411
Maria, 119, 148, 184v, 411
Maria Janse, 89
Styntie, 287, 411
Styntie Janse, 89, 126
Volkert, 411
Volkert Janse, 89
Volkie Volkertse, 179
Van Hoogkerke, Luykas Luykase, 89
see Hooghkerk, 184b
Van Hoorn, Pieter Janse, 89
Van Houten, Jan Cornelise, 86
Roeloff Cornelise, 86, 184c,
VanHun, see Hun, 184b
Wyntie Harmense, 87
Van Ilpendam, Adriaen, 228, 229, 278, 396, 397, 407, 418, 419, 446; trustee of Andries Herbertsen, 365; lot, 190
Van Ilpendam, Adriaen Janse, 88, 440
family, 184b
Van Imborgh, Gysbert, 247, 260, 285, 297; surgeon at Wiltwick, 260, 296
Van Imburg (Emburg) family, 184a
Van Inge, Jacob, 185
Van Ingen family, 184b
Mrs. H. S., died, 33
James, 98
Van Isselsteyn, Cornelis Martense, 89
Van Ist (Nest), Jannetie, 184p
Van Ivere, Maria, 127
Sara, 184n
Van Iveren (Everen), Ariaantje, 165
Carsten Frederickse, 86
Frederick Myndertse, 90
Hester, 184p
Johannes Myndertse, 90
Myndert Frederickse, 86
Pietertje, 175
Reinier Barentse, 85
(Smit), Reinier Myndertse, 90
Sara, 149; see Meyndertse, 184b
Zantje (Susanna), 179; see Van Yveren
Van Klinkenbergh, Lysbeth, 136
Van Kulenbergh, Gerrit Janse, 88
Van Laer, Adriaen, 494
Jacob Gerritse, 87
Van Laets, A., 184n
Van Leyden, Adriaen Janse, 231, 241, 263, 310, 313, 354, 396, 370; tapster, 240; defrauds the revenue, 242; ordered to be arrested, 243; see Appel
Jan, 370
Nathaniel Pieterse, 90, 278
Willem Frederickse, 86
Van Loenen, Gysbert, 254
Van Loon, Elsie, 115, 184r
families, 184b
Jacob, died, 77
Jan, 129; lot, 194
Marietje, 184g
Peter, 21
Van Luider, Jacob, 248
Van Luyten, Arent Teunise, 91
Van Marcken family, 184b
Gerritse, 294
Jan Gerritse, 87, 295, 296, 316, 344; farmer of the excise, 295, 315; farms the slaughter excise, 312; inventory of his goods, 340, 343; see Gerritse
Van Marle, Barent, 330, 357, 359, 360, 375, 376, 378, 383, 416; deceased, 357; lot, 187
family, 184b
Van Merkerk, Cornelis Teunise, 91
Van Meulen, Hendrick Gerritse, 87; lot, 223
Van Munichendam, Pieter Cornelise, 86
Willem Albertse, 84
Van Neck family, 184b
Lambert, 280, 332, 394, 395, 400, 496
Lambert Albertsen, 84, 458; account of, 262
Van Nes, A., 122
Aaltie, 179
Ariaantje, 152
Catarina, 180
Cathalyntje, 184j
Catharina, 128, 179
Cornelia, 181
Cornelis, lot, 112, 184, 193, 211
Dirkje, 184v
family, 184b, 184c
Geertruy, 131
Gerrit, Cornelise, 86
Gerrit, lot, 197
Hendrick Cornelise, 86
Hendrick Gerritse, 87
Hendrikje, 177
Jan Cornelise, 86
Jannetie, 184r
Jannetie Gerritse, 87
Maria, 179, 184g
Maritie, 149
Mayken, 152, 184s
Willem, 131
Willem Gerritse, 87
Van Ness, Aaltie, 184g
Anna, 116
Annatie, 183
Catalyntje, 103
Cornelis, 346, 347, 348, 349, 362, 392, 393, 395, 397, 398, 399, 402, 403, 404, 412, 419, 420, 421, 442; married widow of Hendriesse Van Doesburgh, 306; lot, 190
families, 184c
Gerrit, 347
Hendrick, 347
Jan, 347
Jannetje, 184y
Mrs. John, died, 66
John, Jr., 66
Sara, 184l
Van Nest family, 184c
Van Netton, Pieter Pieterse, 90
Van Neurenburgh, Hans or Jans Coenraetse, 85
Van Neuwenhuysen, Domine, 154
Van Nieukerck, Gerrit Claese, 85
Wouter Aertse, 84
Van Nieuwkerck, Cornelis Brantse, 85
family, 184c
GeertieBlantse Peelen, 184e
Wouter Aertse, 284, 415
Van Noortstrant (Van Oostrand) families, 184c
Jacob Janse, 88; lot, 208, 223
Van Norden, Catharina, 154
Van Nordinge, Pieter Nicolaase, 90
Van Northen, Temple, 106
Van Oldenburgh, Jan Gerritse, 87
Van OLinda, 491
Cornelia, Pieterse, 90
Daniel, 111, 436
(Van Der Linde) families, 184c
Jacob, 436
Maritie, 116
Mathys, 436
Pieter Danielse, 354; account of, 436
Pieter, location of his house, 175
Van Oosanen, Jan Claese Bakker, 85
Van Oost, see Van Woert, 184d

Van Slyck, Akes Corn. Gnatsh, 444. 454; house sold, 453
Catharina, 144, 184h
Cornelis Antonissen, 85, 248, 257, 436, 447; called also Broer Cornelis, 257; see Antonissen
Cornelis Teunis, 91
Dirk, 225
Dirk Willemse, 91
Dorothe, 175
Elizabeth, 132
families, 184g
Geertruy, 149
Gerrit Teunise, 91
Hilletie, 351
Jacques Cornelissen, 85, 86, 423, 436; account of, 354; owner of Marten's island, 373
Jannetie, 129, 132, 157
Jopje Claase, 121
Lydia, 184h
Margarita (Jacques), 184m
Marten, 354
Metie Willemse, 170
Pieter, 225
Pieter Willemse, 91
Teunis, 225
Tryntje Willemse, 91, 135
Willem Pieterse, 225, 229
Susanna Jacobus, 102
Van St. Aubin, Jan, 244, 245
Van St. Obin, Jan Jause, 88
Van St. Tobyn; see St. Tobyn
Van Steenbergen, Margarita, 142
Van Sterrevelt, Cornelis Cornelise, 85
Van Stockholm, Pieter Janse, 89
Van Strey family, 184h
Van Stryer, Margarita, 184
Van Stry, Maritie, 171
Van Sweden, Andries Hanse, 87, 326
Van Swellen, Asser Levy, 266
Van Taerling, Elizabeth, 94
Van Thessel (Tassel), family, 184b
Van Tillburg, Catharina, 171
Van Tricht, Abraham, 170, lot, 188, 215, 217
family, 184h
Margarita, 118
Magdalena, 139
Maria, 171, 184o; see Van Tricht
Van Turick, Jan Harmense, 87
Van Twiller, Aert Goosen, 87
family 184h
Van 't Willer (Van Twiller), Johannes, 237; sells his house in the fort, 319; patroon's agent, protects defrauders, 241
Van Ulpendam, Adriaen Janssen; see Van Ilpendam
Van Utrecht, Claes Hendrickse, lot, 191
family, 184h
Jacob Adriaanse, 84, 225
or Schoonhoven, Claes Hendrickse, 87
Van Valkenburgh, Baatje, 161, 184o
Cathalyntje, 161
Cathaline (Cateryn) Lammerse, 136
Catharina, 134, 137
Cornelia, 129
Elida, died, 22
Van Valkenburgh, Elizabeth, 99
Eva, 125, 162, 173, 184h
families, 184h
Gerritje, 136
Gerrit Lambertse, 89
Jannetje, 122
Jannetje Jochemse, 174
Jannetie Lambertse, 89
Jemima, 133
Jochem, 174
Jochem Lambertse, 89, 339
Lambert, 312, 354
Lambert Jochemse, 89
Mrs. Lambert, lot, 221
Lydia, 99
Maria Jochemse, 89
Peter, died, 77
Rachel Lambertse Jochemse, 156
Rebecca, 167
Van Vechten, Abram, 11, 184j
Abraham Dirkse, 86
Aguiete, 161
Anna (Bogardus), 117, 122 437
Annatie, 138
Annatie Dirkse, 86
Ariaantie, 117
Benjamin Dirkse, 86
Catharina, 102, 184i, 184t
Cornelis Teunissen, 91, 127; account of, 437; see Teunisse
Dirk, 437
Dirck Cornelise, 85
Dirk Teunise, 91
Elizabeth, 184o
Engeltie, 163
families, 184i
Fytie Dirkse, 86, 129
Gerrit Teunissen, 91, 485, 507, 508
Grietie Gerritie, 87
Harmen Dirkse, 86
Jannetie, 140, 164, 437
Jannetie Dirkse, 86
Jannetie Teunise, 91
Johannes, 99
Johannes Dirkse, 86, 87
Judith, 153
Leendert, 437
Lena, 184i
Lucas, 437
Lydia, 112
Margarita, 177, 179
Maria, 142
Michael Dirkse, 86
Neeltie Dirkse, 86
Philip Dirkse, 86
Pietertie Teunise, 91, 149
Rebecca, 103
Mrs. S. S., died, 10
Salomon, 437
Salomon Cornelise, 86
Samuel Dirkse, 86
Sara, 128
Sara Dirkse, 86
Teunis, 184z
Teunis Cornelise, 86
Teunis Dirkse, 86, 294, 479, 496; see Dirkse
Teunis Teunise, 202
Volkert, 171
Volkert Gerritse, 87
Wyntie 104
Wyntie Dirkse, 86, see Van Veghten
Van Vee, Pieter Hertgers, 87
Van Veghten, Dirk Volkertse, 91
Ephraim Volkertse, 91
Johannes Volkertse, 91
Van Veghten, Margaret Volkertse, 91
Van Velpen, Adriaentie Cornelise, 178, 490
Van Velsen family, 184j
Sweer Teunissen, 91, 184s, 354, 456; lot, 199; see Teunissen
Theunissen, farmer, killed, 456
Van Vespen, Adriaen Cornelise, 85
Van Vleck, Tileman, 254
Van Vleckburgh, Cristen Cristyssen Noorman, 86
Van Vlierien family 184j
Jeronimus, lot, 207
Lena (Madalena), 136
Van Vliet, Marytje, 151
Van Voorhoudt, Claas Cornelise, 85, 117
Cornelis Cornelise, 85
Cornelis Segerse, 90, 250, 288, 499; see Segers
Lysbet Cornelise, 100
Seeger Cornelis, 86, 299, 382, 388; see Segers, 184i
Van Voast, Albert, died, 67
Van Vorst, Geertruy Cohuse, 166
family, 184j
Gillis, 431
Jacobus Gerritse, 87; account of, 431; proposes to herd cattle, 431
Van Vranken, Alida, 153
Anna Ryckse, 184h
Anneke, 175
Anneke Ryckse, 179
Barber, 100
Catharine, 125
Christina, 166
Claas Gerritse, 87, 210
Evert, 490
(Van Franken, Van Frank) families, 184j
Geertruy, 108, 125, 184z
Gerrit Ryckse, 90
Grieta Gerritse, 87
Hester Ryck, 101
Jannetje, 184k
Maas, 490
Maas Ryckse, 90
Magtel, 101
Maria Ryckse, 129
Maritie, 95, 158
Ryckerk, 102
Ryck Claese, 85, 477, 490
Sara, 111
Ulderick, 111, 491
Van Vredenburgh family, 184k
Maria, 121, 123
Van W., Peter G., 184k
Van Wagenen family, 184k
Van Warlwyck, Claas Janse, 88
Van Weenen, Zacharias Sickels, 90, 255, 256, 259; see Sickels
Van Wesep, Gysbert Cornelise, 86, 230, 365, 413; lot, 212; see Cornelisse
Van Westbroeck, Cornelis Teunise, 91
(or Bos), Cornelise Theunise, 400, 409
(see also Bos) family, 184k
see Van Velsen
Van Whitbeck, Catharine, 455, see Van Witbeck
Van Wie, Abigail, died, 28
Agnietje, 184v, 184w
Alida, 179, 184k
Anna, 174

Van Wie, Antie, 183
Cattarina, 124. 174, 176
Catharina (Lena), 184
Catryna, 99
Cornelia, 184, 184e
Elisabeth, 184
Hendrick Gerritsen, 225, 272, 298, 378, 389, see Gerritse
Hendrickse, 184h
Ida, 110
Jannetie Hendrickse, 87
Katharine, 106; died, 48
Magdalena, 144, 174
Margaret, died, 65
Pieter Hartgers, 99
point, 48
Wye, Wey, Verwey families, 184k
Van Witbeck, Catharine, 118, 126, 128
see Witbeck, 184l, and Van Whitbeck
Van Woerd, Gerritje, 130
Neyltje (Hevitje), 162
Van Woert, Alida, 184c
Annatie, 140
Antie, 125
Baata, 179
Catharina, 184o, 184q
Christina, 184q, 184v
Elizabeth, 118,124,151,184a, 184x
Eva, 166
Eva Teunis, 170
families, 184l
Fytje, 184w
Jacob Claese, 85
Jannetie, 118
Margaret, 125, 184c
Marten, 184n
Rachel, 184q
Rebecca, 123
Rutger Jacobse, 216; see Jacobsen, Rutger
Sara, 123, 125
Van Woggelum, Jan Pieterse, 90
Pieter Adriaense, 230
Pieter Pieterse, 90, 492, see Sogemackelyk, 184l
Van Woutbergh, Teunis Willemse, 91
Van Wulven, Heer, 402
Van Wurmdrinck, Cornelis Laurense, 89
Van Wurmer, Alida, 109
Van Wurmdrick family, 184l
Van Wyck, Margarita, 162
Van Wyckersloot, Mrs. Sophia, 376
Van Wye, Ariaantje, 177
Geesie Hendrickse, 87, 106
Harmen Janse Knickerbakker, 88
Van Wytert, Hendrick Janse, 88
Van Yeveren, Femmetie, 138; see Van Iveren
Van Ysselsteyn, Baata, 184
Van Yselstein, Marten Cornelise, 85, account of him, 450, 469; see Esselstein
Van Yveren, Alida, 154, see Van Iveren, and Myndertse, 184l
Van Zandt, Dr., 141
Alida, 134
Charles, 20
families, 184l
Gerrit, lot, 219
Gysbert, lot, 219
Hannah, 138, 156
Van Zandt, Joseph Janse, 89
Mrs. Peter G., 81
William, died, 22
Van Zanten, Annatie, 124
Maria, 121
Zelia, 103
Van der Zee, Eegie, 123
Varleth, Maria, 170
Varley family, 184m
Varrevanger, Jacob Hendrickse, 87
Vedder families, 184m
Geesie, 168
Harmen, 250, 306, 349, 350, 371, 408, 445, 448, 479, 469, 486, 508; sells Stone Arabia, 468
Harmen Albertsen, 84, 256, 281, 284, 306, 307, 364, 407, 478; see Albertse
Harmen Albertse, lot, 186, 223
Rebecca Arentse, 85
Veder, Annatie, 183
Veeder, Agnietie (Annetie), 175
alias de Backer, Symon Volkertse, 178
Anna Margarita, 169
Annatie, 95
Catalyntje, 184n
Catharina, 126, 128, 175
Engeltie, 115
families, 184m
Folkje Symonse, 184s
Geertruy, 149, 184k
Geesie Symonse, 184q
Gerrit Symonse, 91, 152
Helmer Symonse, 91
Johannes Symonse, 91
Magdalena, 95
Mary, 1
Pieter Symonse, 91
Symon Volkertse, 91; lot, 193
Volkert Symonse, 91, 161
Veeling (Veeder) Elizabeth, 122
Veher (Fare), Mary, 146
Vegen, Anna, 99
Velocipedes introduced, 48
Velthuysen, Gysbert Philipse, 90
Veltman, Catharina, 184r
Venton families, 184n
Verbeeck family, 184n
Jan, 186, 226, 230, 246, 247, 250, 251, 252, 257, 260, 261, 262, 263, 264, 265, 266, 268, 269, 270, 271, 272, 273, 274, 275, 277, 278, 282, 283, 288, 293, 294, 296, 299, 307, 321, 322, 323, 327, 328, 329, 331, 332, 333, 338, 339, 341, 354, 355, 356, 357, 358, 361, 362, 363, 368, 374, 375, 376, 378, 381, 382, 390, 391, 392, 393, 395, 400, 404, 408, 409, 433, 435, 436, 437, 451, 454, 455, 457, 458, 460, 461, 462, 463, 464, 465, 466, 467, 468, 469, 470, 471, 496, 500, 501, 502, 504, commissaris, 225; old commissaris, 374; orphan master, 390; lot, 193, 194, 211
Verbraeck, Marten Hendrickse, 87
Verbrugge families, 184n
Verbruggen, Gillis, 386
Johannes, 244
Verduyn, Johan Latyn, 89
Verellen, 256
Vergerls, Margarita, 174
Verlet, Maria, contract of marriage, 345
Susanna, 113
Vermeulen family, 184n
Henderick Gerritse, 194, 419, 420, 446, 486, see Gerritse
Vermilye, Rev. Dr., 20, 21
Vernal day, 473
Vernor, Elizabeth, 132
Mary, 112
Vernoy, Cornelia Cornelise, 85
family, 184n
Rachel, 97
Verplanck, Abigail, lot, 214, 216
Abraham Isaackse, 87
Ariaantie, 142, 155, 182
Catalyn, 162
Catharina, 184x
(Planck) families, 184n
Isaac, lot, 191, 215
Marytje, 184q
Rachel, 142, 184v
William, lot, 191
Vervanger, Dr. Jacob Hendrickse, 303
Verveelen, Daniel, 264, 269, 372, 375, 410; account of him, 286; sells his house and lot, 187, 379
Verwey, Cornelia Teunise, 91, 102
see Van Wie, 184n
Teunis Gerritse, 87
or Van Wie, Hendrick Gerritse, 87
Victory family, 184n
Viele, Anneke, 184w
Arnout, Indian interpreter, 449
Arnout Cornelise, 85, 204, 249, 250, 273, 295, 320, 430, 446, 497, 498, 509; lot, 201; see Cornelisse,
Cornelis, 449
Cornelis Cornelise, 85, 414, 450, 469, 470; account of, 449; lot, 185
Debora, 137
Eleanor, 121
families, 184n
Jacomyna, 123
Jannetie, 152, 155
Lewis, 449
Lysbet Arnoutse, 85, 115
Maria, 128, 173, 179, 183
Maria Arnoutse, 85, 184q
Pieter, 449
Pieter Cornelisse, his plantation, 86, 475
Rebecca, 166
Sara, 123, 176
Susanna, 184s
Teunis, 449
Volkert, 449
Willempie, 161, 184a, 184v
Vieling family, 184o
Vigne, Maria, 184n
Villeroy; see De Garmo, 184o
Vinhagel, Aeltie, 445
Anthony, 445
Ariaantje, 104
Dirck, 445
Geetruy, 184b
Jan, 190, 245, 250, 270, 277, 281, 296, 422, 440, 457; the cowherder to obey, 431; master tailor, 445
Jan Dirksen, 337, 338
(Pinhaam) Maritie (Margarita), 179
Willem, 445

Vinhagen, Anna (Johanna), 1
Elizabeth, 151, 180
(Vinhaeghen) Eva, 96
families, 184o
Jan, 216; lot, 186, 195
Jan Dirkse, 86
Margarita, 182
Maria, 158
Marytje, 180
Vinkel, Elizabeth, 167
Vinner, John, 111
Vis, Jacob, 502
Visbach, Elizabeth, 105
Geertruy, 152
Visbeeck family, 184o
Gerrit, 184a, 302
Visscher, Alida, 172
Annatie, 115, 119, 143
Ariaantje Harmense, 87, 184s
Bastiaen Harmense, 87
Catalina, 100
Dirkie 123
Egbertie, 114
Eleanor 116
Elizabeth, 131, 184h
(De Vyselaer) families, 184o
Frederic Harmense, 87, 130, 184s, 249
Geertje Harmense, 184g
Geertruy, 96, 111, 181
Harmen Bastianse, 85, 246, 306, 337, 338, 366, 407, 413, 414; lot, 194, 214, 216
Hester, 170, 174, 181
Hester Bastiaense, 85
Hester Harmense, 87
Jannetie, 141
Johannes Harmense, 87; lot, 214
Magtel, 146
Maretje, 184j
Maria, 129, 130
Maria Harmense, 87, 184s
Maritje, 141
Nanning Harmense, 87
(or Visger), Jacob, lot, 200
Sara, 184m, 184p
Sara Harmense, 87, 184y
Tierck Harmense, 87
see Visser, Visger, &c. 184o
Vlas, Marten Cornelise, 86
Vlensburgh; see Flansburgh,
Voert family, 184p
Voetje family, 184p
Volansby; see Folansbe, 184p
Volchers, Maria, 153
Volkertse, Grietje, 184i
Simon, 408; see Veeder
Voorhees families, 184p
Vos Andries, lot, 199
Barbara, 162
Cornelis, 109, 359, 375, 383 his house: 357; lot, 187
(Vosje, *alias* Van Schoenderwoert) families, 184p
Hans, 302; see De Vos
Jacob Cornelise, 86
Vosburgh, Abraham, 109, lot, 106
Abraham Pieterse, 90, 260, 327, 416, 427 carpenter, 227; see Pieterse
Annatie, 174, 180, 183
Catrina, 133
Christina, 109,
families, 184q
Geertie (Cantje, Catharina), 157
Geertruy (Charity), 141
Geertruy, 165, 177, 184r, 184t, 427, 459; lot, 215
Isaac, 126
Vosburgh, Jacob Abrahamse, 1, 491
Jannetje Pieterse, 90
Maritie Abrahamse, 184s
Maritie, married Thomas Janse Mingael, 260
Pieter Jacobse, 88, 244, 247, 507
Vosch, Cornelis, 269, 301; sells his house and lot, 372
Vose, Rodney, 42
Vossen kil, 267, 272, 282, 361
Voter, aged, 36
Vranken, Annatie, 123
Vredenburgh, Heiltie, 184a
Jannetie, 179
Vreelandt, Johannes, 491
Vretje (Fratien) Christina, 165
Vrooman, Adam Hendrickse, 87
Bartholomew Hendrickse, 87
Domine Barent, 181
Engeltie 93, 184x
Eva, 137
Eva Hendrickse, 87, 184h
families, 184q
Hendrick Meese, 90
Jan Hendrickse, 87
Jannetie, 102, 122, 184h
Magdalena (Lena Huyck, Hogh), 184c 184r
Maria, 170
Matthys Pieterse, 90
Pieter Janse, 89
Pr. Meese, 90, 169, 247, 414, 415 478, 479, 503; sells his house and lot, 187, 199, 200, 201, 282
Wouter 129
Vroome; see De Vroome
Vrydag family, 184r
Vryman, Adriaen Claese, 85, 244
Vyffhoeck, 447
Vylenspiegel, Claes Teunise, 423
Vylspie, Claes, 354
Vyselaer family, 184o
Jan Cornelisse, 86, 202, 497, 498; purchases mill at Poesten kil, 456; lot, 201; see Gow
Wade, Dr., James, died, 11
Wadhams, Very Rev. E. P., 38, 79, 80
Wadman, John, 115
Wadsworth, presents megatherium, 5
Wageman Elizabeth, 143
family, 184r
Wagenaar family, 184r
Jacob Aertse, 84
Maria B., 150
Waggener, Margaret, 150
Waggoning, 54, 55
Wagner, Mrs. John, died, 65
Wainwright, Robert, died, 27
Wakefield family, 184r
Waldbillig, Mrs. Henry, died, 13
Waldron, Catharina (Cornelia), 180, 184k
Catharyntje, 121, 184
Cornelia, 107
Edward, drowned, 77
Elizabeth, 150
Eva, 184x
families, 184r
Geertje, 128
Jannette, 137, 180
Mary, 166
Waldron, Neeltie 180
Pieter, 178
Rebecca, 184y
Willem, lot, 219, 221
Wales family, 184r
Walker family, 184r
Frank, 9
Mrs G. S., died, 70
Colonel John, 8, 9
Robert A., died, 28
Mrs. Gen. W. H. T., died, 41
Walking match, 28
Wall, Bridget, died, 58
Wallace, Ann, died, 32
Walles (Wels) family, 184r
Walley families, 184r
Mary, 94
Wallis, Anna Barbara, 137
Wallis, Ann, 96
Wally, Hannah 154
Walsh, Dudley, 6, 12
Edward, died, 27
Francis, died, 67
Mrs. John, died, 79
Walter family, 184r
Walters, Carolina, 110
Elizabeth, 184s
Walton, Susanna, 131
Wand family 184r
Wands, Margaret, died, 32
Wapto, Indian, 342
Ward, Bridget, died, 77
family, 184r
J. C. & Son, 42
Mrs. Thomas, died, 27
Warmington, 115
Warmond family 184r
Warn (Ward), Catharina, 184r
families, 184r
Warner, Caty (Catharina Warrant), 151
Elizabeth, 131
families, 184r
Maritie, 174
Warners, Tryntje 123
Warren, C. & Co., 42
family, 184r
Sara, 139
Washburn family, 184r
Washington's birth day celebration, 47
General, 9
street lots, 54; Methodist church demolished, 16
Wasson, Mrs. John B., died, 60
Water fountains introduced, 21 works, 17, 83
Waters, Catharina, 184y
(Walters) family, 184r
Jannetie, 140
Waterson, Benj. J., died, 17
Watkins, Charles A., 80
family, 184r
House, 80
Watson, Eleanor, 145
families, 184r
Wattawit, a Mohican, 334, 353; mark of, 335
Way family, 184r
T. P., 53
Wayland family, 184r
Wayne, Samuel R., died, 60
Weason, Elizabeth, 107
Weaver family, 184r
G. S., 16, 53
Mrs. John, died, 43
W. H. & Co., 42
Webber family, 184r
Sarah, 154
Weber, Mrs. Joseph, died, 19
Webner, Agnes, 172

Williams, Elizabeth, 123
families, 184u
General, 17
Henry S., died, 18
Jane, 145, 150
Margarita, 103
Maria, 184x
portrait of, 29
Sarah, 129
Thomas, lot, 220
William H., 32
Williamson family, 184v
Mary, 151
Willis family, 184v
Hester, 93
Willow Flat, 436
Wills, Christopher, died, 77
Wilsie, Catharine 184v
Eleanor, 139
Wilson families, 184v
Mrs. George W., died, 46
Isabel, 105
James, 36
James A., died, 60
James D., died, 27, 28
Jannet, 172
Jean, 105
Maj. John, died, 58
Margarita, 105, 154, 182
Molly, 106
Richard, lot, 221
Samuel, lot, 194, 211
Sara, 107
Sarah, died, 36
Wilton family, 184v
Wiltwyck, Esopus, now Kingston, 260, 296, 350
Winchester, Samuel, died, 59
Wind tempest, 21, 77
Wine, excise of, 315, 316, 366, 367, 389; rate of excise, 338
Wing, Geertruy, 165
James, died, 17
Dr. Joel A., 17
Winne, Aagie, 173
Aaltie, 177
Adam Pieterse, 90
Agnietje, 151
Alette (Aleeta), 109
Allette Pieterse, 90
Anna, 135, 184j
Antje, 168, 169
Barnard V., died, 66
Bata, 119
Catelyntje, 184y
Catharina, 184n, 184t
(Van der Bergh), Catharine, 143
Charles H., died, 36
Christina, 184h
Collette Casparse, 85
Daniel Pieterse, 90
Mrs. David F., died, 60
Dirkie, 122, 175, 184z
Elizabeth, 138, 184t
families, 184v
Francois Pieterse, 90
Giles K., died, 21
Hendrickie, 121
Hester, 184l
Jacobus Pieterse, 90
Jan, lot, 206
Jannetie, 184k
John, died, 66
John T., died, 37
Killiaen Pieterse, 90
Lena, 141
Livinus Pieterse, 90
Lydia, 148
Lyntje, 118, 184w
Margarita, 184c
Margaret, 104
Maria, 161, 177, 184g
Winne, Marten Pieterse, 90
Marytje, 183, 184, 184t
Peter, lot, 201
Pieter, lot, 215, 494
Pieter Pieterse, Jr., 90
Rachel, 95, 110, 122, 125, 130
Rebecca, 100, 184m, 184z
Sara, 128, 142, 184r
Susanna, 176
Tanneke, 113
Tanna, 152
Thomas, 126
Tomas Pieterse, 90
Winnings family, 184w
Wisselpenninck, Reinier, 255, 383; suit against the church, 382; sells his house and lot, 389
Wisselspenningh family, 184w
Witbeck, Andreas, 109
Andries Janse, 88
Andries Jr., 166
Angenitje, 166
Antje, 184
Catalyntje, 178
Catharyntje, 184b
Dorothea, 184g
Elizabeth, 113, 122
Engeltie Andriesse, 85
families, 184w
Geertje, 184
Geertruy, 184l
Geertruy Janse, 88, 178
Geesje (Geefie, Geetje), 129
Gerritje, 175
Hendrick Janse, 88
Jannetie, 139, 180
Johannes Andriesse, 85
Johannes Janse, 88
Jonathan Janse, 88, 177
Lena, 184i
Lucas Janse, 89
Luykas Tomase, 91
Lysbet Janse, 89
Machtel, 150
Maria, 179
Maritie Janse, 89
Rebecca, 164
Sara Janse, 89; see Van Witbeck
Withardt family, 184x
Jan or Johannes, 253, 333, 340, 398, 502; lot, 187, 188
Witmond family, 184x
Witrel, Catharina, 151
family, 184x
Witt, Merrick, died, 35
Tjerck Claase, 400, 401; see De Witt
Woeds, Tanneke, 184l
Wolff, Abel, 285
Elizabeth, 120
Wolffen, Anna, 151
Wolford, Mrs. John W., died, 81
Wood, Hon. Bradford, R., 71
Daniel W., died, 40
family, 184x
John, died, 77
Miss Mary Ann, died, 15
Mrs. Theodore S., died, 82
Woodbridge, Mr., 52
Woodcock family, 184x
John, 125
Wooden pavement adopted, 36
Woodin, Mary, died, 55
Woodruff family, 184x
Phœbe, 145
Woodward J., Jr., 16, 53
Mrs. John, died, 69
Woodworth family, 184x
John, 184u
Woolett & Osborn, 72
Wooley, Eliza, died, 21
Woollett & Ogden, 32, 75
Wooster, Mrs. Susannah, died, 70
Worden, Robert, 55
Woud family 184x
Wouter, 348; Keesie, 230; wheelwright, 352
Woutersen, Keesie (Cornelis same as above, 247, 264
Wray, Jennet, 112
Wreight family, 184x
Wresch family, 184y
Wright, William B., died, 1
Wrightson, Thomas, died, 64
Writh (Wrigth), family, 184y
Wybesse, see Spoor, 184y
Wyburn, Mrs. Martha, died, 17
Wyckersloot, Sophia, 184a
Wyckoff, Dr., Isaac N., died, 5, 49
Mary Catharine, died, 11
Wyman, Mary Elizabeth, died, 64
Wynantse, Gerrit, 84
Melgert, 84
Melgert, lot, 217
Wyncoop, Alida, 120
Johannes, 171; see Wynkoop
Wyngaard, Annatie, 165
Cathalyna, 173
Elizabeth, 112
Hester, 104
Johannes Tomase, 91
Lucas Gerritse, 506; see Gerritse
Luykas Johannes, 185
Margaret, 167
Margarita, 126
Margareta Luycasse, 184g
Wyngaart, Ariaantje, 149
Catelyntje, 110
Claas Luykase, 89
families, 184y
Gerrit Luykasse, 89
Jan Luykase, 89
Luykas Johannes, 89
Luykas Luykase, 89
Lysbet Luykase, 89, 126
Margarita, 153
Magtel, 133, 184x
Maria, 173
Maritie, 97
Marya Luykase, 89
or Backer Lucas Gerritse, 87
Sara, 105, 184p
Wynkoop, Catharina, 184r
Cornelis (or Kees), 211, 252, 261, 507; sells his house and lot, 404
Elizabeth, 141
families, 184y
Marytie, 96
Sara, 123, 142; see Wyncoop
Wynter, 247
Wyp, Keesie, wounded, 246
Wyser, Johanna, 107

Yacht; see Jacht
Yager, Geertruy, 184
Yates, Abraham, Jr., 184z
Ann, 173
Annatie, 140, 180
Annatie (Hannah), 168
Catharina, 128
Catharyntie, 104
family, 184y
Frederick L., died, 71
Hiram, died, 49
Hubertje, 140, 184w

www.ingramcontent.com/pod-product-compliance
Lightning Source LLC
Chambersburg PA
CBHW032103220426
43664CB00008B/1117
* 9 7 8 3 3 3 7 0 9 8 6 4 3 *